Urban Projects

A guide to the preparation of projects for new development and upgrading relevant to low income groups, based on the approach used for the Ismailia Demonstration Projects, Egypt

Edited by
Forbes Davidson and
Geoffrey Payne

To Lucky
with all best
wishes
Geoff Payne
September 2000

Liverpool University Press
for Department for International
Development
2000

Abstract

This manual is based on field experience in many countries, but particularly that gained in Ismalia from 1977 to 1980 in designing and implementing the first 'sites and service' and upgrading project to be adopted formally and implemented in Egypt. The manual closely follows the technical process employed in carrying out the project and concentrates on approach rather than particular solutions This allows it to be used in many situations. The manual is organised in five stages. Each stage is described and subdivided into a group of closely related tasks covering topics such as the identification of target population and its housing needs, project site and site development options, and proposals for institutional and financial framework. Technical notes cover: socio-economic surveys, land survey methods including the use of aerial photographs, estimating land values, pricing of plots, public participation, technical assistance to plot holders, appropriate scales, methods for assessing layout efficiency, and discount factor tables. An appendix describes the background to the El Hekr (Hai El Salam) Project and summarises the position after twenty years.

Descriptors: feasibility studies, detailed studies, options for development, detailed development proposals, implementation.

Identifiers: upgrading of low income low standard urban areas, development of new urban areas, self help housing, technical assistance.

Department for International Development, London.

ISBN 0 85323 685 2 *paperback*

First edition © Crown copyright, 1983. Reprinted by permission of the Controller of Her Majesty's Stationery Office.

First published in 1983 by Liverpool University Press

Reprinted 1986

Second revised edition
© *Crown copyright, 2000*

Second revised edition published in 2000 by Liverpool University Press 4 Cambridge Street Liverpool L69 7ZU

All rights reserved

No part of this publication may be reproduced, stored in any retrieval system, or transmitted, in any form or by any means, electronic, mechanical, photocopying, recording or otherwise, without prior permission of the copyright owner.

A British Library Cataloguing in Publication Data record is available

ISBN 0 85323 685 2 *paperback*

Credits

Manual preparation team – first edition

Clifford Culpin and Partners
Editors
Forbes Davidson
Geoffrey Payne

Contributors
David Allen
Alistair Blunt
Forbes Davidson
Ian Green
George Jelinek
Geoffrey Payne
David Sims

Production staff
Fiona Isles
Suzanne Colvin
Hilary Wright

Ove Arup and Partners
Contributors
Brian Campbell
Ian Dick
Roger Tomlinson

Roger Tym and Partners
Contributors
Roger Tym
Kenneth Wren

Additional contributors to second edition
Claudio Acioly
Forbes Davidson
Duncan Mara
Geoffrey Payne
Kevin Tayler
Uno Winblad
Maria Zwanenburg

Manual designed by
David Milbank Challis

Illustrations and figures by
Peter Branfield

Typeset by
Northern Phototypesetting Co. Ltd,
Bolton

Printed in England by
Redwood Books,
Trowbridge

Foreword

The original *Urban Projects Manual* by Forbes Davidson and Geoffrey Payne et al was first published seventeen years ago. It has been continuously in print ever since, and has proven to be so popular, with such clear demand for this kind of publication, that the publisher has wisely promoted this second edition, with the first major updating of the text and references, in 2000.

What has made the *Urban Projects Manual* so popular? I think it is worth taking a quick look at its origins in order to gain an understanding of its relevance to the present day, and the future.

In 1974 *Culpin Planning* was involved in the preparation of development plans for Ismailia, one of the three cities in the Suez Canal region of Egypt. A specific part of their mandate was to prepare demonstration projects which required them to work within the local ministry as a multi-disciplinary team. A comprehensive understanding of each aspect of the proposals and their impact was built up. They established principles for creating appropriate and affordable developments for all sections of society, including specifically the poor. They applied a market-driven approach to development finance and used this to create a surplus which could then be reinvested in the reduction of costs for the poorest households. A balanced community could then develop in the new area of the city.

This holds many similarities to the goals and aspirations of so many people anxious to develop appropriately in the fast expanding parts of cities in the developing world today. The concerns we have for the poorest in our societies are even more acute today, with such growing numbers in our cities at the beginning of the twenty-first century. Understanding the principles for a constructive and balanced way forward is vital. The *Urban Projects Manual* provides a basis for that understanding.

The aim of the process is to work with the communities, and within given cost and resource levels, to produce development plans which are affordable to all, including the poor. This can only be done by basing proposals on what people can afford, rather than imposing arbitrary official definitions of standards and procedures. This takes thinking from first principles about what is appropriate and reduces initial costs so that the poor can get on the housing ladder. The higher standards come later when, and if, people can afford them. At the same time, the best way of generating a surplus for cross-subsidising to the poor is to include a proportion of higher income housing, together with higher value commercial and small scale industrial activities. In other words, the aim is to create more holistic mixed use urban developments rather than simple housing estates or conventional 'sites and services' projects. This is why the Manual is called an Urban Projects Manual, rather than a Housing Projects Manual.

It is, after all, the local professionals, together with the local development activists, and their local government counterparts who will be responsible for implementing the approaches to development for new urban areas. They all need the kind of practical guidance that comes from experience and best practice. Capturing that experience in an understandable format has taken great skill, using illustration and graphics as an integral medium of communication. The result is a practical capacity-building tool that people actually want to use.

The UK Department for International Development is pleased to have been able to support this second edition of the Urban Projects Manual. The updated text and references have brought the documentation up to an appropriate standard for use as a basic development tool for urban professionals and their client communities at the start of the twenty-first century.

Michael Mutter
Senior Adviser
Infrastructure and Urban Development Department,
UK Department for International Development

Preface to the first edition

Many articles, books, lectures and conferences in recent years have analysed the problem of housing the low income groups of the Third World. Statistics from most countries show that the demand for housing far outstrips the potential of government agencies to meet it. The result is normally overcrowding in the city centres coupled with squatter areas, shanty towns or 'informal development' on empty sites and on the margins. If Governments are to help overcome the present problems in the housing process they must adopt realistic housing policies.

The problem is basically of how best to allocate scarce resources to benefit all sections of the population. One way of doing this is for Government to limit itself to what it can do best - the allocation of land and provision of infrastructure.

Housing itself is an extremely important subject, but cannot and should not be separated from its context of people, culture, employment, services, transportation – i.e. the whole urban system. Similarly 'low income' households may refer to two thirds or more of the population. They should not be seen in isolation. What is more important is that urban development projects should cater for all groups. They must not exclude those with low incomes.

The Manual is intended as a guide to a normal way to plan for and implement projects which upgrade and develop urban areas. The Manual was originally designed for the staff of the Governorate of Ismailia in Egypt, but by focusing on the approach and techniques it is hoped that it will be useful to a much wider readership.

The Manual has been prepared by bringing together contributions by the many authors credited on page ii, most of whom worked as a team during the preparation of the Ismailia Demonstration Project. The responsibility for the final form of the text lies with Clifford Culpin and Partners.

I should like to acknowledge the indirect contribution of other members of the Ismailia Master Plan and Demonstration Project teams, in particular Christopher Berry, Garry Gray, Desmond McNeill,

Preface to the second edition

Tomasz Sudra, John Turner and Isabel Vargas. Thanks are also due to Roy Brockman, George Franklin and Alan Knight for comments and suggestions, and Ernest Barnes of ODA for support.

Finally I thank the Ministry of Housing, New Communities and Land Reclamation, the Governor and Governorate of Ismailia, the Board and staff of the Hai El Salam Project and the people of El Hekr for their support and assistance.

Forbes Davidson

Joint editor
Clifford Culpin and Partners

January 1983

In updating the text of the manual, we were surprised how little needed changing. This is because much of the content is technical, while the major changes have been in approach, in particular, who is responsible to do what. The target group of professionals remains the same, but nowadays it is even more likely that the professionals are working outside the government

We hope you will find the manual useful. Remember never to take it too literally. It should be a source of ideas rather than a blueprint. Whatever you do, always remember to apply common sense. It is perhaps the most neglected tool.

Forbes Davidson and Geoff Payne

Co-editors

August 1999

Editors' note: data on prices and costs in the case studies with reference to the El Hekr project was applicable when the project was developed, and has not been updated to current rates.

Contents

Page

- vii Introduction
- vii Background
- vii How to use the Manual
- viii Basic framework explanation
- ix Use of Manual framework when time and/or staff are limited
- x Manual framework

Stage 1 Feasibility studies

Task group/Task

Page		
2	1	Statement of objectives
3	**1A**	**Target population**: identifying the target population and its housing needs
3	1A/1	Identifying economic characteristics
4	1A/2	Identifying household characteristics
4	1A/3	Identifying housing demand
5	**1B**	**Project site**: outline assessment and selection
5	1B/1	Assessing site availability
6	1B/2	Initial evaluation of site location
6	1B/3	Identifying site area and shape
7	1B/4	Identifying existing land tenure
7	1B/5	Identifying site boundaries
7	1B/6	Initial assessment of site topography and landscape
8	1B/7	Initial assessment of ground conditions
8	1B/8	Identifying pollution problems
9	**1C**	**Site development**: assessing initial site development options
9	1C/1	Initial assessment of housing layouts and densities
10	1C/2	Initial assessment of plot development
10	1C/3	Initial assessment of commerce and industry
11	1C/4	Initial assessment of requirements for public facilities and recreation
11	1C/5	Identifying other land uses
11	1C/6	Initial assessment of circulation and transportation
12	1C/7	Initial assessment of requirements for utilities
12	**1D**	**Institutional and financial framework**
12	1D/1	Assessing the capacity of the institutional framework
13	1D/2	Identifying the financial framework
13		*Assessment of costs and their allocation*
14	IE	Feasibility studies: analysis

Stage 2 Detailed studies

Task group/Task

Page		
18	**2A**	**Target population**: survey of the target population and its housing needs
19	2A/1	Economic characteristics of households
19	2A/2	Household characteristics
20	2A/3	Household attitudes to their locality
20	2A/4	Household attitudes to plot characteristics
20	2A/5	Relationship between households and their dwellings
21	A/6	Potential for community involvement
21	2A/7	Nature of housing demand
22	**2B**	**Project site**: detailed analysis of project site
22	2B/1	Site location
23	2B/2	Site area and shape
23	2B/3	Land tenure
24	2B/4	Site boundaries
24	2B/5	Site topography and vegetation
24	2B/6	Ground conditions
25	2B/7	Local climate
26	**2C**	**Site development**: survey and analysis of existing site development
26	2C/1	Existing housing layouts and densities
27	2C/2	Existing plot sizes and shapes
28	2C/3	Existing buildings
29	2C/4	Public facilities and recreation provision
30	2C/5	Commerce and industry
30	2C/6	Other existing land uses
31	2C/7	Circulation and transportation
31	2C/8	Existing utilities
32	**2D**	**Institutional and financial framework**
32	2D/1	Institutional framework
32	2D/2	Financial framework
32		*Assessing costs and their allocation*
33	2D/3	Assessing the ability to pay
33	**2E**	Detailed studies: analysis

Stage 3 Developing project options

Task group/Task

Page		
36	**3A**	*No tasks at this stage*
36	**3B**	*No tasks at this stage*
36	**3C**	**Site development**: formulating site development options
37		*Plot development*
37	3C/1	Housing: layout and density
37		*Density*
38		*Layouts*
40		*Selecting options*
41	3C/2	Housing: plot sizes and shapes
43		*Selection*
45	3C/3	Housing: buildings
45		*Selection of options*
46	3C/4	Commerce and industry
47		*Selection of options*
47	3C/5	Public facilities and recreation
47		*Education*
48		*Recreation*
49		*Landscaping*
49		*General*
49	3C/6	Incorporation of other land uses
50	3C/7	Circulation and transportation
50		*Circulation*
50		*Transportation*
51		*Parking and servicing*
51		*Constructionstandards*
51		*Selection of options*
52	3C/8	Utilities
59		*Selection of options: networks*
59		*Selection of options: on-plot sewage facilities*
60	**3D**	**Institutional and financial framework**
61	3D/1	Selecting the institutional framework
61		*Type of organisation*
61		*Liaison*
62		*Keypoints*
62	3D/2	Land tenure
62		*Selecting the form of land tenure: general*
63		*Selecting the form of land tenure for residential plots*

Contents

Page			
63			Selecting the form of land tenure for commercial and industrial plots
64	3D/3		**Developing financial options**
64			*Selecting the financial framework: general*
65			*Selection of preferred option for costs and their allocation*
66			*Determining the ability to pay for project costs*
67			*Determining the factors affecting project costs*
68			*Determining means of cost recovery*
69			*Selection of appropriate internal subsidies*
69			*Residential cross-subsidies*
70			*Cross-subsidies from commercial industrial developments*
70			*Determining external subsidies*
70			*Calculating cash flow*
70			*Notes on elements of cash flow statements*
71	3E		**Selection of project options**
72			*Evaluation checklists*
72			*Meeting household needs*
72			*Physical planning*
72			*Implementation*
73	**Stage 4**		**Detailed proposals**
	Task group/Task		
74	**4A**		No tasks at this stage
74	**4B**		No tasks at this stage
74	**4C**		**Designing site development**
75	4C/1		Housing layouts
75			*Boundaries*
75			*Layouts: general*
75			*Layouts: blocks*
75			*Layouts: clusters*
76			*Layouts: upgrading projects*
76			*Layouts: high income plots*
76	4C/2		Housing: building
76			*Owner-managed building*
76			*Assistance to owner-builders*
76			*Agency built housing*
77	4C/3		Commerce and industry
78	4C/4		Public facilities and recreation
78			*Public facilities*
78			*Recreation space*
78			*Landscaping*
79	4C/5		Road layouts
79			*Determining site levels and need for regrading*
79			*Standards*
79			*Definition of road-lines*
79			*Phasing*
79			*Construction standards*
80	4C/6		Utilities
80			*Staged provision*
80			*Utility network*
80			*On-plot utilities*
81	**4D**		**Institutional and financial framework**
81	4D/1		Institutional framework
82	4D/2		Financial framework
82	**4E**		Phasing
83	**Stage 5**		**Project implementation**
84			General notes
85			Example of proposals for administrative and financial framework for implementation
97			Technical notes for implementation

Page			
97			*Monitoring*
98			*Monitoring and evaluation*
99			**Technical notes**
	Technical note		
100	1		Socio-economic surveys
100			*Role of socio-economic surveys*
100			*Relationship between surveys*
100			*Survey types and examples*
100			*Review of existing information*
100			*Public meetings*
100			*Selective meetings*
100			*Scanning surveys*
101			*Case studies*
101			*Detailed surveys*
101			*Survey practice*
102			*Analysis of social data*
104			*Example of household scanning survey form*
106			*Case study guide*
106			*Comments to interviewer*
106			*The guide*
111			*Example of edited case study from Ismailia*
112			*Example of part of detailed survey questionnaire*
114	2		Implementation: land marking in improvement/upgrading areas
114			*Work sequence: reservation of public land (Task A)*
115			*Work sequence: detailed block plans/plot rationalisation (Task B)*
116	3		Carrying out intermediate land surveys
116	4		Implementation: measuring plots
117	5		Preparing sketch plans using aerial photographs
117	6		Interpreting aerial photographs
118	7		Implementation: design of layouts related to setting out
118	8		Implementation: design and location of site markers (monuments)
118	9		Estimating land values
119	10		Pricing of plots
120	11		Implementation: public relations and public participation
120			*Local social/political structure*
120			*Means of communication*
120			*Local commitment to aims of the project*
120	12		Implementation: selecting applicants
121			*Verification of information*
122	13		Implementation: enforcement
122	14		Implementation: technical assistance to plot holders
123	15		Appropriate map and plan scales
124	16		Assessing layout efficiency
124			*Infrastructure network efficiency*
124			*General*
125	17		Reference tables
125			*Discount factor*
125			*Present worth of an annuity factor*
126			*Capital recovery factor*
132	18		Standards
132			*Upgrading of standards*
133	19		Participating in problem identification, planning, design and implementation
133			*Background and objectives of the note*
133			*What is participation?*
133			*Context of participation*
134			*Who participates in what*
134			*How?*
136	20		Capacity building
136			*Background and objectives of the note*
136			*What is capacity and why is it important?*

Page

136		*Who needs capacity, and how much?*
136		*Integration of a capacity building strategy*
137	**21**	Land tenure policy options
140	**22**	Site development and design briefs
140		*Site development briefs*
140		*Urban design briefs*
142	**23**	Innovative sanitation systems
142		*Alternative systems*
144	**24**	Use of Geographical Information Systems (GIS)
144		*How does GIS work?*
144		*Potential benefits of using GIS*
145		*Steps to implementation*
146	**25**	Gender sensitivity in urban projects
146		*Stages 1 and 2: Feasibility and detailed studies*
147		*Stage 3: Site development*
147		*Stage 4: Designing site development, project implementation and monitoring*

148 Appendix 1
Profile of El Hekr (Hai El Salam) Project, Egypt

155 Sources of information

159 Glossary

161 Index

Figures and Tables are listed on the following page.

Contents

Page	Figure		Page	Figure		Page	Figure	
4	1	Household income distribution	76	48	Incremental development	139	92	Likely consequences of improving tenure rights in unauthorised settlements
6	2	Site location features	77	49	Commercial core area			
6	3	Site area and shape	78	50	Open space provision	148	93	Ismailia area master plan
7	4	Land tenure	84	51	Relationship between 'action planning' and normal planning process	148	94	Ismailia master plan
7	5	Site boundaries				149	95	El Hekr: situation before start of project
7	6	Topography and landscape						
8	7	Ground conditions	87	52	El Hekr Project Agency: proposed organisation	149	96	El Hekr: income distribution
9	8	Existing area: layout and densities	92	53	Plot classes	149	97	El Hekr: community plan
10	9	House type: traditional materials, one storey, medium quality	101	54	El Hekr household scanning survey: sample distribution	152	98	El Hekr project: progress to March 1980
10	10	House type: modern materials, two storey, high quality	102	55	Analysis card: example	Page	Table	
			103	56	Analysis sheet; example	4	1	Ability to pay for shelter: examples
14	11	Preparation of feasibility study checklist	104	57	Bar graph: household size	33	2	Ability to pay for shelter: calculation
15	12	Checklist for analysing project feasibility and/or selecting sites	104	58	Linear graph: annual household income	38	3	Housing density options
			104	59	Pie chart: employment distribution	40	4	Relationship between density and land requirement
24	13	Ground conditions: detailed survey	106	60	Structure of case studies	40	5	Relationship between density and land requirement at optimum level of private use
25	14	'Mackintosh' probe	114	61	Land marking tasks			
25	15	Example of climate graphs	114	62	Public land reservation: no accurate base map	41	6	Comparison of characteristics of small and large plots
26	16	Existing layout: detail						
27	17	Layout efficiency	115	63	Public land reservation: accurate base map	44	7	Types of housing provision
27	18	Examples of house plans in existing areas	115	64	Survey and marking in existing streets	50	8	Street hierarchy options
						51	9	Options for road construction standards
28	19	Examples of house types and plans in existing areas	115	65	Existing plots showing rationalised lines			
29	20	Building condition/construction in existing areas	115	66	Rationalisation: final plan and land marking	53	10	Water supply options
			116	67	Intermediate survey	54	11	Sewage disposal options
34	21	Organisation of a master analysis sheet	116	68	Plot measurement in the field	57	12	Surface water drainage options
			116	69	Plot measurement from air photographs	57	13	Electricity supply options
39	22	Cluster				58	14	Rubbish disposal options
39	23	Block	117	70	Camera set up	58	15	Telephone options
39	24	Neighbourhood	117	71	Sequence of photographs	62	16	Land tenure characteristics
39	25	Block layout options	117	72	Distortion in air photographs	66	17	Allocation of costs
41	26	Flexibility of cluster system	117	73	Appearance of building from air photograph	67	18	Comparison of loan repayment rates
42	27	Narrow frontage plots						
42	28	Use of standard module	117	74	Visible parts of building	93	19	Annual charges by plot size: El Hekr new area
43	29	Plot size/shape options	117	75	Differentiating walls and roofs from air photographs			
43	30	Plot development examples				93	20	Annual charges by plot size: El Hekr existing area
46	31	Commercial centre	118	76	Plot layout designed for ease of setting out			
46	32	Local shop				93	21	Capital costs of minimum infrastructure programme: El Hekr
46	33	Commercial core area with adjacent plots designed to cope with expansion of commercial area	118	77	Concrete column marker			
			118	78	Location of marker posts for setting out	94	22	Simplified five year cash flow: El Hekr
			118	79	Marker location for plot setting out	95	23	Estimated network costs for water and sewerage provision
47	34	Primary school location						
48	35	Local recreation space	119	80	Land value areas: Ismailia 1977	98	24	Monitoring: information requirements
48	36	Kickabout area	119	81	Land value profile examples: Ismailia 1977			
65	37	Project financial analysis: operational flow chart				103	25	Simple analysis: household sizes by percentage occurrence
			119	82	Plot pricing			
66	38	Calculating ability to pay for project costs	120	83	Selection procedure for applicants	103	26	Simple analysis: cross tabulation
68	39	Allocating total project costs	123	84	Plan scale examples	123	27	Appropriate plan and map scales
68	40	Allocating costs to plots	124	85	Land control types			
69	41	Calculating ability to pay monthly charges	134	86	Triangulation	127	28	Computation of cost benefit ratio: illustration from population project, Trinidad and Tobago
			135	87	Participation and the process outlined in the manual			
69	42	Determining subsidy levels						
70	43	Establishing the cash flow projection	136	88	Capacity building concept	128	29	Example of net present worth and internal economic return calculation: Uruguay, third livestock development project
			136	89	Relation between capacity required, mean of provision and activities			
74	44	Example: detailed plot and infrastructure layout						
			137	90	Capacity building system	128	30	Discount factor
75	45	Blocks, showing alternative plot layouts	139	91	Likely consequences of providing titles to 'owners' of squatter houses	129	31	Present worth of an annuity factor
75	46	Linking of clusters by footpaths						
76	47	Block boundaries in upgrading area						

Page	Table	
130	32	Capital recovery factor
133	33	Participation: advantages and disadvantages
134	34	Participation at different project stages
151	35	El Hekr: costs per plot of options for different levels of infrastructure provision in new areas
151	36	El Hekr: ability to pay for different levels of infrastructure
153	37	El Hekr (Hai El Salam) project: useful figures March 1980
154	38	Hai el Salam project: summary

Introduction

This Manual, initially written for use in Ismailia, Egypt, is intended as a working guide to the preparation of projects for the upgrading of low income, low standard urban areas and for the development of new urban areas in such a way that the needs of low income groups can be satisfied. The Manual is based on an approach which can be summarised as:
- The nature of the housing system must be understood: 'housing system' to be understood as all the complex interrelationships between peoples, needs, market values, construction industry capacity, legal framework, and the existing forms of housing supply, etc.
- The needs, aspirations and resources of people must be understood and proposals relate to these.
- Government intervention should be at the minimum level necessary to improve the operation of the housing system in a way which allows people to meet their own housing needs. Subject to this, intervention must also be *within* the Governments capacity of manpower, technical capability, administrative capability and financial resources.
- Housing for low income groups should not be considered in isolation, but as a normal part of urban development which considers the needs of all income groups for housing, employment, shopping, social activities and the infrastructure necessary to serve them.
- A project should be implementable, at least at a basic level, without major external finance.
- Where desired standards are not possible initially, a project should be designed at a basic level which is capable of being upgraded efficiently.

The approach is emphasised, rather than particular solutions, since every new project must develop its own solutions to its own particular problems. An attempt is made to indicate the range of options available and to describe appropriate techniques, but there is no claim that the Manual is comprehensive or universally applicable.

Background

The Urban Projects Manual was originally published in 1983 and has been continuously in print ever since. It was designed to make accessible the experience that had been gained in designing and implementing the Ismailia Demonstration Projects in Egypt. The approach adopted was to explain in a systematic way the tasks that need to be carried out to develop an integrated upgrading and new development programme aimed at improving access of the poor to shelter.

Its continued popularity is probably due to the way it addresses key issues facing professionals working in the urban sector and illustrates methods with examples. It is still widely used on English language training courses and by the staff of urban development agencies. However, much has changed since 1983 and many of the original references are somewhat dated. The idea to update the Manual came from Johnny Astrand, the Director of the Lund Centre for Habitat Studies, in Sweden who had found the original edition a useful teaching tool in international courses in Lund, but wanted a Spanish version for use on Latin American training programmes.

The main objective of the new edition is to ensure the continuing relevance of the manual to practitioners, first in content and second in language. Although the body of the text remains substantially the same, sections have been updated where necessary, references added to Latin American cases and additional technical notes included, following extensive feedback. The main example, however, continues to be the Ismailia projects.

The key changes that have taken place include:
- *Changing context*. There is now a much stronger general appreciation of the roles of community based organisations and NGOs
- *Changing view or focus.* Focus of attention is more on enabling local communities and less on direct government intervention
- *Developing urban management approach.* There is a trend towards more pro-active local government trying to work creatively with its partners
- *Changing approach to government and participation of stakeholders.* Working in partnership with stakeholders is becoming a more standard way of working, though there is much to be done to make this widely implementable.

The Manual aims to provide the following:
- A logical approach to the identification of problems, the preparation of project proposals and their implementation.
- A guide to the process – the tasks involved, the sequences and the decision making.
- An indication of the range of options available.
- A description of relevant techniques which are not normally taught or found in readily available books.

The Manual should be a guide and stimulus, but not a substitute for thinking.

Introduction

How to use the Manual

The preparation of a project involves a technical process which could be briefly described as 'survey, analyse and plan'. In each of these stages many individual tasks must be carried out involving different topics, such as surveying the characteristics of the population or the forms of sanitation used. The products of these tasks are then analysed, decisions taken and the process moved to the next stage.

The Manual is organised in the way a project is carried out, that is in stages. Within each stage it is subdivided into groups of tasks which link closely together – for example those concerned with development of the site such as road and layout design are linked together, and those concerning administration and finance are similarly grouped. The tasks which will be carried out at approximately the same time are described in one stage.

To follow the progress of one topic e.g. finance or sanitation through different stages will require referring forward to successive stages. To make cross references easy, each topic is identified by a letter e.g. site development is C; so 4C refers to Stage 4 (Detailed proposals) and Topic C (Site development).

The framework is shown in a simple form below. This is repeated with details of all tasks on the following pages and a small scale version is repeated on each page to indicate where in the process any task is.

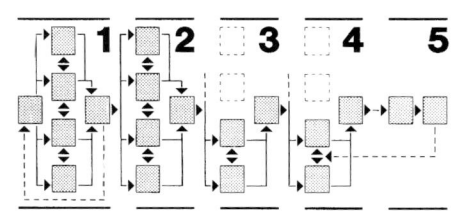

Framework diagram showing process of project preparation

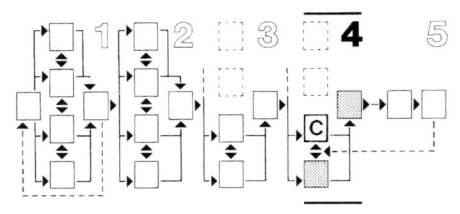

Framework highlighting Task group 4C in Stage 4

xii Framework

Basic framework explanation

Stage 1
Feasibility studies

These are brief and selective studies of the most important topics to determine whether the project is likely to meet its objectives, or whether they have to be modified. The basic purpose is to avoid the wasted effort involved in taking research and design to too detailed a level before a decision is taken to abandon or develop the project.

Stage 2
Detailed studies

This stage covers the research and investigations required to understand the problems and opportunities involved, both existing and projected. It will provide descriptions and measures or 'parameters' for which, and within which, the project will be designed. Examples are the likely number of families, the existing means of housing, problems involved, likely amounts of money available, the administrative system available and the nature and cost of the site.

Stage 3
Developing project options

This is a process of trying to meet the objectives within the situations revealed by the detailed studies. Different possibilities are developed to a 'sketch plan' stage, and those which appear feasible are compared in order to select one for detailed development. The decision may be technical or political, preferably with technical advice.

Task group 2A
- Economic characteristics — 2A/1
- Household characteristics — 2A/2
- Attitudes to locality — 2A/3
- Attitudes to plot characteristics — 2A/4
- Relationship households/dwellings — 2A/5
- Community involvement — 2A/6
- Housing demand — 2A/7

Tasks in Task group 2A

Stage 4
Detailed development proposals

This is the development in detail of both the physical design and the financial and administrative aspects. It is the preparation for implementation and should be tied as closely to implementation as possible. Later stages of detailed design may run in parallel to implementation.

Stage 5
Project implementation

Implementation is the key to the whole process as, without it, the work done is useless. The experience of implementation is probably the most useful input to a successful project, and for this reason it is good to start the first phase as soon as possible, preferably before detailed design is carried out for all stages of a project. For the purposes of the Manual an example of the administrative and financial framework necessary is given, together with some notes on techniques useful in implementation.

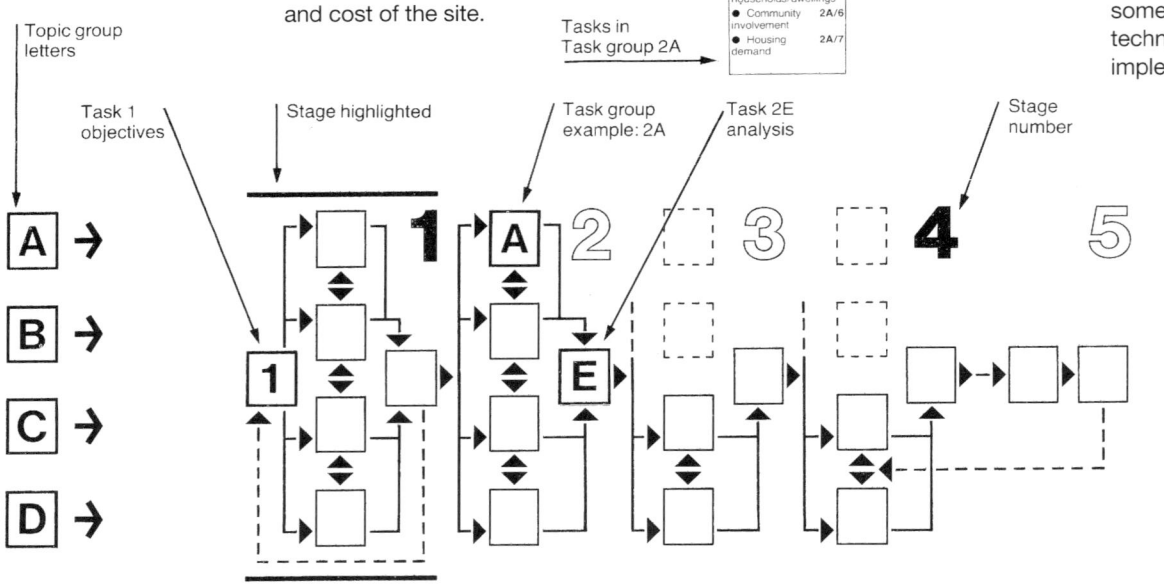

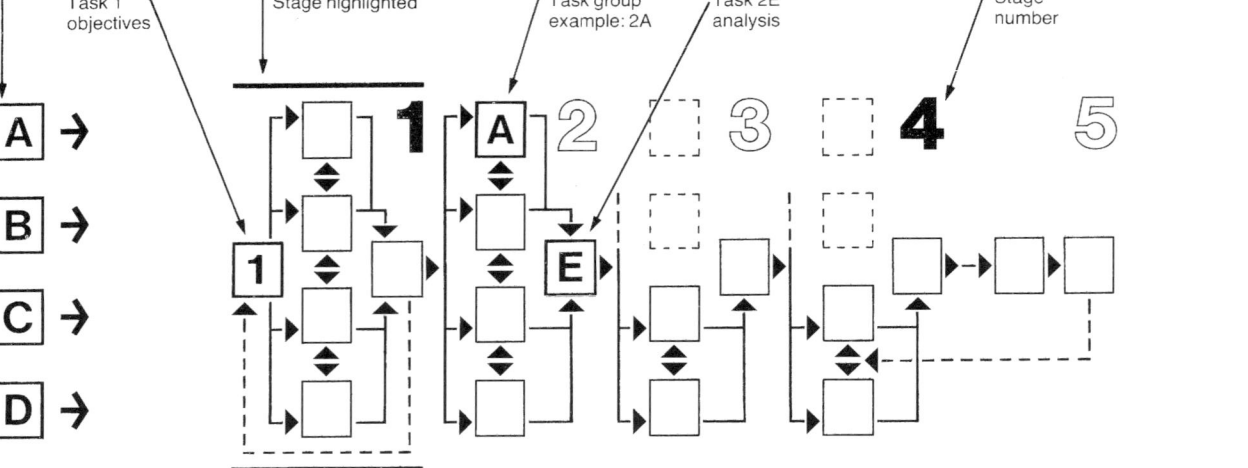

Explanation of the small scale framework, which is repeated on each page to indicate the location of a Task group and its Tasks in the overall process

Topics

In the preparation of a project, four main Topic groups are highlighted:
Target population (A);
Project site (B);
Site development (C);
Institutional and financial framework (D).
To simplify cross referencing, letters are used for identification purposes.

Task groups

This refers to groups of tasks each related to one topic, in one stage, for example, population or site. They are identified by letters A, B, C and D. For example, the population related tasks in Stage 2 are Task group 2A.

Tasks

The tasks are mainly self-explanatory. The intention is to indicate the type of information required, the range of options to be examined and the co-ordination with other tasks. When specific techniques are referred to which are not found in easily available reference books these are explained in the 'Technical notes' section. They are numbered relative to their Task groups, e.g. Task 2A/1 is the first task in Task group 2A.

Use of Manual framework when time and/or staff are limited

Stage 1
Feasibility studies

Subject to a review of existing information and the project objectives (Task 1) being satisfied, carrying out all the Tasks in Task groups 1A, 1B, 1C and 1D and Task 1E will be a short-cut route to preparing a project, though normally more detailed work should be carried out, particularly in Topic groups A and D.

Stage 2
Detailed studies

If Task group 1A studies do not provide a thorough understanding of the target population, its needs and problems and the nature of the housing system then all the Tasks in Task group 2A should be undertaken, in particular. the case studies (see Technical note 1). Further all the Tasks in Task group 2D should be undertaken as institutional and financial issues form the bridge between detailed proposals and their implementation. Finally, the analysis, Task 2E, wiil define the parameters of the project. It is important that information derived from the case studies be checked, as far as possible, from other sources.

Stage 3
Developing project options

The Tasks outlined in Task groups 3C and 3D can be incorporated as part of Stage 2, Task groups 2C and 2D respectively. Task 3E Selection of project options, can also be carried out as an extension of the analysis, Task 2E.

Stage 4
Detailed development proposals

As a minimum all the Tasks in Task groups 4C and 4D and task 4E, Phasing, should be carried out. Detailed design for later phases of the project should be left until they are about to be implemented. The Manual can only provide limited guidance at this Stage as no two projects are similar in every detail.

Stage 5
Project implementation

The detailed nature of implementation will depend on local circumstances and conditions. The Manual is not intended to cover thoroughly the enormous subject of implementation, but rather to highlight certain aspects which are critical to the design of a project. If a new Agency is established to implement a project, experience suggests that as a minimum three years should be allowed to cover the implementation Stage.

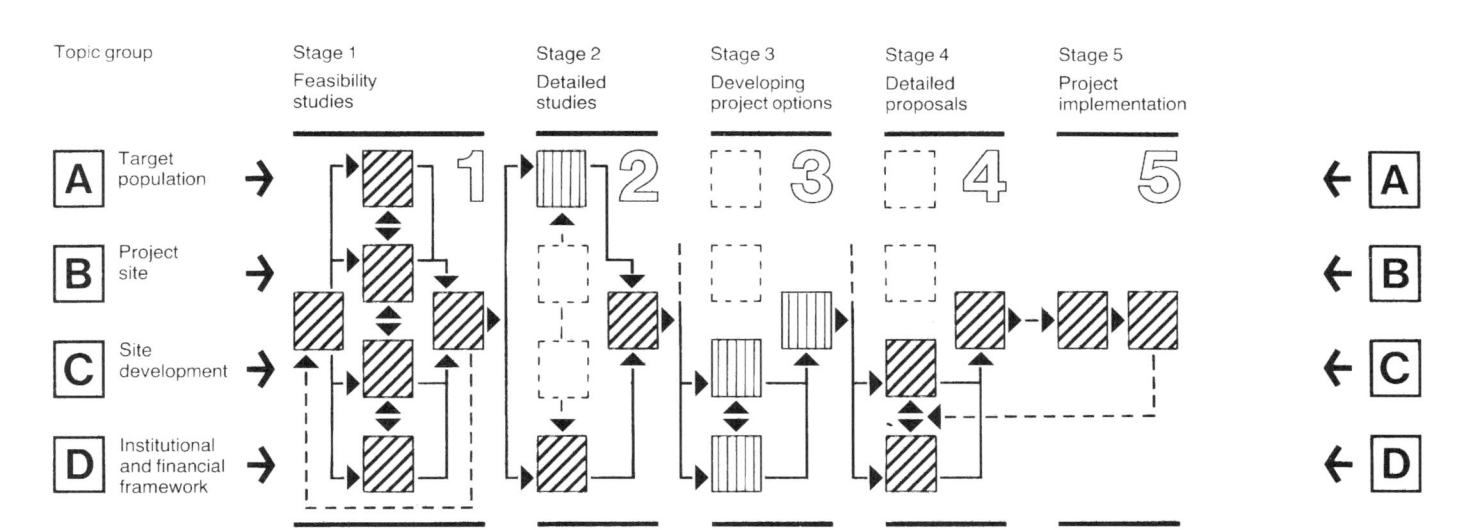

Diagram indicating the essential minimum Tasks to be undertaken. Task group 2A studies are only necessary if the Tasks in Task group IA need amplification. Task group 3C, 3D and 3E studies can be combined with Stage 1 and 2 studies as appropriate.

Framework

Manual framework

The framework shown here is the key to the organisation of material in the Manual. It is based on the work sequence likely to be undertaken in project preparation, but is, of necessity, a simplification. Not all Tasks and Task groups shown in one column will be carried out at exactly the same time, but there should be the maximum of co-ordination between those working on different Tasks. It is vital that co-ordination occurs during analysis, selection and implementation.

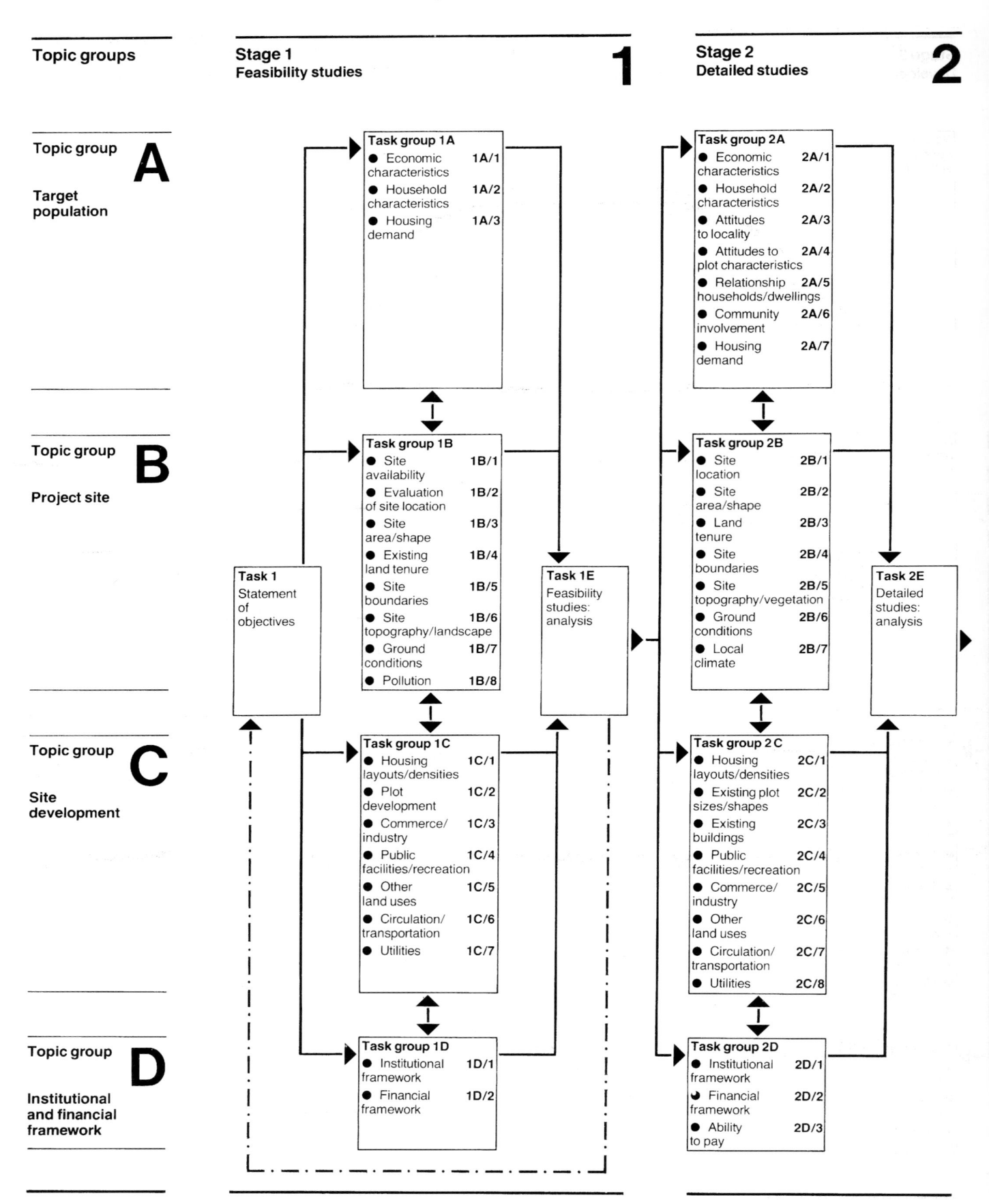

Topic groups

Stage 1 — Feasibility studies

Topic group A — Target population

Task group 1A
- Economic characteristics — 1A/1
- Household characteristics — 1A/2
- Housing demand — 1A/3

Topic group B — Project site

Task group 1B
- Site availability — 1B/1
- Evaluation of site location — 1B/2
- Site area/shape — 1B/3
- Existing land tenure — 1B/4
- Site boundaries — 1B/5
- Site topography/landscape — 1B/6
- Ground conditions — 1B/7
- Pollution — 1B/8

Task 1 — Statement of objectives

Task 1E — Feasibility studies: analysis

Topic group C — Site development

Task group 1C
- Housing layouts/densities — 1C/1
- Plot development — 1C/2
- Commerce/industry — 1C/3
- Public facilities/recreation — 1C/4
- Other land uses — 1C/5
- Circulation/transportation — 1C/6
- Utilities — 1C/7

Topic group D — Institutional and financial framework

Task group 1D
- Institutional framework — 1D/1
- Financial framework — 1D/2

Stage 2 — Detailed studies

Topic group A — Target population

Task group 2A
- Economic characteristics — 2A/1
- Household characteristics — 2A/2
- Attitudes to locality — 2A/3
- Attitudes to plot characteristics — 2A/4
- Relationship households/dwellings — 2A/5
- Community involvement — 2A/6
- Housing demand — 2A/7

Topic group B — Project site

Task group 2B
- Site location — 2B/1
- Site area/shape — 2B/2
- Land tenure — 2B/3
- Site boundaries — 2B/4
- Site topography/vegetation — 2B/5
- Ground conditions — 2B/6
- Local climate — 2B/7

Task 2E — Detailed studies: analysis

Topic group C — Site development

Task group 2C
- Housing layouts/densities — 2C/1
- Existing plot sizes/shapes — 2C/2
- Existing buildings — 2C/3
- Public facilities/recreation — 2C/4
- Commerce/industry — 2C/5
- Other land uses — 2C/6
- Circulation/transportation — 2C/7
- Utilities — 2C/8

Topic group D — Institutional and financial framework

Task group 2D
- Institutional framework — 2D/1
- Financial framework — 2D/2
- Ability to pay — 2D/3

Framework xv

Full descriptions of Tasks and their page numbers are given in the Contents, pages v and vi.

The small scale version of the framework, at the top of each page, indicates the specific Task group being discussed and its relationship to other Task groups in the overall technical process of project preparation.

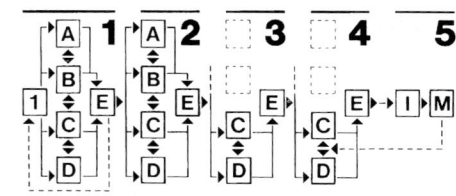

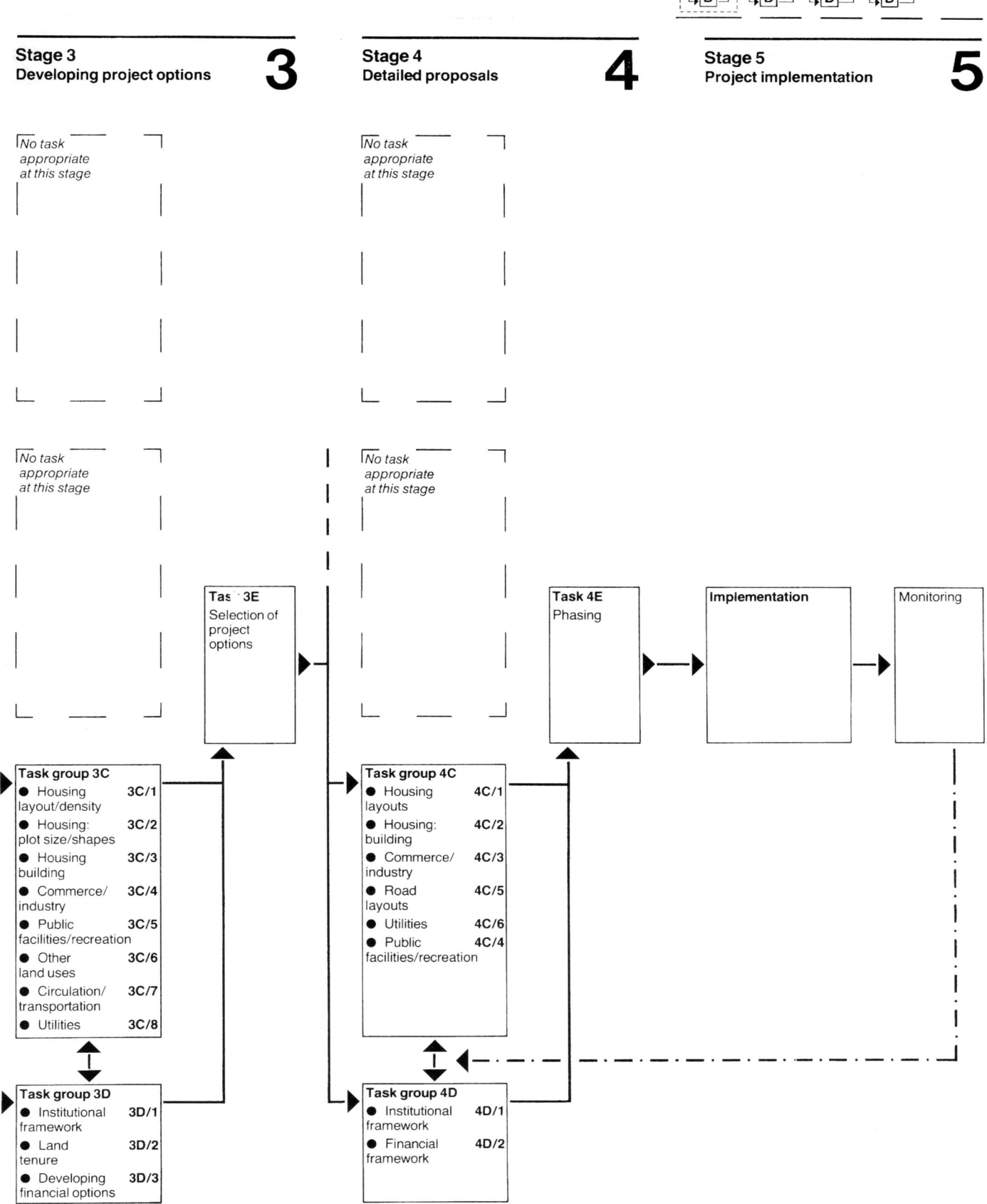

Stage 3
Developing project options 3

> No task appropriate at this stage

> No task appropriate at this stage

Task 3E Selection of project options

Task group 3C
- Housing layout/density — 3C/1
- Housing: plot size/shapes — 3C/2
- Housing building — 3C/3
- Commerce/industry — 3C/4
- Public facilities/recreation — 3C/5
- Other land uses — 3C/6
- Circulation/transportation — 3C/7
- Utilities — 3C/8

Task group 3D
- Institutional framework — 3D/1
- Land tenure — 3D/2
- Developing financial options — 3D/3

Stage 4
Detailed proposals 4

> No task appropriate at this stage

> No task appropriate at this stage

Task 4E Phasing

Task group 4C
- Housing layouts — 4C/1
- Housing: building — 4C/2
- Commerce/industry — 4C/3
- Road layouts — 4C/5
- Utilities — 4C/6
- Public facilities/recreation — 4C/4

Task group 4D
- Institutional framework — 4D/1
- Financial framework — 4D/2

Stage 5
Project implementation 5

Implementation

Monitoring

Stage 1
Feasibility studies

Feasibility studies* form the initial part of project preparation. Their purpose is to establish whether or not a project might be successful before committing substantial funds and/or commitment to it. Investigations should therefore be limited to a quick assessment of the most important aspects.

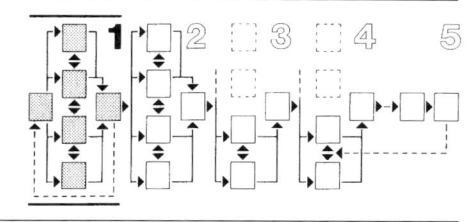

This involves the following tasks:
- Studies to identify the 'target population', or the group intended to benefit from the project. The studies should indicate the housing needs of the target population, taking into account its resources and the amounts people are able to pay for housing and related services.
- Studies to identify sites for new settlement or the upgrading of existing housing areas. They involve an assessment of the suitability of a site and its likely land and development costs.

These studies enable the needs and resources of the target population to be compared with initial proposals and costs. Where this indicates that proposals are relevant to people's needs and that people can afford them, the project can be submitted for approval to the authorities and/or community. If this is obtained, work can start on the Tasks discussed in Stage 2.

If, however, it is considered that the proposals or costs are unacceptable to the target population, an examination will be needed of other sites, different forms of provision, subsidies, or a combination of these alternatives. Projects involving high standards of provision, high land costs or expensive journeys to work will provide the greatest difficulty. In the case of upgrading projects, a high proportion of rental accommodation will also threaten the success of a project, since it will be difficult to predict whether owners or tenants will benefit and what effect improvements will have on rents. If, for example, landlords pass on the costs of improvement to low income tenants, people may be forced out thereby defeating the purpose of the project.

Where changes to the site or the proposals indicate that a project will be successful, outline approval can be requested. Should such changes still prove unacceptable, the project will have to be abandoned unless the cause is financial, when it may be considered eligible for a subsidy. For projects intended to be suitable for large scale

---

* In this Manual 'feasibility studies' refers to short preliminary studies. In World Bank language they would be termed 'pre-feasibility studies', with feasibility studies being equivalent to Stage 3

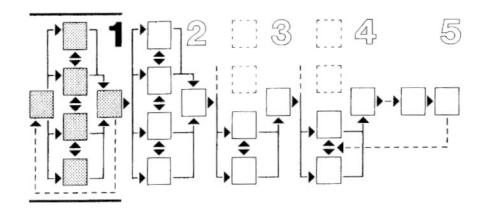

application, this option should generally be avoided unless there are special factors, such as the high cost of land or flood prevention works.

Subsidy in housing is an emotive subject. On the one hand, many countries have for a long time subsidised housing, especially for low income groups; on the other, international lending agencies, such as the World Bank, promote financially self supporting projects which can be developed on the scale necessary and not restricted by a shortage of government funds. It is clearly important to minimise dependence on subsidies in order to reduce market distortion and increase the chances for replicating projects at the scale needed to accommodate increasing numbers of people. The best way to achieve this is to maximise opportunities for generating an internal cross subsidy within a project through incorporating an element of higher value uses, such as commerce or middle income housing. Alternatively, it may be possible to effect a cross subsidy between projects. However, there will always be situations where some households will be unable to participate without an additional external subsidy. By reducing this to the minimum and quantifying the amount required, however, project planners in a good position to identify the type of subsidy required to meet the specific needs of the target population and minimise market distortion. The Ismailia Demonstration Projects are an example of this approach. They were carried out on a self-financing basis with minimum infrastructure (i.e. public standpipes and pit latrines), but were designed to operate efficiently with full water-borne sanitation if sufficient funds become available.

Feasibility studies, therefore, represent a microcosm of the whole project preparation and planning process. They provide a general indication of what is needed, what can be provided and the suitability of project sites. Initially they will require considerable effort, but as more projects are carried out and individuals and institutions gain experience, a more pragmatic approach will be possible.

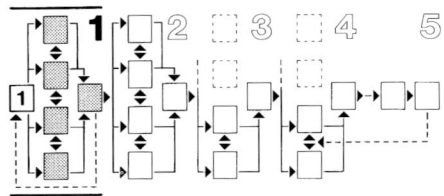

Task 1
Statement of objectives

The starting point of any project preparation must be a statement of objectives – what is to be achieved? for whom? where? when? and with what resources? The objectives will vary with each case. They may be given by politicians and/or the community to those responsible for preparing the project; they may be developed by the technicians or they may be arrived at jointly. Whatever the course, it is vital that the objectives are clear, expressed as simply as possible and have political support.

An example of a set of objectives, those used for the Ismailia Demonstration Projects (Appendix 1, page 148) are shown below. These objectives formed the framework within which proposals were developed and were used as tests to determine the preferred options.

The aim of the Demonstration Projects was to show how the policies proposed in the Master Plan were applied in detail; the guiding objectives were derived from the Master Plan. These links with Master Plan policies are shown, subject by subject, in the following section. Here it should be emphasised that housing, implementation, and the importance of the economic base were the main policy issues taken from the Master Plan, and that objectives formed for the Demonstration Projects were based mainly on these aspects. The most important criteria were as follows:

Proposals should be:
1) relevant to low income groups, which form the majority of the population;
2) capable of implementation with minimal subsidy;
3) based on the best possible understanding of the existing situation in its social, cultural, economic and physical aspects;
4) able to be administered without the need for a high level of sophistication and continued support from outside expertise;
5) realistic, i.e. should be implementable within the existing administrative and executive structures and not require fundamental legal or organizational reform;
6) implementable as soon as possible;
7) capable of modification with experience and with changing external factors;
8) replicable at other sites in the future.

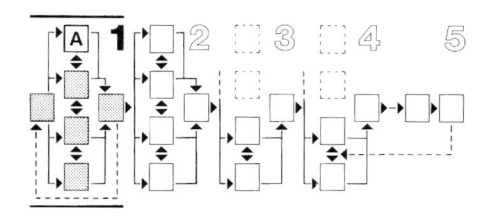

Task group 1A
Target population: identifying the target population and its needs

1A/1	Identifying social organisation 3
1A/2	Identifying economic characteristics 3
1A/3	Identifying household characteristics 4
1A/4	Identifying housing demand 4

Task 1A/1
Identifying social organisation

This Task group requires the answers to four main questions:
- What is the social organisation of the community?
- What problems do people face?
- What are their economic and social characteristics?
- What is their motivation and potential contribution to solving their problems?

The way in which the answers are obtained will vary for upgrading and new settlement projects. For upgrading projects, where people are already living on the project site, it will be simple to obtain essential information from existing data and from a series of short surveys or case studies, as discussed in Technical note 1 (page 100).

For new settlement projects, the task will be more difficult, since no existing households will be available on the project site. It may therefore be advisable to conduct brief surveys in the nearest area where the population is also low-income and can be used as a guide. Alternatively, information and experience from other new settlement projects can be used, providing it is up to date and accurate. See Technical note 19 on Participation (page 133).

It should be emphasised that the estimates involved at this stage are to be used to gain a general outline only and need not be exhaustive.

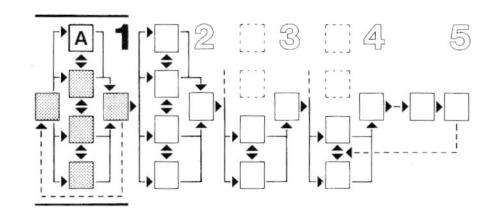

Task 1A/2
Identifying economic characteristics

Although a number of criteria may be applied in order to define the target population for a housing project, it is sensible for any project intended to benefit low income households to pay particular attention to economic characteristics.

The initial definition will need to be very broad, since it is not uncommon for 80 per cent of urban populations to have incomes below the level necessary to afford existing forms of legal housing. Such groups should be the basis for the 'target population'. However, the important point is to address the needs of all sections by reducing the entry costs to legal housing as far as possible and assisting those unable to afford entry to obtain rental accommodation within housing developed by those who can afford to participate. Where appropriate, it may also be desirable to include middle and higher income groups to generate an internal cross subsidy and a social balance in the locality. This is discussed on page 69.

The target population will not be able to include, however, all those households below this upper limit. No matter how basic proposals are, there will always be some households who cannot afford them. Provision for this group will generally be limited to the encouragement of additional low-cost private and public rental accommodation.

In new settlement projects, the target population can therefore be defined as households with insufficient incomes to afford conventional housing, but sufficient to be able to build or organise the building of their own houses.

In upgrading projects, the target population will already have some form of accommodation. They will therefore need to pay only for any improvements to their existing superstructures, together with the cost of local utilities and their share of total project costs. Assuming that the ability to pay for project proposals applies equally to new settlement and upgrading

4 Stage 1

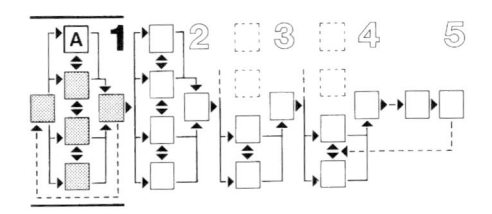

projects, upgrading projects will therefore be able to reach households with lower incomes.

It is useful to obtain information concerning:
- Household and individual incomes (both net and gross) and an indication of their regularity.
- Household expenditure, especially on housing and related services, but also food, clothing, medical costs, education, heating and travel to work.
- The maximum amount which households are able to set aside each month for housing and related services. For feasibility studies, this can generally be taken as 20 per cent of total net household income.
- The level of savings, or other assets available for deposits.

― Project area income distribution
•••• Typical national urban income distribution
―·― Minimum income level required to afford modest legal housing
― ―· Minimum income level required to afford any expenditure on housing or services
 Range of income levels for typical target population

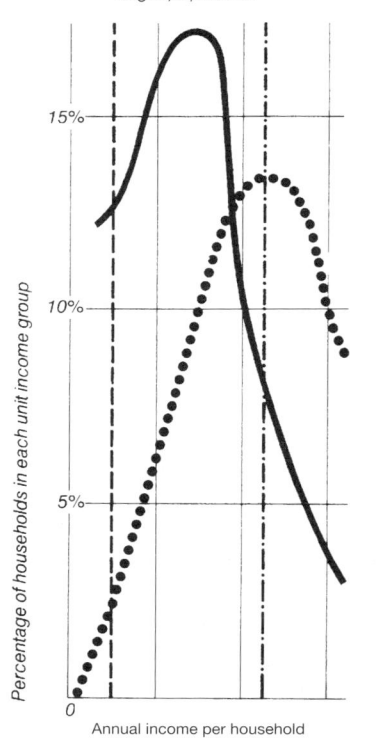

Figure 1
Household income distribution

Task 1A/3
Identifying household characteristics

Important information includes:
- Household size (i.e. the number of people living together as a social unit).
- Household structure (i.e. their relationship).

This information is important in estimating the number of people in households, existing housing densities and the rate at which new households are created. (see Technical note 1, page 100 for methods of collecting this information).

Table 1
Ability to pay for shelter: examples

Annual income ranges: limits & mid-points (LE)	Income for shelter (%)	Monthly (LE)	Annual (LE)	Total(Le) available assuming amortisation at 7% over 20 years
525	15	6.7	78.8	833
	20	8.8	105.0	1113
	25	10.9	131.3	1390
630	15	8.1	94.5	1001
	20	10.5	126.0	1334
	25	13.3	157.5	1666
840	15	10.5	126.0	1334
	20	14.0	168.0	1778
	25	17.5	210.0	2223
1050	15	13.3	157.5	1666
	20	17.5	210.0	2223
	25	22.1	262.5	2779
1365	15	16.8	202.3	2132
	20	22.4	269.5	2853
	25	28.0	337.1	3570
1680	15	20.7	246.8	2615
	20	27.3	329.0	3483
	25	34.3	411.3	4354
210	15	29.1	346.5	3672
	20	38.5	462.0	4893
	25	48.3	577.5	6318
2940	15	36.4	435.8	4613
	20	48.3	581.0	6153
	25	60.6	726.3	7690

LE = Egyptian Pounds 1999

Task 1A/4
Identifying housing demand

The assessment of housing demand has to distinguish between *effective* demand (i.e. what people are able to obtain) and *potential* demand (i.e. what housing people would prefer if they had a choice). To be realistic, emphasis should be placed upon existing economic characteristics of the target population rather than optimistic views of future improvements, since this may commit people to having to pay more for housing than they can afford. This indicates the level of demand for housing which can be afforded in a city, but care should also be taken to estimate the *type* of demand which is relevant to a project. For example, does experience or survey evidence suggest that some types of housing are more popular among different income groups than others? The information on incomes and the amounts available for housing will enable a more precise definition of the target population to be made. This can then be related to population forecasts for the whole urban area.

In order to estimate the extent of total demand for housing in any given urban area, it will be necessary to calculate the total number of households within the target population and the proportion which is likely to be involved in a project. This estimate of total housing demand should be projected for the full period during which a project will be implemented.

An indication of the *nature* of demand for housing should also be obtained. This need only indicate the main aspects, such as the priorities which people in each category of the target population have expressed for upgrading or new housing, the type of tenure, plot, size, location or utilities needed and any others considered relevant.

This information can only be obtained by asking questions directly to the target population. Some form of field survey will therefore be necessary. Methods of conducting surveys are discussed in Technical note 1 (page 100).

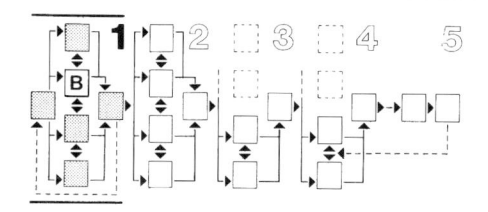

Task group 1B
Project site: outline assessment and selection

1B/1	Assessing site availability	5
1B/2	Initial evaluation of site location	6
1B/3	Identifying site area and shape	6
1B/4	Identifying existing land tenure	7
1B/5	Identifying site boundaries	7
1B/6	Initial assessment of site topography and landscape	7
1B/7	Initial assessment of ground conditions	8
1B/8	Identifying pollution problems	8

This Task group requires an outline study of possible sites, including their availability, location and main physical characteristics.

There are two basic situations in which preliminary site studies are required. The first is when only one site is being considered, in which case the question to be answered is: 'Are there any major problems with the site which will affect the success of the project?' The second situation is where there is a choice of sites, in which case the second question is not simply: 'Will it work?' but: 'If it works, how will it work relative to other sites?' This type of study usually requires more information and an initial list of sites should also record whether they are suitable for new settlement, the upgrading of existing site development or a combination of the two. Since upgrading will generally involve the removal of at least some residents to other areas, there will often be an advantage in combination projects. In carrying out this Task, reference should also be made to Task group 1C (page 9) and Task 1C/2 (page 10).

The information obtained on each potential site should be recorded in note form and/or plotted on a series of maps. The scale of such maps will depend upon the area of the site and the amount of information available, but 1:10 000 would probably be the smallest useful scale and 1:500 the largest practical one (see Technical note 15, page 123). Maps should be based upon the most recent and accurate surveys available and checked against air photographs where possible (see Technical notes 5 and 6, page 117). Important details should be checked by visiting the site and walking over it. These site maps will provide the base upon which information on all physical aspects of the site are recorded. When visiting a site it is important not to raise expectations of the community. Discussion with local leaders is important and the local community can be a useful resource in surveys.

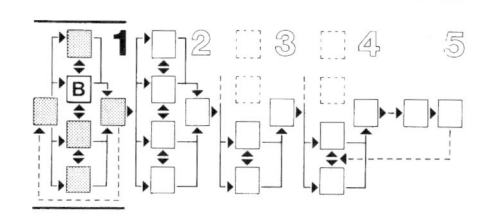

Task 1B/1
Assessing site availability

In most cases, potential sites can be identified by:
- Discussion with the relevant central or local government agencies.
- Reference to metropolitan and local planning proposals.
- Checking on the ground and discussing with local communities and those dealing in land.

The availability of all sites will be influenced by their tenure category and price and reference should therefore be made to Task 1B/4 (page 7). Potential sites should then be marked on appropriate scale plans. In all cases where the availability of a site is confirmed, the Tasks outlined below should be carried out.

It will also be advisable to check if any land disputes or litigation affects the selected site or sites, as this will seriously affect site suitability.

6   Stage 1

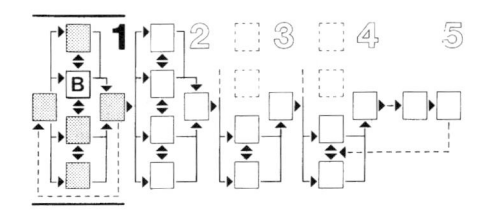

Task 1B/2
Initial evaluation of site location

This requires the examination of a site's position relative to the urban area of which it is a part, and its relationship to growth trends and development plans.

The main question is one of accessibility. This includes:
- Access to existing or potential employment opportunities. Sites which involve long or expensive journeys to work may be difficult to develop unless cheap and efficient transport can be guaranteed.
- Access to public facilities such as shops, schools and hospitals.
- Means of access (i.e. road and transport links).

In the case of upgrading projects, the fact that low income households are already living in an area means that some of the above Tasks will not be applicable. In such cases, the major consideration will be whether upgrading can be undertaken as a self-contained process; that is, can displaced households be found alternative accommodation within the project site after the necessary utilities and facilities have been installed? If this is not possible, it will be necessary to provide access to housing, or sites elsewhere for those households to be displaced.

If a potential site is in a politically or militarily sensitive location, particular care should be taken in carrying out the studies and an assessment should be made of any positive or negative effect upon project feasibility.

Task 1B/3
Identifying site area and shape

It is important to establish at the beginning that a site is of a suitable size and shape to make a project feasible. The need to put all urban land to the best possible use will make even very small sites suitable for some form of development, but larger sites will provide more planning options and will enable a single project to cater for the needs of more people. A preliminary estimate should therefore be made of the site area available for a project.

The shape of a site will also exert an important influence upon its possible development or improvement. In general, the more regular a site is, the greater will be the chance of achieving an efficient layout. (See technical notes 3 and 24).

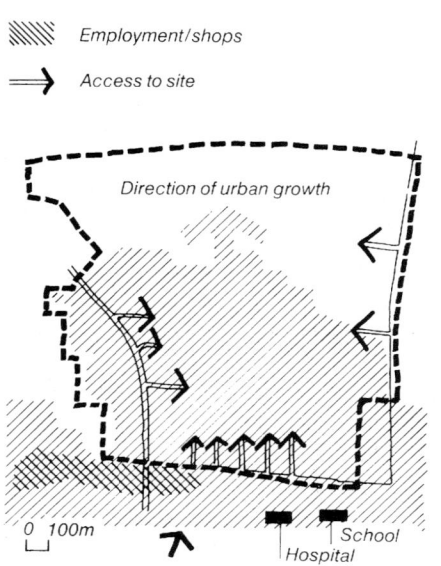

Figure 2
Site location features

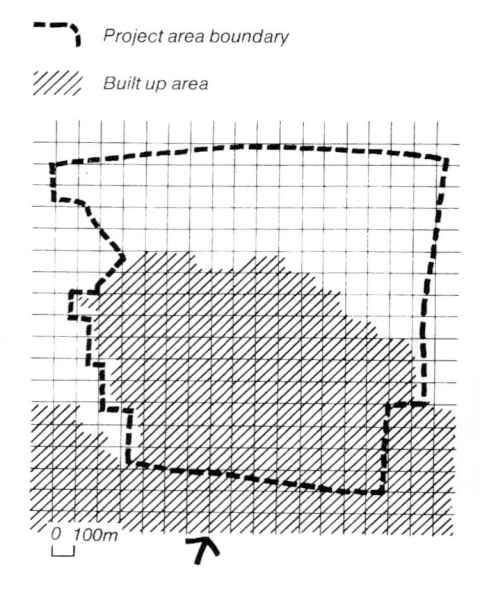

Figure 3
Site area and shape

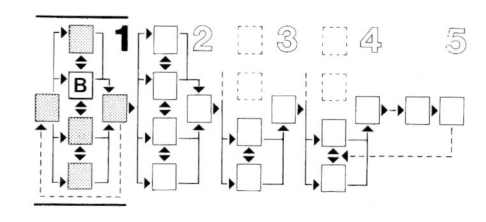

Task 1B/4
Identifying existing land tenure and value

The suitability of an area for a project will be influenced by its existing tenure and ownership. In cases where the land is held in freehold tenure, its cost may be so high that households within the target population may be unable to afford project costs. Where the entire site is under public ownership, however, the task of planning site utilization will be greatly simplified.

Information will be necessary on the existing type or types of tenure on the project site and the approximate areas these cover. This can usually be obtained from the land registry or property taxation departments, though a special check is recommended in areas subject to speculative transfers or where records may be out of date. A broad estimate of land costs should be prepared on the basis of Technical note 9 (page 118). All information should be plotted on a copy of the site plan and in note form as appropriate.

It will also be advisable to check if any land disputes or litigation affects the selected site or sites, as this will seriously affect site suitability.

Task 1B/5
Identifying site boundaries

The nature of site boundaries, together with the characteristics of adjoining development, will determine the points of access to the site and will influence road planning and housing layouts within the site. They will also determine the degree to which the site can be linked to or separated from adjoining development. All defined boundaries such as rivers, canals, highways or railways should be recorded on the site map and their implications noted.

Task 1B/6
Initial assessment of site topography and landscape

The existence of steep slopes, for example, will reduce the chances of fully developing or upgrading a site. They will also affect project site and individual structure development costs. All available information should be obtained from government departments and a short site visit made, when any steep slopes or other features should be plotted on the site map. It may be advisable to omit unsuitable parts of the site, or to designate them for development as public open areas.

During the topographic survey, the main characteristics of the natural landscape should be recorded. Existing planting can be a valuable feature, especially during the early stages of a project, and should be noted so that as much as possible can be incorporated.

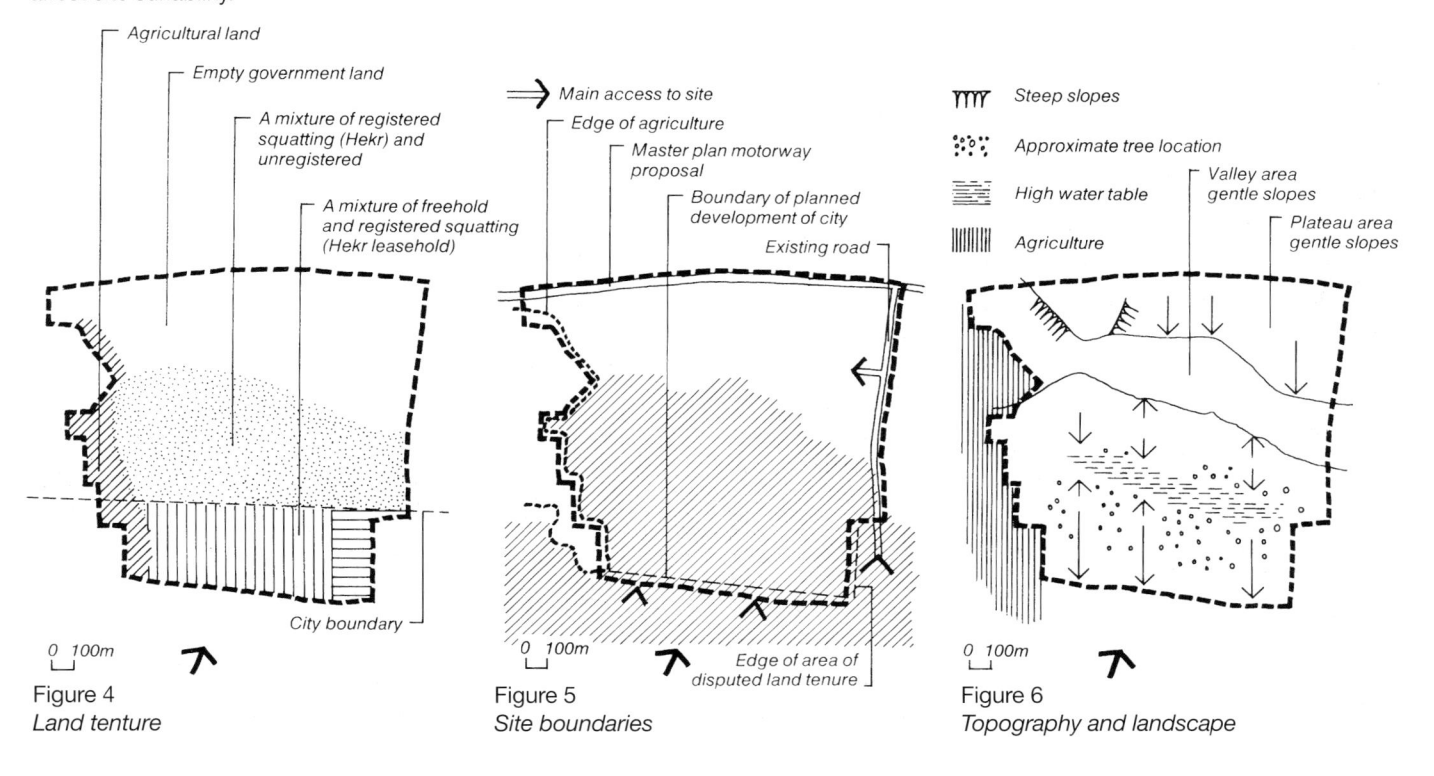

Figure 4
Land tenure

Figure 5
Site boundaries

Figure 6
Topography and landscape

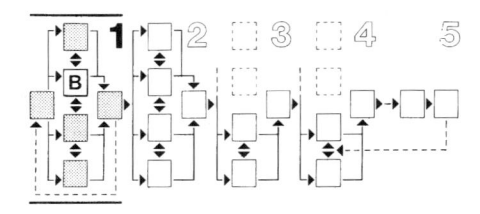

Stage 1

Task 1B/7
Initial assessment of ground conditions

These important studies should be based upon all available information and a short site visit.

Means of information collection include:
- Plot all existing *borehole* and *trial pit* information for the site and its immediate vicinity. This can usually be obtained from local government departments, contractors and public health organisations and will indicate any problems involved in providing utilities to the site or building on it.
- Refer to the site maps and, if possible, to stereo aerial photographs. To an experienced engineer these should highlight most major hazards, and even an inexperienced engineer should be able to identify hazards such as mobile sand dunes or a high water table.

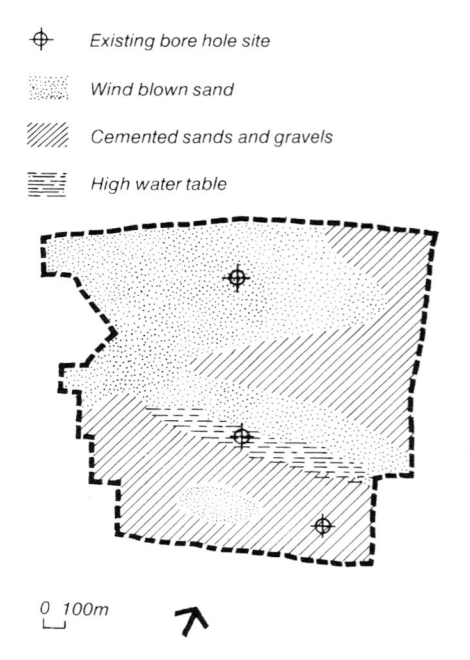

During a visit to the site the following points should be noted:
- The nature of the geological structure. This should include, e.g. the extent and location of any rock outcrops or sand dunes.
- Any cracking of existing buildings or other signs of movement. This may indicate expansive clay soils, salt crystallisation, or load deformation.
- Old quarries, mines or pits which have been backfilled. These generally provide a poor basis for building.
- The presence of aggressive chemicals or salts in the soil or ground water which could corrode cement in buildings or their foundations. Dead trees may indicate a recent rise in a salty water table and the splintering of stone or brickwork may indicate chemical attack.
- The possibility of flooding, earthquakes or other natural hazards. If present these may require considerable protection works and should therefore be identified quickly.
- In the case of new settlement projects, an assessment should be made of any practical reasons why the area has not already been developed.

All this information should be recorded in note form and included on copies of the site plan.

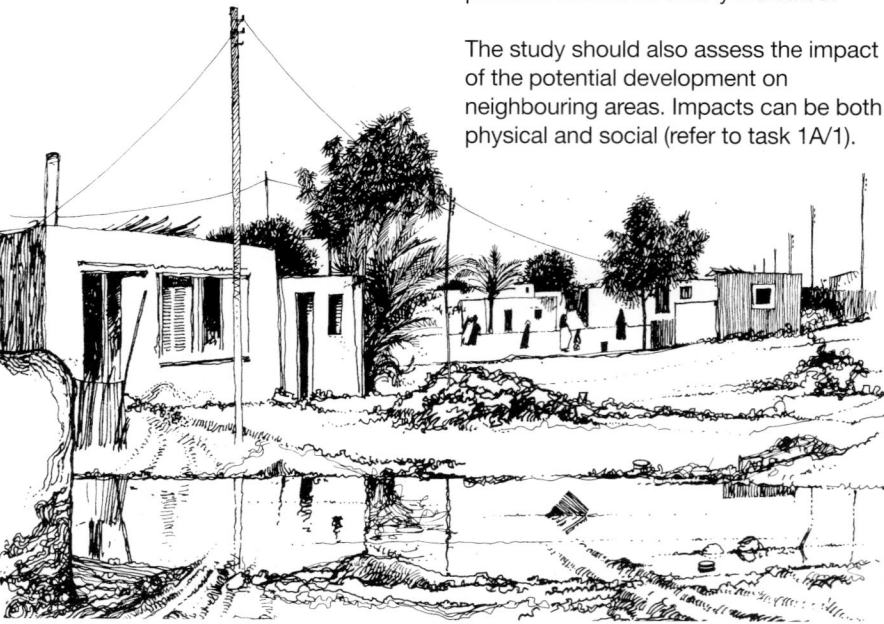

Task 1B/8
Identifying environmental problems

Pollution is one aspect in which prevention is not only better than a cure, but also cheaper. A study should be made to see if there are any significant levels of pollution near the site which could affect the feasibility of the project. The study should consider:
- Abnormal levels of dust or other airborne matter.
- Gases and fumes, particularly industrial emissions.
- Sewage, effluent or industrial waste carried by water in the ground or in streams.
- Any other sources, especially those which may pollute wells.

The severity and frequency of the various forms of pollution should be estimated and an assessment made of their possible effect upon the project. In general, development close to a major source of pollution should be discouraged, especially if the site is downstream of the source, or downwind of the prevailing winds.

Information on pollution can normally be obtained from specialised public agencies. It should be recorded on copies of the site plan. Areas affected by different types of pollution should be clearly indicated.

The study should also assess the impact of the potential development on neighbouring areas. Impacts can be both physical and social (refer to task 1A/1).

Existing bore hole site
Wind blown sand
Cemented sands and gravels
High water table

0 100m

Figure 7
Ground conditions

Stage 1

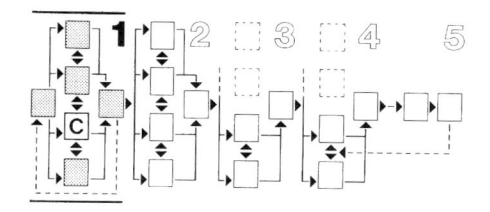

Task group 1C
Site development: assessing initial site development options

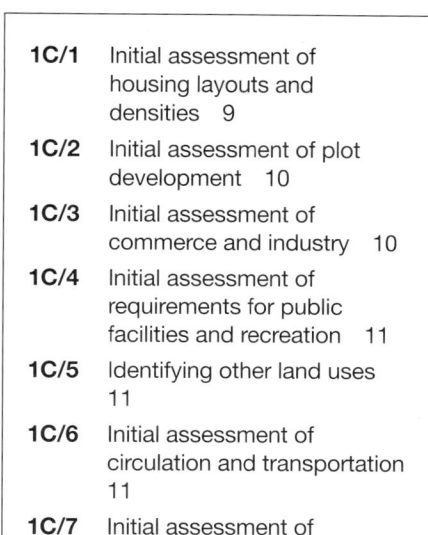

1C/1	Initial assessment of housing layouts and densities 9
1C/2	Initial assessment of plot development 10
1C/3	Initial assessment of commerce and industry 10
1C/4	Initial assessment of requirements for public facilities and recreation 11
1C/5	Identifying other land uses 11
1C/6	Initial assessment of circulation and transportation 11
1C/7	Initial assessment of requirements for utilities 12

This Task group consists of two main elements. The first studies existing accommodation of the target population. For upgrading projects these can be carried out on the project site, but for new settlements an existing area accommodating low income households would provide useful information. This could be the same location in which studies of the target population are carried out (see Task group 1A, page 3). The second is preparing outline proposals for site development and should concentrate on achieving an effective use of available land.

Since the purpose is to establish project feasibility, generally it will be sufficient to cover the main features of existing development and project proposals.

All information should be plotted on copies of the site plan or set out in note or tabular form as appropriate. When this information is recorded, preliminary proposals can then be made for development of the project site. These will be based upon the estimate of housing needs and resources as obtained during Task group 1A (page 3), and the constraints and opportunities identified in 1B (page 5), 1C (page 9) and 1D (page 12). Reference should be made to the compatibility of the potential development to master plan or other proposals for the area.

Each Task can now be discussed in sequence.

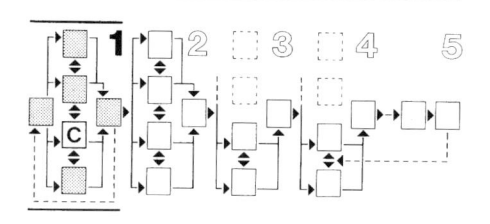

Task 1C/1
Initial assessment of housing layouts and densities

For new settlement projects, it will be necessary at this stage to identify any constraints which may prevent an efficient layout from being developed.

For upgrading projects, the main considerations will be to assess the existing layout as a possible basis for operations (see Task 1C/6, page 11). This involves assessing any problems which may arise in providing an efficient street layout and utilities network. Evidence of house improvement may indicate that there is an effective demand for an upgrading project. Lack of improvement may be due, however, to insecurity of tenure.

Densities will also be important. Where these are very high, the installation of utilities or public facilities will be more difficult and expensive and may well involve substantial demolition and social disruption. Lower densities will not generally present these problems and it will be easier to find a site within the project area for any households who have to be moved. It is also easier to accommodate displaced households nearby when a new site is being developed adjacent to the upgrading area.

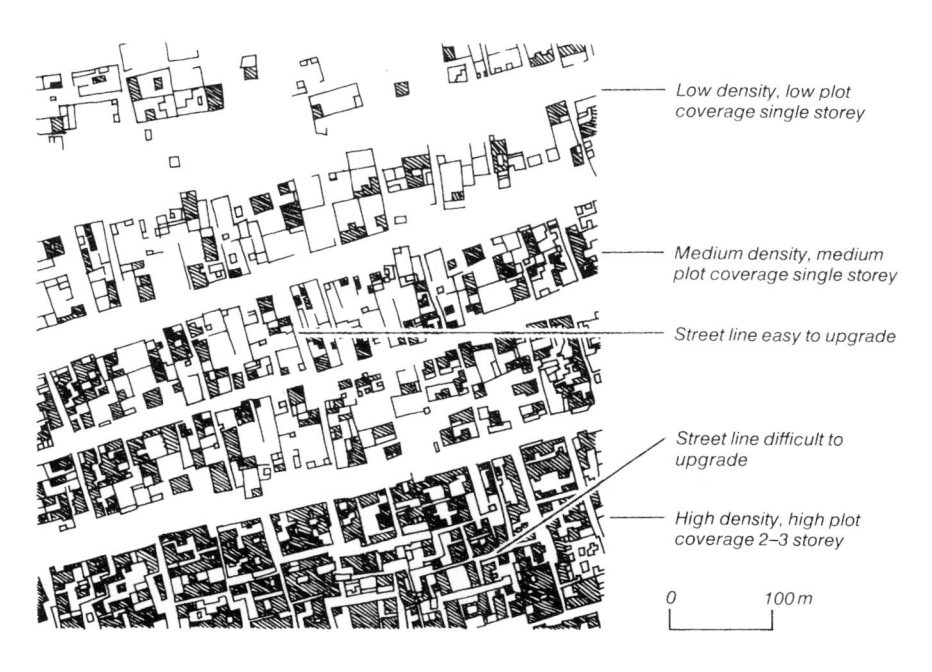

Figure 8
Existing area: layout and densities

- Low density, low plot coverage single storey
- Medium density, medium plot coverage single storey
- Street line easy to upgrade
- Street line difficult to upgrade
- High density, high plot coverage 2–3 storey

0   100m

Stage 1

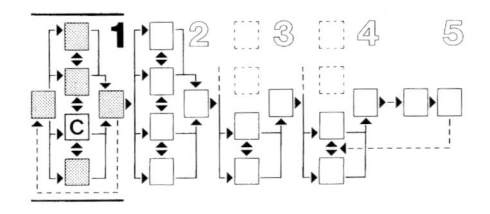

It will be necessary to estimate the future likely densities for the project site, since this will determine the number of households participating in a project. For upgrading projects, this can be done by applying densities found in sample areas of the more consolidated parts of a site to the remainder. Total project populations can then be obtained by multiplying average density totals by the total area of a project site. An estimate of total numbers of households can then be obtained by dividing the total population by the average household size (see Task 1 A/2, page 4). The same method can be used for new settlement projects using data from an existing area accommodating the households similar to target population.

Information can be obtained in several ways. Existing plans or census data can be useful but a site visit should always be made, discussions held with local residents and representatives and a consolidated part of existing development surveyed.

Information from the studies should be recorded on copies of the site plan and/or in note form.

Task 1C/2
Initial assessment of plot development

Plot development refers to the type and extent of buildings on a piece of land. This Task need not be covered in great detail at this stage since it is unlikely to exert a major influence on project feasibility. A brief study of how plots are being developed gives a good framework for preparing initial options.

The main focus of preliminary studies should be on assessing the following:
● Whether or not it is feasible for each household to be provided with an individual plot in new housing areas.
● The ability of existing plot sizes accommodating the target population to meet household needs.
● The existence of any problems which may arise in installing utilities to each plot.
● The types of existing superstructures (i.e. houses, tenements and apartments) their condition, number of storeys and general suitability for upgrading.
● The nature and extent of building necessary to meet at least short term household needs and the ability of households to provide this for themselves.
● The extent of any changes to plot or building lines which will be necessary before upgrading can take place.

Information can be obtained by reference to detailed maps or aerial photographs of the site, or of other areas accommodating the target population. A short site visit should also be made for checks with local residents (see Task group 1A, page 3).

Task 1C/3
Initial assessment of commerce and industry

Commercial and industrial development serve important functions for a potential project. They provide the opportunity for employment; they provide services and, through their influence on land values, provide a potential for a land agency to make money which can be redistributed within the project.

A brief study should be made of existing and potential commercial and industrial development and its implications for project feasibility. Information can be obtained by reference to local shops and workshops, Chambers of Trade or spot interviews. It should be carefully recorded on site plans and/or in note form.

Figure 9   (*left*)
House type: traditional materials, one storey, medium quality

Figure 10   (*right*)
House type: modern materials, two storey, high quality

Task 1C/4

Initial assessment of requirements for public facilities and recreation

For upgrading projects, the study of any existing public facilities provision (e.g. schools, health clinics) is vital before considering the possibility of providing new facilities. This involves a brief study of existing types and levels of provision relative to problems which exist and attainable standards. Official government standards may be very high but may be a long term aim. Discussions with local education and health officials will probably reveal a realistic or attainable basic standard which may be the initial objective of the project.

This study should include:
- The number of schools, the ages they cater for and the number of places (official), the number of children actually attending and problems which exist. Comparison with standards will give a first estimate of deficits.
- Types of health care and capacity of facilities compared with health problems in the area and official standards of provision.
- Other social or public facilities and their capacities compared with standards.

Information can usually be provided by government departments, though a spot check will be useful. The location of each facility should be plotted on copies of the site plan and/or in note form.

For new settlement projects, it will be necessary to identify any constraints which will prevent the normal provision of public facilities or recreation. It will also be necessary to determine whether the project has to meet deficiencies occurring outside its boundaries.

Task 1C/5

Identifying other land uses

The purpose of studying these at this stage is to establish any constraints or opportunities which they may imply for a project. The existence of a military camp or polluting industrial plant obviously may reduce the chance of achieving a successful project. Any such areas should therefore be identified, mapped, and their implications for a project assessed.

Task 1C/6

Initial assessment of circulation and transportation

The purpose of this Task is to assess roughly the work required to produce a road and transport system which:
- Provides opportunities of access to employment, social facilities and shopping.
- Provides a simple street layout, within which utility networks can be provided efficiently.
- Provides a standard of access which satisfies minimum project requirements and the capital budget.

Matters which need examination depend on whether an upgrading or new settlement project is being considered.

In upgrading projects, existing street conditions should be recorded by classifying and recording on a plan the:
- Street widths.
- Type of frontage development.
- General traffic conditions especially any particular problems.
- Public transport.

The object is to be able to rank alternative sites in a way which expresses the extent of work required to provide a transport and circulation system which meet defined project objectives. Of particular importance is the extent of demolition required to rationalise and improve street layouts and the suitability of existing street patterns to provide improved utility networks.

In new settlements, the opportunity for linking sites to the local or regional road network should be examined and potential problems on the site recorded. The conditions which may cause construction problems include:
- Ground conditions.
- Cost of links to adjacent road networks.
- Topography of site.
- Existing buildings or other property.

In upgrading areas and new settlements, a preliminary estimate of construction costs should be made to provide an input to the economic assessment of the viability of site improvement or development.

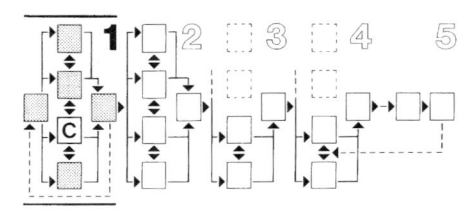

Task 1C/7
Initial assessment of requirements for utilities

For most upgrading projects, utilities (e.g. water supply, sewerage) provision will be the most important element. Existing standards will provide useful information on which to base new proposals, though the location and layout of future utility mains is more important. In many cases, some demolition or relocation of existing buildings will be necessary, though this should be kept to the minimum.

For both upgrading and new settlement projects a brief study should therefore be made of provisions existing for the target population, problems arising, and the potential difficulties of installing new utilities. This should include details of:
- The extent, nature and quality of water supplies.
- The means of collection and disposal of sewage and surface water.
- The extent of electricity supplies.
- Any health hazard or problems.
- Any existing proposals for improving utilities.
- Any projects being carried out on the site.

Information on these aspects can usually be obtained from local government departments or public health authorities, though a short site visit should also be made. The study should not be confined to the site itself, but should include an examination of available off-site networks and their capacity to provide the necessary level of improved service. The principal utilities concerned will be water supply, electricity supply and sewage disposal systems.

Information should be plotted on copies of the site plan and/or in note form.

Task Group 1D
Institutional and financial framework

1D/1	Assessing the capacity of the institutional framework	12
1D/2	Identifying the financial framework	13

Task 1D/1
Assessing the capacity of the institutional framework

This Task has to provide the answer to one question: Is the existing institutional framework for housing and urban development projects appropriate to the type of project being proposed and, if not, what changes appear necessary? The 'Institutional framework' includes NGOs and CBOs and private sector in addition to government institutions.

Since upgrading or new settlement projects based upon the expressed needs of the target population may represent a major change of policy or practice, the ability of existing institutions to carry them out should be examined carefully. Particular attention should be given to the need to co-ordinating the various aspects of a project, such as employment, in addition to housing. Finally, the institutional framework will have to be capable of meeting special local needs and the objectives of national housing policy.

For project feasibility, it will be necessary to establish that the organisation responsible for a project will possess the necessary *authority*, *finance* and *personnel*.

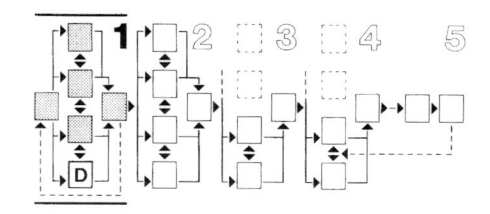

Task 1D/2
Identifying the financial framework

The financial framework can only be considered adequately within the institutional framework for a project.

Assessment of costs and their allocation

It will not be possible generally to prepare detailed cost estimates, since the proposals and data on which they are based will be provisional. The best approach is to identify any elements upon which costs are likely to be critical or different from local experience and to assess these as accurately as possible. Average rates can then be applied to all other elements to obtain a preliminary estimate of total project cost.

When preparing outline costs, particular care should be given to:
- Land costs. These may well prove to be the single most important factor in determining the feasibility of a site for housing low-income groups, and must be based upon the market value of the land.

Land values will depend to a large extent upon the tenure status of the site (see Task 1B/4, page 7). They will also vary, however, according to location and a central city site generally will be many times more expensive than one in a suburban area. Within a given location, access to main roads will increase land costs and so will a higher level of services provision.

The actual price which a piece of land can command will depend on all the factors mentioned and on the urban land market. Not all land will be free to vary in price according to market forces and government or institutional land is generally excluded from the market, though its conversion in or out of the market may be possible.

Where a 'free' land market operates, estimates of likely land value can usually be obtained from local land registration or property tax departments, land agencies or legal landowners. Another method is discussed in Technical note 9, (page 118). Where land is under public ownership or control and is therefore excluded from the 'free' market, an 'opportunity' cost, (i.e. an amount which the land would be likely to command if sold in the free market), should be estimated. This can also be done by comparing prices on similar sites in private freehold tenure.*
- Infrastructure. The type and level of provision (i.e. roads/water/sewerage) and public facilities indicated as appropriate by the surveys of the target population (see Task group 1A, page 3). To enable as many as possible of the target population to participate in the project, initial proposals should be kept to a minimum, as they can always be upgraded later if households can afford more, or if subsidies are available. It is critical to separate out costs which will not be the responsibility of the project. Examples are schools or electricity supply.
- The extent to which project costs are to be recovered from the target population.
- The possible costs related to special ground conditions which have to be considered in the provision of utilities or building, especially if land fill, drainage or other works are required.
- Approximate costs for all types of building used, or expected to be used, by the target population. Where the proposals for new settlement exclude government built housing units, this will mean an estimate of costs which households will have to meet in building or organising building themselves.

When all aspects have been considered, total project costs can be estimated. An allowance should then be made for physical contingencies, inflation, administration and interest charges and the likely level of default (non-payment). Estimated figures should not be made artificially low in an attempt to make the project appear to reach people in income groups lower than can actually be achieved. The preliminary estimates of the costs applicable to households will vary according to the arrangements for cost allocation as discussed above.

Total preliminary costs per household can then be identified. These costs will vary depending on the assumptions which have been made, for example, on the level of infrastructure or whether a 'shadow price' has been charged for government land. They will later be compared with levels of 'affordability' or what families are likely to be able to spend on housing, to help determine the nature of the project.

The information on costs for any particular set of proposals will inevitably be very approximate. They should be adequate, however, to enable the feasibility of a project to be assessed. Where a number of sites is being considered, the unit costs of each type and level of provision should be the same so that the relative merits of each site can be assessed.

The ability of the target population to meet the possible costs of the project will be indicated by information obtained in Task 1A/1, (page 3). Since household incomes are relatively fixed, any gap will have to be bridged by modifying the project proposals. This is discussed in Task group 1E (page 14). An example is shown in Table 36, Appendix 1, page 151.

---

* In calculating feasibility, the 'opportunity cost' of land should be included as a cost. It may be excluded at a later stage, when this would represent a hidden subsidy.

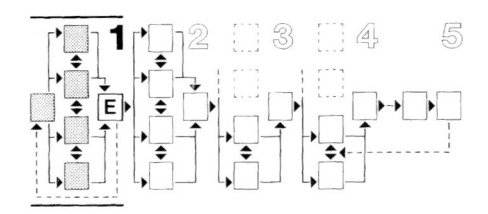

14 Stage 1

Task 1E
Feasibility studies: analysis

How can the analysis of project sites and proposals be made? In view of the range of points described in the previous Tasks, there can be no simple answer and methods should be related to local experience and resources. Sophisticated approaches should be avoided, since the decision on feasibility can only be as accurate as the information on which it is based and that will generally be provisional and incomplete.

Of possible methods, the tabulation of information against a checklist provides a simple and useful way of:
- Making sure that all the relevant points are covered.
- Forming a basis for comparing information from different sites, where a choice is being made.

A checklist has to resolve the problem of *rating* each point, that is, how will it achieve project objectives. Some points are also more important than others, and that in turn raises the problem of *ranking* them in order of importance.

In using the checklist, a simple five point rating system can be used. One method is as follows:
- + +   Indicates that a point is very favourable to a project.
- +   Indicates that a point is favourable.
- + −   Indicates that a point would not create any particular problems.
- −   Indicates that a point would create some difficulty.
- − − Indicates that a point would make the success of a project very difficult to achieve.

The checklist cannot attempt any ranking of the various points, since the relative importance of each will vary with local conditions. Reducing the list of points to the minimum will, however, make comparison easier.

For clarity, the checklist should follow the Task sequence in the text as closely as possible. Where there is any doubt concerning the rating of any particular point, reference can be made to the appropriate part of the text.

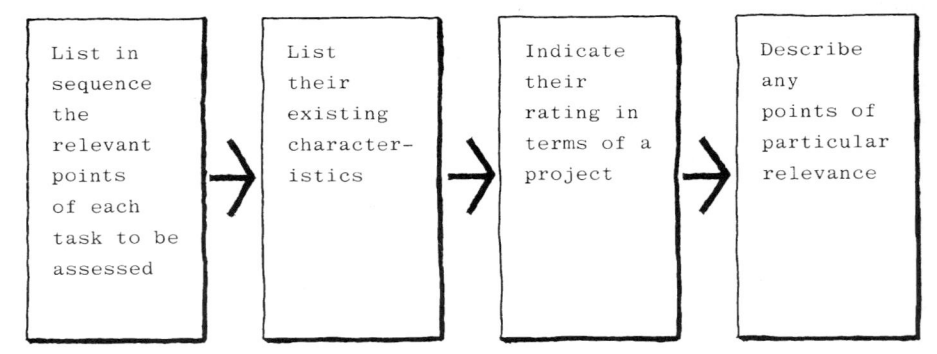

The checklist can be organised as shown in Figures 11 and 12.

This analysis is, of course, only a preliminary one. *The rating of each Task will indicate the degree to which a project is likely to succeed. The possibility of the target population being able to afford project costs is probably the most critical test.*

If the analysis shows the most important elements favourable and a minimum of unfavourable assessments, it would suggest that the project site and proposals being considered are feasible. Where there are more than one site or set of proposals, the analysis will indicate the combination most likely to produce a successful project. These can then be submitted for approval to the authorities. Once this is obtained, work can begin on the Tasks described in Stage 2.

If the analysis shows that, on balance, the project site or proposals are *not* suitable, it will be necessary to establish the reasons. In most cases, one or both of the following may be responsible:
- The site is unsuitable. This may be because the land cost is too high, the amount of work needed on it may be too expensive, or there may be a large number of tenants living on it, making upgrading more difficult. If this is the case, it is likely that another site will need to be selected, unless a subsidy is available.
- The proposals are not suitable. This may well be because they cost more than the target population can afford to pay or do not reflect adequately its housing needs. If this is the case, proposals should be modified until they *are* suitable. The same exercise of relating them to the project site and the resources of the target population will then need to be repeated.

If subsequent reviews suggest that the project may become feasible, it can be submitted for approval to the authorities. Should the analysis show that despite modifications, it is still unlikely to be feasible, it should be abandoned and an alternative site or set of proposals chosen. The only possible exception could be if the cause is excessive costs due to abnormal local factors, such as flood prevention requirements, high land acquisition costs or landfill. In exceptional circumstances, it may be considered appropriate to apply for an external subsidy to enable very low income households to participate in a project. In such cases, it is vital to identify the extent of subsidy required and select the cost element or elements which will meet the needs of the target groups, minimise market distortion and maintain options for future changes if required. These factors will determine whether the subsidy should be applied to the cost of land, interest rates, services, materials, or other items. It is also important that subsidies are transparent. The project will only be able to proceed if the required level of subsidy is available.

| List in sequence the relevant points of each task to be assessed | → | List their existing character-istics | → | Indicate their rating in terms of a project | → | Describe any points of particular relevance |

Figure 11
Preparation of feasibility study checklist

Figure 12 (*right*)
Checklist for analysing project feasibility and /or selecting sites

Example of sheet used in selection of El Hekr site, Ismailia

Stage 1   15

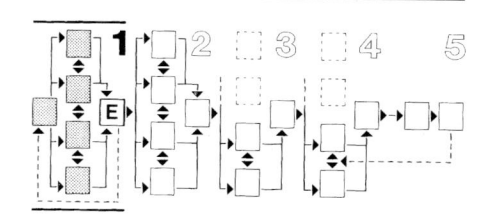

NUMBER	CRITERIA	++	+	+−	−	−−	COMMENTS	REFERENCE TO MANUAL TASKS
1	Sufficient size of area	●					Sufficient area for Demonstration Project both new and upgrading, its future stages, necessary relocations and services, population of existing area 20 000	1B/3
2	Local concentration of diverse employment (including low skill)			●			Some in older section of El Hekr more in adjacent Arashia and bazaar area 1 km (15 minutes walk) away	1B/2
3	Proximity to main concentration of diverse employment in the city (including low skill)	●						1B/2
4	Proximity to specialised employment centre			●			Limited, more in adjacent area (5 to 10 minutes walk) or in main bazaar	1B/2
5	Local subsistence shopping			●			0.8 to 1.5 km away (depending on section of El Hekr)	1B/2
6	Proximity to main bazaar of the city		●					1B/2
7	Food purchase from local farmers					●	Practised on limited scale at present	1B/2
8	Possibility of own subsistence farming and animals		●				Most rapidly improving area of the city (Arashia) immediately adjacent	1B/1
9	Proximity to other low income residential areas		●				No constraints. Some relocations may be needed for improved site, layout, services and facilities	1B/5
10	Compatibility with present land uses in the area		●				Insufficient information	1B/1
11	Compatibility with committed land uses in the area			●			Control of urbanisation of El Hekr essential to prevent invasion of future University land	1B/1
12	Compatibility with present surrounding land uses		●				Insufficient information	1B/5
13	Compatibility with committed surrounding land uses		●				Positive mix already existing will be enhanced by new site programme	1B/1
14	Possibility of fine grain social stratification of the section of the city		●				Area of strongest urbanisation pressure in Ismailia	1B/5
15	Agreement with general present growth trend of the city	●					No constraints	1B/1
16	Possibility of continuing directly from present growth	●					Upgrading and new sites programme essential to prevent growth inconsistent with Master Plan	1B/1
17	Agreement with Master Plan		●				Very rapid rate	1B/1
18	Intensity of new construction in the area or adjacent		●				see number 9	1B/5
19	Rate of improvement in the area or adjacent		●				Limited at present, demand evident	1B/5
20	Existing community centre in the area or adjacent		●				Limited at present, demand evident	1B/1
21	Potential of local employment		●					1C/3
22	Off-site (trunk) infrastructure (existing or relative cost of new)			●			Adjacent area fully serviced. Electricity and standpipes within El Hekr	1C/7
23	Public transport (existing or relative cost of new)			●			Main bus terminal about 1 km away - buses to all directions. Demand for service in the area	1C/6
24	Other services (existing or relative cost of new)			●				1B/2
25	Facilities (existing or relative cost of new)			●				1B/2 1C/6
26	Land ownership and tenure		●				Government ownership of open desert land. Hekr leasehold in built-up area	1B/1 1B/4
27	Natural and topographical features		●				Sand desert stabilizes when settled, dry	1B/7
28	Environmental factors		●				Relatively elevated, well ventilated. Generally healthy, dusty on edges on windy days	1B/8
29	Other relevant site constraints and advantages		●				Low density and adjacent sparsely settled land permit new services, relocation and expansion	1B/5
30	Opportunity cost of land			●			Low. Area of proposed new sites being squatted over at present. Will be completely and chaotically settled if no action is taken	1B/4
31	Impact on economic viability (families)		●				Good location in respect to employment and subsistence shopping supports economic potential of families	1A/1
32	Impact on economic viability (project economy)		●				Present rate of construction and improvement in the area assures project viability	1B/2 1C/3
33	Political acceptability		●				No very sensitive decisions (eradication, expropriation, etc.) necessary	1B/1
34	Visibility			●			Largest spontaneous urbanisation in the city. Its control as main step to orderly urban growth	1B/2
35	Demonstration value (typicality of situation)	●					Upgrading of new spontaneous urban area, and guiding urbanisation of open fringe land	1B/2
36	Potential for generating improvement in other areas		●					General
37	Benefits for areas and population beyond the project		●				Services and facilities for new area and first stage of upgrading will benefit entire present population	General
38	Housing tenure (users)		●				Majority owner-builders on Hekr land. Rental demand small but will increase soon	1B/4
39	Housing tenure (owners)		●				Own houses on Hekr land	1B/4
40	Physical improvability of structures		●				Likely to follow improvement process demonstrated in Arashia and oldest section of El Hekr	1C/1
41	Need of property line changes to improve the area			●			Some limited adjustments needed	1C/1
42	Capacity to pay		●				Insufficient information	1A/1 1D/2
43	Willingness to contribute		●				Demonstrated by investments in response to installation of main electricity lines	1A/3

(38–43: APPLY TO UPGRADING AREA ONLY)

++ very supportive/very positive/very easy   + supportive/positive/easy   +− no problem   − some problem/negative/difficult   −− big problem/very negative/very difficult

16   Stage 1

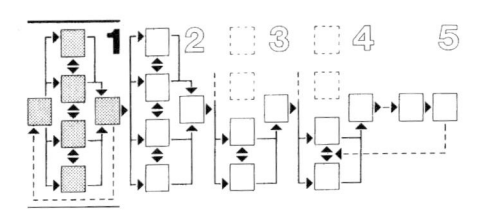

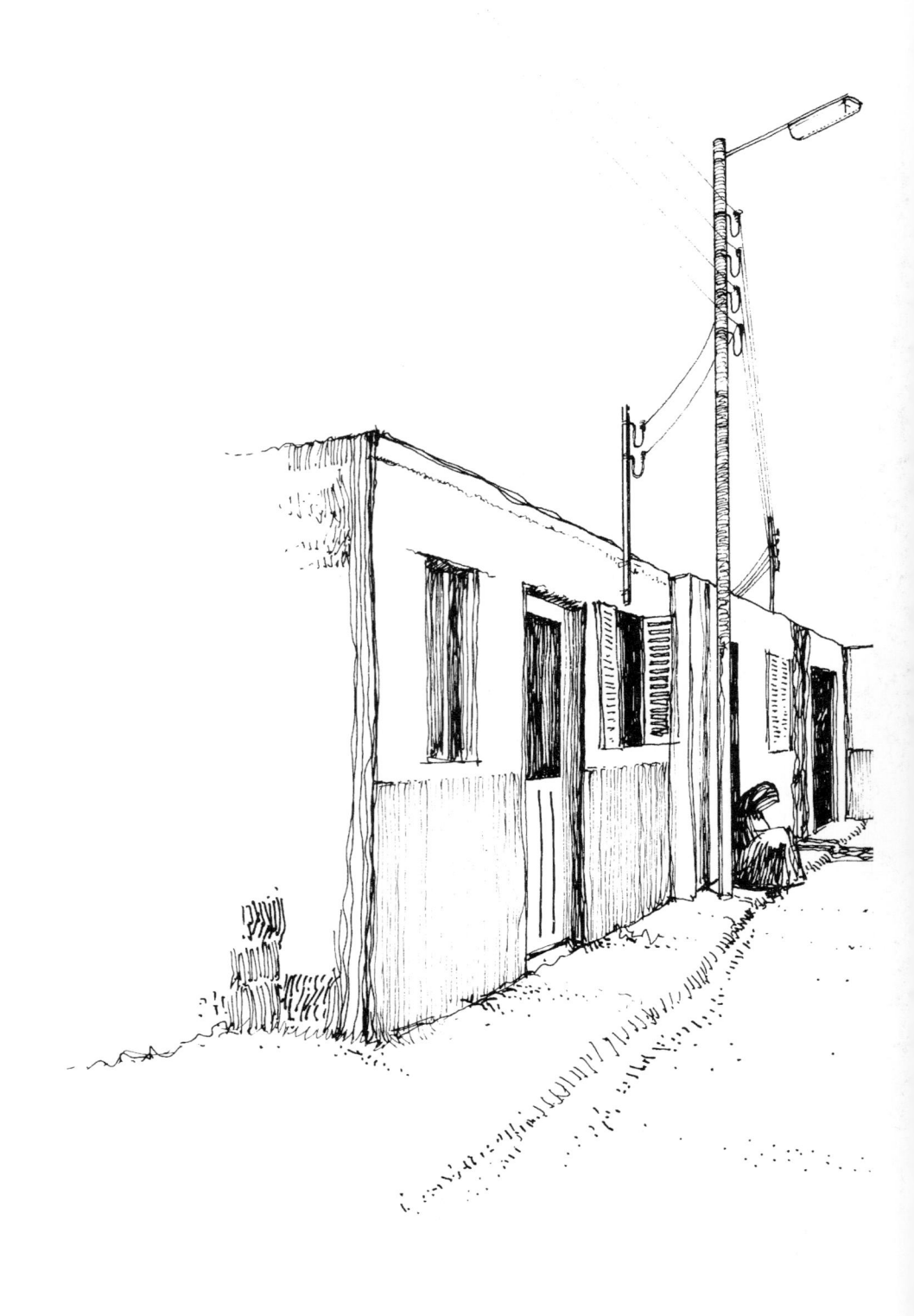

Stage 2
Detailed studies

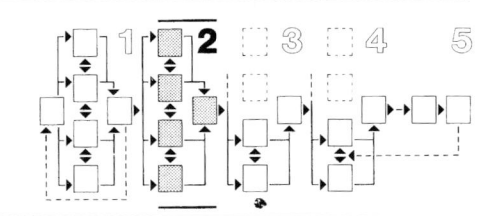

This Stage presents a number of studies which will need to be carried out before project proposals are developed. They form the main part of project preparation and can begin as soon as the Feasibility studies have been completed and outline approval for the project has been obtained.

The purpose of Detailed studies is to provide information essential for project planning. This includes these Tasks:
● Studies to determine the detailed characteristics and housing needs of the target population. These will involve original surveys as well as discussions with the representatives of communities and relevant government departments.
● Studies of all points of the project site as they will affect the project, including existing site and plot development and land tenure. Information obtained during the Feasibility studies will provide a useful reference; but more detailed information will be required. Further discussion will also be necessary with the representatives of government departments to obtain details of strategic or local planning proposals which could affect the project.

For upgrading projects, it will be possible to carry out these studies mainly within the project site. For new settlement projects, there will be no people living on the site and no on-site development. It will therefore be necessary to select a representative population on a nearby site which can be studied, to gain the necessary information.

The following notes describe each of the Tasks involved.

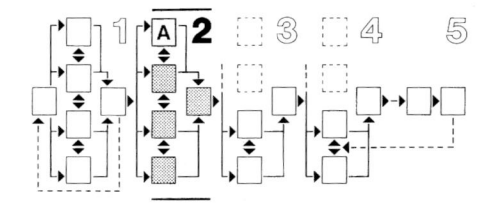

Task group 2A
Target population: survey of the target population and its housing needs

2A/1	Organisation of the community 19
2A/2	Economic characteristics of households 19
2A/3	Household characteristics 20
2A/4	Household attitudes to their locality 20
2A/5	Household attitudes to plot characteristics 20
2A/6	Relationship between households and their dwellings 21
2A/7	Nature of housing demand 21

The purpose of these Detailed studies is to collect, in a systematic way, information about households which make up the target population and the operation of the housing system. This includes incomes and expenditure, existing housing and other aspects of domestic life. The studies should also attempt to discover how the housing system operates and people's housing preferences. This will prevent unnecessary confusion, for example, regarding the type of housing which people are able to pay for and the type they are *willing* to pay for.

The content of the studies should be developed from what is already known about the target population and the project site, (see Task group 1 A, page 3). For example, if something of particular relevance to the project site is identified (e.g. a local reluctance to accept credit, or irregularity of incomes) then these points should be investigated in detail.

The information needed will naturally vary from one project to another. No single list of points will be totally applicable, though the one described below gives an indication of the scope and level of coverage which should be aimed at. Within each Task, some information will *always* be needed and some *may* be optional; the choice of which to use should be based upon local circumstances.

How can the necessary information be obtained? There are two main methods:
● A review of existing information. This may consist of data from official statistics and information from central government, local agencies and possible university or other research. Care will be needed to check how and when information was collected since unreliable information is worse than none.
● Original research. Basically, this consists of two types, formal and informal. Among the former are large scale social surveys which aim to collect information on a statistically significant basis to arrive at generally sound conclusions on a limited number of questions, such as household size or employment.
Among informal approaches are group discussions with local leaders, meetings with local residents and case studies of individual households. These are not intended to provide statistical information, but enable a deeper understanding of the problems to be gained. The two are complementary and should be used together where possible. Methods of carrying out original research are discussed in Technical note 1 (page 100).

There is no substitute for the views of the target population in preparing housing proposals. Direct approaches also provide an excellent opportunity to explain the nature and purpose of a project. This should not be done, however, in such a way that it raises false hopes or expectations.

Specific information on the physical aspects of housing and the project site can usually be obtained from the interviews. Before undertaking original social research, it is very important to co-ordinate with the physical survey team to ensure that all relevant information is gathered (see Task groups 2B, page 22; 2C, page 26; and Task 2C/1, page 26). This will also facilitate the co-ordination of social, economic and physical information which will be necessary if the project is to succeed. (See technical note 1 on conducting socio-economic surveys).

Task 2A/1
Organisation of the community

Community organisation should be checked at an early stage so that existing organisations can be fully involved in the planning process. The degree of organisation of the community will influence the form of participative working. There is no standard pattern, just as there are no standard communities.

Information to be checked:
- What community based organisations exist in the area?
- What is the official representation?
- Are there traditionally organised groups?
- What informal systems exist? Examples include savings groups.
- Is there any evidence of self help or other organisation for development?

Organisations and individuals identified at this stage may play a vital role in planning implementation and management of the project.

Task 2A/2
Economic characteristics of households

The importance of this subject means that it should be investigated more thoroughly than any other. Studies should therefore provide a detailed knowledge of all sources of income and types of expenditure, including savings and capital wealth.

Reliable information is usually difficult to obtain, partly because it is a sensitive subject which people are reluctant to discuss with strangers. For many low income households, an added factor is the difficulty of being able to budget if incomes and expenditure are irregular. It is further complicated by non-cash income in the form of home-produced foodstuffs enabling some households to save even on very low incomes. Every care should be taken to cover the following points as accurately as possible:
- The occupations of all household members, including any non-resident members, who contribute to household income.
- The gross and net incomes of all household members and an indication of whether or not an increase is expected in the near future.
- Total net household income, including any secondary sources, such as rent from letting rooms or cash from the sale of domestic produce.
- In the absence of data on incomes, affordability can be indicated by assessing existing expenditure on housing and related items and asking respondents what additional amounts they could spend for the housing of their choice.
- The cost of the household's existing plot and dwelling and the basis of payment (i.e. cash or credit and freehold or rent).
- Any savings or loans and their extent.
- The nature and cost of any house extensions or improvements carried out by plot occupants.
- The maximum amount which households can afford each month for housing and related services.

This information will enable an estimate to be made of the existing economic status and expectations of households, together with their ability to participate in the project.

Additional information may include:
- The place of work for all employed household members, but particularly the household head.
- The method of travel to work.
- Household priorities for spending any additional income if it became available.

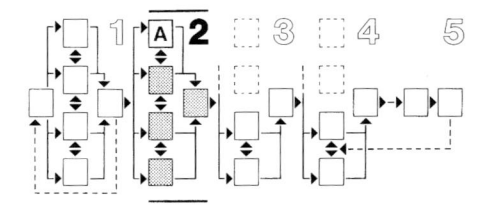

Task 2A/3
Household characteristics

This point will be essential in building up a social and demographic profile of the target population. Essential information about a sample of the population includes:
- The number of people in the household, including any absent.
- The age of the household head (usually the senior income earner).
- The age and sex of all household members.
- The household type, i.e. nuclear, extended or single person.
- Household health, especially relating to the presence of endemic diseases, such as bilharzia or chaga disease, which may be attributable to environmental factors. This information will enable estimates to be made of the distribution of household sizes and the potential for new households to be formed.

Additional information may include
- Length of residence in the project town or city.
- Length of residence in the project area.
- Birthplace of the household head.
- Reason for migration to the project town or city.
- Location and type of first residence in the project town or city.

This information will provide a valuable insight into migration patterns to and within the town or city. Most points can easily be included in even a short survey.

Task 2A/4
Household attitudes to their locality

Information on household attitudes to the area in which they live and especially on the provision of local utilities and facilities will be important in indicating the extent of any inadequacies. This will provide a basis for both upgrading and new settlement projects. Much of the information required may already have been obtained during the Feasibility studies (see Task groups 1 B, page 5; and 1C, page 9), or the Detailed studies of the project site (see Task 2B, page 22; and Task 2C/1, page 26).

Essential information includes:
- An indication of the advantages and disadvantages of the locality.
- The *use* of all facilities, including school shift systems and enrolment levels.
- Household attitudes to existing levels of provision for utilities and facilities and priorities for the future.

Before this information can be used in developing proposals discussions will be necessary with government departments or public agencies to relate existing provision to projected standards and budgetary allocations. Where immediate provision is unlikely, the reservation of adequate sites, especially for public facilities, will still be appropriate so that they can be developed in the future. Information about this will be useful in indicating priorities for new settlements.

Task 2A/5
Household attitudes to plot characteristics

This study is applicable to both upgrading and new settlement projects as it provides information on existing plots occupied by the target population, including household attitudes towards them. Since the size and shape of a plot directly influences what can be built upon it and how it can be used, it is important that significant and reliable information is available. Reference should also be made to Task 2C/2, (page 27). All information on plots should be collected as part of the social surveys (see Technical note 1, page 100).

Essential information includes:
- Household attitudes towards their existing plots related to the existing tenure status of the plot (i.e. freehold, leasehold, private rental, officially recognised squatter owner, unrecognised squatter owner, squatter tenant or member of co-operative).
- The unit area of the plot and its frontage.
- The number of households and the total number of people living on the plot.
- The extent and nature of all on-plot utilities, including water supply, sewage disposal and electricity, and attitudes towards these.

Useful additional information includes:
- The date the plot was obtained.
- The proportion of the plot which is built upon (i.e. the plot coverage ratio).
- The area of any private or shared open spaces.
- The uses to which the plot is put in addition to housing, such as shop, or workshop.

Task 2A/6
Relationship between households and their dwellings

Information about this will be applicable to both upgrading and new settlement projects. If existing housing has been produced by its occupants, it may be of particular interest in developing proposals for new settlements. Reference should be made to Task 2C/1 (page 26). For survey methods see Technical note 1 (page 100).

Essential information includes:
● Household attitudes to their existing dwellings and priorities for change.
● Existing tenure status of the dwelling on the same basis as that for the plot.
● The number of habitable rooms on the plot and, in particular, the number available to each household. The existence of a kitchen, bathroom or toilet should also be noted.
● The number of storeys.
● The phasing of construction.
● The main structural materials used (i.e. modern, traditional or mixed) and any difficulties in obtaining them.
● The financing of construction (e.g. cash, commercial loan, or other sources).
● The organisation of construction (e.g. self build, self organise, local contractor).
● Building condition (i.e. very good, good, average, poor or dangerous)

Useful additional information includes:
● The date on which the dwelling was acquired.
● The area of all habitable rooms.
● The uses to which the dwelling is put in addition to residence.

Task 2A/7
Nature of housing demand

Before proposals can be developed for either upgrading or new settlement projects, information will be needed on the total extent of housing demand within the city. Reference should also be made to Task 1A/4 (page 4).

Current income alone can be misleading, it is also important to understand the importance of family expectations. The following categories of demand relative to expectations may be considered appropriate:

1 Very low income households with no expectation of improvement.
2 Very low to low income households expecting some improvement.
3 Low to moderate income households with no expectation of improvement.
4 Low to moderate income households expecting some improvement.
5 Moderate to higher income households.

Definitions for each category will, of course, have to be made according to local conditions. In general it will be found that households in categories 2–5 inclusive will be able to participate in either upgrading or new settlement projects. Category 1 will usually only be able to participate in upgrading projects, where total costs may be less. These categories take into account that household attitudes depend not only on current income but on expectations.

In assessing demand, it is important to understand what type of housing is desired. Studies should obtain information on:
● The type of housing preferred (e.g. individual family house, apartment, tenements or rooms).
● Preferred tenure category (e.g. ownership, customary or rental).
● Preferred methods of obtaining dwelling (e.g. self-help build, buy complete dwelling or build through co-operative).
● Preferred locations.
● Priorities for provision of utilities.

Where possible, information on the categories of demand by income levels should be compared with the preferred housing types. This will indicate any significant relationships between them.

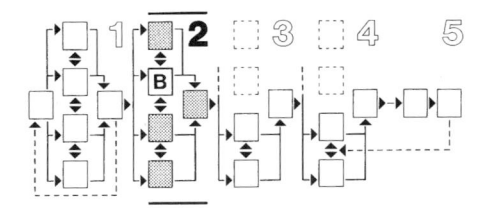

Task 2B
Project site: detailed analysis of project site

2B/1	Site location 22
2B/2	Site area and shape 23
2B/3	Land tenure 23
2B/4	Site boundaries 24
2B/5	Site topography and vegetation 24
2B/6	Ground conditions 24
2B/7	Local climate 25

A detailed and up-to-date knowledge of the project site is an essential prerequisite for any project. It involves:
- The location of the site.
- The physical characteristics of the site.

The studies should expand on the information obtained during the Feasibility studies (see Task group 1B, page 5), and special attention should be given to any aspects which are likely to influence project proposals.

Existing information from other sources should also be checked as it may be adequate and only require updating or expanding. Possible sources include maps and plans, aerial photographs, registers, urban development or master plan files and independent research sources.

Where these sources are not totally adequate, some form of site survey will be required. Before this is done, however, it is important to co-ordinate with the social survey work, as much information as can be collected in one survey.

The information collected will be of interest on its own and in conjunction with other information. The information gathered will vary with local conditions and the following checklist provides only an indication of the range and level of coverage which should be aimed at. In most cases, it will be easiest to record information on the site plan.

Task 2B/l
Site location

This study should provide detailed information on:
- Existing master plan or other urban development plans which may affect the project site.
- Location of existing or potential employment suitable for target population.
- The distance to major public facilities such as schools and hospitals.
- Existing or potential transportation linking the project site to other areas and particularly to major employment centres.
- Existing or potential provision of off-site or on-site urban utilities.

The location of the site will directly affect accessibility and therefore the ability and willingness of low income households to participate in new settlement projects. It will also influence the main priorities for upgrading projects.

Necessary information can usually be obtained from the government agencies, consultants who have been working locally, or public agencies. All information should be field checked.

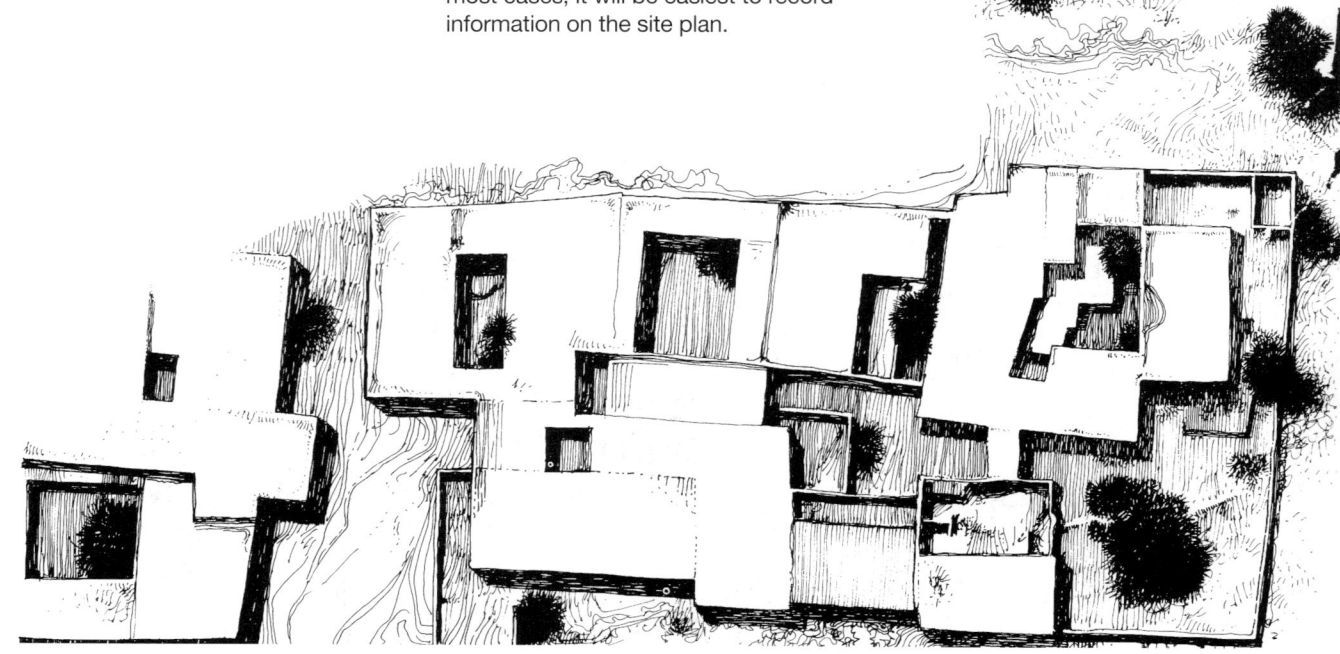

Stage 2

Task 2B/2
Site area and shape

This study should identify any problems which may make it difficult to produce an efficient layout for the project. It may also be useful to prepare the necessary base mapping for all the other tasks at the same time. This should include all existing features located within or immediately adjacent to the project site and be based upon existing maps, aerial photographs, or preliminary land surveys. Ways of carrying out such studies are discussed in Technical note 3 (page 116), and Technical note 24 (page 144.)

When the site has been plotted on scaled maps, its total area should be estimated and recorded.

Task 2B/3
Land tenure

Outline information obtained on land tenure during the Feasibility studies, (see Task 1B/4, page 7) will have indicated the various tenure categories on the project site and their implications. More detailed information will be necessary to develop proposals.

The Detailed studies should obtain accurate information on the area and boundaries of each tenure zone or land parcel. Particular attention should be paid to any areas likely to present difficulties, or be subject to speculative transfers.

The range of tenure types will vary from one area to another. In addition to public or private freehold ownership, customary or other local tenure categories should be included, together with an outline of any land use rights which may apply. A list of possible tenure types will include:
- Freehold.
- Leasehold.
- Public rental.
- Private rental with contract.
- Private rental without contract.
- Membership of co-operative.
- Customary tenure.
- Squatter occupation – officially recognised.
- Squatter occupation – not officially recognised.
- Squatter rental.
- Others (e.g. tied to employment).

How can the required information be obtained? Two main methods can be used:

A review of existing information. This can usually be obtained by reference to local land registers or property tax departments and probably provides the quickest and most accurate information. In areas where registers are not up-to-date, or speculation exists, additional spot checks are also advisable. Information on land disputes may be obtained from the local court records. All details should be recorded on the site plan.

Original research. This involves including questions on land tenure in any social surveys or household case studies (see Task group 2A, page 18). The latter in particular can provide an idea of changes in land tenure over several years, so that trends can be identified and their implications assessed. All information should be recorded carefully on the site plan and the implications of the information analysed in terms of its effect upon the project. For further information on land tenure issues and options, see Technical note 21 (page 137).

Stage 2

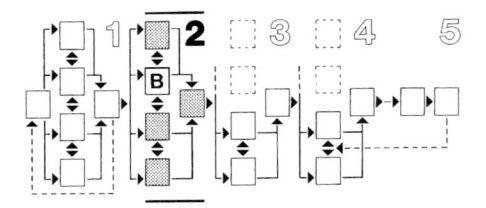

Task 2B/4
Site boundaries

Details of areas adjacent to the project site and any planning proposals for them should be noted on the site map. The existence of any political or administrative boundaries should also be obtained through the relevant authorities and plotted.

During the preparation of proposals for the project, it will be necessary to decide if connections to adjacent areas should be encouraged or restricted. Where adjacent areas are considered compatible, it may be appropriate to increase links, e.g. direct road and path connections. Industrial plant or major highways, however, may require restricted links.

Task 2B/5
Site topography and vegetation

The landform of the site will directly affect future proposals, especially for utility networks. Any areas unsuitable for building need to be identified and appropriate sites selected for any necessary water storage reservoirs. Utility networks can then be planned by indicating drainage catchment areas.

Where possible a full topographic survey of the entire project site should be carried out, and checked against aerial photogrammetric plans. Where this is not possible simpler forms of survey should be carried out as described in Technical note 3, page 116. Maps should be drawn at a scale large enough to show all relevant details, see Technical note 15, page 123.

Existing natural landscape features, especially trees, not only provide a human environment in the early stages of the project, but encourage residents to initiate and maintain planting in areas under their own control. This is particularly important in new settlements when initial development may consist of small, temporary structures. All details of natural landscaping should therefore be surveyed and plotted as part of the land survey programme.

Task 2B/6
Ground conditions

Where Detailed studies are necessary they should investigate any specific problems. The survey should consist of trial pits on a regular grid, with the dimensions dependent upon site conditions. Where the Feasibility studies indicate that conditions over the site do not vary, the spacing of trial pits at intervals of 1–200 metres may be adequate. Where variations exist this spacing may need to be reduced and if conditions are considered critical to the success of a project, a spacing of 30 metres may be necessary.

Trial pits may be supplemented by probing to establish bearing capacities. These have two purposes:
- To identify the various soil types and their engineering properties.
- To establish the presence of rocks, ground water and any aggressive chemicals.

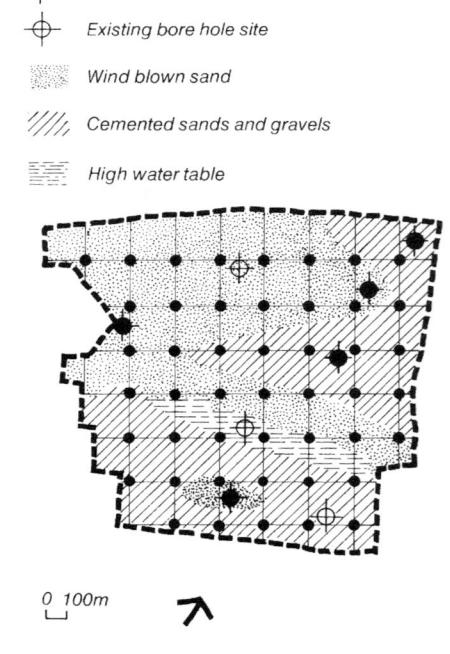

Figure 13
Ground conditions: detailed survey

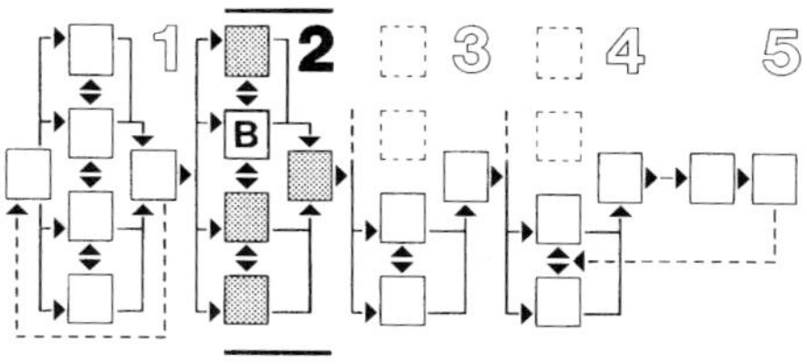

Stage 2

The results of these surveys will provide information on the presence of moving sand dunes, high water tables, aggressive salts or filled ground, as well as the nature of the soils. Additional data on bearing capacities may also be obtained, although this is unlikely to be significant in low-rise housing unless the land has a very low bearing capacity.

Generally, expert advice and/or interpretation of results is recommended for these surveys and specialist staff should be available during the excavation of trial pits.

Once the information has been obtained and processed it should be recorded in note form and on the site plan. Any parts of the site likely to present problems should be clearly annotated, and the implications for the project noted.

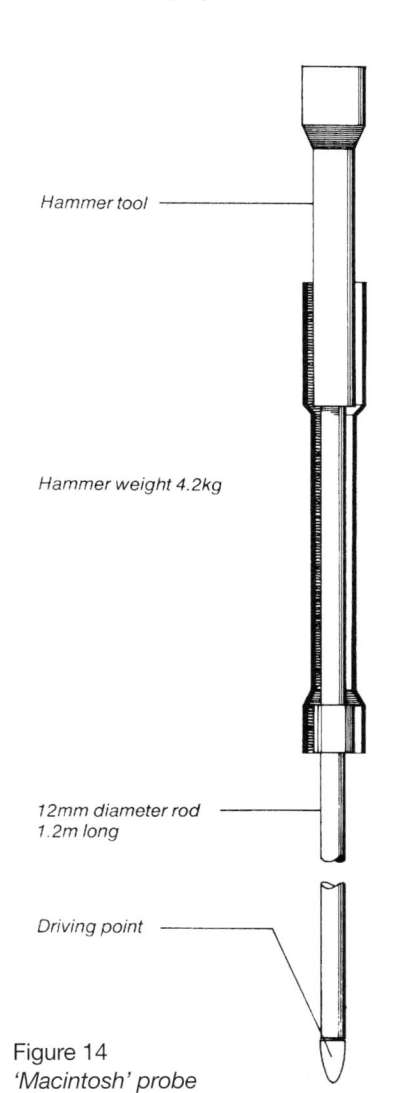

Task 2B/7
Local climate

An examination of local climatic factors is necessary. There are two main reasons for this: to ensure that the favourable points of the local climate can be maximised and the negative ones minimised by careful design, and to provide an adequate basis for engineering designs, especially for roads and drainage systems.

An adequate study should include the following points:
- Temperature and relative humidity, including daily and seasonal variations.
- Rainfall, including seasonal variations.
- Wind, including seasonal variations in direction and strength.
- Cloud cover and its seasonal variations.

Data on climatic conditions can usually be obtained from the authorities and will relate to the nearest city or airport meteorological station. This does not take account, however, of the very local climatic effects caused by topography, areas of water or changes in vegetation, and it may be necessary to obtain data on any such changes which affect the project site. This can usually be obtained in discussion with local residents and should be recorded on graphs or tables for each main point. The vulnerability of the site to any extreme conditions such as seasonal storms should also be noted for their effect upon project proposals.

This information will suggest which type of layout will provide the most comfortable conditions. For example, exposure to prevailing winds at some times of the year may help increase body comfort, while at other times of the year, protection may be necessary. Houses and streets should be orientated so that they provide the most comfortable conditions possible throughout the year.

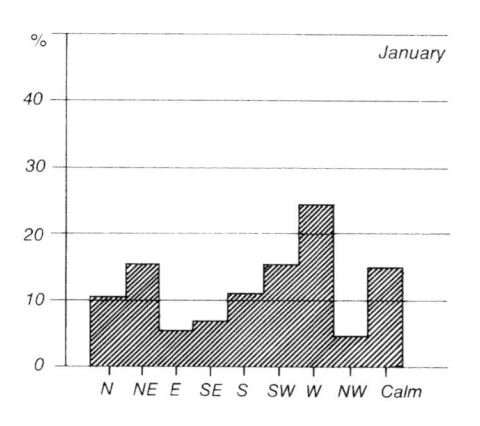

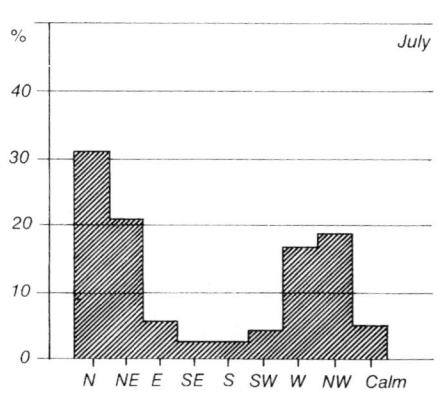

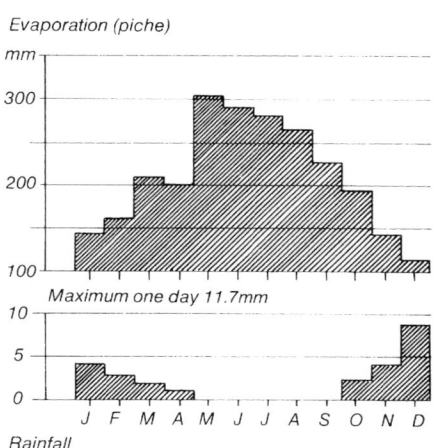

Figure 14
'Macintosh' probe

Figure 15
Example of climate graphs

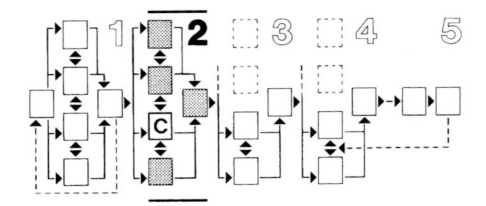

Task group 2C
Site development: survey and analysis of existing site development

2C/1	Existing housing layouts and densities 26
2C/2	Existing plot sizes and shapes 27
2C/3	Existing buildings 28
2C/4	Public facilities and recreation provision 29
2C/5	Commerce and industry 30
2C/6	Other existing land uses 30
2C/7	Circulation and transportation 31
2C/8	Existing utilities 31

The purpose of this group of Tasks is to obtain detailed, accurate and up-to-date information on the nature and layout of existing areas accommodating the target population. For upgrading projects, the Task can be carried out on the project site. For new settlement projects, the nearest site accommodating the target population should be selected. This can be selected in conjunction with the social studies discussed in Task group 2A (page 18).

It should not be assumed that the types of existing development will be appropriate for the future, though housing which has been produced in part or whole by the people living in it may be considered more likely to be suitable than that which has not. This is because there is a greater chance that locally planned housing reflects the needs as well as the resources of its inhabitants.

The Feasibility studies (see Task group 1C, page 9) will have provided useful information on existing site development. This will not be adequate to develop proposals and more Detailed studies will be necessary. Such information can be obtained either from direct physical surveys or by asking residents for their views. While a combination of these methods will be advisable generally, much of the necessary information can be obtained easily during the course of social surveys, and close co-operation should be established with those responsible for Task group 2A (page 18).

All information obtained by the studies should be recorded in note form and/or on the site plan.

Each aspect can now be discussed in turn, though in practice all are closely related.

Task 2C/1
Existing housing layouts and densities

The purpose of this Task is to provide an understanding of housing development, its good points and its problems, for existing areas accommodating the target population. This forms the basis of the proposals for both upgrading and new development. Areas planned or built by local residents will be particularly useful as examples since the layouts will probably incorporate many of their needs.

The study should expand on that carried out in Stage 1 (see Task 1C/1, page 9) and should include:
- The total land area occupied by housing plots.
- Average density levels for housing areas (i.e. people per unit area).
- The type of layout used, especially the relationship between individual plots and the street pattern.
- An estimate of the extent to which the layout uses land efficiently.

The study need not include the whole area of a settlement, but should include a typical neighbourhood with its shops and other facilities. For a large settlement, it may be necessary to analyse more than one area to obtain a representative sample. When the selected area or areas have been measured, the proportion of land occupied by housing can be calculated by superimposing a grid of 10 x 10 metre squares on the map, aerial photograph or sketch plan, and counting the number of squares out of the total occupied by housing plots.

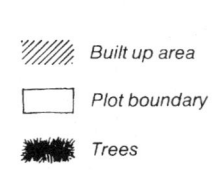

Figure 16
Existing layout: detail

Stage 2   27

Using the same neighbourhood areas, the number of house plots should be counted as accurately as possible. This figure will give a total number of plots per unit area.

Reference to the social surveys (see Task 2A/4, page 20) can then provide the average number of people living on each plot. When multiplied by the number of plots per unit area, this will give an estimated total population for the whole site.

A brief study of existing housing layouts should indicate the reasons why the particular solution was adopted. For example, small communal areas may be used for children to play in, for women to talk while working or for social purposes. This information can be obtained by conducting a brief site survey to record the special groupings of house plots and public areas and the way the latter are used.

The layout surveys will help in assessing the efficiency with which available land accommodating the target population is used.

How can an efficient layout be defined and measured? Since all land has a value, the first criterion must be that the higher the proportion of private land, the lower its unit cost will be, since there will be less public land to be paid for and more people occupying private land to pay for it. Conversely, a layout which provides a high proportion of roads, or other public areas, will place a heavier financial burden on the population. One measure of efficiency is, therefore, the proportion of land in private use. Technical note 16 (page 124) explains how both existing and proposed layouts can be tested for the efficiency with which they use available land. 'Private' here includes privately owned or semi-privately owned or managed. For example, an area surrounded by a group of houses and maintained by the inhabitants would count as semiprivate.

These surveys will indicate what land-use categories need to be proportionately increased to make better neighbourhood housing layouts.

Figure 18 (*right*)
Examples of house plans in existing areas

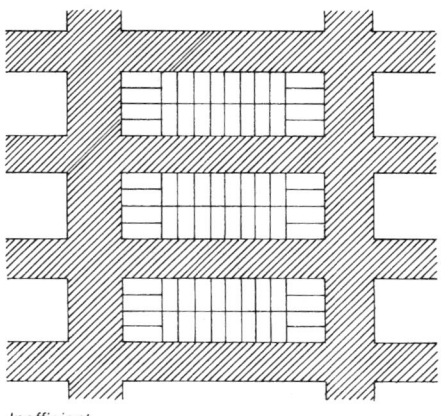

Inefficient
Layout contains larger proportion of public space

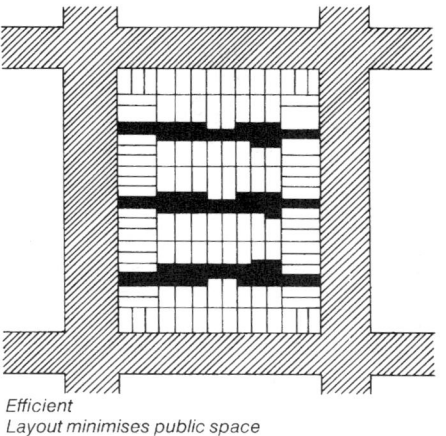

Efficient
Layout minimises public space

▨ Public space   ▯ Plot boundaries
■ Semi-private space

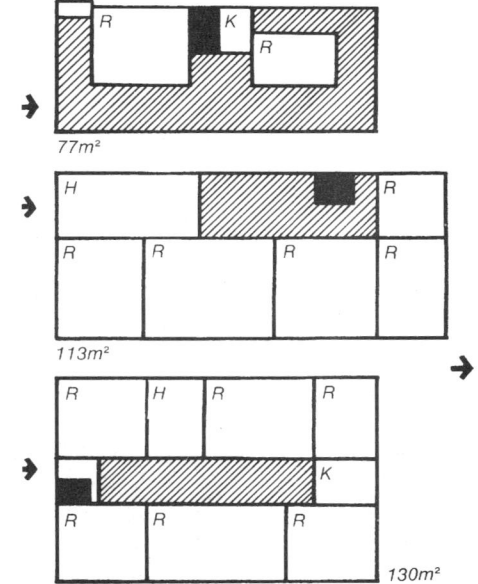

Figure 17
Layout efficiency

77m²
113m²
130m²
99m²

0   5m

Task 2C/2
Existing plot sizes and shapes

This study should provide information on the range of existing plots accommodating the target population and the dimensions which are important for new settlement projects.

The size and shape of a plot exerts a strong influence on what can be built on it, what it will cost and how it can be used. It is a very important element to households, therefore it deserves careful consideration.

The Detailed study should cover these points:
● The sizes of typical plots representing the range found on the site.
● The frontage of plots relative to their size. For example, do larger plots also have wider frontages?
● The plot coverage (i.e. the proportion of the plot area covered with buildings), and any variations in coverage relative to plot size. For example, it may be found that very small plots require an excessively high plot coverage ratio, while large ones have a low coverage and may waste space.
● The sizes of plots accommodating more than one household (see Task 2A/4, page 20).

Useful additional information may be obtained on:
● The ways in which plots have been developed, relative to their size and frontage. For example, do wider or larger plots offer greater flexibility in use, or do smaller, narrower ones noticeably restrict flexibility?
● The degree of consolidation or improvement of plots relative to their

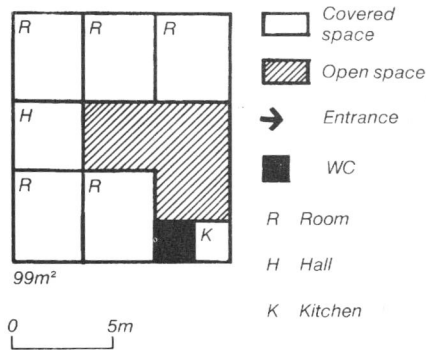

☐ Covered space
▨ Open space
➔ Entrance
■ WC
R Room
H Hall
K Kitchen

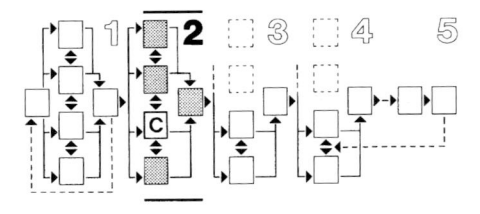

size and frontage. For example, what types of plot appear to be necessary for people to be able to build good houses?
● The orientation of plots, especially where this increases control of climatic conditions. For example, are plots facing the sun, or prevailing winds, more comfortable than those facing away from them?

The information on existing plot sizes, shapes and development will provide a basis for proposals on upgrading and new settlement projects. For the latter, this will apply particularly if existing plots have been planned and developed by their occupants. Before changing existing provision, the implications of such changes should be examined carefully. It may be found, for example, that smaller plots are more economical and therefore enable projects to attract lower-income households, but it may also mean that it becomes difficult to provide additional rental accommodation or expensive multi-storey construction is necessary. In general, it will be found that narrow, deep plots reduce the cost of roads and public utilities, though the extent of this should be calculated.

Task 2C/3
Existing buildings

A detailed knowledge of the existing buildings available to the target population is essential for both upgrading and new settlement projects. It should include points such as the type, materials and condition.

The Detailed studies should indicate the range of housing types including:
● *Individual houses*. These may vary in size, form and quality, though it is common for owners to extend and improve them over time. They may be found in all parts of a city and can be owner-occupied or rented.
● *Rooming houses*. These consist of buildings containing rooms for private rental. They may be single or multi-storey. Space and utility provision standards are often very low and this type is usually restricted to low-income parts of a city.
● *Private apartments*. These often consist of better quality and are usually multi-storey buildings for sale or rent.

They are usually found in the most developed or consolidated parts of a city.
● *Public housing*. These are rental units and often consist of a set of rooms in a large block. Space and utility provision standards are often high though their condition may be poor. They can be found particularly in outer areas of a city where open public land is available or private land is cheaper to acquire.

The distribution of the building types should be mapped. Since it is common for types to change (e.g. for houses to become rooming houses and even apartments)l any evidence of such changes should also be recorded, as it would indicate processes of consolidation which a project should take into account.

All available information on building ages should also be obtained and related to the data on building types. This information can generally be obtained from property taxation departments, land survey offices or local residents. This will provide a useful indication of building consolidation rates which should be allowed for in either upgrading or new settlement projects.

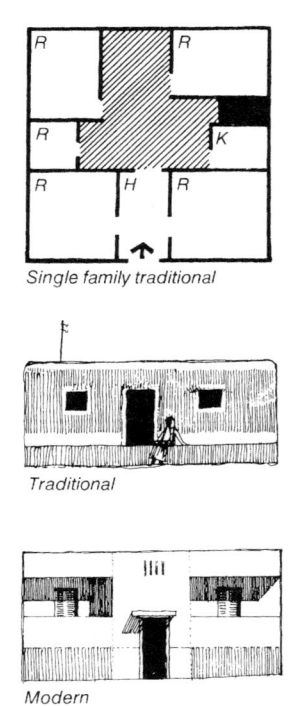

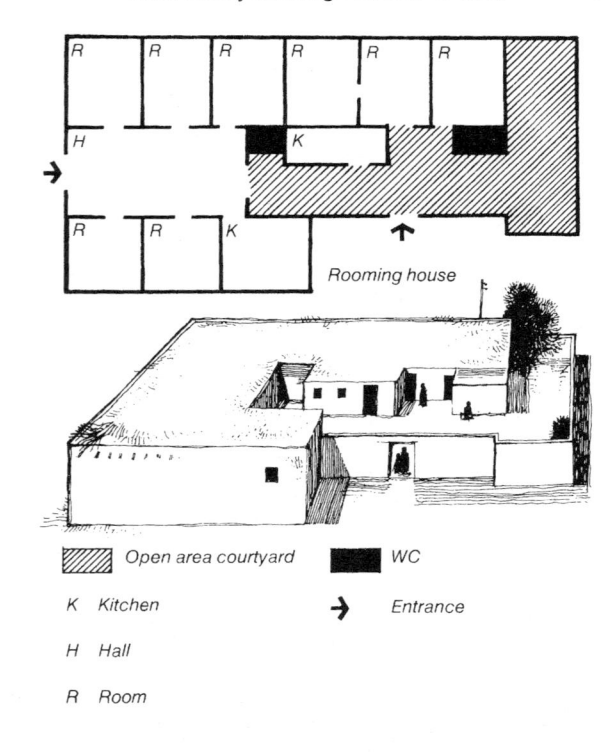

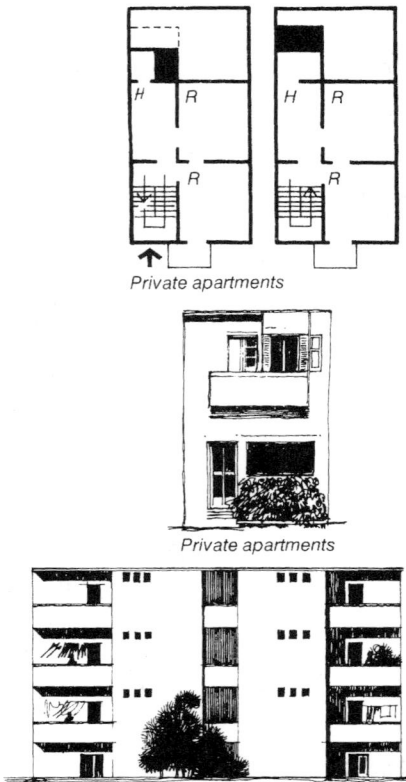

Figure 19
Examples of house types and plans in existing areas

Stage 2

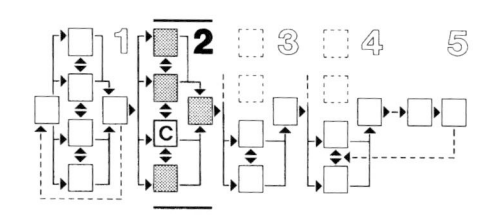

The survey of *building materials* should indicate the types of building industry and technology existing on the site and the locations from which materials are obtained. Any difficulties which residents or local builders face in obtaining sufficient quantities of materials at reasonable cost should be carefully identified and their implications noted. A simple classification should be adequate such as:
- *Traditional*. This includes mud-brick, rammed earth and timber, or any other material used in a traditional, labour intensive way.
- *Modern*. This includes fired brick, steel, reinforced concrete, or any other material used in a capital intensive manner.
- *Intermediate*. This includes materials such as sand-cement blocks or a mixture of modern and traditional materials.

Building condition within each category should also be noted. This will be important when plans considering demolition of existing structures are being prepared, since it will show where such demolition will have the least physical impact. When recording building condition, a simple classification such as 'good', 'medium' or 'poor' is sufficient. It is also useful to indicate structures which are significantly better or worse than the local average.

Finally, information should be collected on the general arrangements of rooms and private open spaces in each of the main house types. The ways in which are as are used should also be noted as this will be important in considering future house layouts or plot sizes and shapes. Local traditions, for example, may require a room at the front of the dwelling for entertaining visitors or a yard to keep poultry. Cultural and climatic factors should also be considered in assessing existing dwelling layouts.

Information on all these aspects can be obtained from the Feasibility studies (see Task 1C/2, page 10), studies of the target population (see Task group 2A, page 18), and informal discussions with local builders and residents. A site survey is necessary. All data should be recorded in note form and/or on the site plan.

Figure 20
Building condition/construction in existing areas

Task 2C/4
Public facilities and recreation provision

Existing facilities within or accessible to the project site will provide an indication of the services available and the degree of surplus or under provision.

A detailed study should be made of the following aspects:
- Health facilities, including both in-patient and out-patient, local and central, medical and dental units. The land occupied by each should be measured and related to official standards. Operation and maintenance should be assessed.
- Educational facilities, including nursery, primary, secondary and college levels and the land areas occupied by each measured and related to official standards (see Task 1C/4, page 11). Levels of attendance and the ability of government to provide adequate numbers of teachers should also be assessed.
- Social facilities, including provision for public meetings, entertainment and worship. All services available to specialist groups should also be noted. Land areas available for or used for recreation should be noted and measured.
- Others, such as police and fire stations or local government offices.

Information on existing provision should be collected and recorded. Where possible population areas served by each facility should be noted. This can be done by analysing the social survey data (see Task 2A/5, page 20) to see where people in each housing area go for public facilities and recreation.

An estimate should also be made of any inadequate or surplus provisions. This can be estimated by reference to the social surveys (see Task 2A/3, page 20) and by discussion with local government agencies. Finally, any budgetary allocations which may affect future provision should also be obtained from government departments or public agencies.

The study should enable priorities to be identified for both upgrading and new settlement projects. All information should be plotted on the site plan and/or in note form.

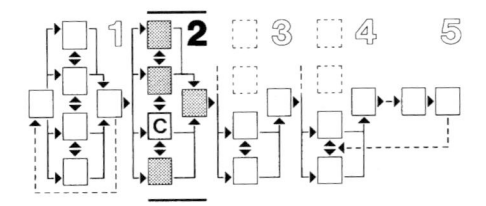

Task 2C/5
Commerce and industry

Information obtained during Stage 1 (see Task 1 C/3, page 10) will have provided useful information on any existing commercial and industrial establishments serving the site. More Detailed studies will be necessary for proposals to be developed. Establishments should be classified into types. This will enable an estimate to be made of any potential increase in employment which may be appropriate for each main type of establishment.

In general, commercial activities can be defined as 'population serving' establishments, both those offering personal services and those engaged in retail activities. Thus, cafes, restaurants, laundries, bakers or shops can be considered commercial while manufacturing and repairs establishments can not.

Industrial activities can most fairly be classified according to their scale as follows:
- Larger scale establishments employing 100+ workers on individual sites and dependent upon uninterrupted supplies of all main utilities and raw materials.
- Smaller scale establishments employing between 10 and 100 people.
- Workshops and very small craft industries employing up to 9 full-time workers, usually owner operated with some assistance from friends or relatives.

Details of the location and type of formal commercial and industrial activities can then be obtained by reference to local government registers and confirmed by carrying out a site survey. All information should then be plotted on the site plan and annotated as necessary.

Because of the number of possible variables, it will be difficult to estimate the potential increase in commercial or industrial activity and further studies will be required. For commercial activity, these can be carried out by:
- Estimating the average mark-up rate, (i.e. the percentage added to the wholesale price of a product to obtain its retail price), and
- Using this to postulate a minimum turnover for a shop in order to yield a typical local monthly income.

For example, if a typical mark-up rate is 25 per cent and average monthly incomes for shopkeepers locally are estimated as 50 currency units, the total turnover required to produce this income is 200 units. This figure can then be used to estimate the total turnover for all commercial activity on the site and the proportionate amount spent by each household. The proportion of this total to household expenditure patterns (see Task 2A/1, page 19) will indicate any scope for increased local commercial activity. For example, if the turnover for each shop is 200 units and there are 10 shops in the locality, total monthly turnover is approximately 2000 units. A comparison of this sum with household expenditure patterns (see Task 2A/1, page 19) will indicate the proportion of total cash spent in these shops and any potential for an income in the number of shops provided.

For *industrial activity*, it should be possible to obtain an outline of total potential levels by relating existing levels of employment in industry to both existing and anticipated population levels. When compared to consolidated low income areas in other parts of the city, the extent of any potential increase should become apparent, in view of the dynamic nature of local employment and commercial/industrial activity. This study will provide a guide only to potential activity and provision should therefore be made to permit the conversion of existing premises to increase industrial/commercial activity if local demands exist.

Task 2C/6
Other existing land uses

This study will be important in identifying any special needs or problems in developing or upgrading the site.

It will be necessary to carry out a site survey in order to determine the precise nature and extent of other land uses. When this has been done, the information can be plotted on a copy of the site plan and its implications for the project assessed. For example, any major public installation, such as a sewerage works, may need an area of open land between it and a housing development.

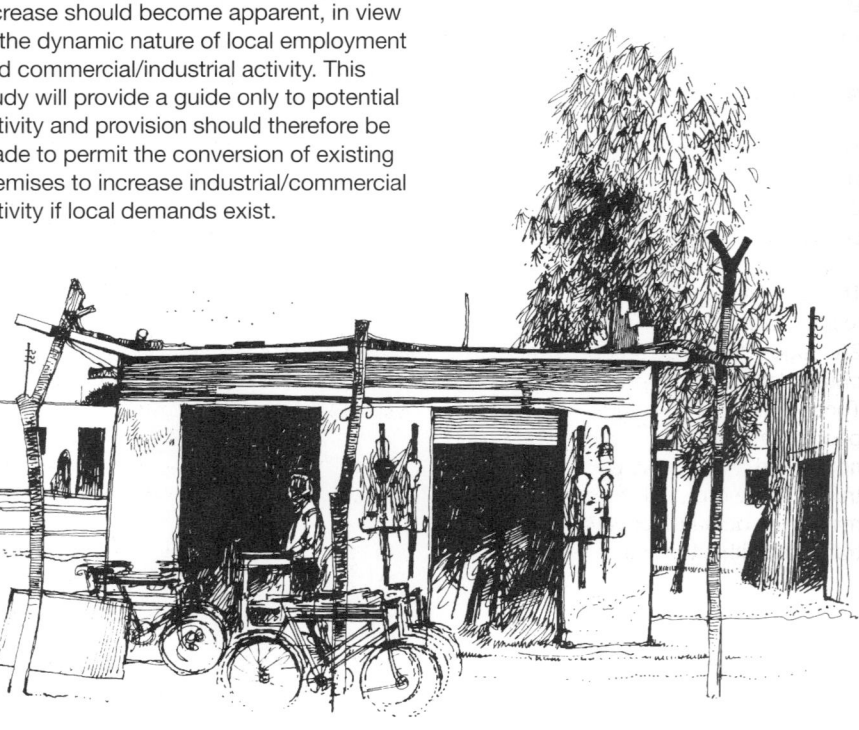

Task 2C/7
Circulation and transportation

The Detailed studies must provide the information from which options can be developed. It will be necessary to obtain physical information concerning the engineering and planning for the potential site and to obtain from social surveys some information on the transport normally used by the target populations. In general the detailed information required is similar in both upgrading and new settlements, although, for upgrading projects it is necessary to have adequate mapping, or aerial photography, to record existing building or property lines.

The Detailed study should cover:
- The location factors and condition of adjacent roads from which access to the site may be obtained.
- Proposals for road works or new routes which may directly affect the site or affect the adjacent street system.
- An inventory of existing streets describing Rights-of-way (ROW), function surface condition and where appropriate traffic volumes.
- The pattern of pedestrian routes and public transport.
- Identification of opportunities to provide links to adjacent roads and points of traffic conflicts or congestion.
- Parking provisions and problems.

The engineering characteristics of site soils should be assessed (see Task 2B/6, page 24) and an investigation made of local construction methods and standards.

The social surveys of the target or residential population (see Task group 2A, page 18) provide an opportunity to obtain data on travel characteristics. These data will allow assessment of how people travel to work and the amount of household expenditure given over to travel. This will provide a basis for determining the demand for various modes of transport within the site.

Task 2C/8
Existing utilities

The Detailed study of the site and the surrounding area should establish the extent of existing utilities and their adequacy. Particular attention should be given to the capacity of existing provision, since this will probably be inadequate for the project. Off-site utility networks will impose limitations on the location and level of service that can be provided for the project, so they should also be included in the analysis. Information should also be obtained from utility provision agencies on their existing projects for the area and their long term policy objectives, as these may affect the project.

These should be included in the study:
- The nature of water supply, including its quality, reliability and source. If an area has a consistently good quality ground water, it may be possible to continue using it in the future. The location of public and private wells should be noted and samples tested. Areas of 'polluted' and 'non-polluted' water should be shown on the site plan. The efficiency of other systems, such as distribution tankers, should be assessed.
- Water distribution system, including the location, sizes and capacity of mains, branches and standpipes. Any surplus capacity should be estimated.
- Sanitation system, including areas served by pit latrines, septic tanks, aqua privies or public mains. Notes should be made on the quality of the existing provision. Information can be obtained from the household surveys (see Technical note 1, page 100).
- The location, size, capacity and condition of all sewerage mains, branches and connections.
- Surface water drainage systems, including soakaways and sewers, their location and condition and any spare capacity.
- Electricity supply network, including rating and capacity, main and secondary distributors and any areas fully or partly served.
- Telephone system, including the extent of provision and location of all cables, an indication of whether they are above or below ground, and public access to the system.
- The method, frequency and effectiveness of rubbish (garbage) disposal.
- The type of construction materials and techniques used in providing utilities.
- The way in which existing utilities are used. This can indicate likely demand for each type of utility.
- The design and construction standards adopted by utility provision agencies for their own projects. These will provide a useful guide, though they should not be considered appropriate for *all* projects.

Utility provision agencies provide a prime source of information, but this should always be checked on site to make sure it is sufficiently detailed and up-to-date. A limited survey may also be necessary to check the way utilities are actually used. For example, how do water consumption levels change according to the type of provision from standpipes to individual taps? Research suggests that consumers will use the amount of water they receive as being their minimum requirement. Probably in the range of 10–15 litres per capita daily (LPCD). This low level of provision may contribute to water pollution and consequent health risks. A range of 150–200 LPCD is often considered necessary. Details of all existing utilities should be marked clearly on the site plan. Connections to off-site networks should also be shown. Information on construction standards or the use of utilities can be recorded in note form. This information will indicate the nature and extent of under provision or surplus capacity.

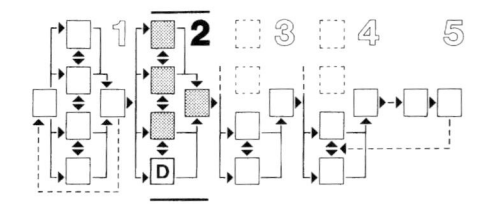

Task group 2D
Institutional and financial framework

2D/1	Institutional framework	32
2D/2	Financial framework	32
2D/3	Assessing the ability to pay	33

Task 2D/1
Institutional framework

The purpose of this Task is to assess the suitability of existing institutions for carrying out the preparation, planning and implementation of projects. For an individual project, the extensive modification of existing institutions or the establishment of new ones will not always be justified, but where projects form part of a long term programme it will be essential that an appropriate institutional framework be established.

Ideally, the designated institutions responsible for the project will possess sufficient authority, financial resources and personnel to undertake all stages of the project. At the same time, they should be sensitive to local variations in demand. Analysis of the existing institutional framework should therefore assess the appropriateness of existing structures or the changes which may be required for the project to be able to achieve its objectives. This will mean examining the existing decision making routines of the organisations concerned with land development, and assessing their capacity to meet current work loads. "Institutional capacity" refers to community and private organisations as well as government.

Task 2D/2
Financial framework

The main purpose is to obtain information which can be used to assess costs and the ability of the target population to meet costs. Some of the required information will have been obtained during the Feasibility studies (see Task 1D/2, page 13) but more detailed and accurate information will be required to develop proposals for the project.

Assessing costs and their allocation

The main cost item which can be identified at this stage is that of land. Rapid urban development or speculation may create sudden changes in land values, so detailed studies will be necessary.

Influences on land values include:
- Market demand for development of all kinds.
- Tenure status.
- Location.
- The size and shape of land parcels and particularly the extent of frontage on main roads.
- Land use controls and zoning.
- Levels of servicing, e.g. the availability of main drainage.

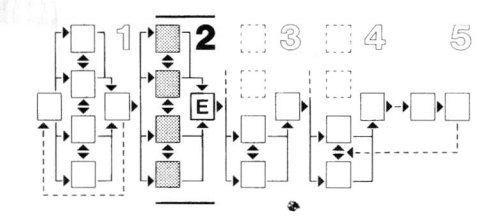

In addition, the fact that a site has been selected for a project may well affect the price to be paid, especially if parcels are held in freehold tenure. Allowances should also be made for the likely change in land values, especially as acquisition procedures could take considerable time. A method of estimating relative and actual land values is described in Technical note 9 (page 118). For information on options for varying land values to generate added value for internal project cross-subsidies, see Technical note 22 on site planning and design briefs (page 140).

For sites under public ownership or control, it will be necessary to estimate an opportunity cost (see Task 1 D/2, page 13) since this will represent the cost of lost potential revenues. It should therefore be considered as an effective cost to the project.

Estimates should also be made of other project costs applicable to the site. For example, would any flood prevention works be required or special provision needed to obtain adequate drainage? An attempt to estimate these costs should be made, based on experience of other situations where such works have been needed.

Task 2D/3
Assessing the ability to pay

To analyse the ability of households to pay for housing, a proportion of total household income may be allocated for housing and related expenditure (e.g. housing taxes, electricity). In practice this proportion is likely to vary with incomes, since households with higher incomes will have an increased surplus over and above the amount required for necessities such as food and clothing.

For most low-income households, a range of between 10–30 per cent of net household income is generally appropriate for calculating the ability to pay.

It is vital that information on household incomes is reliable and up-to-date. The appropriate proportion can then be applied to income levels within the target population. This will produce a range of monthly payments which can be afforded for housing, including all financing charges, utility costs and property taxes. In addition, a total capitalised sum obtained by amortised annual payments for a specified period (say 25 years) at appropriate interest rates can be calculated as in Table 2.

Table 2
Ability to pay for shelter: calculation

Household income	1000
Amount for housing, say 20%	200
less 10 units property tax *less* 50 units utilities *less* 30 units loan repayments	90
Net available for mortgage repayments 110	
Capitalised over 25 years at say 10% – affordable capital sum	998

Task 2E
Detailed studies: analysis

The exact nature of Detailed studies, and therefore also their analysis, will depend upon local conditions and the type of project being proposed. Most of the information collected will be useful in two ways; first as material in its own right, and second in combination with other information.

The purpose of this analysis is to determine the characteristics of the target population, the existing housing available to it and future needs which people have for housing and related services. In addition, it will be necessary to identify any constraints or opportunities which the project site provides in meeting these needs.

When conducting the analysis, it is important to ask what effect any of the information will have on project proposals. This is essential if research is to improve the quality of decision-making on projects.

As with the Feasibility studies, there are several ways in which the analysis can be made. Whether automated or manual methods are used, the emphasis should be put on those which clearly identify the choices and limits of the project. This is particularly important in the Detailed studies because although most operations will be relatively simple, there will be many of them.

For the socio-economic studies, a check-list, or master analysis sheet, has many advantages and is the method which is recommended. An alternative system for analysing information from social surveys is that of data analysis cards. In this system, each interview is allocated its own card containing the coded answers to each question. It is a quick method of analysing smaller surveys, but becomes unwieldy for larger ones. Simple analysis can also be carried out by computer. Details can be found in Technical notes 1 and 19. For the physical studies of the project site, comparison of the various site maps will be necessary and this is

34   Stage 2

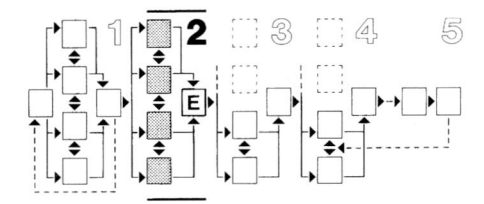

why consistency of scales is so important. To assist comparison, it may be useful to superimpose plans on top of each other in the form of overlays. In this way a mass of material can be shown for each part of the site at the same time.

The sheer amount of socio-economic information to be analysed or compared may make it difficult in practice to contain all the relevant information on a single analysis sheet. If this is the case, it may be desirable to separate the analysis into two or more parts, though considerable cross-reference will be necessary between them.

Before analysis, data from social surveys should be checked to make sure that it is all in a suitable form. In the case of answers to questions which have been preceded, this will be a straightforward process of recording either the actual observations, (i.e. yes/no), or codes in the appropriate column. Where answers have not been pre-coded it will generally be necessary to categorise them into codes so that they can be processed and comparisons made between one set of observations and another. This may be difficult for subjective or open ended questions, especially those asked during case studies. Brief notes may therefore be necessary on the most important aspects and space should be left for these when designing the master analysis sheet.

Information on the physical studies of the project site and plot development present a different problem in that it will be in several forms including notes, tables and annotated plans. Care will be necessary to ensure that all data is in a compatible form for analysis.

The method of *rating* data for the detailed analysis will vary from one aspect to another, so that the system proposed for Feasibility studies will not be generally applicable. It may, however, be used where appropriate, as in the analysis of existing building condition.

Since the relative importance of each aspect will vary from one project to another, no system of *ranking* information can be recommended and the importance of each aspect should be assessed according to local circumstances.

In preparing the master analysis sheet, each aspect discussed in the text should be checked, though not all will need to be included. For ease of reference, the analysis sheet can follow the sequence in the text.

The detailed master analysis sheet should be organised as in Figure 21.

The master analysis sheet will show at a glance the relevant information on any particular aspect and the other aspects with which it should be compared.

Analysis of data from social surveys, will include the full range of answers given as well as the frequency of each answer for the entire sample. In many cases, it will be sufficient to know the number of the total households who give a specific answer, such as the number of people who work near their dwelling. This information can be obtained by counting the frequency of each observation from the tabulation (master analysis sheet).

The actual process of analysing and comparing information will require detailed discussion between all those responsible for each aspect of the project. Those concerned with providing utilities will therefore be particularly interested in the topography and geology of the project site, existing levels of provision and priorities for the future. For this reason each member of the project team will need to have access to all information which will be relevant in carrying out his work.

Finally, when analysing information on any specific subject, remember that data obtained by one method (such as social surveys of the target population), can provide valuable information on other aspects (such as the existing housing on the project site).

At the end of this analysis the following points should be clearly understood:
● The type or types of housing and related services *presently* available to the target population.
● The type or types of housing and/or related services *needed* by the target population.
● The *ability* and *willingness* of the target population to pay for them.
● The extent to which the target population (including individual households and local organisations) is able and willing to take *an active role* in providing such housing and services.
● Any problems regarding the site and its suitability for the project.
● Problems or opportunities of the site as these will affect project design and costs.
● Problems or opportunities of on-site development as they may affect project design and costs.

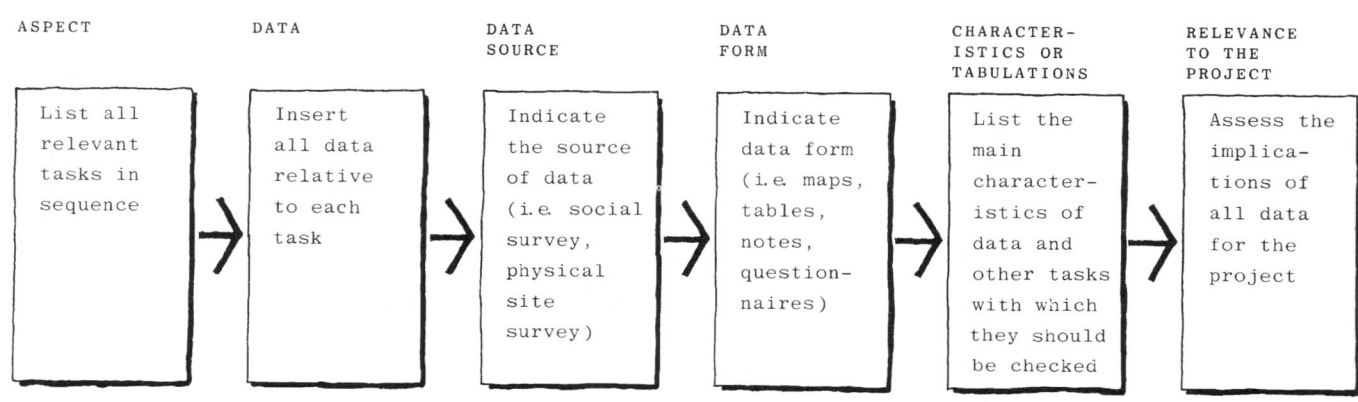

ASPECT	DATA	DATA SOURCE	DATA FORM	CHARACTERISTICS OR TABULATIONS	RELEVANCE TO THE PROJECT
List all relevant tasks in sequence	Insert all data relative to each task	Indicate the source of data (i.e. social survey, physical site survey)	Indicate data form (i.e. maps, tables, notes, questionnaires)	List the main characteristics of data and other tasks with which they should be checked	Assess the implications of all data for the project

Figure 21
Organisation of master analysis sheet

Stage 3
Developing project options

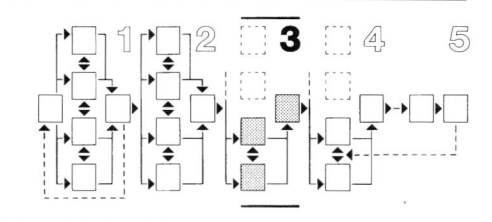

This Stage represents the key part of project planning when all the options which are likely to be relevant to the project are identified, their relevant advantages and disadvantages assessed and a preferred group of options selected.

The main criteria to be used in assessing options will be based on success in achievement of the objectives of the project. However, the most important test will be whether the proposals will be appropriate to the people who will live in the project area. Their needs and resources should form the basic criteria against which options are measured.

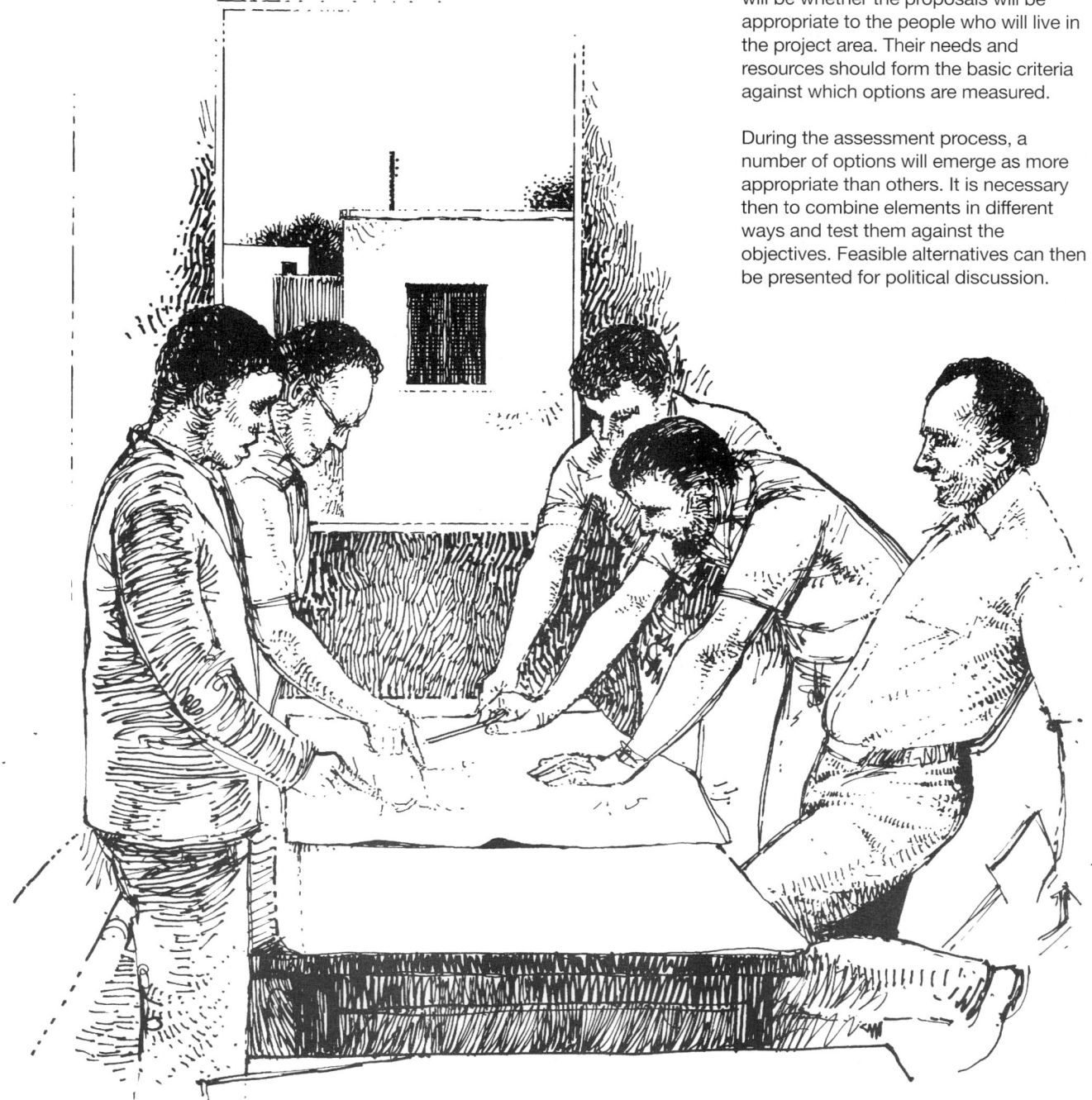

During the assessment process, a number of options will emerge as more appropriate than others. It is necessary then to combine elements in different ways and test them against the objectives. Feasible alternatives can then be presented for political discussion.

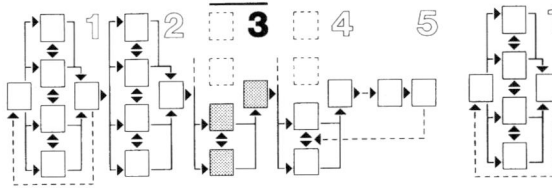

Task group 3A

No Tasks at this stage

Task group 3B

No Tasks at this stage

Task group 3C

Site development: formulating site development options

3C/1	Housing: layout and density 37
3C/2	ousing: plot sizes and shapes 41
3C/3	Housing: buildings 45
3C/4	Commerce and industry 46
3C/5	Public facilities and recreation 47
3C/6	Incorporation of other land uses 49
3C/7	Circulation and transportation 50
3C/8	Utilities 52

In considering the various options for developing the site, it will be important to bear in mind site characteristics (see Task group 2C, page 26) since these will determine which options are the most appropriate for each project.

Although any housing project must be primarily to increase the quantity, quality and availability of housing; its contribution to urban and economic development should not be ignored. An appropriate project will be one in which the full range of urban activities including housing, work and recreation are included.

This requires that careful consideration be given to land use planning for each aspect of site development and particularly to the relationship between housing and other land uses. The chance of achieving a satisfactory solution will increase if site development options can encourage flexibility and a mixture of land uses. Treating the project site as a *settlement* or general urban area, rather than purely a *housing* project is one way of maintaining the maximum number of options This involves:
● The integration, where possible, of new development and any existing urban areas so that deficiencies in the latter can be compensated for by increased provision in the former.
● Allowing for the progressive intensification of land use. This is a common feature in most urban areas and enables development to proceed efficiently from low initial density of use to consolidated or intensive use over time.
● Allowing for changes in land use and mixed land uses.

The actual range of options available will be restricted in practice by the income levels of the target population and thus the amounts households can afford for housing and related services (see Task 2A/1, page 19). The lower the income level, the smaller the range of possible options for initial development. In all projects, however, it will be important to offer house-holds a choice, and even at low levels of income, variety can be achieved in the way options are combined.

A critical factor in developing options is likely to be the way in which site development can be phased. This includes both the successive implementation development over different parts of the site and the upgrading of the area from initial to higher levels of development.

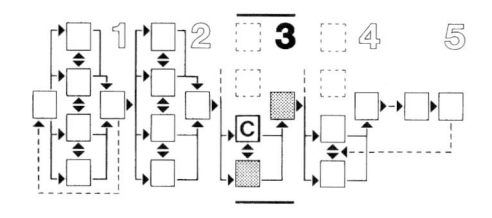

Plot development

Options regarding the size and development of individual plots will depend upon several considerations, the most important which will be what the target population is able and willing to pay for. There can be no standard solution, for the simple reason that no two households will have identical needs or resources. Households in upgrading projects may place a high priority on secure tenure, utilities or public facilities, while the greatest initial need of those in new settlements is likely to before some form of building .

Because of the wide range of needs, it is necessary to identify the limits of provisions which are likely to be appropriate for each aspect. It will be most important to determine the *minimum* acceptable level for each element. Additional provision can then be allocated according to the needs and resources of the target population. The lower the incomes of households are, the more important it will be to establish an *appropriate* minimum level.

The phasing of future upgrading of the house should be left to individual households who can decide according to their own priorities. Although this will result in varied levels of upgrading, any attempt to enforce a standard programme of improvement will only penalise poorer households.

Task 3C/1
Housing: layout and density

The purpose of this Task is to develop and select options for the planning of urban areas, so that they will be appropriate to the housing needs of the population.

For upgrading projects, the existing layout and density levels will inevitably restrict options. In new settlement projects, the information on existing areas, especially that obtained from the surveys of local residents, will provide a guide to the options which can be developed.

Although the general disposition of land uses over the site will form the first step in designing layouts, and this will require s reference to Task group 2B (page 22), it will also be important to define the basic unit of layout design. This may range from a small group of plots to the entire project site. In general, however, a useful scale will be that of the *neighbourhood*, since this is usually a unit with which people can identify and is often the basis of public administration and the provision of public facilities.

The main determinant of a neighbourhood will be its population. This will naturally vary according to the criteria by which it is defined, but if the number of people necessary to support a local primary school is used as the basis, a population of about 5000 people may be involved. (The number depends, of course, on the capacity of local primary schools).

Density

Within the framework of the neighbourhood unit, it will be necessary to assess options for net and *gross housing densities.** In upgrading projects, existing densities in the more consolidated parts of the site will indicate those which should be anticipated in other parts. These levels will also indicate what densities may be expected in new settlements. *It is, however, important to remember that densities cannot be easily controlled overtime, since they are a reflection of demand and supply. A layout planned for low or medium densities, for example, may absorb more people by sub-division of large plots, building of additional accommodation on existing plots or simply the housing of more people in existing buildings. It is important that options allow for intensification of use over time when these pressures are likely.*

Among the options for influencing density levels are the following:
- The layout of housing areas and the efficiency with which land is used.
- Levels of multi-occupancy.
- The size of individual plots.
- Planning legislation, especially that relating to the extent of building permitted on a plot.

When assessing density options for new settlements, the points outlined in Table 3 (page 38) should be considered.

Of all the above considerations, the most important is likely to be that of land cost (see Task 2D/2, page 32). Where this is expensive or represents a large proportion of total project costs, high or very high residential densities will represent the only realistic options. If these options are unacceptable, the possibility of a subsidy should be explored. (see Task 3D/3, page 64).

---

* Net density includes all land occupied by residential plots. It differs from gross density in that the latter includes land occupied by roads and public facilities

Stage 3

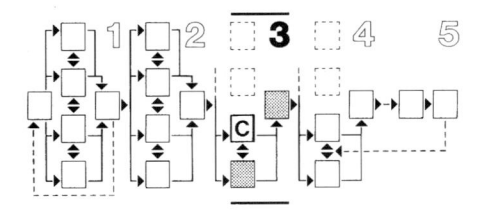

Table 3
Housing density options

Gross density	Characteristics	Advantages	Disadvantages
Low *average say 100 persons per hectare*	Generally synonymous with individual dwellings for each household and abundant private and/or public open space.	● Ample opportunity to extend houses cheaply. ● Long-term flexibility over future land use. ● Possibility of on-plot disposal of sewage. participate when land costs are high.	● High costs for utilities, administration and maintenance. ● Fewer households available to share increased initial costs ● Difficulty of enabling low-income households to
Medium *average say 200 persons per hectare*	Usually involves individual dwellings per household, though there may be some multi-occupancy. Private and public open space adequate.	● Scope for some expansion of dwelling. ● Reduced cost of roads and utilities relative to low densities. ● Reduced unit costs per household compared to low densities. ● Moderate flexibility in future local development. ● Possible on-plot disposal of sewage.	● Possible high land cost for low-income households, especially if costs are high or incomes very low.
High *average say 400 persons per hectare*	May be achieved with single household dwellings, though probably with some multi-occupancy. Private and public open space limited.	● Significantly reduced land, road, transport and utilities costs. ● More households can be accommodated in initial development. ● Increased opportunities for generating local services and employment. ● Increased chance of accommodating low and very low-income households where land costs are high.	● Restricted opportunities for house expansion and high costs of vertical expansion. ● Reduced flexibility over long term development. ● Increased costs of house building. ● Difficulty of providing adequate layout on each plot. ● Difficulty in providing on-plot disposal of sewage (e.g. pit latrines).
Very high *average say 600 persons per hectare*	Generally requires multi-storey, multi-occupancy housing, though possibly with some single household dwellings. May be single storey but with extremely small plots. Private and public open spaces restricted and used intensively.	● The lowest unit land costs for a given land price. ● Greatest scope for generating local services and employment. ● The largest possible number of households can be accommodated initially ● The maximum proportion of very low-income households can be accommodated.	● Very little opportunity for house extension. ● Very limited flexibility over long term development. ● Possible social tension and disruption. ● Possible excessive load on infrastructure networks and no possibility of low-cost on site sewage disposal. ● Probable high cost of construction per unit area of housing.

Layouts

An important aspect which must be considered is the *design of the layouts* to be adopted for a typical neighbourhood unit. This involves the organisation of primarily residential plots into a hierarchy of groups which can include the following:
● 'Clusters', or groups of plots surrounding a common circulation space which is largely for the use of households which share it. Their area will vary according to the size of plots and the extent of multi occupancy.
● Blocks, or areas containing a number of clusters and surrounded on all sides by public roads.
● Neighbourhoods. The size of these has already been discussed. Where a number of neighbourhoods are grouped together it will be necessary to provide additional public facilities (see Task 3C/5, page 47).

The most important factors in achieving an efficient layout for any given net density level will be the proportion of public, semi-public and private areas and the cost of installing public utilities. As discussed in Task 2C/1 (page 26) the higher the proportion of private land the lower its unit cost will generally be, and for infrastructure, the less the total length of circulation the cheaper. In the case of upgrading, the information on existing layouts will indicate where improvements are desirable and possible. For new settlements, the number of options will naturally be greater.

How can the proportion of private land in a layout be maximised to help achieve an efficient layout? The simplest means is to reduce the unit length and width of roads and other public circulation spaces to the minimum commensurate with safe and efficient circulation. This can be done by using plots with relatively narrow frontage (see Task 3C/2, page 41). Within housing blocks, the use of communal open spaces and clusters can help achieve a layout which minimises public maintenance. A large number of possible combinations exists, as shown in the illustrations.

When water-borne sewerage is included as a project option, either at an initial or at a later stage in development, it is essential that the layout allows the lengths of pipes to be minimised as this involves very

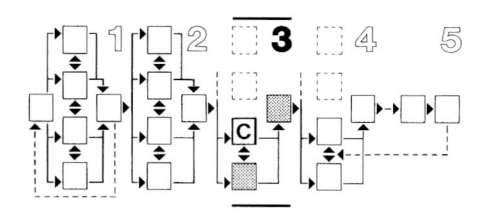

Stage 3

significant costs. Co-ordination between layout design and infrastructure design is essential.

Achieving an efficient use of land will obviously help to reduce total project costs and therefore the costs to each household. Care should also be taken, however, to create layouts which are appropriate to local social and cultural practices and physical conditions. Layouts should also be practical to set out on the ground (see Technical note 7, page 118).

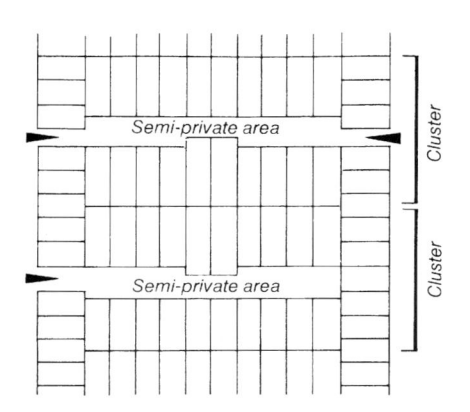

Figure 22
Cluster

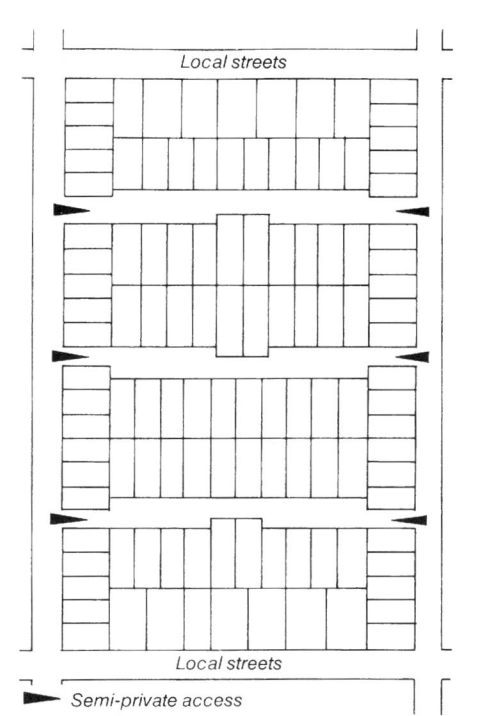

Figure 23
Block

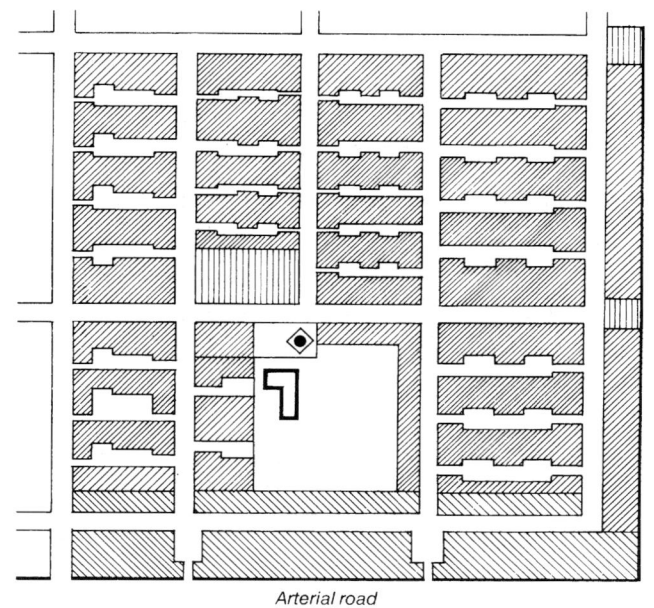

Figure 25 (above)
Neighbourhood

Figure 25 (below)
Block layout options

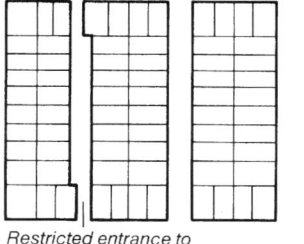

- Low cost plots
- Concession areas at market price
- Open space
- Mosque
- School

Restricted entrance to discourage through traffic

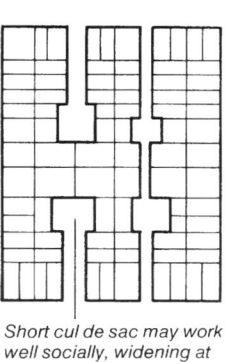

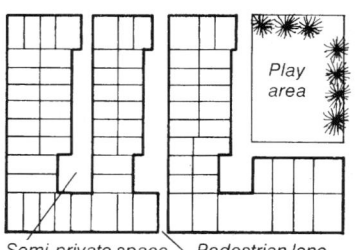

Semi-private space cul de sac improves security

Pedestrian lane improves accessibility

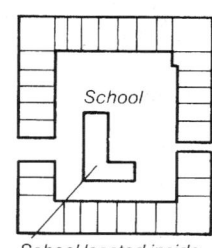

School located inside block maximises revenue generating street frontage plots

Short cul de sac may work well socially, widening at end for vehicle turning

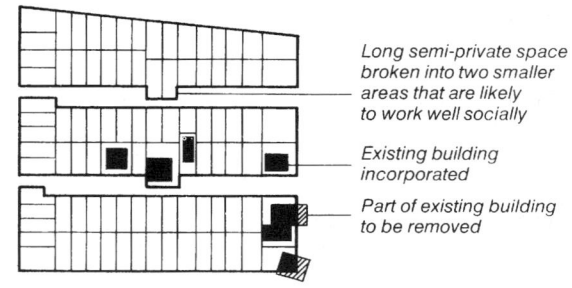

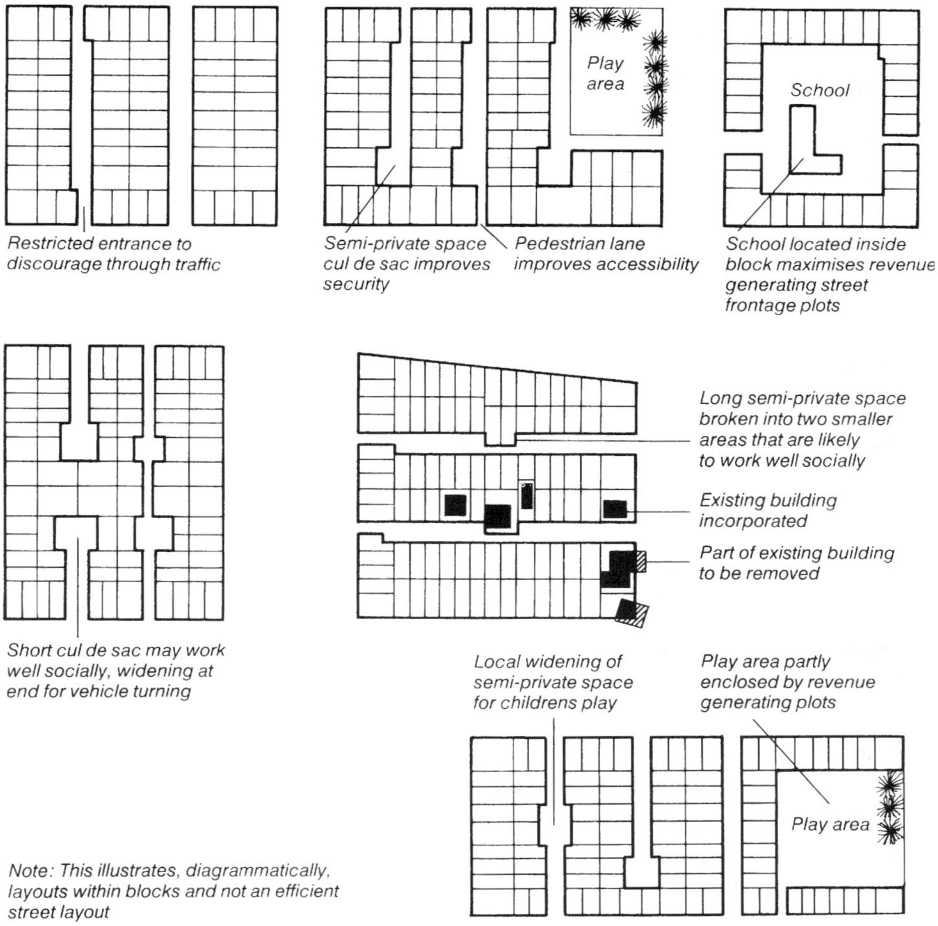

Local widening of semi-private space for childrens play

Long semi-private space broken into two smaller areas that are likely to work well socially

Existing building incorporated

Part of existing building to be removed

Play area partly enclosed by revenue generating plots

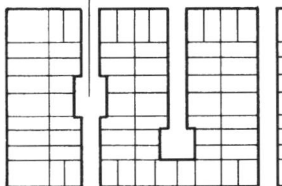

Note: This illustrates, diagrammatically, layouts within blocks and not an efficient street layout

Stage 3

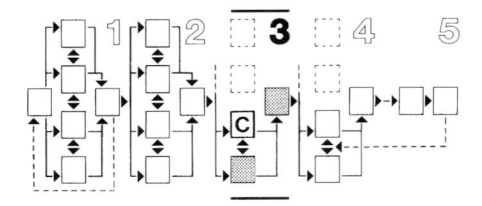

Selecting options

Selection of feasible options for housing layouts and densities is based on testing them against the Project objectives (page 2).

Before plans can be prepared, it will be necessary to determine the population of a typical neighbourhood. This should be based upon projected population for consolidated development since initial populations will be lower. It will then be possible to select net density levels (again at consolidated development) from the range discussed. Net density levels can be selected for both upgrading and new settlement projects according to the levels considered acceptable under local conditions. A range of 200–600 people per hectare is likely to be appropriate for most projects.

Once net density options for consolidated development have been selected, it will be possible to calculate the area required for a given neighbourhood population. This will be determined by the gross density (i.e. the area occupied by roads, other public land and semi-public areas such as schools, as well as residential land). Gross density levels will therefore be determined largely by the layout, especially the proportion of land occupied by housing plots. Where this proportion can be measured, the area required can be calculated as shown in Table 4.

In *upgrading projects*, the gross density at consolidated development will be largely pre-determined and will enable the area required by a typical neighbourhood to be calculated. For example, if net density in a consolidated part of an existing area is 500 people per hectare, and 50 per cent of the total land was occupied by private land such as house plots, the area needed for a neighbourhood of 5000 would be:
50% x 500 = 250 (gross density)
5000 250 = 20 hectare.

The neighbourhood area can then be related to the area of the project site to determine the total number of neighbourhoods and the projected total population of the project. Alternatively, existing political or administrative boundaries can be used.

In *new settlement projects*, layout options will be greater and the area required for a typical neighbourhood will therefore be more difficult to predict until the layout has been designed. It may be helpful, however, to select the proportion of land in private use as a basis for layout design in order to estimate the total area of a typical neighbourhood. Experience suggests that where at least 60 per cent of all available land is allowed for private use, an optimum use of land will be achieved. If this is adopted as a basis for design, the area required for typical neighbourhoods at different net density levels is as shown in Table 5.

Once the area of land required for a typical neighbourhood has been estimated, it will be possible to calculate the number of neighbourhoods that can be accommodated on the project site, their approximate boundaries and the total projected population of the project. Also it will be possible to prepare initial layout options for housing areas. For example, if atypical neighbourhood occupies 20 hectares and the site contains 100 hectares of land available primarily for housing, 5 neighbourhoods (or about 25 000 people) can be accommodated).

Alternative layouts should be designed and tested for the efficiency with which they use land and the efficiency of infrastructure layouts. (see Technical note 16, page 124). The preferred option will be one which reduces public land and the costs of utilities provision to the minimum and is sufficiently flexible to allow for subsequent intensification or changes of land use. An important element in achieving this will be the *cluster layout*. Providing that the size of blocks is not too large, clusters can vary in shape and size (page 39) to make the optimal use of available land. They can also accommodate a variety of plot sizes and shapes, thereby adding to the flexibility of the layout. This cannot be achieved so easily or economically in a standard land subdivision, as shown below on the right because the size of a block is restricted by the depth of individual plots. This in turn limits development of an efficient infrastructure system. This is not the case for the cluster layout on the left.

If it is decided to designate open spaces within the clusters as private land for the use of residents adjoining them, the cost will have to be borne by the residents, though total project costs, to which they will have to contribute, will be reduced accordingly. The design of small open spaces serving groups of individual plots and for which the residents are responsible for maintenance and use, gives residents greater control over the land in front of their plots. The layout of these spaces should, however, be designed to prevent unauthorised encroachment. This can usually be achieved by restricting their width.

The actual size of clusters and blocks will, of course, vary according to the preferred

Table 4
Relationship between density and land requirement

Neighbourhood population	Net density people per hectare	Proportion of land in private use	Gross density people per hectare	Land area needed (hectares)
5000	400	35%	140	35.7
5000	400	50%	200	25.0
5000	400	65%	260	19.2

Table 5
Relationship between density and land requirement at optimum level of private use

Neighbourhood population	Net density people per hectare	Proportion of land in private use	Gross density people per hectare	Land area (hectares)
5000	200	60%	120	41.7
5000	400	60%	240	20.8
5000	600	60%	360	13.9

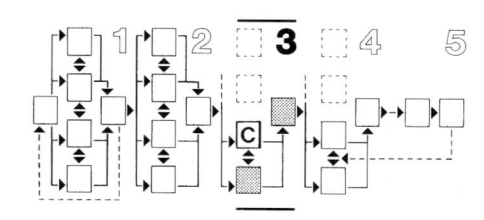

Stage 3   41

options on road Rights of way (see Task 3C/7, page 50) and individual plot sizes as discussed in Task 3C/2.

Layouts should also allow for middle and possibly higher income group housing to be provided within the project. The potential for this will have been indicated within Task 3D/3 (page 64). The ability to provide the required area of higher income housing will depend in practice upon site characteristics and any existing site development. In upgrading areas there may already be a wide variety in income groups.

Where conditions permit, suitable locations and areas of land should be selected. In addition to an attractive environment it will be necessary for higher income areas to possess good accessibility and appropriate levels of infrastructure in terms of the higher charges being made. This will need close co-ordination with the planning and phasing of all infrastructure networks, so that the cross-subsidy generated by such development can provide an impetus for the project as a whole.

Figure 26 *(below)*
Flexibility of cluster system

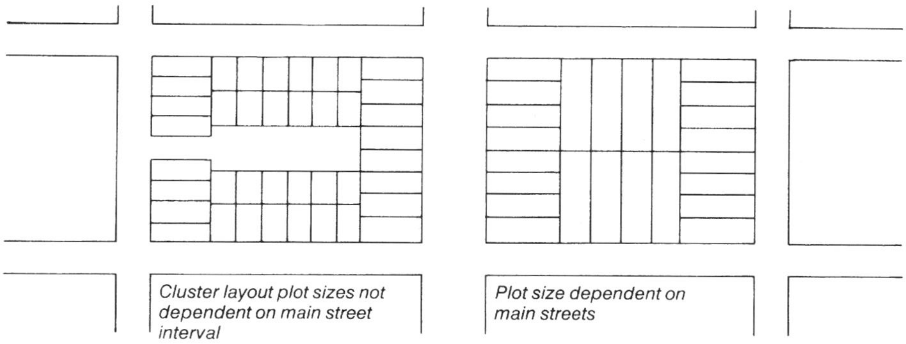

Cluster layout plot sizes not dependent on main street interval

Plot size dependent on main streets

Table 6
Comparison of characteristics of small and large plots

Plot type	Advantages	Disadvantages
Small plots *less than 70m²* 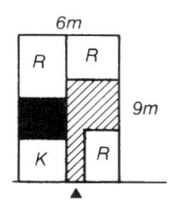	● Reduced land costs of plot allowing more money to be available for building and on-plot utilities. ● Reduced layout and site utility costs. ● More households can be provided with a plot in any one area. ● Reduced risk of higher income groups benefiting from project.	● Reduced opportunity for house expansion without seriously reducing private open space. ● More difficult and expensive to develop housing on the plot. ● Dependent for cost savings on layout. Inefficient layouts could lead to higher costs due to the larger proportion of public open space. ● Reduced possibility of on-site disposal of sewage.
Large plots *more than 140m²* 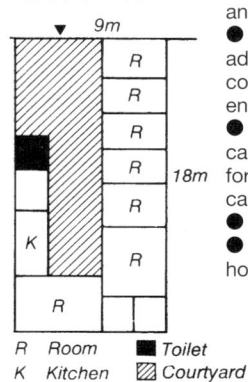	● Private open space for growing food, keeping domestic animals, and working. ● Space available for providing additional rooms for rental or commercial use. This can encourage consolidation. ● A wider range of dwelling types can be provided so that traditional forms (such as courtyard plans) can be included. ● Possibility of on-site pit latrine. ● Greater comfort, especially in hot-humid climates.	● Higher total land costs for each plot. ● Higher layout and site utilities cost. ● Reduced number of households which can be accommodated on their own plot, where land is scarce. ● Greater risk of project anracting higher income groups than those intended.

R Room   ■ Toilet
K Kitchen ▨ Courtyard

Task 3C/2

Housing: plot sizes and shapes

This element will generally only apply to new settlement projects. Its importance in achieving a successful project has already been mentioned in Stage 2 (see Task 2C/2, page 27).

By referring to the studies carried out in Stage 2, it will be possible to determine the smallest plot capable of accommodating a dwelling and private open space adequate for the needs of an average size household. This will provide a basis for a minimum plot size likely to be acceptable under prevailing local conditions. Similarly, the sizes of plots on which high levels of consolidation have been successfully achieved will indicate an appropriate maximum plot size for the project. Particular attention should be given in both cases to the minimum frontage necessary to permit the full and efficient development of different plot sizes.

Existing provision is not necessarily, of course, an adequate guide for future needs and reference should therefore be made to the views of the target population, as obtained in Task 2A/4 (page 20). This should provide an indication of the size or sizes of plots which households consider appropriate and an indication of their ability to pay. Experience of surveys in several countries suggests that *households usually have a clear and realistic idea of what is appropriate for their needs*.

In addition to these studies, design tests should be carried out on a range of *plot sizes* to determine an appropriate minimum and maximum limit. When carrying out these tests, the points noted in Table 6 should be considered.

These considerations should be applied to the range of plot sizes considered suitable for the project. It will also be important, however, to consider options for plot *shapes*. Research suggests that square plots or rectangular ones where the frontage is on the longest side, lead to considerably increased circulation and utility network costs. As can be seen below, the most economic result for any given area is

Stage 3

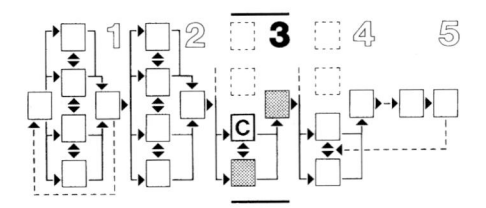

with rectangular plots of which the frontage is the shortest side.

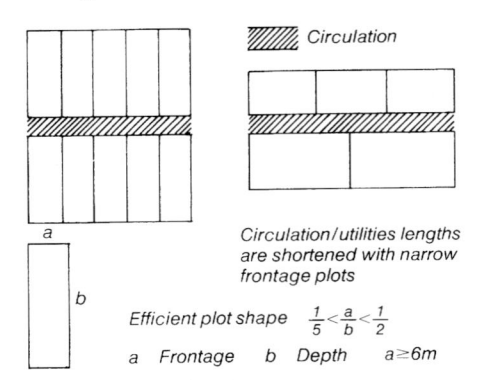

Figure 27
Narrow frontage plots

Efficient plot shape $\frac{1}{5} < \frac{a}{b} < \frac{1}{2}$
a Frontage   b Depth $a \geq 6m$

In this example, plots of equal size and a ratio of 2:1 in the length of sides to frontage produces a reduction in total site area required and the amount of circulation space. The layout on the right results in a 20 per cent increase in total land area, and a 100 per cent increase in that of circulation. In general, options for plot frontage should therefore aim to provide the narrowest frontage compatible with the efficient development of each plot size.

The options identified should allow for local trends in housing design and plot layout. They should also include an allowance for on-plot sewage disposal in cases where households may not be able to afford full sewerage provision, and where physical and legal conditions permit.

A *range of plot sizes* will normally be necessary. This has a number of advantages, including:
● It enables the varied needs and resources of different households to be accommodated.
● It provides considerable flexibility in designing layouts and enables any imbalance in demand and supply to be corrected during later phases of the project.
● It enables a proportion of households who wish to invest in larger dwellings to do so, thereby increasing the potential for rental accommodation within the project.
● It provides a number of alternative methods of charging for different plot sizes, making an internal cross-subsidy possible.

When costs have been estimated for each option (see Task 3D/3, page 64) it should be possible to identify the acceptable range and particularly the area required for the smallest plot size.

In preparing detailed plans, a series of design studies will be necessary so that the most appropriate dimensions for plot frontage and depth can be calculated. A useful step in designing a range of plots is to create a *basic design module* suitable for both enclosed and open spaces. The size of the module will be determined by the following considerations:
● It should be the same dimension in both directions, so that modules can be added on any side.
● It should allow for the thickness of structural walls built of materials in common use, so that the space remaining will be adequate for rooms and open spaces.
● It should relate to any standard building materials dimensions.
● It should be related to the survey information on existing plots accommodating the target population (see Task 2A/4, page 20; and 2C/2. page 27). This will provide a basis for determining a suitable design module, provided that existing plots are considered by their occupants to be suitable.

This information should then be tested to assess the size of a module which is most appropriate to the project. In areas using metric units, a module of 1.5 x 1.5 metres or 3 x 3 metres may well be satisfactory. If thick walls are likely, this may be increased as necessary. The decision on which dimension is appropriate should be based on that which is suitable for the smallest plot size and gives the most flexible range of increments. This will favour the selection of the smallest convenient dimensions.

The next step is to determine an acceptable minimum plot frontage. This also involves a number of considerations as follows:
● It should be sufficient to provide space for an entrance hall and a room at the front for guests, tenants or commerce.
● It should not be so large that the economic provision of utilities is prejudiced.
● It should make possible an efficient development and use of the plot.

Once the range of plot frontages has been determined, plot depths can be obtained by dividing the total area of the minimum plot size (see page 41) by the plot frontage. The total area may need to be modified slightly so that it is compatible with the nearest module dimension. If this results in a minimum plot area which will cost more than households can afford, it will be necessary to revise the dimensions of the design module.

The advantages of using a modular design system are:
● Ease of preparing a range of standard designs.
● Ease of preparing layouts.
● Flexibility of being able to alter layouts.
● Economy of production of small unit, prefabricated building materials.

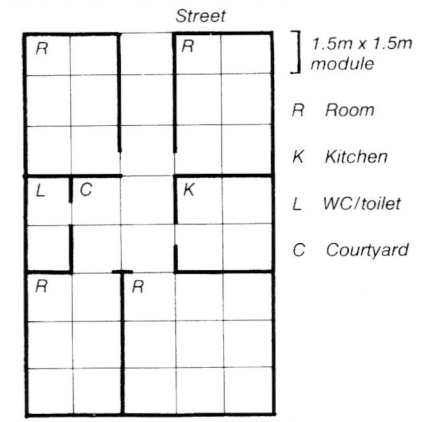

1.5m x 1.5m module
R Room
K Kitchen
L WC/toilet
C Courtyard

Plot layout based on 1.5m module

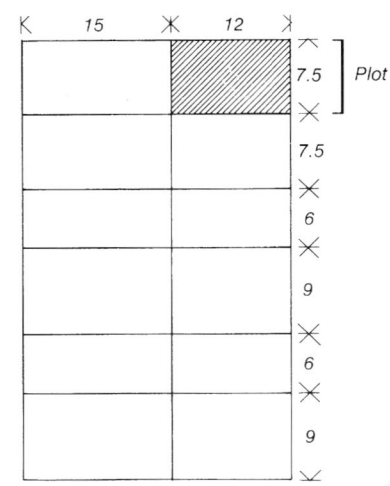

Block layout based on 1.5m module plots

Figure 28
Use of standard module

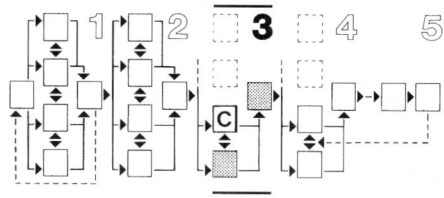

Stage 3   43

Selection

The difficulty of predicting household needs suggests that a range of sizes and shapes should be provided wherever possible. This enables households to make the selection themselves and also reduces the work (and costs) of the implementing agency.

Where this approach is adopted, it will be necessary to select an appropriate minimum plot size which conforms to household needs and resources. Then a maximum plot size on which it is possible to construct a large, possibly multi-storey, building can be determined, together with an intermediate range of sizes to meet all project requirements. It must be possible to incorporate each size easily into the preferred housing layouts.

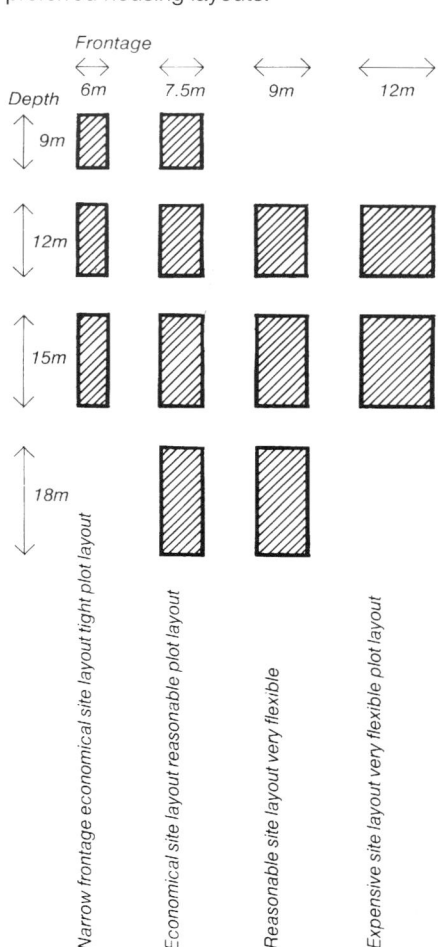

Figure 29 (*above*)
Plot size / shape options

Figure 30 (*right*)
Plot development angles

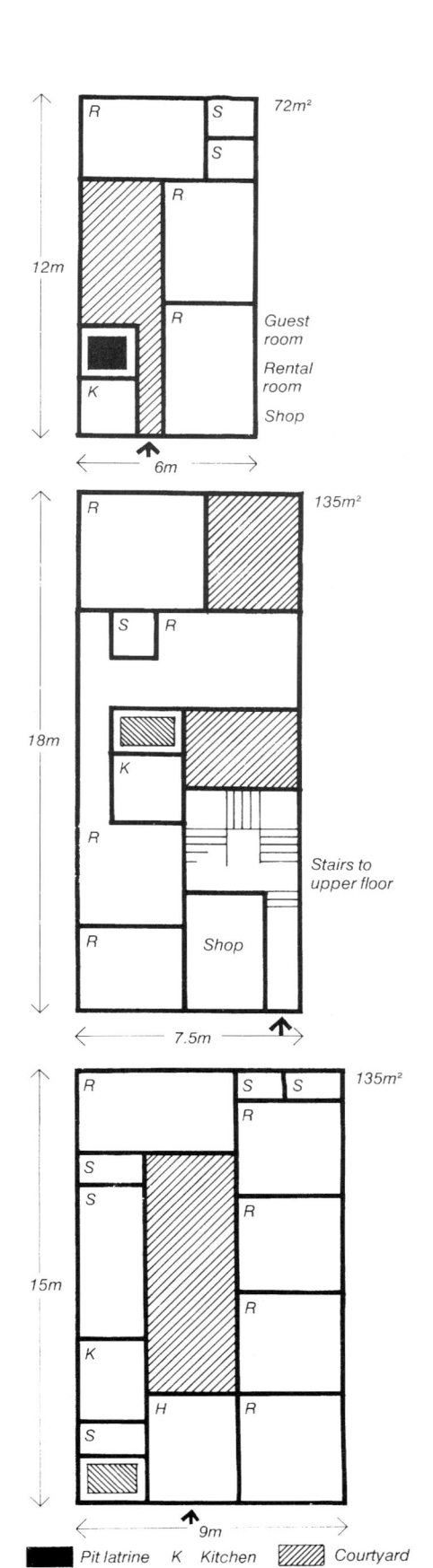

When selecting this range the following points should be considered:
- The minimum plot should be able to accommodate an average size household in a dwelling which satisfies required space, ventilation and daylighting standards.
- The range of sizes should be capable of accommodating the range of users identified (i.e. the households which make up the target population).
- All plots should provide for a yard or other private open space.
- Where possible, space should be available for the construction, at ground level, of rooms for extended families or nonpaying guests, rental accommodation or commercial activity.
- Access to such rooms should be direct from the street, cluster or private yard (where that is at the front of the plot).
- Suitable arrangements should be made for the installation and servicing of on-plot sewage facilities where necessary (e.g. the emptying of pit latrines).
- Construction of at least one upper storey should be possible.
- Within the financial arrangements proposed, households should be able to afford plot costs.
- Plot sizes and shapes should be designed so that both public and private costs are minimised.

The cost of each plot should include the appropriate proportion of land costs for site development. How increase in plot sizes will affect utilities costs should be calculated, too, as this will mean additional road and pipe lengths. The effects of such increases will generally be less critical than land costs, but should be taken into account.

When establishing the preferred options for plot size, it should be remembered that once a plot is marked out on the ground it is extremely difficult to increase its size, regardless of household needs or the layout. *Where a choice has to be made between plot size, utilities or superstructure, priority should be given to providing an adequate plot.*

Stage 3

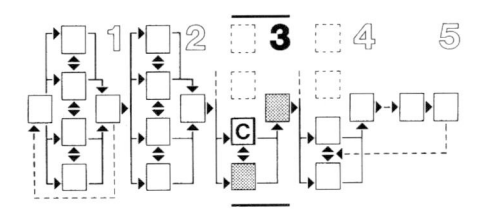

Table 7
*Types of individual housing provision**

Type of provision	Characteristics	Advantages	Disadvantages
Fully pre-built by implementing agency	A complete dwelling including all construction work to public utilities and ready for immediate occupation.	● Agency can control design, construction, cost and even use of dwelling to ensure full conformity with all official standards. ● Immediate occupation possible.	● Extremely high cost especially when related to income levels of target population. This means the low income population cannot be accommodated without a major subsidy. ● Necessarily high rents lead to higher default in Payments ● Reduced public funds for other sections of the population or for the provision of public utilities and facilities. ● Inflexibility in meeting the varied needs of households. ● Discourages households from using their dwelling as a means of generating additional income by constructing additional rooms for commercial or rental use. ● Reduces incentives for occupants to invest in improvements or maintenance of their dwelling and consequently the increased burden placed upon the project agency. ● Usually eliminates small local builders and fails to generate local employment.
Partly re-built by implementing agency	Various possible methods include the pre-built provision of a service 'slab' containing connections to public utilities, a sanitary core unit, a shared firewall, or posts and roof.	● Enables control to be exercised over the main elements of superstructures such as the location of on-plot utilities. ● Facilitates immediate occupation of the plot. ● Reduced cost in relation to full pre-built provision. ● Increased flexibility compared to fully built house. ● Enables households to invest in the completion of their dwelling.	● Possible high cost relative to income levels of the target population. ● Reduces scope for employment of local builders. ● Reduces design options for final dwelling. ● Increases level of compulsory payments by occupants compared to unbuilt plot.
Completely built by plot occupants.	The complete dwelling is built by the users either during or before occupation of the plot.	● Gives maximum control over finance, design and use of dwelling to its occupants, thereby increasing user satisfaction. ● Generally much cheaper than other options as local builders can be used. ● Minimises compulsory repayments by occupants. ● Reduced cost to agency leading to increased opportunity for replicating project. ● Increased scope for using housing as a means of generating additional income and rental accommodation. ● Creates maximum local employment. ● Enables construction to be phased, relative to availability of money.	● Immediate occupation is dependent upon climatic conditions and location. ● Depends upon availability of local labour and materials.

* If land costs are too high to permit individual plots for each household, vertical provision may be necessary. In this case unit costs can be reduced by leaving all internal construction to be completed by householder, creating a form of vertical sites and services project.

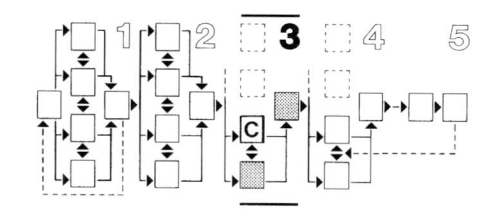

Task 3C/3
Housing: buildings

The Detailed studies (see Task 2C/3, page 28) provide information on existing housing These studies should indicate the smallest and cheapest form of building capable of meeting the needs of an average size household under prevailing local conditions. This will provide essential information for the financial assessment (see Task 3D/3, page 64).

Reference should also be made to the needs of the target population, as expressed in Task 2A/5 (page 20). This should indicate the number of rooms and the area of private space which households consider necessary.

In addition to this information, design tests should be carried out to identify appropriate building options. As with the design tests for plot sizes and shapes, these should be based upon trends in housing design and construction so that future as well as present needs can be met. Reference should also be made to applicable building regulations, as this could eliminate some options, at least in the short term.

Options for the way in which individual buildings are to be provided can then be identified. Basically, there are three choices, the characteristics, advantages and disadvantages of which are outlined in Table 7. A major factor in assessing these options is that while some form of government action is necessary for the provision of land and infrastructure, the building of the house is one element which households can manage themselves. International experience of settlements in which households have been responsible for building their own homes shows clearly that, in most cases, there is a greater chance of matching needs and resources than is possible with government built housing. Equally high, or higher, physical standards may also be achieved over time.

Increasing awareness of the disadvantages of pre-built housing has led to many projects which attempt to increase the role of the occupants in house construction. Partly pre-built options are a notable step in this direction, but for very low-income households, even this may prove too expensive. The ability of households to provide all or part of the building will, of course, depend upon the availability of building skills and of inexpensive and sound building materials. A study should be made to assess what problems exist, and ways to supply the necessary skills and/or materials.

Before options can be selected it will be necessary to prepare cost estimates. These should be based upon current unit rates for the type of construction involved and include an allowance for inflation. In some cases, it may be considered advisable to subsidise materials for self-help construction, or to provide low-interest loans for their purchase, so that households can obtain durable materials for each stage of construction (see Task 3D/3, page 64).

Selection of options

Of all elements in the housing process, the building itself represents one of the largest cost items. It is also the one which most directly affects each household. The preferred option will therefore be the one which gives households the chance to decide what type and cost of house they need. Experience shows that where it is possible, people are most likely to obtain housing which meets their needs and resources. Their ability to do so is shown by the extent to which housing is at present produced by its occupants. In Egypt this process is currently adding more units to the national housing stock than all public housing efforts combined.

In selecting the preferred range of options the first need to be assessed should be if any completed or core units are needed. If so these points should be considered:
● It should be possible to use forms of construction which are familiar to people and appropriate to the project site.
● The necessary labour and materials should be available.
● What pre-built superstructure which site conditions, such as climate or location, may be required to enable households to occupy their plots.
● The unit costs of different forms of provision should be compared, and related to what households can afford (see Task 3D/3, page 66).

The first step in selecting preferred options will be to determine the type and minimum size of superstructure which households regard as necessary, at least in the short term (see Task 2A/5, page 20 and Task 2C/3, page 28). The next step is to determine the amounts which households can afford for building, based upon the proportions of total housing expenditure allocated (see Task 3D/3, page 66). This total can then be divided by the unit cost of the cheapest form of construction suitable to meet short term needs, to obtain a range of superstructure options which households can afford.

Where a choice has to be made between the levels of provision for plots, utilities and superstructure. It is important to note that an initially modest superstructure provision is normal in most low income housing developments. This is because households rarely have adequate capital to finance high quality building in a single phase. A modest initial structure has the merit of not absorbing scarce capital resources and thereby over-burdening a household. It also enables improvements and extensions to be carried out when savings are available to finance them.

Apart from any partial superstructure required for the installation of full on-plot utilities, or because of site characteristics, the provision of pre-built housing is usually unnecessary and undesirable. Attention should be focused instead on ways of providing potential settlers with the means to build their own houses. The main constraint upon this activity is usually lack of money to purchase building materials. It may therefore be advisable to introduce a complementary building materials loan scheme, under which beneficiaries can borrow the amount needed to purchase materials for the erection of, say, one room or supply of roofing materials. Small loans could be offered for periods of between 5 and 10 years at the same rate of interest adopted for mortgages or other loans. Similarly, training of building workers or providing loans to help small contractors to obtain essential equipment can give a major stimulus to local house building and generate many employment opportunities.

Stage 3

Task 3C/4
Commerce and industry

Figure 31
Commercial centre

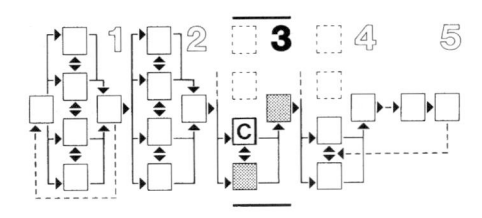

Figure 32 (*above*)
Local shop

Figure 33 (*below*)
Commercial core area with adjacent plots designed to cope with expansion of commercial area

▨ Commercial plots

▧ Plots likely to develop commercial use over time

→ Direction of likely expansion of commercial use

The study of commercial activity in existing areas accommodating the target population (see Task 2C/5, page 30) and the analysis of local demand (see Task 3D/3, page 64) will indicate the potential extent of any new activity.

The advantages of encouraging a range of commercial and industrial activities include:
- They provide local employment and earning potential, which in turn increases the amount which households can afford for housing.
- They increase the amount of money spent within the project site.
- They attract investment into the project and enable a cross-subsidy* to be generated which reduces total costs to the target population.
- They provide convenient services, and thus improve the quality of life in the area.

The layout options for commercial or industrial activity will vary according to their scale. Large scale commercial activity will generally require a central location on the site with direct frontage to local roads in order to attract sufficient investment and custom. Large industrial units, however, can usually be located in peripheral parts of the site but still require good access.

* A cross-subsidy is a subsidy in which a profit or surplus achieved in one aspect of a project is used to offset costs in another.

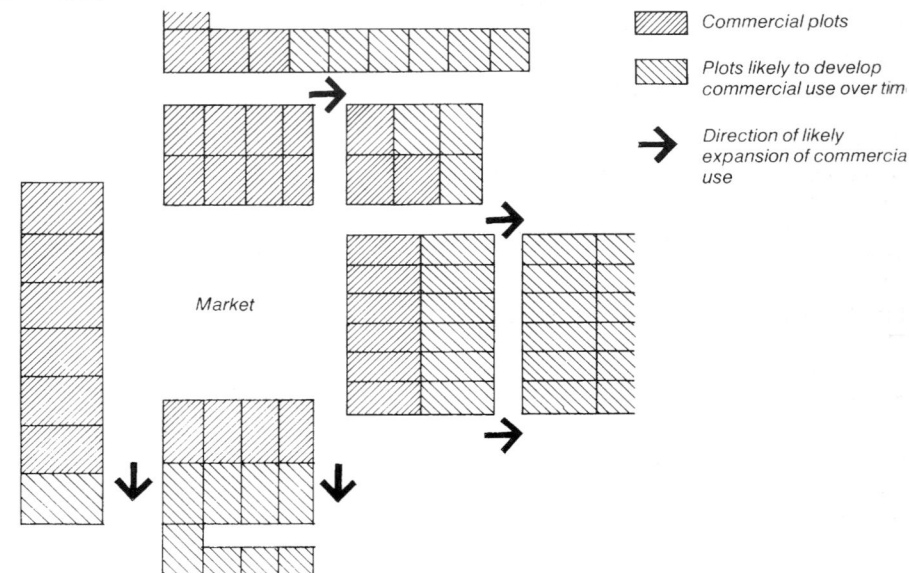

For small-scale family businesses, the option of permitting residential plots to be used for industry or Commerce (including rental accommodation), should be considered, as overheads are reduced and full advantage can be taken of informal family employment. This is perhaps the most effective way to encourage local enterprise. Provision should also be made for workshop areas for noisy uses such as panel beating.

In upgrading projects, the design options for large scale activities will be more restricted than in new settlements, though options for small scale activities may be greater because of the existing demand. Where projects combine upgrading and new settlement, opportunities for both types will be increased still further, especially if the large scale activities are located so that they are equally accessible to both new and existing areas. Similarly, *the provision of a commercial 'core' can provide flexibility for future development if it is surrounded by plots which are designed to be suitable for either commercial or residential use.*

Stage 3

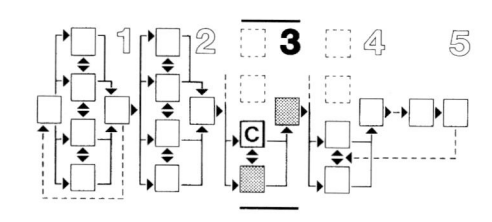

Selection of options

The selection of commercial and industrial development options will be based upon the alternatives discussed related to the project options and the financial analysis (see Task 3D/3, page 64). Decisions will be required on the scale of provision and distribution of both small and larger scale activity.

On balance, the advantages of encouraging small scale commercial activity on residential plots are likely to be greater than any disadvantages incurred through the loss of potential revenue. This risk can be further reduced by charging a higher unit price for all plots in locations of commercial potential such as those on main roads or at intersections (see Technical note 10, page 119). This approach is easy to administer and may be particularly appropriate in upgrading projects where commercial activity may already exist in residential areas. It has the further merit of simplifying land use planning for the neighbourhoods, since only limited special provision is required.

For larger scale commercial activity, the only effective option is likely to be a central location on the project site, with direct access to main local roads and utilities. This will provide maximum accessibility to all parts of the project site and maximise the attraction of commercial investment. The location of commercial activities in combination with major public facilities will enhance the investment potential and also help to generate a lively and attractive mixture of development available to local residents. *It is recommended that specific provision of land or buildings for commercial use be limited to a minimum core area. Plot sizes, shapes and layouts around this core should be designed so that commercial use can expand efficiently into these areas in the future as population and demand increase.*

In *upgrading areas*, the relationship of any new commercial activity to existing development will be important in ensuring the viability of both. Where possible, the *extension and intensification of existing centres will be the best solution*, as it will increase the value of existing investment as well as providing a secure demand for future activity.

The same considerations will also apply to *large-scale industrial development*, though it will not be necessary to provide an expensive central location or direct street frontage. Access to main roads and essential services will be important, however. It may, therefore, be advisable to locate industrial areas immediately behind commercial sites which need to front onto main roads. This enables links between both uses to increase. Alternatively, industrial development may be able to occupy land which would be unsuitable or unattractive for other uses.

As in predominantly housing areas, layouts for commercial or industrial development should be designed to put all land to optimum use. It should be possible to achieve a proportion of private (i.e. revenue generating) land which is as high, if not higher than can be achieved in housing layouts (see Technical note 16, page 124). This may not be the case in upgrading projects, where existing development will restrict opportunities.

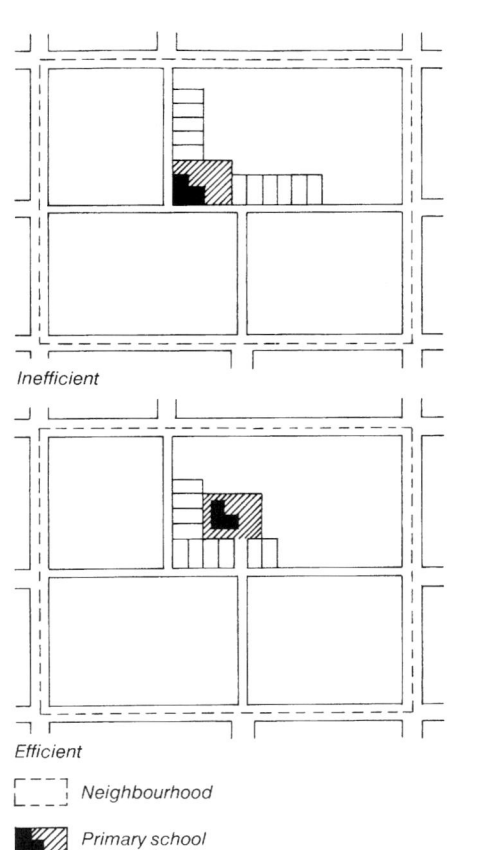

Inefficient

Efficient

☐ Neighbourhood

▨ Primary school

Figure 34
Primary school location

Task 3C/5
Public facilities and recreation

These land uses include a wide range of provisions such as schools, health clinics, parks and landscaped areas provided by various public agencies. The studies of existing provision available to the target population (see Task 2C/4, page 29) and the social studies (see Task 2A/3, page 20), should indicate the extent of any inadequacies and the order of priorities.

The ability to satisfy existing needs will depend upon resources, including, in the case of upgrading projects, the availability of land. Where budgetary restrictions show that full provision cannot be met initially, it will still be important to designate adequate sites so that the facilities can be included later.

Design options for each facility will be determined largely by the requirements of the agencies themselves, balanced against competing land uses. Every effort should be made to ensure that some provision is available to all parts of the project site at all stages of project development.

Education

The most important item in site development will probably be provision of school sites, as schools generally make the greatest land demands. Schools should be located as near as possible to the centre of the areas which they serve, though the location options in upgrading schemes depend in practice upon available space. Primary schools should be near the centre of the neighbourhoods which they serve. They *do not*, however, need to front directly onto main local roads or occupy sites more suitable for revenue generating uses such as commerce or housing. The *extent* of public facilities provision will vary according to the size of the project and the number of people to be served. For example, a single neighbourhood of about 5000 people will require a primary school, but a project for several neighbourhoods will also require a secondary school and possibly a college. The same principle

48   Stage 3

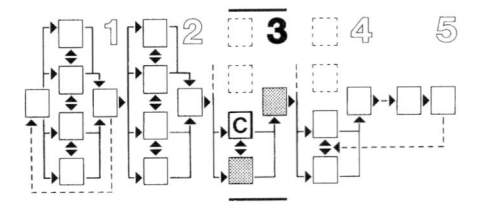

applies to health facilities. The applicable agencies should therefore be consulted to find out the most suitable level of provision, but their requests must be considered in relation to the needs of competing land uses. Payment for the land and buildings required for educational facilities can normally be expected to be met from educational budgets, rather than from urban project budgets.

Recreation

Options for *recreational space* should include a range for both formal (e.g. organised games) and informal use (e.g. parks, play spaces).

The extent of *formal recreation* space will be determined largely by available space and official standards, limited by the ability of the target population to bear the costs. The location should be as central as possible to the areas the spaces serve, though this need not be a valuable area of the project site. Access will be important, but a location behind commercial, industrial or public facility areas would be suitable. Naturally, are as for formal games should be reasonably level and of a suitable surface. Preferred locations should therefore be selected with reference to the Detailed site studies (see Tasks 2B/5 and 2B/6, page 24.

Informal spaces may be provided on a more pragmatic basis. On balance, the advantages of locating a large number of small open spaces relating to housing clusters or local access roads will prove to be most economical and socially acceptable, since it provides space for children to play under supervision from their homes. Finally, it may also be desirable to provide some 'hard' areas suitable for older children. These may also be located within housing areas, though they should be distinct from general open areas surrounding house plots.

Particular care will be required to ensure that recreation spaces will be socially acceptable and that any existing planting, especially trees, is incorporated into the layouts. These should therefore be checked against the information on existing site landscaping obtained in Task group 2B (page 20).

Figure 35   *Typical view of a kickabout area*

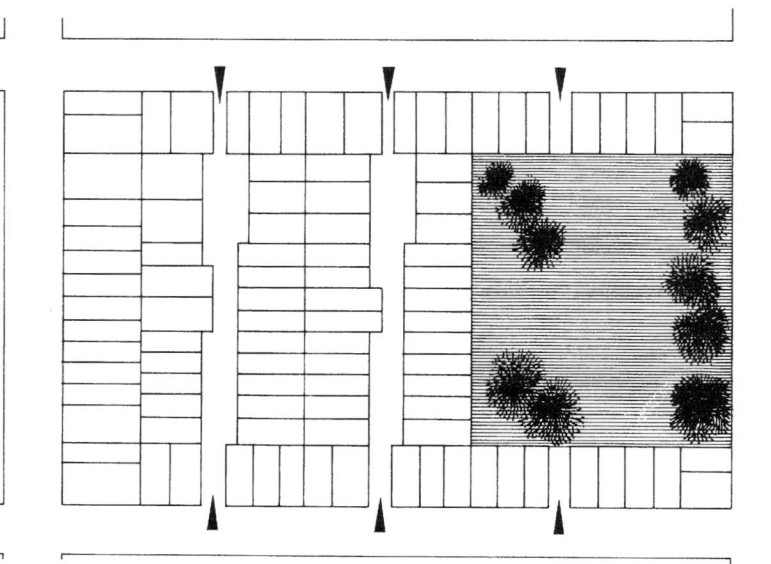

Figure 36   *Typical arrangement of a kickabout area in a block*

Stage 3

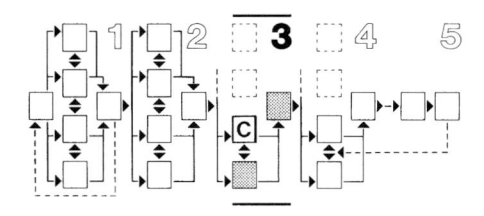

Landscaping

The options developed for landscaping must take account of these questions:
- What is the purpose of the landscaping? For example, is it to provide shade or simply to make an area look attractive?
- Who will pay for the landscaping initially, who will maintain it, and at what cost?
- What are the climatic, soil, water and social constraints?

Design proposals must be developed within the above constraints. Options to reduce public costs include:
- Private maintenance of garden areas in front of houses. This can have the same effect as street tree planting schemes.
- Maintenance of sports areas by clubs.
- Maintenance of small public gardens by commercial establishments, e.g. cafes.

General

Outline proposals for public facilities should be checked with authorities who will be concerned in provision of facilities, to ensure they are acceptable.

Task 3C/6
Incorporation of other land uses

The Detailed studies of the project site (see Task 2C/6, page 30) will have identified any other land uses which will need to be taken into account in developing proposals for the project site.

Options for incorporating, modifying or removing these other uses will obviously depend upon their nature and on government policy for land use zoning. Where necessary, discussions should be held with the agency, group or individual responsible to determine the best approach, though there will usually be (considered) advantages in permitting a mixture of land uses. This is, after all, a common characteristic in most urban areas, including high, medium and low income areas. A flexible approach allows local needs to be met without bureaucratic delay. Limitations on land use should exist where this is particularly important, for example, for school sites, industrial sites, and market, but elsewhere limits should restrict only uses which cause bad pollution especially smoke, smells and noise.

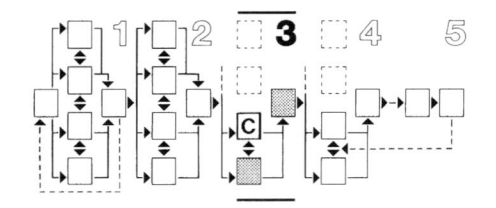

Task 3C/7
Circulation and transportation

The layout of streets should provide adequate and safe means of vehicular and pedestrian circulation. Studies of the target population and existing areas accommodating them (see Task group 2A, page 18; and 2C, page 26), will provide useful information from which circulation options can be developed. This involves three things: circulation, transportation methods and parking.

Circulation

In *upgrading projects*, the existing street pattern will generally limit circulation options. In such cases the objective should be to rationalise the street pattern to obtain the most efficient use of land. In *new settlements* it will be possible to consider a wider range of options; these will take account of the opportunity to provide links to the existing or proposed adjacent urban street system and of the arrangement of plots into blocks and neighbourhoods, as discussed in Task 3C/1 (page 37).

The circulation options for upgrading and new settlements are developed here as a road hierarchy which is related to the strategic urban road network. The function of the elements in this hierarchy is described in Table 8.

Requirements for the total street width, or Rights-of-way indicated in the table allow for carriageway, sidewalks and any landscaping. The requirements of local legislation and regulations will also have to be considered.

Transportation

The surveys carried out in Stage 2 will provide information on the travel requirements and habits of the target population. This information will allow *transport options* to be developed. The question of general accessibility is discussed in Tasks 2A/3 (page 20) and 2B/1 (page 22).

The transport options should take into account:
- Pedestrian and bicycle circulation.
- Public transport (buses, shared taxis, trams, rail).
- Vehicular circulation (cars, service vehicles, possibly with differentiation

Table 8
Street hierarchy options

Street type	Function	Total street width or Rights of Way (metres)	Number of lanes	Recommended spacing (metres)
Access street	Provides direct access to plots, and circulation between blocks. Pedestrians predominate.	8–12	1–2	varies with plot sizes
Local street/distributor	Provides plot access and vehicular circulation between neighbourhoods. Potential bus routes.	15–20	2–4	80–200
District distributor street	Bounds neighbourhoods and provides plot access. Caters for general urban vehicular circulation and through traffic. probable bus routes.	20–30	4	400–1000
Arterial street	Minimal frontage access city or regional vehicular movement. Probable bus routes.	20–30	4–6	1000–5000

Stage 3

between motorised and animal or human drawn vehicles).

The provision of public transport, and its cost, will generally be under the control of private individuals or of another authority with whom options should be discussed. However, the availability of a flexible and efficient circulation system will ensure that a good service is possible. The design of public transport routes will have an effect on spacing of District Streets since pedestrian routes and walking distances should be related to public transport routes; routes should be within 10 minutes walk of the population which they serve.

Parking and servicing

Parking options consist of on-street or off-street provision. The demand for car parking will be indicated by information obtained during Task 2A/1 (page 19) but it is unlikely to be great, even in the future, in low income areas. Adequate off-street, or off-carriageway parking space should be allowed for industrial and commercial areas.

Requirements for servicing commercial and industrial activity should be considered when defining options for commercial and industry, (see Task 3C/4, Page 46).

Construction standards

The range of options must include possible road construction standards. Local construction practice, site soil condition (see Task 2B/6, page 24) and climate should be considered before developing options relating to each element of the street system. For example, unstable or soft ground conditions may require a higher construction standard than consolidated ground conditions. The standard of construction required for each element is also related to its function. The standard should be related to traffic intensity and in particular the intensity of heavy vehicles. Table 9 gives the range of options which should be considered.

The functional requirements for each type of street will be determined on the basis of Stage 2 surveys. In general the cost of higher standard roads (Arterial and District Streets) will not be attributable directly to the project since they will form part of the total urban street system.

The various options should be costed so that they can be related to the financial framework (see Task 3D/3, page 64) and the phasing of road construction considered in relation to provision of services and site development (see Task 3C/8, page 52).

Selection of options

The selection of transport and circulation options is based on:
- Financial objectives of the project.
- Layout efficiency.
- Operational efficiency.

The *financial objectives* are discussed in Task 3D/3 (page 64). The financial requirements will determine which construction options can be afforded.

The *street layout* has a significant effect on the pattern of utility networks which use streets as Rights-of-way. The selection of Rights-of-way and spacing of the various street types making up the street hierarchy should be based on testing the options, to find which results in the most efficient utility layout. Plot size and planning of layouts will affect the layout of streets and the two must be coordinated (see Task 3C/1, page 37). The design approach proposed for residential plots should allow an efficient street layout to be selected. Generally, the shorter the total length of the street network, the shorter, and therefore cheaper, will be the utility network.

In general the testing of circulation options will be based on optimising utility networks while taking into account plot area requirements (see Technical note 16, page 124). The testing of *layout efficiency in upgrading projects* will require consideration of demolition requirements of each option. *Where demolition is required, it should be kept to the absolute minimum by careful design*.

The *operational efficiency* of a circulation option is dependent on:
- Traffic capacity and functions.
- Accessibility by mode.
- Parking provision.

The selection of *Rights-of-way* for each street in the hierarchy depends on the *function of adjacent plots*, (see Table 8, page 50). In general Rights-of-way should be kept to the minimum width compatible with traffic demand. For streets not giving access to interiors of plot clusters the minimum width of carriageway should allow for two-way traffic (i.e. 5 metres).

Table 9
Options for road construction standards

Construction	Comments
No provision: minimal regrading of in situ soil to provide drainage.	Dependent on local soil and rainfall conditions for suitability. Appropriate for very light traffic. Very cheap.
Sub-base only: grading and compaction of sub-grade with gravel surface.	Suitable for staged construction, forming the first pavement layer; drainage by side ditches; light traffic only. Depends also on rainfall pattern. Low cost.
Stabilised soil: in situ soil stabilised with bitumen or cement.	*As immediately* above. Highly dependent on local soils. Low cost.
Sub-base and road base. (granular base material or stabilised soil.)	May be surfaced with DBST* as part of stage construction final step. If unsurfaced maintenance required. Suitable for moderately trafficked roads. Kerbs should be considered with drainage in kerb channel. Moderate cost.
Base course asphaltic concrete additional structural layer on sub and road base.	Kerbs required. May be used as running surface in staged construction; as minimum requirement for heavily trafficked roads. Moderate cost.
Wearing course (asphaltic concrete).	Final structural layer necessary on heavily trafficked routes. High cost.

* Double Bitumen Surface Treatment

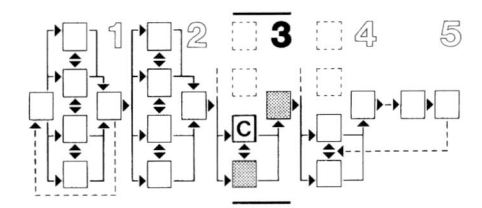

Rights-of-way should be chosen with a view to *future traffic requirements*. If traffic demands are low in the short term the Rights-of-way selected should allow for the later upgrading of carriageway by widening or providing a dual carriageway.

Layout options should be tested to see which provides the safest and most direct *pedestrian circulation* and the best overall access between residential areas and public transport routes. In some projects *cycle routes* should also be considered.

Specific *parking* provision will be required in commercial and industrial areas of the project. Provision should be made for off-carriageway parking in commercial areas. In other areas it is important that some parking space is available either on street or in access roads, but large scale specific provision is unlikely to be justified.

Here is a *checklist* of points to be considered in the selection of circulation and transportation options:
● Are links required to the strategic urban roads network? These may determine the location of District Streets.
● The location of industrial and commercial activity should relate directly to District Streets. Thus the appropriate siting of such uses will interact with factors determining location of District Streets.
● The hierarchy of streets should ensure that traffic on a particular element is compatible with adjacent land uses. For example, through traffic should be catered for on Arterial or District Streets, and Access Streets should be arranged so that through traffic is deterred from using them. The safety of pedestrians should be a key consideration in designing the circulation hierarchy.
● The various options should be tested for circulation efficiency (see Technical note 16, page 124).
● The appropriate total street widths for each element in the road hierarchy will depend on planning factors and on the actual requirement set by expected traffic flows. The widths for Arterial and District Streets, which form a city-wide function, will be determined by the level of traffic in the whole urban area. The widths for Local and Access Streets should provide for vehicular access to plots and within neighbourhoods. The minimum carriageways should generally allow for two-way traffic, i.e. 5 metre carriageway. The additional width required will be determined by planning requirements for sidewalks or landscape areas.
● For streets performing a mainly vehicular traffic function, the width should be sufficient to allow safe sight lines at junctions. T junctions at Access Street/Local Street will minimise this requirement.
● The widths in District and Local Streets should allow for off-carriageway parking in areas of commercial activity.
● The appropriate number of traffic lanes will be a function of traffic flows. Where traffic flows will be low in the short or medium term, total street widths intended, for dual carriageways may be provided, but with a single carriageway at first. This can then be widened when traffic flow warrants it.

In upgrading projects, the layout options should be tested in relation to the extent of demolition required. The relative quality of buildings affected by different layouts should be considered. If necessary, street widths may be modified locally to minimise demolition.

The selection of the standard of construction will depend on policy decisions and on the budget and allocation of costs (see Task 3D/3, page 64). However, a minimum requirement should always allow access to all plots to allow servicing (construction, fire appliance, utility and servicing). The level of construction required will depend on local ground conditions (see Tasks 2B/5, page 24; and 2B/6, page 24) and rainfall pattern. A basic network of paved streets should be provided to permit bus routes to be established; in general, this will require a paved street within 300–500 metres of all plots. Before submitting public transport proposals for approval, it is advisable to check them with the specialist agencies.

In the interests of economy, the preferred solution should reduce the area, total length and the costs of roads to the minimum necessary while ensuring efficient circulation of people and vehicles throughout the project site. Since conventional road planning frequently over-provides for circulation relative to effective demand, considerable cost savings should be possible.

Task 3C/8
Utilities

The Detailed studies of the target population (see Task group 2A, page 18) with project site (see Task group 2B, page 22), the financial framework (see Task 2D/2, page 32) and utilities (see Task 2C/8, page 31), will have provided all the information necessary to identify the constraints for the development of utilities. The design standards and project objectives concerning the level of provision per person relate to the analysis of these Detailed studies.

This task has three objectives:
● Establishing those options for each utility which satisfy the design standards and project objectives.
● Carrying out preliminary designs for each option.
● Selecting those options which best meet the project objectives.

In general, the two principal aspects which need to be considered in depth are water supply and the sewage disposal system. Their relationship to the health of the population is a vital element in any housing project, but particularly so in low income projects, where densities are likely to be higher than in other areas. Every effort should therefore be made to ensure that access to safe drinking water and the sanitary collection and disposal of sewage, are achieved.

Several options exist for each utility. The lower the incomes of the target population, the more these options will be restricted, since utilities generally represent a significant proportion of total costs for low income housing projects. For this reason, it is essential to make sure that care is taken in assessing and selecting and the appropriate options.

An indication of options for each utility is shown in Tables 10–15. Notes on the characteristics, advantages and disadvantages of each are given, though the list is not complete.

Stage 3   53

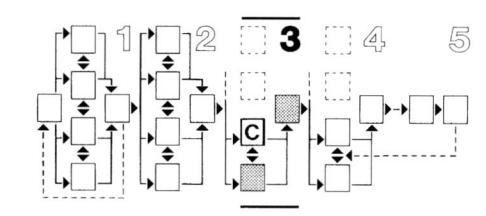

Table 10
Water supply options

Type of provision	Characteristics	Advantages	Disadvantages
Communal well	Large capacity well to serve a reasonable number of plots.	● Quality of water can be good if appropriate sanitation systems are used.	● Moderate capital cost, though less than individual on-plot wells. ● Dependent upon geology and depth of water table. ● Inconvenient. Volume of water used dependent on distance from well. ● Risk of contamination.
Water tanker/water vendor	Supply from tanker or from kiosks.	● Low initial cost to provider. ● Water can be good quality.	● Very high running costs. ● Difficult to control quality. ● Inconvenient. ● Often expensive to consumer.
Existing water course or pond	Generally requires modification to bank of river, stream or pond to facilitate removal of water, though it could be pumped to outlets remote from source.	● Low capital cost.	● High risk of contamination by users and/or upstream conditions. ● Dependent upon climate. ● Inconvenient. ● Volume of water used dependent upon distance to source
Communal storage	Various possible methods include dammed-up streams or river to reservoir, storage tank with gravity or pumped supply and treatment works if necessary. Distribution from a central point via communal taps or standpipes.	● Quality of water can be controlled if access to stored water is prohibited, or treatment provided between storage and outlet.	● Capital cost dependent on type of system used. ● Inconvenient. ● Volume of water used dependent upon distance to source.
Public standpipes	Piped network throughout development with standpipes at strategic locations. Can be associated with an on-site storage facility.	● Moderate cost. ● Good quality of water if from treatment plant. ● Enables individual on-plot connections to be made when people can afford it, if piped network is adequate.	● Risk of wastage of water from damaged fitments and negligence. ● Slightly inconvenient. ● Efficiency and risk of pollution dependent upon spacing of standpipes.

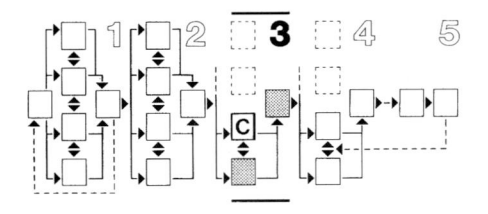

Stage 3

Table 10 continued

Type of provision	Characteristics	Advantages	Disadvantages
Individual water butt 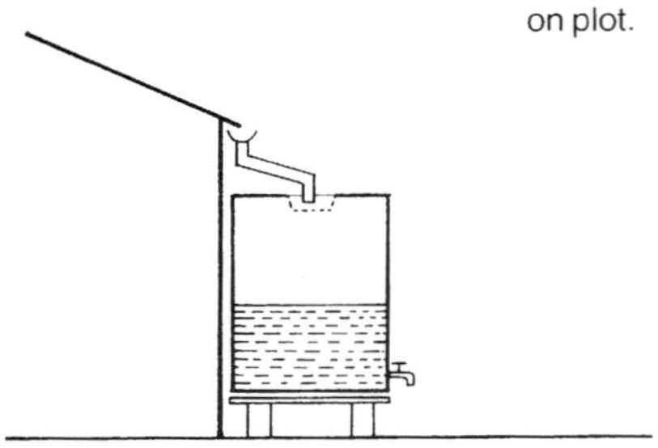	Water collected from roofs and stored on plot.	● Convenient. ● Good quality. ● Low capital cost.	● Small storage volume. ● Very dependent on climate. ● Risk of contamination if stored for long periods.
Individual well on plot 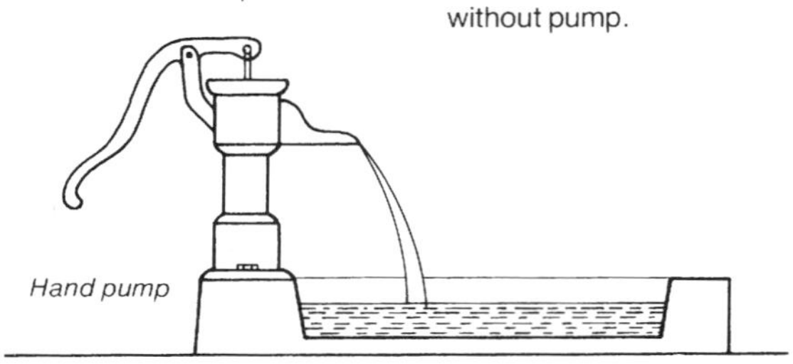	Individual well or borehole with or without pump.	● Convenient. ● Quality can be very good.	● Can be high capital cost. ● Dependent on local geology. ● Risk of contamination from sewage if pit latrines are used.
Individual piped supply – single tap	Fully piped network from treatment plant to plots. Individual connections can be phased as residents can afford it, if adequate mains are installed in street. Single tap only provided on plot.	● Good quality. ● Readily accessible in moderate quantities. ● Significant health benefits. ● Can operate with lower grade sewage disposal systems.	● High capital costs. ● Increases volume of sullage water to be disposed compared with no connection.
Individual piped supply – multi-tap	Generally as for single tap, but mains required to be larger and multiple taps or outlets provided to each plot enables water flushed toilets to be used.	● Good quality. ● Readily accessible in large quantities. ● Maximum health benefits.	● High capital costs. ● Requires fully piped sewage disposal system.

Table 11
Sewage disposal options

Type of provision	Characteristics	Advantages	Disadvantages
Communal system. Various levels from pour flush latrine to piped network	The basic concept is to provide a block of toilet facilities connected to any of the following sanitation systems: pour-flush latrine aqua-privy septic tank piped sewerage.	● Possible reduced costs compared with individual provision. ● Can be installed in densely populated areas without requiring extensive demolition.	● Inconvenient. ● High maintenance costs due to damage and neglect. ● Can become unhygienic and under-used if not kept clean. ● If subsequent up-grading is carried out, the capital cost of toilet blocks would have to be written off. ● Often socially unacceptable.
Night soil collection 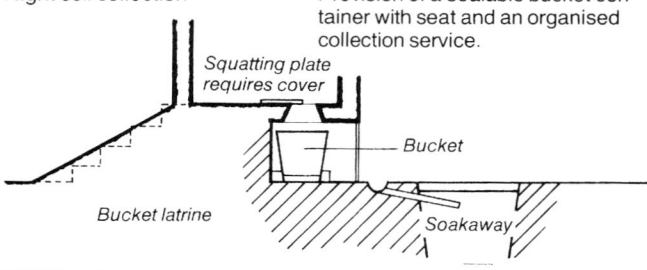	Provision of a sealable bucket container with seat and an organised collection service.	● Comparatively low capital cost if treatment is already available with collection vehicles.	● High maintenance cost. ● Comparatively high health hazard to users and collectors.

Stage 3 55

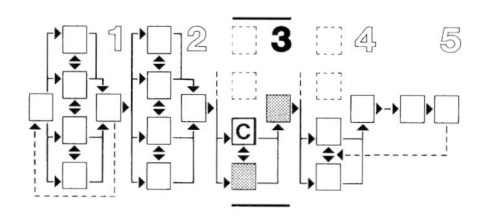

Table 11 continued

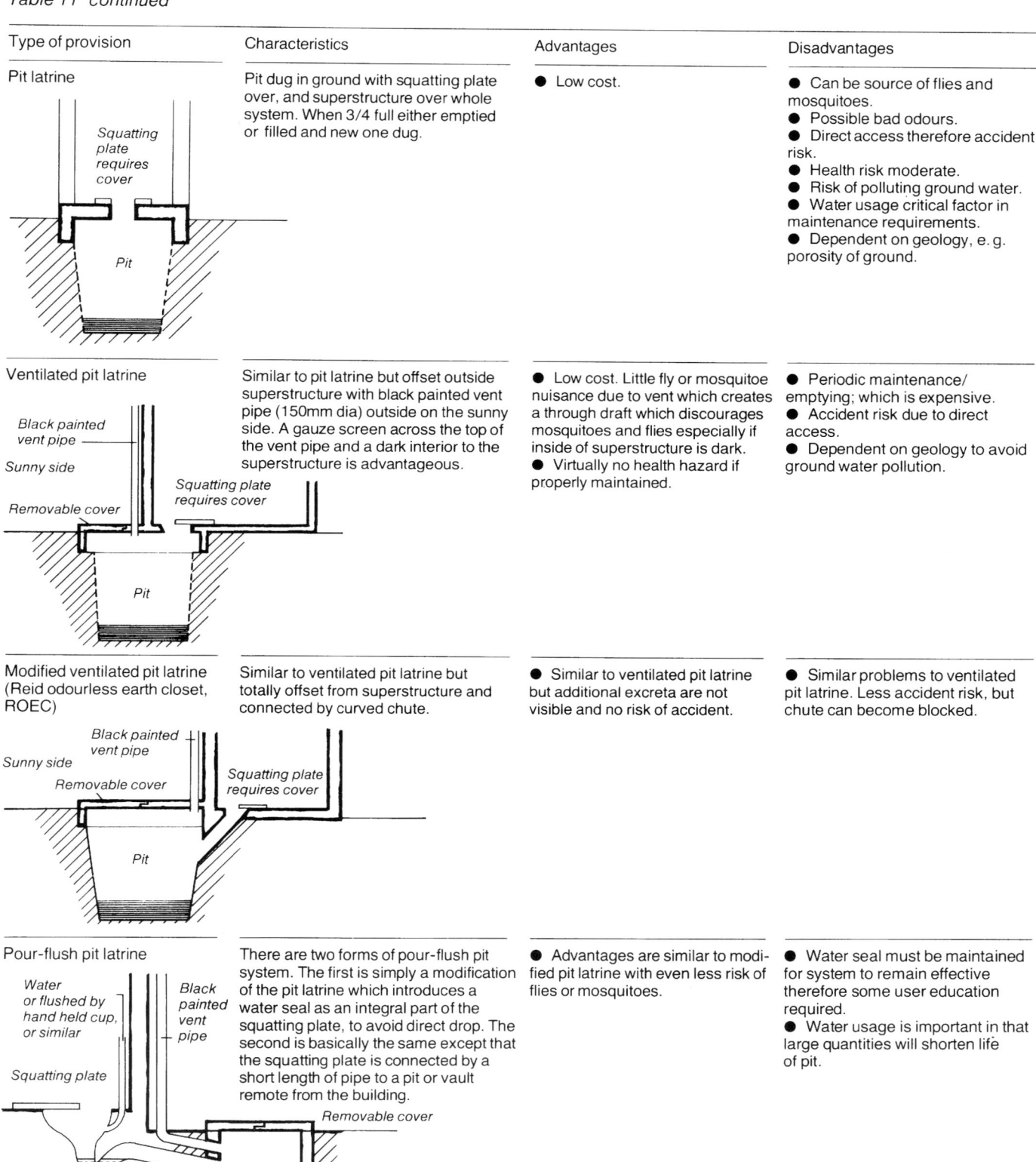

Type of provision	Characteristics	Advantages	Disadvantages
Pit latrine	Pit dug in ground with squatting plate over, and superstructure over whole system. When 3/4 full either emptied or filled and new one dug.	● Low cost.	● Can be source of flies and mosquitoes. ● Possible bad odours. ● Direct access therefore accident risk. ● Health risk moderate. ● Risk of polluting ground water. ● Water usage critical factor in maintenance requirements. ● Dependent on geology, e.g. porosity of ground.
Ventilated pit latrine	Similar to pit latrine but offset outside superstructure with black painted vent pipe (150mm dia) outside on the sunny side. A gauze screen across the top of the vent pipe and a dark interior to the superstructure is advantageous.	● Low cost. Little fly or mosquitoe nuisance due to vent which creates a through draft which discourages mosquitoes and flies especially if inside of superstructure is dark. ● Virtually no health hazard if properly maintained.	● Periodic maintenance/emptying; which is expensive. ● Accident risk due to direct access. ● Dependent on geology to avoid ground water pollution.
Modified ventilated pit latrine (Reid odourless earth closet, ROEC)	Similar to ventilated pit latrine but totally offset from superstructure and connected by curved chute.	● Similar to ventilated pit latrine but additional excreta are not visible and no risk of accident.	● Similar problems to ventilated pit latrine. Less accident risk, but chute can become blocked.
Pour-flush pit latrine	There are two forms of pour-flush pit system. The first is simply a modification of the pit latrine which introduces a water seal as an integral part of the squatting plate, to avoid direct drop. The second is basically the same except that the squatting plate is connected by a short length of pipe to a pit or vault remote from the building.	● Advantages are similar to modified pit latrine with even less risk of flies or mosquitoes.	● Water seal must be maintained for system to remain effective therefore some user education required. ● Water usage is important in that large quantities will shorten life of pit.

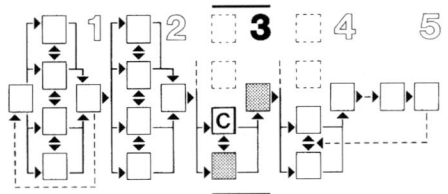

Stage 3

Table 11 continued

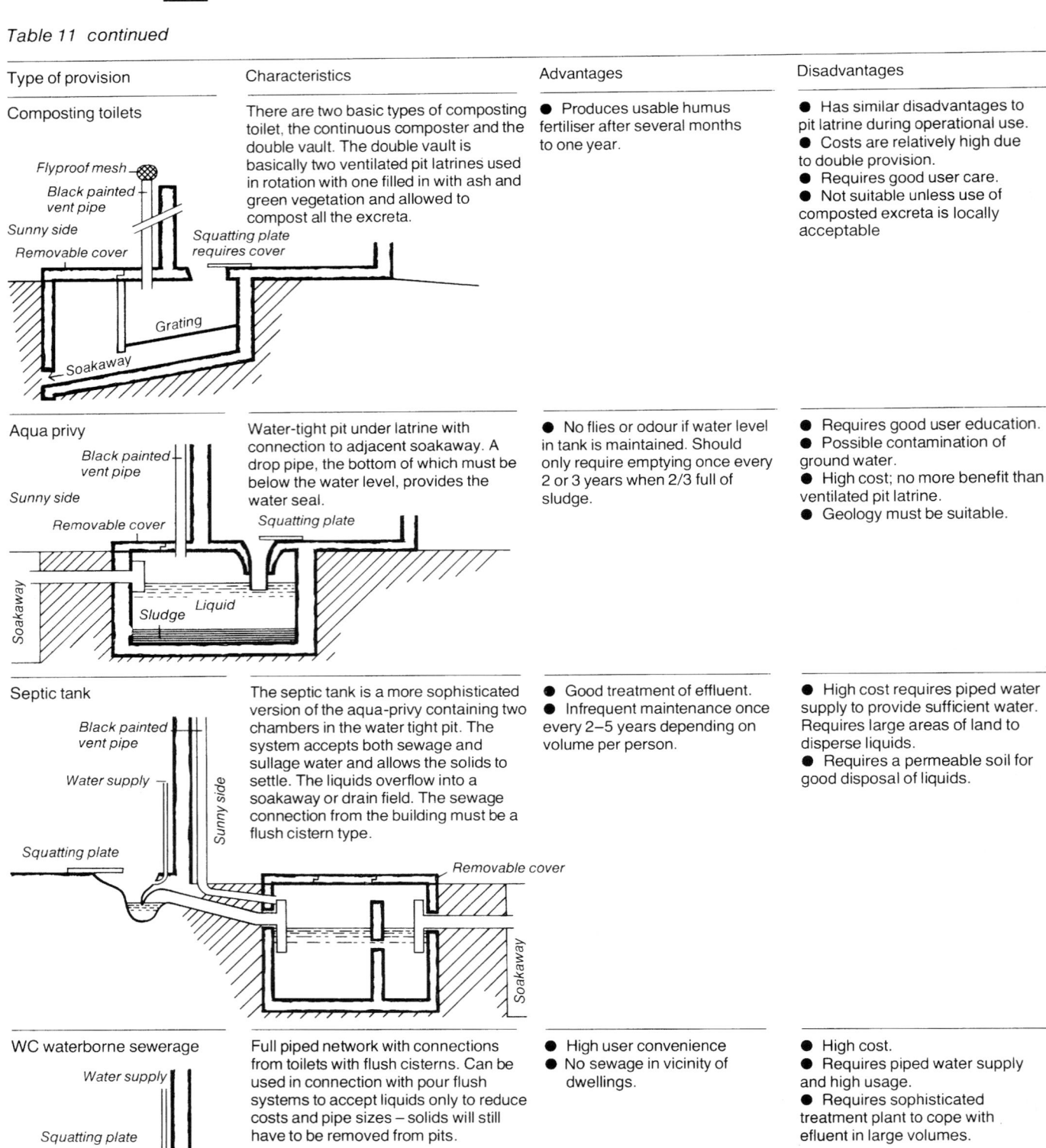

Type of provision	Characteristics	Advantages	Disadvantages
Composting toilets	There are two basic types of composting toilet, the continuous composter and the double vault. The double vault is basically two ventilated pit latrines used in rotation with one filled in with ash and green vegetation and allowed to compost all the excreta.	• Produces usable humus fertiliser after several months to one year.	• Has similar disadvantages to pit latrine during operational use. • Costs are relatively high due to double provision. • Requires good user care. • Not suitable unless use of composted excreta is locally acceptable
Aqua privy	Water-tight pit under latrine with connection to adjacent soakaway. A drop pipe, the bottom of which must be below the water level, provides the water seal.	• No flies or odour if water level in tank is maintained. Should only require emptying once every 2 or 3 years when 2/3 full of sludge.	• Requires good user education. • Possible contamination of ground water. • High cost; no more benefit than ventilated pit latrine. • Geology must be suitable.
Septic tank	The septic tank is a more sophisticated version of the aqua-privy containing two chambers in the water tight pit. The system accepts both sewage and sullage water and allows the solids to settle. The liquids overflow into a soakaway or drain field. The sewage connection from the building must be a flush cistern type.	• Good treatment of effluent. • Infrequent maintenance once every 2–5 years depending on volume per person.	• High cost requires piped water supply to provide sufficient water. Requires large areas of land to disperse liquids. • Requires a permeable soil for good disposal of liquids.
WC waterborne sewerage 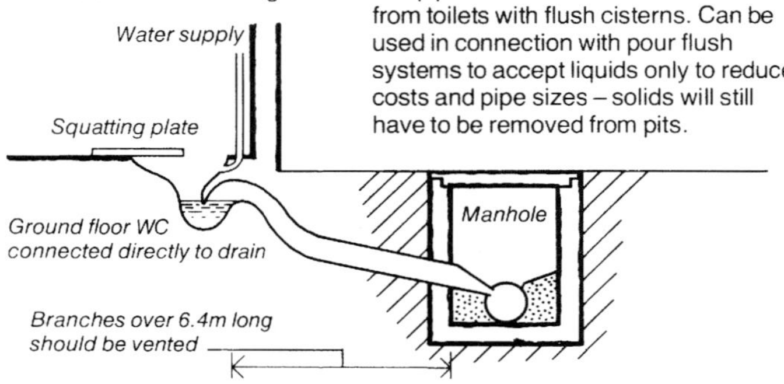	Full piped network with connections from toilets with flush cisterns. Can be used in connection with pour flush systems to accept liquids only to reduce costs and pipe sizes – solids will still have to be removed from pits.	• High user convenience • No sewage in vicinity of dwellings.	• High cost. • Requires piped water supply and high usage. • Requires sophisticated treatment plant to cope with efluent in large volumes.

Stage 3   57

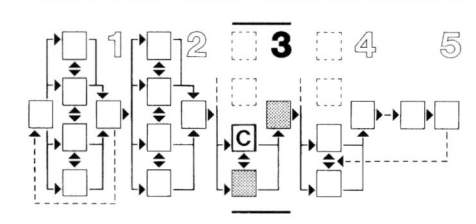

Table 12
Surface water drainage options

Type of provision	Characteristics	Advantages	Disadvantages
Any of the following options can be used in combination			
Transporting options			
No provision	Water finds its own way along roads and paths.	● No capital cost to agency.	● Depends for adequacy on very low rainfall. ● Can be inconvenient especially during rainy periods. ● Dependent on site topography and geology.
Open channel	Open channels adjacent to paved areas carry water to outfall point.	● Disposes of water adequately. ● Moderate cost. ● Extent of network can be varied without great disturbance.	● Can restrict vehicular or pedestrian access across roads. ● Dependent upon topography for outfall point.
Disposal options			
Natural water-course	Water led into river and stream and allowed to run off site downstream.	● Low capital cost.	● Dependent on existence of stream and adequate topography.
Soakaways	Water allowed to filter into ground from either purpose made soakaways or soakage ponds in natural depressions.	● Moderate capital cost.	● Cost dependent on solution. ● Dependent upon geology and rainfall. ● Temporary flooding likely.
Storage	Water stored for re-use in natural basins or purpose made facilities. Can be used to prevent downstream flooding due to sudden water run-off.	● Water retained for local use. ● Low to moderate costs possible.	● Dependent upon geology, topography and climate.
Piped network	Piped mains used in conjunction with road gullies. Can be combined with foul sewerage system to reduce costs and assist with cleansing, though treatment works will need to be larger.	● Maximum layout flexibility. ● Maximum use of Rights of way for vehicles/pedestrians.	● High capital cost. ● Can silt up in arid climates.

Table 13
Electricity supply options

Type of provision	Characteristics	Advantages	Disadvantages
Not provided	No installation of mains electricity within project site. Residents make their own provision for heat, light, cooking and power. Communal facilities such as schools may use generators.	● No capital cost to agencies except for communal facilites.	● Inconvenience. ● No security lighting possible. ● Unreliability of alternatives. ● High maintenance costs for communal facilities equipment. ● High cost to occupants.

Stage 3

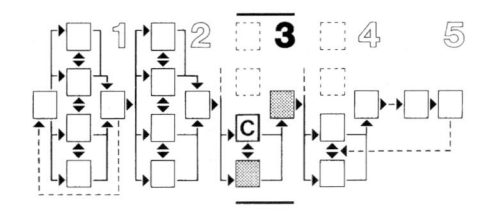

Table 13 continued

Type of provision	Characteristics	Advantages	Disadvantages
Street lighting only	Lighting for security of streets and footpaths.	● Provides convenience and security. ● Costs to project are relatively low.	● Can be illegally tapped.
Full connections	An intermediate form of provision is not necessary since additional capital costs are not high. Plot occupants can obtain connections when they can afford it.	● Convenient. ● Level of security lighting can be varied as funds permit. ● Low costs to households for electricity.	● Possible high cost depending on mains equipment required, though this may be borne at least in part by the electricity authority.

Table 14
Rubbish disposal options

Type of provision	Characteristics	Advantages	Disadvantages
Nil	Plot occupants responsible for disposal. Nature of rubbish dictates means of disposal: vegetable matter can be composted or fed to animals. Most natural products can be allowed to compost. Man-made products generally require disposal in tips or similar facilities.	● No capital cost to agency.	● Can create major health hazard. ● Clutters roadways and blocks drainage.
Communal disposal points	Large capacity containers located at convenient points adjacent to roads.	● Comparatively low maintenance and collection costs. ● Can help overcome health hazard problem.	● Some inconvenience to residents.
On-plot collection	Regular collection of refuse from each plot.	● Minimise health hazard. ● Convenient.	● Higher running costs than communal collection points. Low quality of rubbish means little potential for recycling – thus unlikely to operate commercially in low income areas.

Table 15
Telephone options

Type of provision	Characteristics	Advantages	Disadvantages
Not provided	No provision on project site.	● No capital cost to agency.	● Inconvenient especially in local or personal emergency.
Communal provision	Telephone installations in public facilities and possibly also in kiosks or local shops, etc. Restricted number of lines.	● Provides an emergency service without placing great demands upon telephone exchange capacity.	● Fairly high capital costs for small number of telephones. ● Subject to vandalism.
Plot connection available	Telephone cables sufficient for the majority of plots available in vicinity and also exchange with adequate capacity.	● Provides full access when people can afford it.	● High capital cost, especially if new exchange facilities are required. ● Unlikely to be many households who can afford connection.

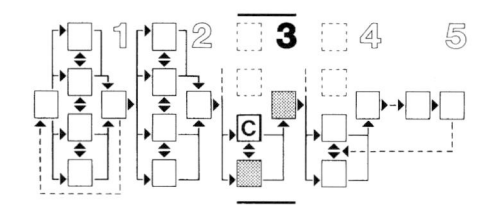

In developing each option, reference should be made to project objectives (both short and long term) and to the priorities of the target population as expressed in the household survey (see Task group 2A, page 18). The practicability of each option should be assessed in relation to the characteristics of the project site, especially its topography, ground conditions, climate (see Tasks 2B/5, page 24; 2B/6, page 24; and 2B/7, page 25) and the financial framework (see Tasks 2D/2, page 32; and 3D/3 page 64).

There are many variations to the options shown in the Tables. Some of these may be based upon local custom or adapted to suit local conditions. All can provide a basis for designing suitable options.

It is possible that several options will satisfy project objectives and the needs of the target population. Some of these are independent of each other, though water supply, sewage collection and disposal options are closely related, as Tables 10 and 11 indicate.

Water is required on each plot for several purposes including drinking, cooking, personal hygiene, laundry, cleaning, flushing of excreta and garden irrigation. *Sullage* includes all the waste water, other than that connected with sewage. It requires careful disposal.

The most appropriate means of disposal will depend on the climate and geology of the site as well as the quantity of water to be used. The various disposal options range from tipping in yards, in streets, to seepage pits, storm water drains or piped sewers.

The outcome of this Task should be one or more 'packages of options'. Every option should be compatible with the others in the package. They should satisfy the project objectives, the needs of the target population and be socially acceptable to them (see Task group 2A, page 18). Designs for each option must be developed to a degree of detail that enables preliminary cost estimates to be made.

Selection of options: networks

The first stage in selection of options is to produce designs for the utility networks which can be costed in sufficient detail to assess their economic acceptability for the project (see Task 3C/3, page 45). The designs must include consideration of the options discussed to see if they apply to the project site and to the various options for plot sizes, shape and layouts as developed in Task group 3C (page 36). The cost will be the main determinant of the system selected.

The most convenient unit for designing on-site utility networks is the neighbourhood. Trunk networks can then be designed on the basis of demand from each neighbourhood and aggregated to form the design for the whole site. Connections to off-site mains networks must be made at suitable locations. Assessment of factors such as the availability of spare capacity in the off-site networks will usually mean discussions with the appropriate agency.

The possibility of future upgrading of the utility networks should be considered during this Stage. Such planning will minimise later disruption to plot occupants and help to reduce costs, so increasing the possibility for future improvement. The various options or sets of options should be designed to different levels of provision from the minimum feasible level to the likely maximum level. Each set of options can then be costed and valued.

The design of the utility networks should take account of available materials, existing construction methods and local design standards. Alternatives should also be examined. For example, it may be possible to reduce costs by the selective use of more expensive materials.

The selection of preferred sets of options will depend primarily upon their costs relative to the project's budget. To minimise costs for future upgrading, it may be advisable to provide a higher level of provision for parts of the system than is initially required. This applies particularly to trunk utility networks, for which the additional material costs may be less than the cost of later replacement. The feasibility of this additional provision will depend upon the forecast date at which the increased provision will be required, the cost of increasing the capacity initially, the utility network involved and the likely cost and disruption in upgrading at a later date.

Where it is very unlikely that a waterborne sewage system can be afforded in the short term, it may still be useful to produce outline designs for a system so that site layouts can be designed for efficient drainage when and if resources are available.

Selection of options: on-plot sewage facilities

This is likely to be the cheapest option, and in many cases the only one. Social acceptability of the option is essential and this can be gauged by responses to the household surveys (see Task group 2A, page 18) and informal discussions.

The plot occupancy rate is one of the most important factors in designing on-plot provision and the information obtained during the detailed studies of the target population will provide an excellent basis for calculating future trends. The level of water consumption per person will have been assessed for each water supply option and the volume of sewage per person will be known from the Detailed studies. This basic information enables a reasonable estimate of the volumes of sewage and sullage per day to be assessed. The volume of all pit disposal systems is based upon the daily volumes to be processed, and serious consideration must be given to the expected life of the pit. The maintenance costs incurred by plot occupants for emptying should also be included in cost estimates.

Ground condition also influences the effectiveness of pit systems (see Task 2B/6, page 24). This will affect both the volume of provision necessary and the cost of construction.

All options for on-plot utilities should be designed to the degree which enables approximate costs to be estimated. The cost of each option per plot can then be obtained by combining the on-plot cost with the appropriate proportion of the on-site costs.

Stage 3

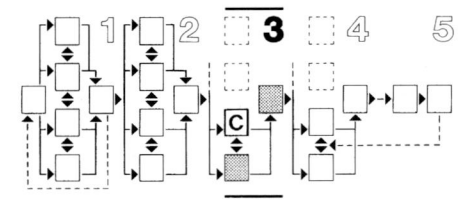

The selection of preferred options will inevitably be a compromise since the target population is unlikely to be able to afford full provisions to the standard generally envisaged by government agencies. The preferred options should, however, satisfy the main project objectives and the priorities of the target population as analysed in the Detailed studies (see Task 1, page 2; and Task group 2A, page 18).

In selecting preferred options for upgrading or new settlement projects, a series of levels of provision can be established which represent a long term upgrading process. Each of these levels will mean a total cost which may or may not be affordable by the target population. An example of levels of infrastructure provision related to affordability is given on pages 150 and 151.

There will also be other project costs to be borne by the target population. These include land, community facilities and house superstructure. Obtaining the correct balance between these is probably the most difficult part of the selection process. This choice must not compromise the provision of utilities to such an extent that the project objectives cannot be achieved.

Throughout the Manual, reference has been made to the ability of the target population to help themselves and the need to encourage this. The same point applies to on-plot utilities, though it may be necessary to provide advice and possibly supervision to ensure that design and construction are satisfactory.

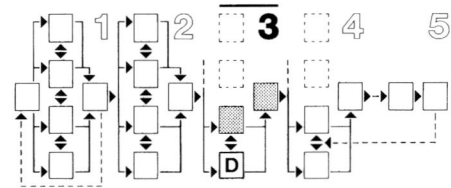

Task group 3D
Institutional and financial framework

3D/1	Selecting the institutional framework 61
3D/2	Land tenure 62
3D/3	Developing financial options 64

A variety of institutional arrangements present themselves as appropriate methods for preparing, developing and managing urban development projects. Judgements have to be made in each case of the competing merits of representative government, which is often not capable of incisive and decisive action, and an appointed body which is often very effective but may be less democratic.

Existing housing development institutions very frequently will be preoccupied with a standard and cost of house and associated infrastructure which is considerably beyond the means of the typical low income household. For such institutions, the main questions are the ease with which they could change the nature, and the image, of what they produce, and the adaptability of its workforce to a changed product. On the other hand, to create new institutions will often strain the supply of qualified technical and management staff, and could result in wasteful duplication.

Above all other considerations, whatever institutional form is considered, there must be an executive function, with adequate independence from other authorities. The powers should include the right to buy, sell and lease land and property; borrow funds; lend on mortgage and hire purchase; design, build, supervise all necessary building and associated operations; enter into contracts and sue, and be sued; engage on the payroll all necessary managerial, technical, operational and clerical staff and, finally, be fully accountable for its own trading operations in such a way that it can clearly be seen whether the overall financial objectives of the undertaking are being achieved.

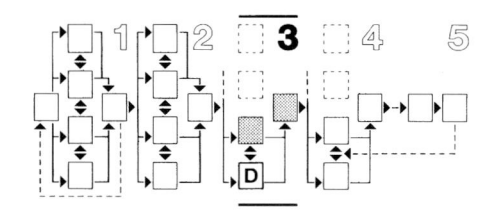

Task 3D/1
Selecting the institutional framework

An essential element in any successful administrative unit is the political backing necessary to ensure the co-operation of other agencies in the provision of utilities and other components of the project. Certain/y in the initial stages of such a programme, both high level and local political support is a prerequisite of success, to overcome prejudices, ensure an adequate supply of sites for development, and obtain the agreement of other national and local agencies concerned in the provision of key services.

Type of organisation

International experience has shown that the innovative nature of upgrading and serviced site projects often calls for the creation of a new administrative unit with specific responsibility for such a programme. Existing agencies, such as Housing Ministries or Departments, Public Works Departments and Public Housing Agencies, may not have the legal powers necessary to act as an effective development agency. In addition, they often hold fixed views based on a long term involvement in conventional housing programmes. As a result, they may find difficulty in developing more modest but appropriate solutions.

Any successful organisational solution must recognise the role that can be adopted by the target population group itself. Highly organised settler groups can help achieve a reduced involvement by the public authorities in housing, and thus reduce costs. They can also, in some circumstances, obtain political support. Beyond a basic minimum design and construction programme, settlers can be successfully encouraged to organise themselves in the provision of a level of housing and services best suited to their particular needs and resources.

Finally, *a major requirement of any organisational arrangement is that of flexibility and adaptability to change.* During the process of implementation, it may become apparent that changes of an administrative and organisational nature are called for, perhaps arising from the response of the settlers themselves, or from the growing competence of the administrative unit or agency created for the project.

The preferred option may consist of the establishment or development of an agency for project design and implementation which strikes a balance between independence of action and strong relations with local government. In this way fresh approaches can be developed with a clear understanding of local needs and conditions.

Naturally, the organisation and staffing required for an implementing agency can only be determined in relation to the scope of its activities and the size of the project. Bearing in mind the objective of producing solutions which the target population can afford, the aim must be to ensure that administrative costs are kept to the minimum if households are not to be penalised. An example of staffing proposals is given on pages 86 to 88.

This suggests that the activities of the implementing agency should be limited to the key elements of development and concentrate on providing those which people cannot provide for themselves. This should include land development, the provision of infrastructure, some public facilities and a simple system for the encouragement and control of house building.

Liaison

There are many advantages in the implementing agency having considerable autonomy, the main one being speed and effectiveness of action. The degree of autonomy will depend largely on the amount and source of funds. Where the major parts of the programme are funded externally formal liaison will be needed.

To ensure that there is sufficient time for each infrastructure provision agency to approve the level of services necessary and make adequate budget provision, early and effective liaison arrangements must be set up for each project. There are some advantages in having two formal liaison groups, one covering the provision of infrastructure and the other the provision of public facilities. This is not imperative, but it may facilitate the discussion of two very different types of components. The groups' terms of reference should be:
- Effective arrangements for the exchange of data, plans and programmes.
- Discussions and agreement on the level and standard of provision.
- Determination of the responsible agency for design and implementation of components as well as planning their detailed phasing.
- Agreement on costs, plus the level and timing of budget provision.
- Investigation and resolution of any difficulties arising in the scheduled development of each project.

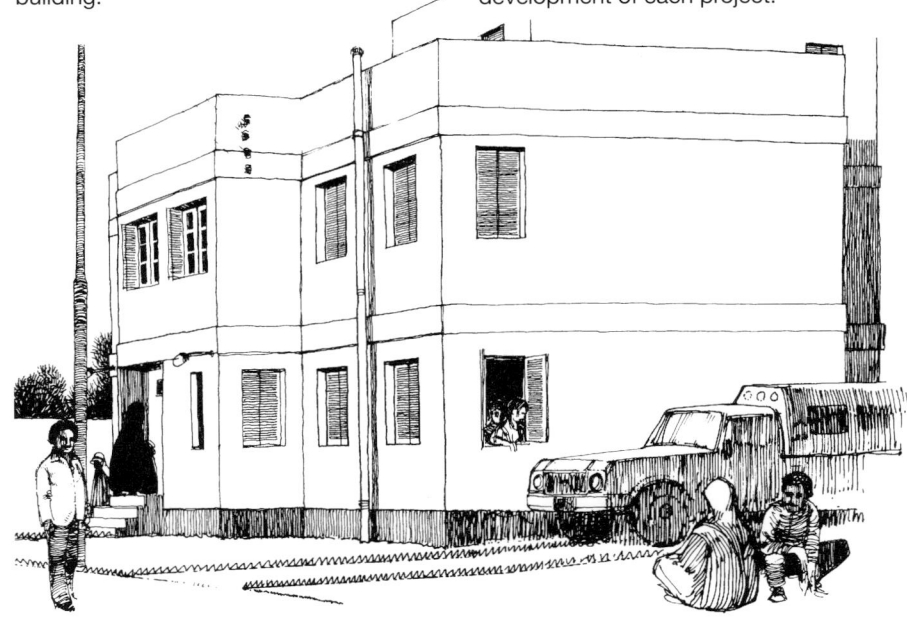

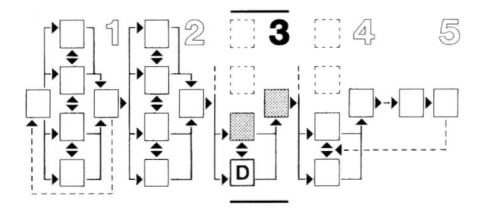

It is possible that initial discussions in the liaison groups will be conducted by the local representatives of national agencies. If so, the machinery should allow for them to consult with their headquarters where necessary. It may also be necessary for the national agency responsible for upgrading and new settlement projects (if one exists), to have formal communication with these national agencies when difficulties arise in the provision of components.

Efficient arrangements need to be made for the allocation of approved funds where these are provided through a central government budget agency. Forecasts of likely investment must be made by the project agency and advances made, perhaps on a quarterly basis, with adjustment if necessary.

It is clear that the various agencies will be unable to agree on every conceivable occasion the precise terms of allocating costs. Adequate arrangements therefore need to be made to settle differences, so that delays in the programme can be avoided. Activities such as allocation of land and use of funds should be transparent and fully accountable.

Key points

The selection of the preferred option for institutional framework of the project is one of the most important decisions to be made as it will have a critical effect on the effective implementation of the project. Key qualities are likely to include:
● Proposals must be developed in close relation to the political realities of the local situation.
● Proposals should be possible within the existing legal framework.
● Proposals must relate to local staff resources.
● The implementing agency should have control of funds which can be recycled and which enable it to carry out a basic development programme.

Capacity of existing institutions will often need to be developed and this should be integrated in development plans. For a discussion of this refer to Technical note 20, p. 136.

An example of proposals for the setting up of an implementing agency is given in Stage 5.

Task 3D/2
Land tenure

Land tenure refers to the kind of *rights* and *title* in which land is held. There are many forms of land tenure ranging from individual to communal and public, and variations may also exist between the nature of rights and title. In areas where sites are developing rapidly, changes in land tenure may occur faster than land registers are able to record and considerable confusion of exact forms of tenure in a given area may result.

Some of the most common options are presented in Table 16, together with notes on their characteristics.

Table 16
Land tenure characteristics

Tenure category	Characteristics
Private freehold	● The individual ownership of land in perpetuity. This is the most secure form of tenure and therefore the one most likely to encourage households to invest. Full market forces may, however, encourage displacement of low income residents. It normally provides limited possibility of control by the implementing agency.
Leasehold	● The individual or collective occupation of land for a specified time. This provides security of tenure but for a limited period and may therefore discourage investment, especially if the lease is short. It may also be difficult to administer in areas where it is not familiar. ● It retains long term control of development in the hands of the owners providing more opportunity for control. ● It excludes land from the operation of the 'free' market or at least mitigates its effects. Increase in land value returns to the freehold owner. ● Leasehold from a public source may provide greater security and therefore incentive to invest than from a private source.
Co-operative	● A form of collective ownership in which both title and rights are vested in the co-operative. Individuals possess rights to a share of the land subject to specified terms and conditions. No rights of transfer normally exist other than through the co-operative. ● It is a secure and inexpensive way for groups of people to obtain access to land and to encourage investment on it. ● It enables groups to increase their control over the development of the land and to reduce government responsibility and costs. ● It requires a stable income for all members to prevent defaults. ● It requires a disciplined code of mutual support and management which may take time to develop.
Customary (traditional)	● This can take several forms. It is particularly common in areas where land is considered to be a group rather than an individual asset. ● It enables members of a group to obtain secure access to land irrespective of their income, though on condition that they fulfil specified obligations . ● It restricts speculative pressure on land. ● It depends upon a strong social bond between all members of the group which is not commonly found in rapidly developing urban areas.
Religious (e.g. Islamic)	● Characteristics to include waqf (land held for God). ● Mülk land (similar to freehold). ● Miri land (held by the state). ● Tassruf (usufruct).

Selecting the form of land tenure: general

In selecting preferred options, an important consideration is that a basic role of the project will be land development and this will be the prime economic function of the project agency. The existing urban land market cannot be ignored in this process, nor can the dynamics of urban expansion and the inevitable rise in land values. It follows, therefore, that land tenure within the project must be considered within the larger urban land context. The selection of tenure options applies to both plots for housing and for commercial/industrial uses. These need to be discussed separately.

For more details of the policy issues and options regarding urban land tenure and property rights, see Technical note 21.

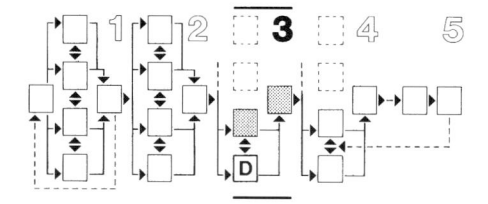

Selecting the form of land tenure for residential plots

The final selection of tenure form will depend on local circumstances, and it is not appropriate to promote one particular form. Both freehold and long lease have similar advantages in terms of security of tenure. Freehold, however, although the most secure form, is also most open to speculation, especially where the initial price is subsidised. The result of speculation could be that the eventual beneficiaries would come from the middle or upper income range, though they would probably be able to afford forms of shelter not available to the target population. Although freehold ownership may have major attractions, there are many advantages to be gained in offering the initial tenure on a leasehold basis with, say, an option to purchase after a period of continuous occupancy during which compliance with leasehold rules and regulations has been observed.

In cases where leasehold or *delayed freehold* is selected, it is necessary, and an obvious advantage, to introduce some form of regulation relating tenure to the development of the plot. Regulations normally would expect to cover two separate areas, those of controlling the quality and density of plot development and of avoiding speculation or exploitation.

The regulations should prescribe conditions which must be fulfilled, in the case of *delayed freehold*, before the right of a freehold option can be exercised. For example, it may be appropriate to require that the building on the plot is of a certain standard in terms of construction materials and layout and does not constitute any nuisance or present a health hazard to the neighbourhood.

The right of option should be exercised only by the original beneficiary of the lease, unless any transfer of lease has prior approval of the project agency. Any lessee, prior to approval of the purchase option, should have paid all dues and demands under the lease and have a reasonable record of payment. All other conditions having been fulfilled, it is recommended that a reasonable period should elapse before such rights of purchase are accepted to allow adequate time for assessment of the lessee and to avoid speculation, but otherwise every encouragement should be given to the beneficiary to take up the option.

Should beneficiaries wish to sell their plots at some time in the future, it is important to introduce adequate safeguards to minimise speculation. One measure that may be considered is a period of grace, once ownership is established, before sales are permitted to third parties. Five to ten years may be considered appropriate; any desire to sell by the beneficiary within the chosen period could be satisfied by the project agency purchasing the plot at cost price plus an allowance for inflation, or the agency's approval being sought for sales to third parties at an agreed price. Local circumstances may suggest a number of other safeguards.

The agency responsible for the project may wish to consider that when the right of option to purchase is exercised, any beneficiary choosing to pay for the plot outright may do so, rather than continue on the basis of monthly mortgage payments. This would assist the project cash flow and should be encouraged, subject to the rigorous enforcement of the safeguards on possible re-sale to a third party, as previously suggested.

Enforcement of these regulations and conditions outlined above would greatly benefit from the participation of co-operative groups representative of the settlers, though all tenure types may benefit from this and some may depend on it. The collective approach is beneficial first in achieving the co-operation of settlers and then in the on-going management and regulation of the newly established community.

The co-operative* group could be concerned in plot development through the organisation of self-help building operations; regulation of on-plot structural standards and the management and maintenance of public facilities. It could also assist in the day-to-day management of the project including the collection and recovery of rentals and amortisation payments. The co-operative should also ensure that exploitation is kept to an absolute minimum. Special care is required when selecting tenure proposals for upgrading projects in informal settings to ensure that tenants and other vulnerable groups will not be adversely affected. The most appropriate approach will invariably be to offer improved property rights which will be sufficient to increase security and investment in housing improvements, but not so much that they result in increased costs or rents for low-income tenants.

Selecting the form of land tenure for commercial and industrial plots

The preferred option will inevitably vary according to local circumstances. However, the pressure for early recovery of capital investment, which may well be critical to the success of the project, suggests that the argument for freehold disposal may be sufficiently compelling for it to be selected for general application, where this is possible.

Where this option is agreed, the freehold price for land must be arranged to give a reasonable impetus to the project. Prices must be reviewed from time to time and be competitive, since they will probably rise during the period of project implementation. Auction of land, or pricing based on market levels is a useful approach. Sale at less than market levels can be used when necessary, but should be recognised as a deliberate and open subsidy. If leasehold of sites is chosen, the terms of the lease should allow maximum flexibility for future development, should certainly include provision for periodic rental reviews and may also include an option-to-purchase after a period of years. A positive marketing policy is necessary to maximise the potential of this element of the project.

Enforcement of regulations once a title document is issued can be very difficult. One option, used with success in Hyderabad, Pakistan*, was to offer titles only after settlers had lived on the site for a minimum period.

---

* Co-operative could mean local political or social units The effectiveness of this approach depends largely on local social organisation as revealed by the social studies (see Technical note 1, page 100)

* United Nations Centre for Human Settlements (Habit, (1990)) *The incremental Development Scheme: A Case Study of Khuda -Ki-Basti in Hyderabad, Pakistan UNCHS (Habitat), Training Materials Series* United Nations Centre for Human Settlements (Habitat) Nairobi, Kenya.

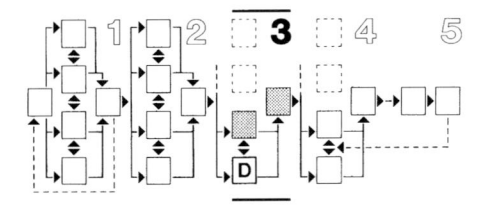

Task 3D/3
Developing financial options

Politically, the simplest approach to the financing of low income housing and urban infrastructure is to assume that public goods such as housing should, in any humane state, be redistributed towards the poor, and that subsidies should make up the gap between what the poor can afford and what 'ought' to be provided for them by way of standards of accommodation and infrastructure. This approach has been found to be very much less than adequate, however. Almost by definition, the large numbers of poor people in developing countries who require accommodation and access to services rule out the automatic assumption that subsidies can be paid on anything but a wholly insignificant scale. The alternative, and preferred, approach is to assume *initially* that the population for whom the accommodation and services are targeted cannot expect any subsidies, and that whatever is to be provided should be financed entirely from the resources at their command, however meagre. This is the only intellectually honest approach to the problem of tackling the issue of poverty in the round: to identify where the starting point is in terms of what could be afforded by the people themselves. In the poorest societies, and in the poorest sections of society, the conclusion may be that very little can be afforded from their own resources, and the costs of setting up an organisation to administer such assistance for these ultra-poor would vastly outweigh the value of the material goods and services that could be provided.

Within the low income group, however, there is a range of incomes, and it is possible by charging proportionately more to those with higher incomes within the group, to effect what is known as 'internal cross-subsidy'. This can be considerably more effective if the project caters also for people of higher income groups, provided that this type of provision is kept in proportion. The starting point, however, should be to find out what the poor can afford themselves (see Task 2A/1, page 19).

It should not be assumed that the poor will always remain poor or that a household's income relative to others will always remain the same. Economic development proposals for these income groups can help to generate real increases in income and wealth, and if these programmes strike at the root of the economic problem, can be of greater economic and social importance in themselves than those programmes restricted to the provision of housing and infrastructure. To help people obtain the means of earning income and of saving to afford decent housing and infrastructure is clearly more desirable than merely disbursing public goods without being concerned about how they may be afforded.

Therefore only when a realistic assessment has been made of what the poor themselves can afford and pay for, can it be right to look at the question of subsidy from external sources, and then only against a realistic assessment of the extent to which the subsidies can be expected to continue to flow and in what quantities. One objective of programmes of this nature is to ensure, as far as possible, that others like them on an increasing scale can be set in motion it is a radical, as opposed to a cosmetic, alleviation of urban poverty.

Broadly there are four main items of cost that have to be provided for: land; infrastructure including economic development programmes; the dwelling itself and the financing cost (i.e. the rate of interest and the loan repayment period). Land poses the most difficult question. It is, strictly, a non-renewable resource, and its price (often quite different from its true value) is usually determined by short-term conditions of scarcity, location, an imperfect market mechanism, and a whole set of institutional factors. The latter expressing to some degree the state's view of the concept of private interests in land and hence its true value. The answers to the questions: 'what is the true cost of land?' and 'should this cost be charged?' are nearly always complex and obscure, and the most important practical problem in identifying the financial structure of these programmes is to ensure that the poor are not charged or required to pay inflated prices for land which will be acquired on their behalf.

The starting point for financing infrastructure and superstructure costs, and the project funding as a whole is that all costs should be recoverable and that the standard and quantity of provision should be treated as a variable. It may be a convention in a particular country or state that the community at large pays for particular elements of urban infrastructure or offers subsidised interest rates and, while the general principle should be that low income group housing projects should be self-financing, clearly it is in the wider context inequitable and politically unacceptable for the poor to have to pay for something which wealthier groups in society do not.

In cases where water supply, for example, is generally very heavily subsidised to all sectors of the community, but the level of subsidy could not possibly be sustained to pay for the new, rapidly expanding low income group programme, a review may well be necessary, leading to possible changes in policy.

For a project, however, it will be necessary to develop options within the existing legal and financial framework. This is because it is not possible to depend on changes, particularly of national policy.

Selecting the financial framework: general

The purpose of this section is to establish a framework within which the preferred options for the project can be selected.

Financial options can be considered adequately only within the institutional framework for design and implementation. In considering the institutional options, emphasis has been placed on the advantage of achieving a political commitment at both national and local levels. This is equally important for the successful financing and recovery of the investment in urban development related to low income groups. At the national level, it is important in ensuring that all agencies which have a role to play, play their part using their usual powers and the provision of financial resources. At the local level it is important in order to obtain support from local agencies in the search for adequate areas for upgrading and new

Stage 3

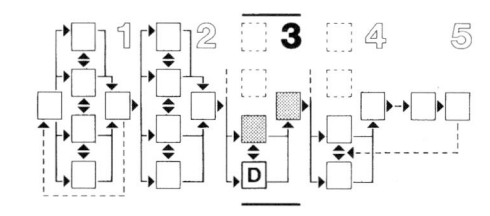

settlement, and in the encouragement of settlers, particularly in seeking their co-operation to contribute towards the costs of development not recoverable from other sources.

The sources of finance for each project are likely to consist of:
- Receipts from settlers from the sale of land or lease-rentals.
- Locally generated resources channelled through a government or community institution.
- Government appropriations (or capitalisation if a 'semi-public' corporation is created).
- Loans from central government.
- Bilateral and multi-lateral agency funds, lent normally by central government, but possibly available direct, usually to finance the foreign exchange costs of each project.
- Reimbursement of project component costs from central government agencies and others where development is initially funded by the project agency.

The detailed financial appraisal of the project involves a number of operations and their organisation. This is illustrated in Figure 37.

The appraisal of financial options will take place within the context of the Feasibility studies discussed in Stage 1. These will have determined that the target population can broadly afford to meet likely project costs. Once feasibility has been established, it will be possible to determine the contributions from government and likely allocations to national and local agencies with specific responsibility for project components. The remaining operations can then be carried out as described below.

Selection of preferred option for costs and their allocation

Costs to be included in each project will consist of:

- *The cost of land acquisitions* (see Task 2D/2, page 32). Where land is already in public ownership, it should be transferred to the project at a cost which reasonably reflects market conditions in that particular locality. Costs will include legal and survey fees and associated administrative expenses. It is possible that this land charge may eventually be waived, but it should be included at this stage of the calculations.
- *The cost of infrastructure* including:
Off-site costs (where these are charged to the project).
Site reticulation costs (i.e. the cost of main utility networks within the site).
Land reclamation.
Costs of removing houses and relocating families* in upgrading areas.
Costs of communal toilets (if any).

* Davidson, Forbes, Zaaijer, Mirjam Peltenburg, Monique Rodell. Mike (1993) *Manual for urben relocation and resettlement* Institute for Housing and Urban Development Studies Rotterdam.

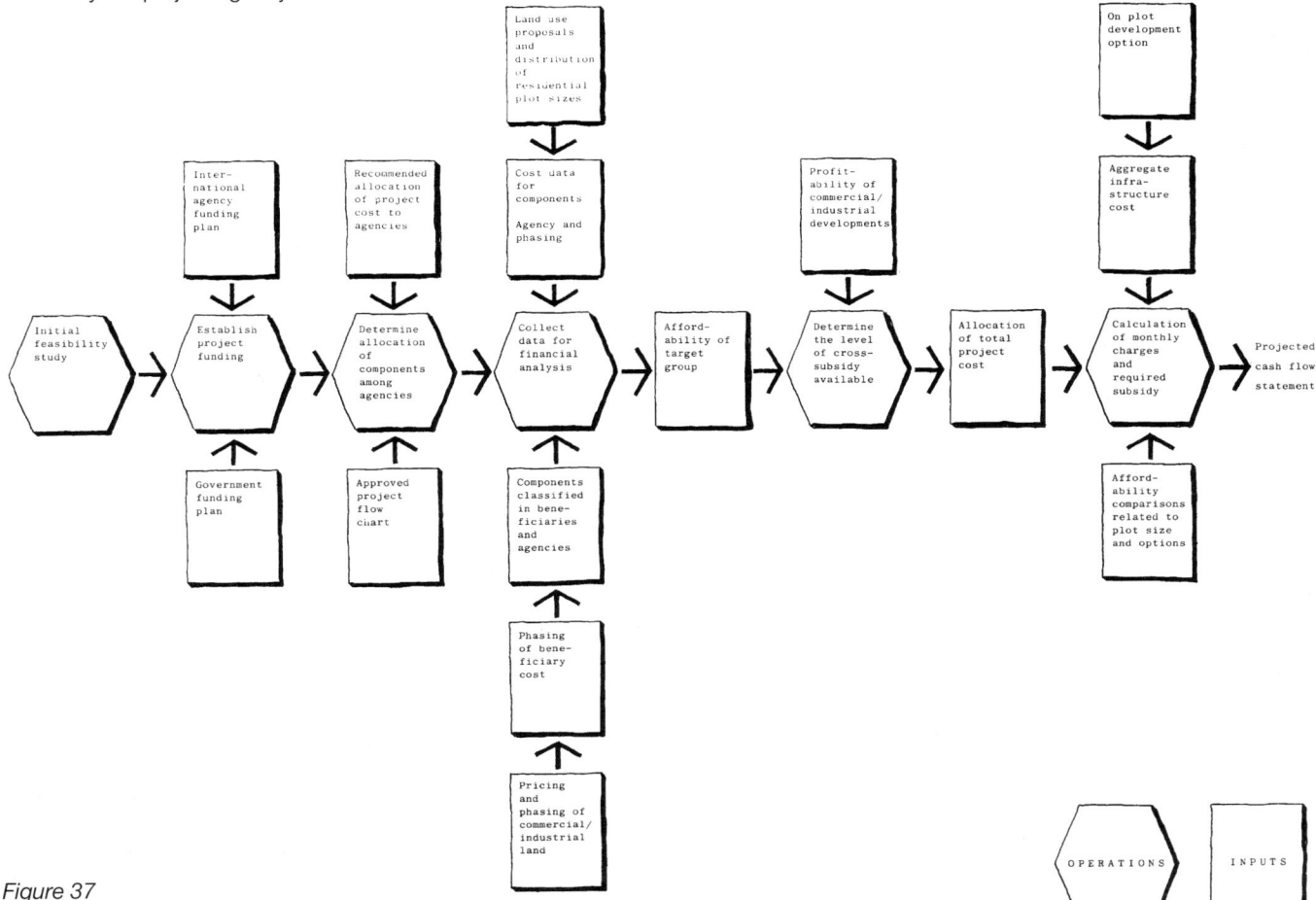

Figure 37
Project financial analysis: operational flow chart

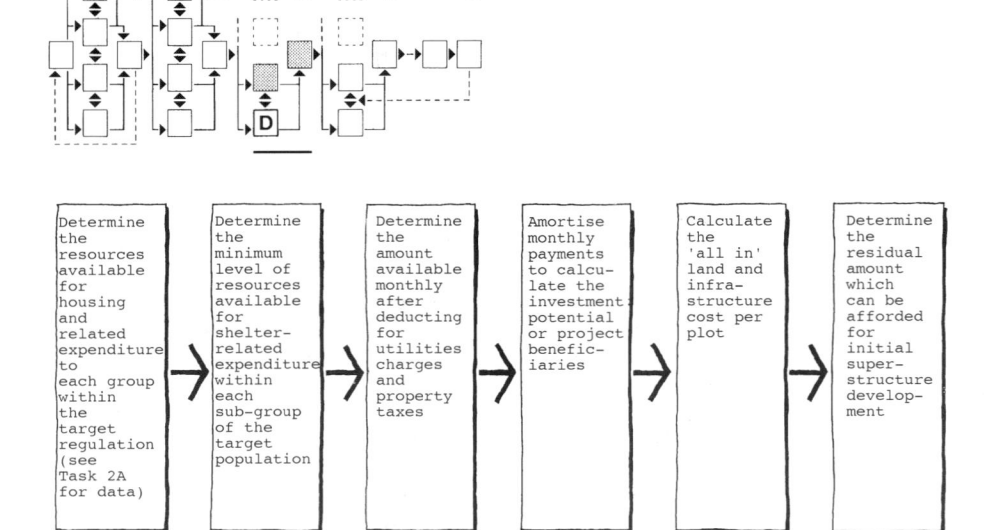

Stage 3

Figure 38
Calculating ability to pay for project costs

[Flow chart boxes:]
- Determine the resources available for housing and related expenditure to each group within the target regulation (see Task 2A for data)
- Determine the minimum level of resources available for shelter-related expenditure within each sub-group of the target population
- Determine the amount available monthly after deducting for utilities charges and property taxes
- Amortise monthly payments to calculate the investment potential or project beneficiaries
- Calculate the 'all in' land and infrastructure cost per plot
- Determine the residual amount which can be afforded for initial super-structure development

Determining the ability to pay for project costs

The Feasibility studies (see Task 1 E, page 14) will have determined that the target population broadly is able to pay the likely project costs. It is now necessary to use data obtained during the Detailed project studies (see Tasks 2A/1, page 19; and 2D/2, page 32) to calculate this more accurately. Where necessary, this information should be updated so that any movement in resource levels can be identified.

The first step is to determine the income distribution of the target population and the monthly payments households can afford, relative to the benefits to be received. Generally one would expect the lowest income levels to pay a lower percentage of their income than those with higher incomes, since much of their income will be needed to pay for necessities such as food.

Essentially, the key elements in total costs to be recovered from project beneficiaries are land, infrastructure, superstructures (if any), administration and financial costs. The cost of the land is probably predetermined and will vary in cost from very little in the more rural locations to very expensive in majorities.

Experience suggests that between 15 and 25 per cent represents the likely range of household income that can be made available for housing. After deducting for property taxation and utility charges, the capital equivalent of the resulting monthly repayment represents the amount which can be afforded for plots and super-structures. From this amount the costs of land and infrastructure for each plot can be deducted. This leaves a residual amount which represents the sum which can be afforded for initial superstructure (building). Where data on household incomes are either unavailable or unreliable, estimates of affordability for housing can usefully be made by collecting data on existing expenditure on housing and estimating any increase which households would be willing to pay for the housing of their choice.

● *On-plot development costs* including:
Service connections.
Sewage disposal.
Pit latrines.
Any specified superstructure (buildings).
● The cost of planning, design and supervision of contracts, including surveys and the cost of producing reports and plans.
● Operational costs, including interest during project implementation; financing charges; the cost of collecting revenues from beneficiaries and other project resources.
● Adequate provision against default in payment by project beneficiaries and for depreciation of assets required for project execution.
● The cost of providing schools, health centres and other social and cultural facilities, where these are charged to the project.

Certain principles should be adopted in seeking to allocate project costs. Where central government and local agencies, in the exercise of their normal functions, would expect to provide some of the project components, costs should be recovered from the agency responsible providing it is within the capacity of the project agency to do so. In some instances, it may be appropriate for the responsible agency to provide such components independently of the initial funding and ultimate recovery.

It is important to ensure that adequate and punctual financing arrangements are made by the various agencies responsible for project components. Formal liaison machinery (see Task 3D/1, page 61) between all parties concerned is of considerable advantage in ensuring a smooth programme.

In the first instance, a schedule of project component costs, identifying the agencies responsible for financing, design and implementation should be prepared as a basis for discussions and agreement with all agencies concerned with the project. This might be prepared as in Table 17.

Table 17
Allocation of costs

Project components*	Agency responsible for:		
	Financing	Design	Implementation
Land acquisition			
Land reclamation or fill			
Flood protection			
Roads			
Drainage			
Water supply			
Sanitation			
Sewerage			
Street lighting			
Public facilities			

* These headings can be expanded or modified as necessary.

There will be a considerable advantage to the implementing agency, in terms of its ability to develop a project quickly, if the basic land development can be financed from its own resources – even if this is only a 'fall-back' position.

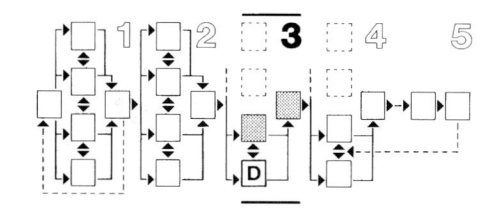

The allocation of costs between these two elements should be determined on the basis of the minimum amount of shelter possible, in order to maximise the area of land and standard of infrastructure provided. This is because additions can be made much more easily to buildings than to the area of land or the services provided to the plot.

The operations outlined in Figure 38 are necessary to arrive at likely levels of investment for infrastructure and superstructure. In carrying out these operations it will be necessary, at least initially, to make assumptions regarding:
● The proportion of net household income available for housing and related services. In the absence of accurate information, it is generally reasonable to assume 20 per cent.
● Land costs. If no accurate information exists, assume that these represent 5 per cent of net household monthly income in terms of monthly charges.
● The allocation of remaining monthly charges for superstructure and household shares of infrastructure (i.e. roads plus on-site and on-plot utilities).

It is important not to confuse the theoretical 'ability to pay' levels with compulsory payments.

Determining factors affecting project costs.

Among the most important factors are:
● *The rate of interest*. The rate charged to beneficiaries for the amortisation of capital costs will reflect the average rate of funds raised by the project agency. It is possible that loans raised will be a mixture of multilateral agency loans (e.g. The World Bank/IBRD), bilateral loans (e.g. Department for International Development, UK) and loans by central government, finance raised by floating bonds, or loans from the private sector. These will vary in accordance with market conditions prevailing at the time of the loan negotiations. However, the average rate is usually lower than commercial rates charged for loans for housing development purposes. *Given a fixed amount of monthly income available for housing purposes, the rate of interest charged has a strong influence on the level of investment which can be afforded*; the lower the rate, the herewith level of investment possible.
● *Amortisation periods*. This involves the period over which a loan is recovered and it also influences the level of investment that can be afforded. Clearly, if a loan to a beneficiary is to be repaid by him over a period of five years, the resultant monthly charge would be far in excess of that if the loan was spread over twenty-five years. See Table 18 for an example. In selecting the amortisation period applicable to the project periods of 15–25 years can be considered normal and these reflect the periods over which the project agency raises its own funds. World Bank housing loans, for example, are currently spread over twenty years, with a short grace period before repayments are due to begin.
● *Subsidies available to the target population*. Following the principles already specified for allocating the costs of components to those agencies who traditionally have responsibility for their provision, an indirect subsidy may have already been provided to the project. It is important to recognise, however, that these agencies must themselves be funded either from government sources (probably through taxation levies), or through user charges (e.g. water and electricity consumption). In other words, somebody must pay eventually for the services provided. Moreover, uncontrolled subsidies usually result in the eventual breakdown of housing programmes and so must be avoided. However, there are usually further possibilities available for relieving households of the total impact of the investment cost. For example, cross-subsidy is possible through the introduction of revenue generating land uses alongside the housing development. This also has the advantage of creating employment opportunities and increasing the proportion of income spent within the project site, thus actually increasing the amounts which the target population can afford for housing.

Table 18
Comparison of loan repayment rates

Principal sum: 100 000	Year	5 years 8%	12%	15 years 8%	12%	25 years 8%	12%
Years: 5, 15 & 25	1	25 046	27 741	11 683	14 682	9 368	12 750
	2	25 046	27 741	11 683	14 682	9 368	12 750
	3	25 046	27 741	11 683	14 682	9 368	12 750
	4	25 046	27 741	11 683	14 682	9 368	12 750
Interest: 8% & 12%	5	25 046	27 741	11 683	14 682	9 368	12 750
	6			11 683	14 682	9 368	12 750
	7			11 683	14 682	9 368	12 750
	8			11 683	14 682	9 368	12 750
	9			11 683	14 682	9 368	12 750
	10			11 683	14 682	9 368	12 750
	11			11 683	14 682	9 368	12 750
	12			11 683	14 682	9 368	12 750
	13			11 683	14 682	9 368	12 750
	14			11 683	14 682	9 368	12 750
	15			11 683	14 682	9 368	12 750
	16					9 368	12 750
	17					9 368	12 750
	18					9 368	12 750
	19					9 368	12 750
	20					9 368	12 750
	21					9 368	12 750
	22					9 368	12 750
Note:	23					9 368	12 750
Principal and	24					9 368	12 750
interest combined:	25					9 368	12 750
yearly rates	Total	125 230	138 075	175 245	220 230	234 200	318 750

Stage 3

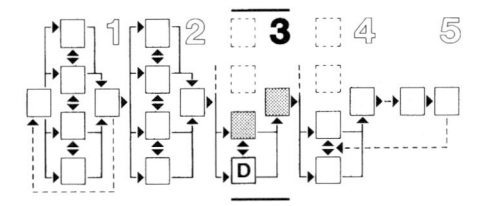

The amount of commercial and industrial development must be determined, however, by the market demand in terms of overall allocation of land for this purpose, and its forecast rate of being developed. One of the problems associated with this kind of development is that some projects have the potential for its inclusion and others do not. The cross-subsidy available on one site may have to be spread over a number of sites to be equitable, otherwise it will benefit only a relatively small number of people.

Having ascertained what the market will bear, then the likely surplus from this form of development can be calculated with reference to the estimated development cost and the income realised through plot sales and leases.

In addition, it is preferable to have price differentiation between plots to reduce plot prices charged to the lowest income households (see Technical note 10, page 119). Internal cross-subsidies of this nature are possible where there exists a fairly wide income distribution among the settlers, the better off subsidising those who can afford the cost of minimum standards only with difficulty.

Determining means of cost recovery

It is now necessary to divide total project costs between components and beneficiaries, including those costs to be borne by other agencies. Figure 39 shows how this analysis can be conducted.

It is important to note that adequate provision should be made in this cost schedule for design and supervision of the contract, usually around 10 per cent and also a physical contingency and a price contingency based on the current movement in prices and materials, should be added for each year of project implementation. Finally, to ensure that all costs are fully recovered, 'financing charges' should be added to cover interest accruing during the implementation period.

The analysis can now concentrate on what households will have to pay. In allocating costs to each plot it is usual, initially, to calculate basic land and infrastructure costs on a square metre basis. Particular plot development costs are normally allocated individually. Plot development options may therefore need separate tabulating. Figure 40 shows the process of distributing plot development costs, in terms of size and number and the various options calculated for each plot. When choosing the plot development options (which are to be added to general land and infrastructure cost allocations) the overall investment range previously estimated (page 66) must be observed. General infrastructure costs per square metre can then be aggregated with the preferred distribution of plot development options (see Tasks 3C/7 and 3C/8, pages 50 and 52), to arrive at total allocated costs per plot.

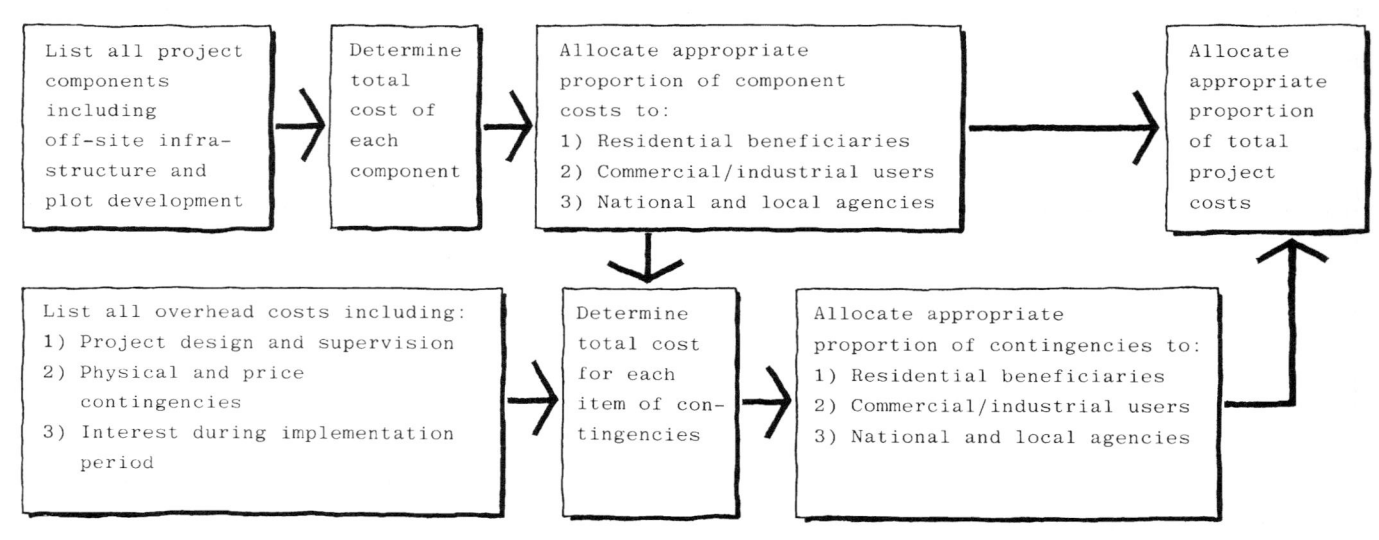

Figure 39 (*above*)
Allocating total project costs

Figure 40 (*below*)
Allocating costs to plots

Stage 3

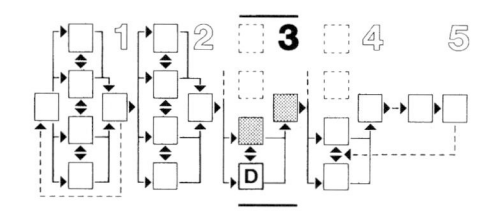

It is likely that particular income groups will select particular plot sizes in a new settlement project, but this cannot be assumed when dealing with an upgrading project. It is thus necessary to examine the implications of cost allocations per plot for upgrading areas. It will then be possible to conclude whether or not the majority of beneficiaries will be able to meet monthly charges without difficulty. The process is outlined in Figure 41.

It is important to remember that the assumptions used in these calculations should not become conditions on implementation. *Development costs which will result in compulsory monthly payments should be kept well within the theoretical amount affordable.*

If a reasonable interpretation of the results of these calculations suggests that monthly total housing costs to households will fall within the acceptable range (say 10–25 per cent), then it can be broadly assumed that the options proposed in Task group 3C (page 36) are feasible.

Should the amounts required be greater than the acceptable range, then further analysis will be called for. If initially preferred options are beyond the means of households to pay for them, then adjustments should be made and the revised options subjected to the same analysis.

Selection of appropriate internal subsidies

An exception to the principle of matching project options with the ability of households to pay for them would be if difficult site conditions resulted in costs being abnormally high for the standard of infrastructure provision necessary. If this is the case, it is appropriate to calculate the subsidy which would be required to bring the costs within the means of the beneficiaries. Basically, there are two options, as follows:

Residential cross-subsidies

The results of the analysis of incomes may indicate that particular groups can afford more than is being provided. This suggests the possibility of internal cross-subsidies, the more favoured groups assisting those where the impact on earnings is much greater.

This 'levelling-up' process for those households able to afford more should not, however, be undertaken without care. Inequitable comparisons between benefits provided and charges being made must be avoided.

The process advocated emphasises the need, from the very start, to determine the broad level of investment which all households in the target population can afford. Failure to do so could lead to a delay in the design of the project as changes are found to be required, but even worse could result in a project that either requires extensive unplanned subsidies or leads to a high level of default in repayments.

The subsidy required if, say, 15 per cent of earnings is the maximum amount payable for infrastructure and plot development, can be calculated (Figure 42).

Determine the initially allocated costs for each plot development option and plot size option → Select the rate of interest and the amortisation period applicable to the project → Calculate the total monthly repayments required for each plot size and plot development option for the interest rate and amortisation period selected

List the total net monthly income for each percentile group → Determine the proportion of total household income allocated for housing and related services → Relate the cost of each plot size and development option to the net monthly household income to determine if costs are within the acceptable range. If they are above, households may not be able to afford the option involved

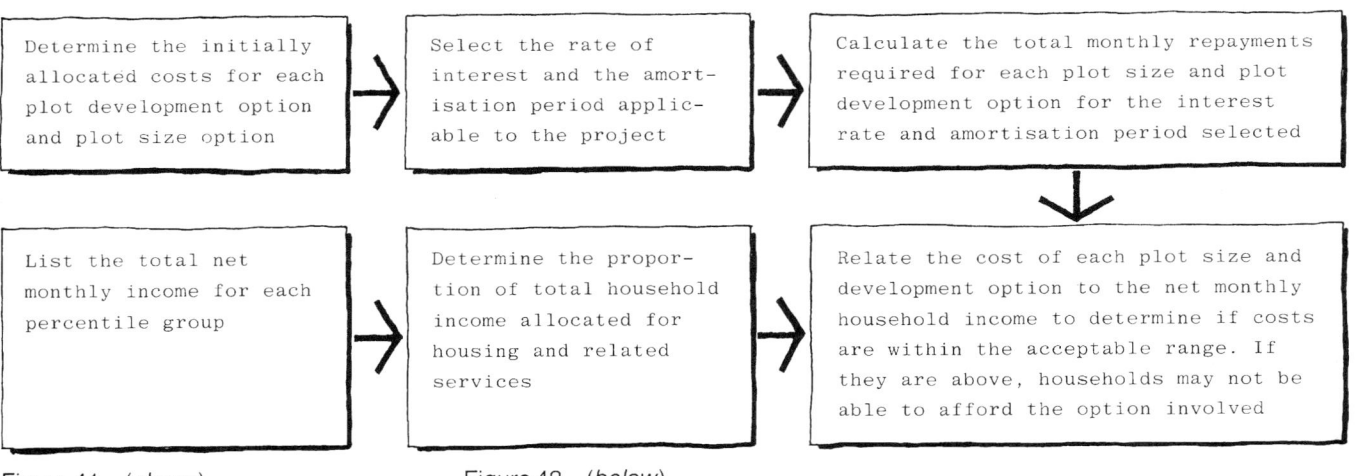

Figure 41 (*above*)
Calculating ability to pay monthly charges

Figure 42 (*below*)
Determining subsidy levels

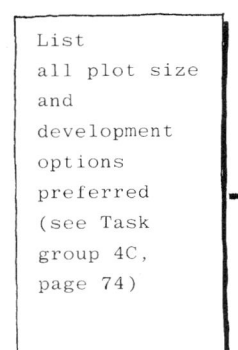

List all plot size and development options preferred (see Task group 4C, page 74) → Relate each option to the pertinent income level and percentile group → Determine the proportion of total monthly household income available to meet the cost of each option and its capital equivalent → Determine the capital cost of each plot size and development option and relate to the equivalent which can be afforded to obtain the capital difference → Determine the capital subsidy required to reduce the allocated cost to a level which represents the equivalent to the acceptable level (say 15% of total income)

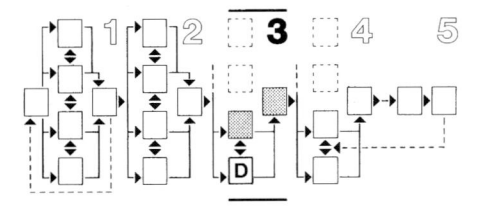

The provision of a percentage, say 10 per cent, of all plots to be sold at a full market price is a good means of:
- Obtaining increased income for use in cross-subsidisation.
- Introducing a wider mix of income groups.
- Possibly introducing a source of rented flats or houses.
- Helping to relieve any pressure for land from middle and upper income groups who might otherwise buy their way into the project, and displace low income groups.

Cross-subsidies from commercial/industrial developments

The financial appraisal has so far determined the level of subsidy likely to be required by various beneficiary households after taking into account relevant standards of infrastructure and land acquisition costs.

The Feasibility studies (see Task 1 C/3, page 10), Detailed project studies (see Task 2C/5, page 30) and previous sections of this financial analysis should have ensured that the aggregate of all subsidy requirements can be met by surpluses created by the presence of commercial or industrial development in the project, or from surpluses on better quality residential plots.

Determining external subsidies

All evidence from housing programmes in developing countries tends to suggest that placing too much reliance on external forms of subsidy will lead to a failure of the programme. It follows, therefore, that upgrading and new settlement projects should be developed, as far as possible, within a self-financing framework.

There is evidence, however, to suggest that *the costs of land acquisition in and around major cities may seriously inhibit viable new settlement projects, based upon the approach so far outlined in this Manual*. Where a national programme exists, it will become clear how large a problem the price of land is. It will be for central government to monitor progress, but the possibility may have to be faced of earmarking some form of assistance to ensure the programme's continuity. This *assistance is probably most effective as a 'one-off' payment*, e.g. to offset excessive land costs, or to help supply the initial infrastructure. This is especially important where site conditions, regulations or particular pressure make it necessary, v to construct a water-borne sewerage system, which is a very expensive item.

Calculating cash flow

In preparing the cash flow, it is suggested that the order of items to be classified should be:
- *Sources*:
Government capitalisation or loans.
Loans from bilateral or multi-lateral agencies.
Central or local government agency contributions.
Income from residents or settlers, less allowance for default.
Income from other revenue producing developments, such as commercial or industrial uses, less allowance for uncollected repayments.
- *Uses/Application*:
Land acquisition.
Development costs:
   Land draining/filling/grading
   All attributable off- and on-site utilities
   On-plot developments
   Building materials loans
   Attributable public facilities provision.
Design and supervision costs.
Administration and overhead costs.
Loan repayments (government and other agencies) including principal and interest.
Working capital.
Net cash inflow/outflow.
Cumulative cash balance/deficit.
Discounted net present value.

The process of establishing cash flow is outlined in Figure 43. Stage 5 provides the example of the cash flow of the El Hekr Project, Ismailia (page 94).

Notes on elements of cash flow statements

- *Sources of funds*: The basis for recovery of costs for the project, either by central government agency or other public sector contributions, should enable the *government's capital investment* in the project to be treated as a loan to the project and therefore recoverable over time. Nominally the basis that can reasonably be assumed is for recovery of such loans to be spread over 25 years at, say, 12 per cent rate of interest. In practice, however, it may be possible to recover Government funds invested in the project at an accelerated rate, especially where profitable elements such as commercial/industrial developments are part of the plan and freehold is chosen as the basis for land disposal.

- *Loans from bilateral and multi-lateral agencies* intended to fund foreign exchange costs of approved projects may be planned to run the full term, e.g. 20 years with a grace period of 5 years.

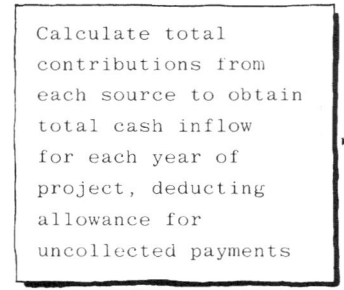

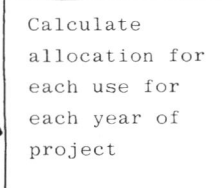

```
Calculate total         Calculate            Deduct total for      Assess any
contributions from      allocation for       uses each year        cumulative
each source to obtain   each use for         from total inflow     surpluses
total cash inflow       each year of         to obtain total       available for
for each year of        project              net inflow            repayment of
project, deducting                           (outflow) each        government
allowance for                                year                  loan on
uncollected payments                                                reinvestment
```

Figure 43
Establishing the cash flow projection

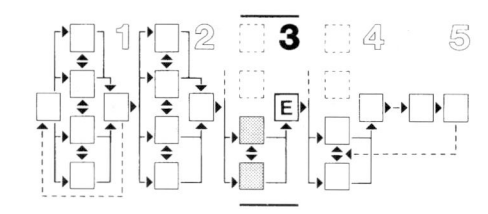

Interest during the grace period can either be capitalised (i.e. added to the original capital sum) or if preferred and feasible, paid independently of the principal sum over the first 5 years.

● *National and other agency contributions* may be planned to be received within the year in which expenditure is incurred. The financial and administrative arrangements proposed for their recovery should be facilitated by the suggestions outlined in Task 3D/3 (page 64). Broadly, the sources of funds: Government loans, loans from international agencies and national and other agency contributions should equal the costs of land acquisition and construction.

● *The timing of the commencement of residential monthly payments* will depend on the phasing programme adopted and the schedule of completion of the plots. Every attempt should be made to release plots to the chosen beneficiaries at the earliest point consistent with the requirements of a continuous implementation programme. This is in order to assist the cost recovery process.

● The appropriate marketing investigation for *disposal of commercial/industrial plots* will determine the price and absorption rate possible. The terms of both freehold and leasehold disposal will also have been ascertained and it is equally a matter of simple arithmetic which is to be preferred on a strict net present value basis. Other considerations are dealt with elsewhere.

● An allowance needs to be made for future *default of beneficiaries*. This will vary from city to city but experience dictates that approximately 9 per cent of monthly charges should be allowed. There is no substitute, however, for an efficient and effective collection system.

● *Land acquisition costs* in projects normally come at the beginning and therefore have an early impact on project funding. *The construction costs*, however, can be phased so as to limit early costs to a minimum consistent with efficient contracting arrangements and the need to generate productive land use in the early part of the programme.

● Adequate provision must be made for *administrative and overhead expenses* likely to be associated with the project. The effect of future inflation should be taken into account in forecasting such costs over the longer term.

From the tabulation of resources and their utilisation a net inflow (or outflow) of funds can be ascertained, both on a year to year basis and cumulatively. Viability of the project should already be assured based on the procedures for recovery adopted. In practice minor cash flow problems may occur, particularly in the earliest part of the programme, where revenues from commercial/industrial sales and residential leases lag slightly behind interest and amortisation payments and recovery of contributions from other agencies are delayed. The projected cash flow is unlikely to show other than minor net outflows on a year by year basis and cumulatively should indicate a surplus of funds for re-investment.

● *Sensitivity analysis*: The projected cash flow statement is based on a series of assumptions ranging from the phasing of construction costs to the realisation of surplus funds from commercial/industrial development and from the timing of national government agency contributions to the speed at which options to purchase land are exercised by beneficiaries. Such assumptions are naturally based on the best information available at the time of the analysis. Some of the assumptions made may be critical to the long term viability of the project, so that the effect of possible changes in these assumptions should be tested and the impact on the cash flow demonstrated.

The policies adopted as a result of the financial analysis in Ismailia are described in Appendix 1 (page 148). The cash flow table can be found in Stage 5 (page 94).

See Technical note 19 for a discussion of participation in planning and management.

Task 3E
Selection of project options

The process of selecting preferred options within each element, which has been discussed in each Task in Stage 3, is an initial sifting to reduce the very large number of total options to a manageable number which appear feasible relative to the objectives of the project and the constraints identified in Stages 1 and 2. This process of selection within each element goes on in parallel with work on other elements. For example, as the financial limitations become clear, so work on infrastructure options will tend to concentrate on, say, the lowest cost solutions, subject to site conditions, health regulations, social factors and many other aspects. To draw all of these interconnections on a flow chart would suggest a very complicated process, while in fact it is no more than common sense. If the Manual makes a particular point of emphasising interconnections it is because they do get forgotten, often because of the way work is organised.

This task involves putting preferred options together to make a comprehensive set of proposals. When more than one real alternative exists these options should be combined into alternative sets of proposals and evaluated. Final selection of the proposals which will be developed in detail in Stage 4 will then normally be by the committee or board controlling the implementing agency, based on technical advice. It is important that the proposals have local political support.

Selection of sets of options should be based on how well they meet the objectives (see page 2) while representing the constraints identified in Stage 2, e.g. site conditions and financial resources. The most important test is that the proposals should be able to meet the needs of the low income groups that the project is aiming to help.

The use of a check list with rankings, as described in Task 1E (page 14), is suggested as a basis for the evaluation. Some key questions are included here as a guide, but it is important that they should be based on the objectives of the project.

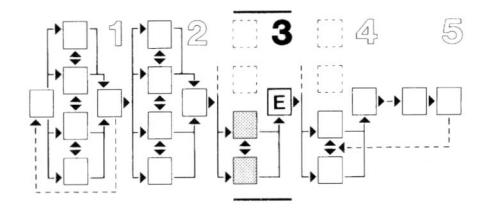

Evaluation checklists

How well do proposals meet project objectives in the main areas outlined below?

Meeting household needs

The order of magnitude of problems is first identified in discussions and in social surveys (see Tasks 1A/3, page 4 and 2A/7, page 21) . The real test of proposals, however, is how they affect individual families as represented by those interviewed in Case Studies (see Task group 2A, page 18). For example, a family's income may seem adequate to make a certain level of payments, based on the scanning survey. The case study might reveal, however, that the income was based on employment in a major construction project which is about to finish, with no alternative work available. Do the proposals depend on relatively high monthly payments over long periods? If that is the case, this particular family would be likely to default. Points of this type include:
● Compulsory payments, particularly regular ones, should be as low as possible, and well within the total proportion that a family is likely to spend on housing.
● The physical framework, e.g. plot sizes, should allow for normal patterns of family life and should not force the adoption of new materials or building types (there will, of course, be exceptions to this where very high land costs reduce the options).
● There should be the opportunity for economic activities renting rooms, operating a shop or small workshop on primarily residential plots to help family finances and to provide jobs.
● Households should be able to obtain a secure form of tenure. This is often the most important single issue.
● Sanitation, if a problem, should be significantly improved by the proposals.
● Households should be able to participate in the development process as much as is possible.

Physical planning

To ensure an efficient use of land, which will be necessary to reduce costs, and a plan which can respond flexibly to peoples' needs over time, a well designed physical plan is necessary. The key points include:
● Proposals should be capable of phased development, with re-design of later stages possible subject to experience in early stages.
● Proposals must respect physical constraints.
● Proposals must use land efficiently, subject to social limitations and allow efficient infrastructure provision.
● Proposals must relate to land uses and plans external to the project site. A project is part of a city or town 's development and should not be seen in isolation. Opportunities for employment generation should exist within the project.
● When possible, legally, land use zoning should be as flexible as possible, with only core areas specified for particular uses.
● A mixture of land uses and income groups will provide greater opportunities for cross-subsidisation.
● Circulation, i .e. roads and footpaths, should provide efficient access to work, shops and facilities.
● Proposals should be sustainable and not have a negative environmental impact.

Implementation

Proposals must be planned with the requirements for implementation in mind. The key elements include:
● Proposals must have political support.
● Proposals must be within the agency's capacity, both technical and administrative. For example, if squatting is tightly controlled long before an organisation is set up to implement a new subdivision programme, then problems can be increased, because of greater pressure leading to breakdown of control. In most cases an agency cannot control and provide all options for housing demand to be satisfied. Other means should be left open. Allowing greater community participation in the development process can allow limited staff to cover considerably more development.
● Proposals should represent the minimum interference in the housing system which will overcome the problems identified.
● Proposals should have a 'basic' form which can be implemented with little or no subsidy, i.e. based primarily on resources obtained from settlers, but upgradable to full standards overtime, as funds become available. This means that a project can go ahead in a short time irrespective of the allocation of funds from central government or international agencies. 'Basic' applies not only to infrastructure, but to services provided such as community development and building loans. These can be introduced later, as and when they prove necessary.
● Proposals should be implementable within existing legal and executive structures. Changes in legislation, though often desirable, are likely to take too long to be effective in the short term.
● Operation and maintenance should be sustainable. This means responsibilities and funding should be agreed before implementation begins.

Stage 4
Detailed proposals

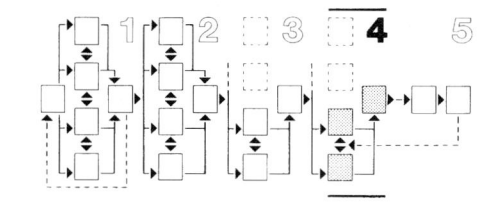

Once a set of options for the project have been approved by the authorities, and local groups have had a chance to discuss and influence them, work can begin on detailed design for the first phase of the project. Detailed design for later phases should be left until they are about to be implemented. In this way it will be possible to incorporate any changes in demand and to build on the experience gained.

The detailed designs prepared in this Stage will only apply to initial levels of development, but they must be designed within the framework of likely final levels. For example, sewage disposal may be by on-plot pit latrines initially, but layouts should be efficient for a water-borne system if possible in the future. The appropriateness of the initial proposals will depend largely upon the information and understanding obtained during the Detailed studies (see Stage 2, page 17) and reference should therefore be made to them as necessary. The tasks in preparing detailed designs require the various individuals and institutions to work together closely and to be very flexible.

It should be recognised that the Manual can provide limited guidance only at this Stage and the following notes are merely intended to ensure that all the main points are considered.

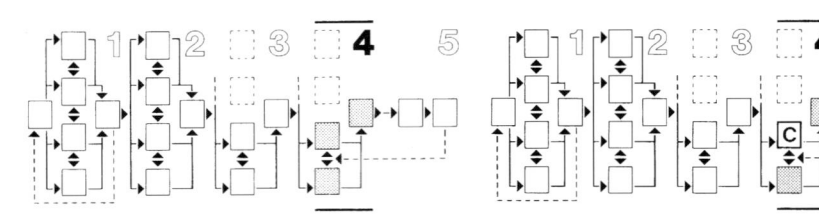

Stage 4

Task group 4A

No Tasks at this stage

Task group 4B

No Tasks at this stage unless further detailed land surveys are necessary

(see Task 2B/4, page 24)

Task group 4C
Designing site development

4C/1	Housing layouts 75
4C/2	Housing: building 76
4C/3	Commerce and industry 77
4C/4	Public facilities and recreation 78
4C/5	Road layouts 79
4C/6	Utilities 80

The purpose of this Task is to prepare the detailed site development plan for the project based upon the proposals prepared in Stage 3.

For new settlement projects, it means taking into account existing site characteristics (see Task group 2C, page 26) and any existing site development accommodating the target population (see Task 2A/3, page 20).

For upgrading projects, it will be necessary to apply proposals to the site, taking existing site characteristics and site development into consideration.

Detailed plans will be required for every item of site development. When designing these, all items must be coordinated, particularly the costs of the detailed proposals in relation to what the target population can afford.

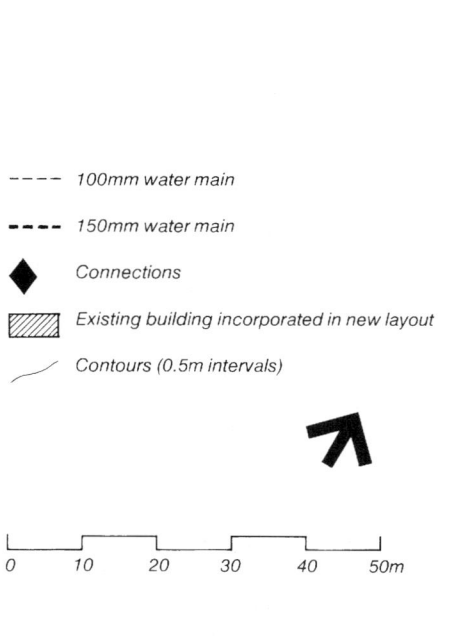

Legend:
- ---- 100mm water main
- ---- 150mm water main
- ◆ Connections
- ▨ Existing building incorporated in new layout
- ⌇ Contours (0.5m intervals)

0 10 20 30 40 50m

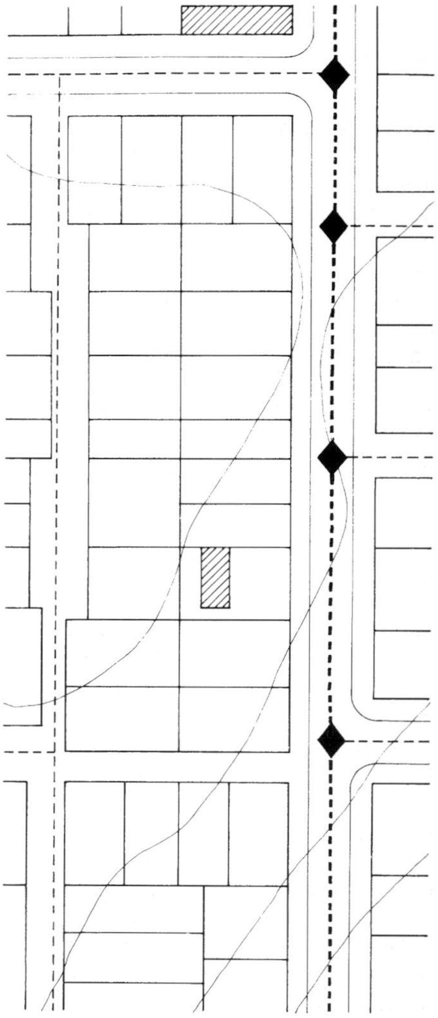

Figure 44
Example: detailed plot and infrastructure layout

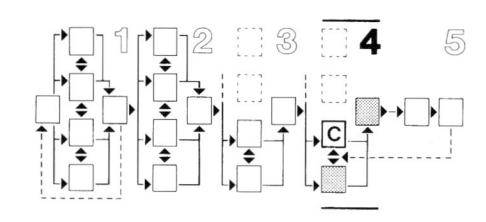

Task 4C/1

Housing layouts

Boundaries

The boundaries of each neighbourhood should be set in co-ordination with the road and footpath proposals and site characteristics. Inevitably this will require some modification in the precise size and shape of neighbourhoods from the sketch plan developed in Task 3C/1 (page 37). Plans should then be drawn to scales such as 1:1000 or 1:2500 (with 1:500 for plot layouts and utilities) and related to the detailed site studies discussed in Task group 2B (page 22).

The definition of neighbourhood boundaries will enable final estimates to be made of projected population levels. These will be based upon estimates of densities in existing fully built up areas and will enable the demand for public facilities to be calculated.

Layouts: general

In designing new settlement projects, site conditions and existing development should be considered. Flexibility will be necessary in applying the options developed in Stage 3 (page 35). Buildings requiring special locations should be considered first. For example, religious buildings may be allocated plots on higher ground or at major road intersections, and plots for commercial activity should be placed in the most accessible part of the neighbourhood.

Layouts: blocks

Within each neighbourhood, various *blocks* can then be related to the main road layout and the neighbourhood facilities. Once again, it will be necessary to adapt the layout principles to site conditions. In addition to providing efficient local circulations, the roads defining each block should be oriented, if possible, to ensure the most comfortable conditions during extreme seasons. When the design of blocks has been completed the detailed plan of local roads and public open areas can be incorporated into the circulation plan (see Task 4C/5, page 79).

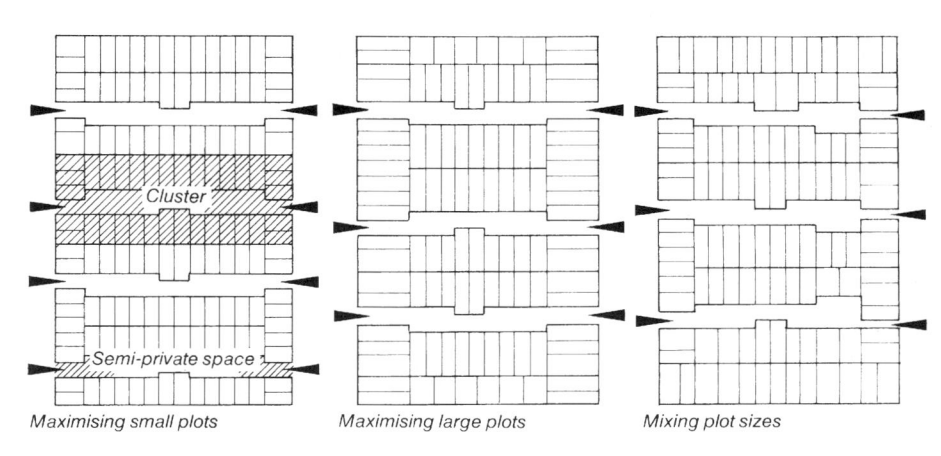

Figure 45
Blocks, showing alternative plot layouts

Maximising small plots | Maximising large plots | Mixing plot sizes

Layouts: clusters

One of the most important design tasks is the detailed design of *clusters* within each block. Clusters are important because they may constitute the immediate environment for a large part of all house plots in a new settlement and may also constitute a large part in an upgrading project. Clusters should be designed as *places* not as open areas surrounded by plots and they should use any existing trees or other useful features.

In some cases, it may be considered appropriate to connect clusters to each other so that, for example, a secondary form of pedestrian circulation can develop in addition to the road system. This improves convenience, but reduces privacy and security. In general, clusters will function best if they are designed primarily for the use of households living within them. Reference to existing layouts accommodating the target population (see Task 2C/1, page 26) may provide a useful indication of possible layouts.

Wherever possible, access to clusters should be from quiet local rather than busy major roads which may present a safety hazard. Clusters should also be oriented to take advantage of prevailing winds and provide shade. The precise size of each cluster will depend upon the sizes of the house plots as determined in Tasks 2C/2 (page 27) and 2C/3 (page 28). Layouts should be designed with concern also for the practicalities of easy layout on the site. This is discussed in Technical note 7 (page 118).

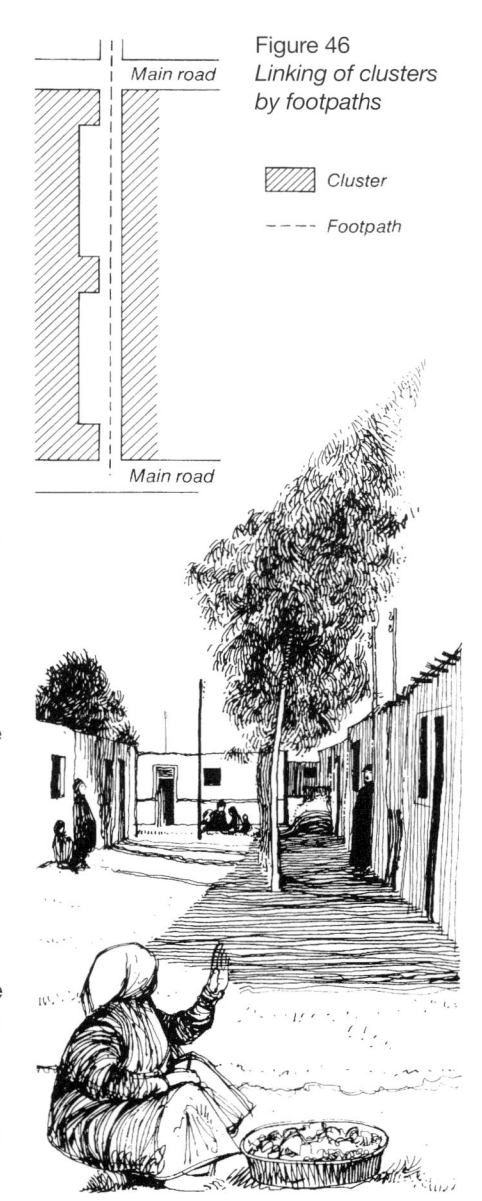

Figure 46
Linking of clusters by footpaths

Stage 4

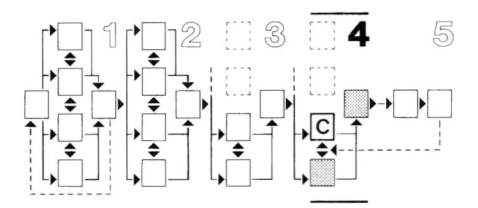

Layouts: upgrading projects

In upgrading projects, the task of regularising clusters and plots depends very much on the accuracy of land surveys and/or air photo coverage. Where survey information is limited it may be more useful to define the boundaries of each block accurately and allow residents to prepare the detailed layout plan for each cluster, with necessary technical advice given by the project agency. For notes on how to carry out this procedure, see Technical notes 2 (page 114) and 4 (page 116).

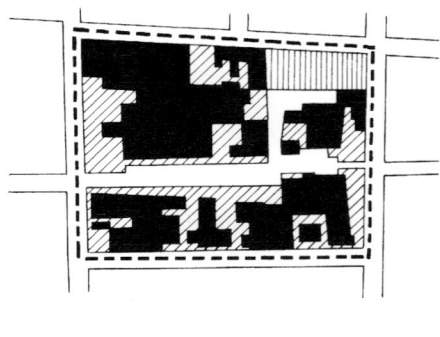

☐ *Semi-private space*
--- *Block boundary*
■ *Built up area*
▨ *Private open space*
▥ *Kickabout area*

Figure 47
Block boundaries in upgrading area

Layouts: higher income plots

Within the locations defined in Task 3C/1 (page 37), detailed plans should be prepared for any higher income plots. The design should allow for environmental standards sufficient to attract middle or higher income applicants.

Task 4C/2
Housing: building

Owner-managed building

Where the costs of pre-built superstructures are greater than the amounts which low income households can afford for them, and this will be the case in most housing projects, the project agency should prepare and make available plots for settlers to build their own houses. In this case the project agency will be able to perform a valuable service to settlers by making available designs for optimal plot and building layouts. This will help households prepare an efficient and appropriate design for themselves, while making sure that later upgrading can take place easily.

Initial development

Intermediate development

Consolidated development

Figure 48
Incremental development

Assistance to owner-builders

Information from case studies (Technical note 1, page 101) and interviews with local builders should identify whether there are any problems about funds for building, availability of materials or lack of skills. Where problems exist, the project should be designed to help overcome them, for example, by provision of loans or technical assistance. It is important to relate assistance of this kind to:
● The proven need.
● The financial and manpower capacity of the implementing agency.

Agency built housing

In general, detailed designs for buildings will only be applicable to new settlement projects, unless substantial modifications or improvements to existing buildings are

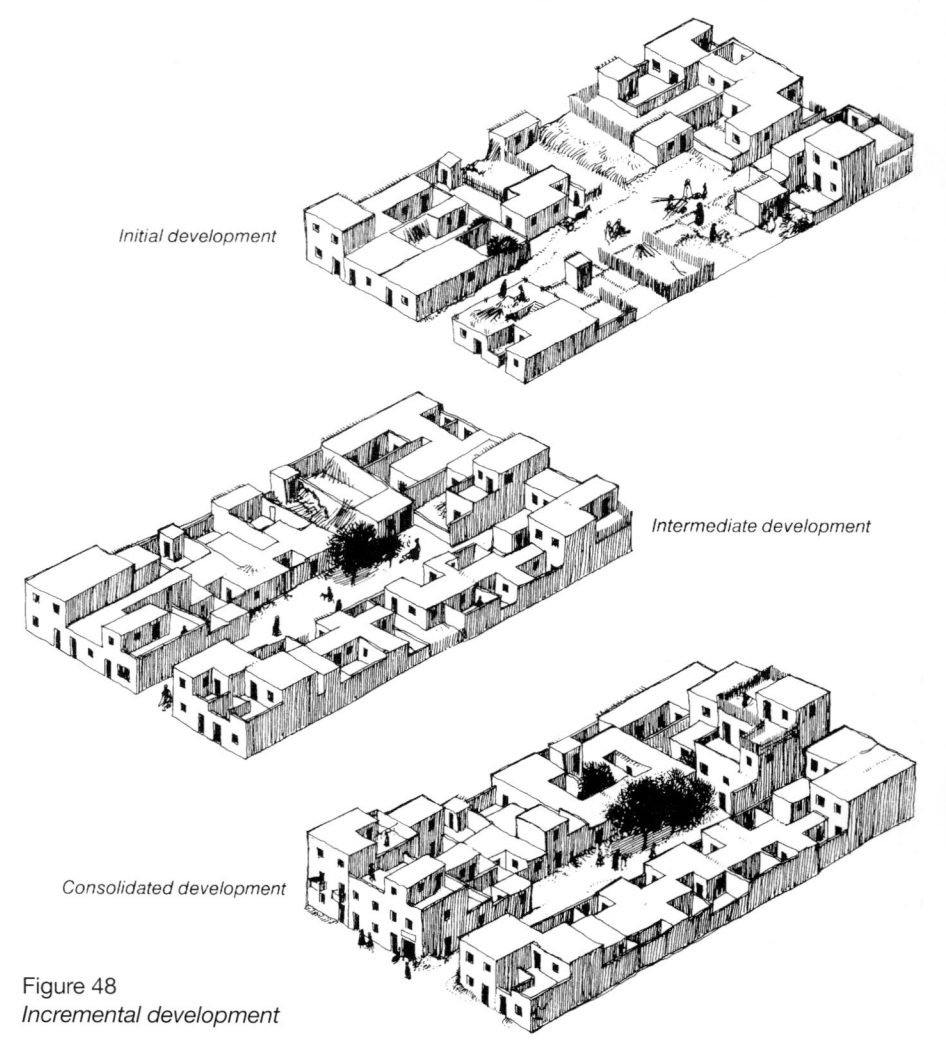

Stage 4

required in the course of an upgrading project.

Where the plot development proposals prepared in Task 4E (page 82) indicate that full or part building of houses by the agency is required *and* is within the cost limits which households can afford, detailed designs for contract purposes should be prepared. In cases of part provision, it will be necessary to allow apart of the total sum allocated for superstructure in the calculations (see Task 3D/3, page 64) to be deducted so that households can provide the remainder for themselves.

The design of pre-built houses should be appropriate to the social needs and customs of the target population (see Task 2A/5, page 20) and to local climatic conditions (see Task 2B/7, page 25). This applies particularly to the sanitary facilities within the dwelling, provision for personal privacy, the preparation and eating of food and the use of private open space. Care should be taken in locating the superstructure on the plot as this can significantly affect costs of installing on-plot utilities connections. There will usually be technical advantages in locating the superstructure section containing utilities at or near the plot frontage (see Task 4C/6, page 80) where connections can be made easily to public mains networks. Reference should be made, however, to the social and cultural aspects of plot development (see Task 2A/4, page 20; and Task group 4C, page 74) to see if this is likely to be acceptable to residents.

Task 4C/3
Commerce and industry

Detailed plans for commercial and industrial development will need to be prepared for all activity not included in primarily residential plots. This involves plot layouts and use specifications for the key sections of all main centres, sub-centres and neighbourhoods. Designs should be made at a scale of 1:1000 or 1:500.

All details of access (for customers and goods), outline plans of utilities provision (both on-site and on-plot) and any special conditions such as the maximum number of storeys should be specified. In addition, sites for temporary markets should be identified and individual plots demarcated for registration.

Main commercial and industrial centre plans should be prepared in greater detail than for sub-centres or neighbourhoods, since land costs and revenues will be greater and more control is therefore necessary. In all cases, care should be taken to design attractive layouts to help these areas develop as effective centres of local life.

It is never possible to forecast accurately the amount of shopping or office space which will be required in the future. It is thus preferable to limit layouts designed for specific commercial use to the minimum likely to be required, and to design plot layouts in the adjacent areas in such a way that if converted from residential use to commercial, or vice versa, they will still be able to be used efficiently.

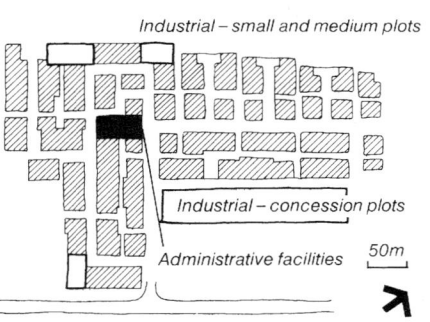

Plan of industrial area

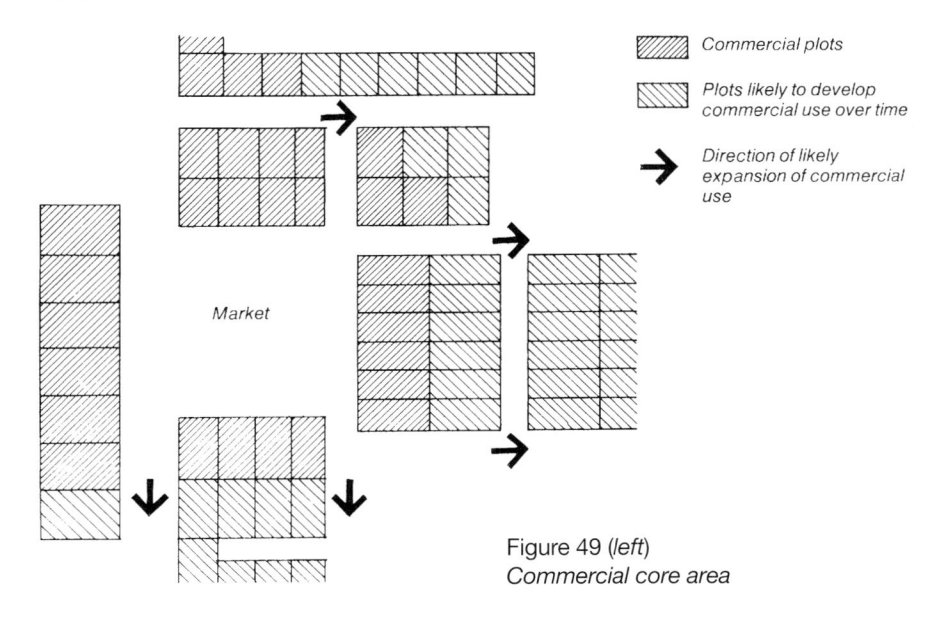

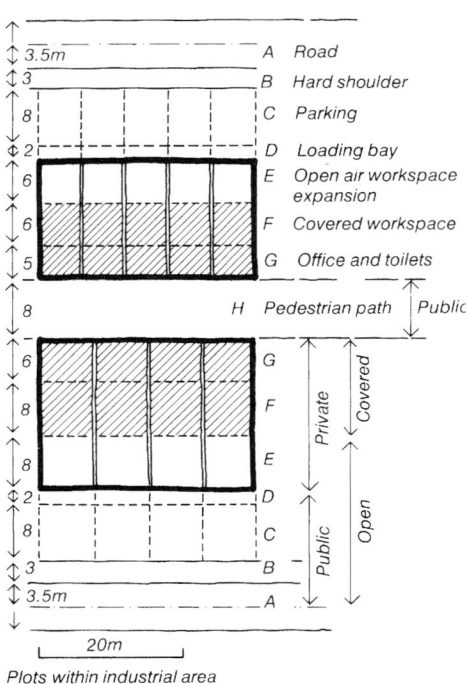

Figure 49 (*left*)
Commercial core area

Plots within industrial area

A Road
B Hard shoulder
C Parking
D Loading bay
E Open air workspace expansion
F Covered workspace
G Office and toilets
H Pedestrian path

78 Stage 4

Task 4C/4
Public facilities and recreation

Public facilities

Proposals for type and land requirements for all public facilities will be required for all main and local units. Plans should be at a scale of 1:1000 or 1:500.

As with commercial and industrial development, details of access, outline of utilities provision and other conditions should be specified.

Recreation space

Boundaries and outline design for all types of recreational space should be prepared as an integral component of the site development plan; they should not be regarded merely as 'left-over' spaces. Detailed design should be prepared immediately before implementation.

Landscaping

Any existing planting, especially trees, should be incorporated to provide local amenity. This will be especially important in the initial phase of new settlement projects, when the site consists generally of modest structures.

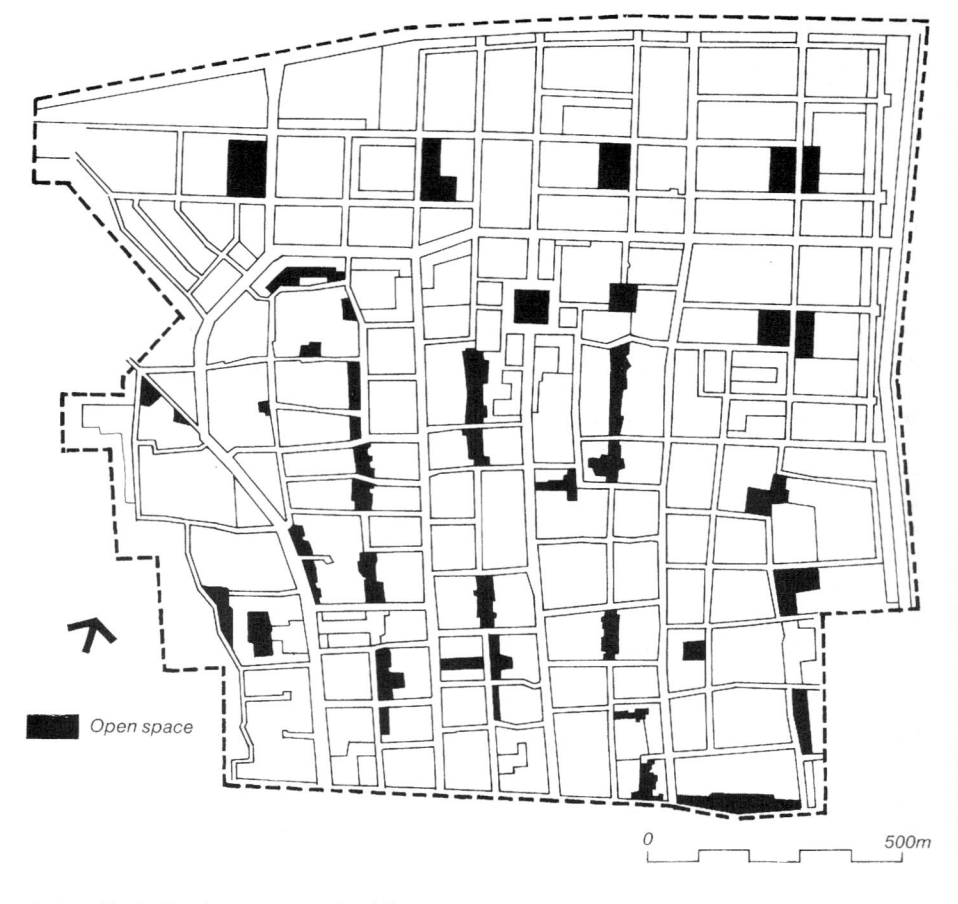

It is unlikely that large areas of public planting will be maintained because of the cost. The most successful means of encouraging tree planting is by private control of open space adjacent to houses or by community planting and maintenance.

Figure 50
Open space provision

Before

After

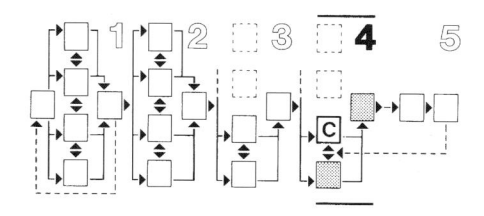

Task 4C/5
Road layouts

In general, detailed design to the level of preparation of contract documents belongs in the Implementation Stage.

The Task carried out in Stage 4 (page 73) includes:
- Determine basic site levels for road and building development.
- Determine basis for setting out and defining Rights-of-way for streets.
- Determine phasing.
- Set construction standards.
- Establish public transport routes.

The nature of the Task will depend on whether an upgrading or a new site is being considered. Upgrading projects will require more work on alignments since the location of existing development will have to be considered.

Determining site levels and need for regrading

In general, the economics of a project will prevent extensive regrading of the site either to improve the drainage pattern or to reduce ground slopes. It is therefore important that road levels and grades will cater for general site requirements for drainage.

In any new sites being developed, it is possible that some plot development will precede road construction. Therefore, as a minimum, road design should be taken to the point where a policy defining road elevations (levels) is established. This will ensure that the foundation level of any development on plots can be related to the expected level at which an adjacent road might be built later in the life of the project. A good quality site survey is desirable for this outline design. The object is to ensure that where road construction follows plot construction, problems of stability or increased expense do not arise because of level differences between on-plot development and the adjacent road way. The design policy will also assist in subsequent phasing of road construction.

Standards

The design standards applied to the vertical alignment of each type of street should reflect its importance in the street hierarchy. Thus district streets should have vertical curves defined by conventional highway engineering standards. However, vertical curves on less important streets need not be considered.

Definition of road-lines

The layout selected in Stage 3 (page 35) must be defined in such a way that it can be set out on site. The combination of plots and clusters into blocks of development can be established by defining the location of the Rights-of-way of the streets bounding each block.

The centre-lines of the Rights-of-way should be determined in terms of the national survey grid or a local grid specially established for the purpose. It is important that design work be based on surveys of sufficient accuracy which are tied into a system of permanent survey monuments (markers). Technical note 2 (page 114) provides some guidelines for work in upgrading areas.

In general, some form of grid is likely to be adopted since this simplifies the design process and setting out. Junction layouts and curved carriageway alignments should be designed in sufficient detail to enable the boundaries of the Rights-of-way (and thus the building lines) to be set out on site, and ensure compatibility with subsequent detailed alignment design.

Phasing

Phasing is discussed on page 82. The specific relevance of phasing to this Task is that it determines the level of design. Road design, for elements of the network expected to be constructed at an early stage, should be taken to a greater degree of detail to facilitate implementation and upgrading at a later phase. For example, full standard road construction should be delayed if construction of sewers is likely to result in a road being dug-up to lay pipes within a few years of the road being built.

Construction standards

The construction standard should be related to each street type and the class of traffic expected to use the road. An assessment of likely traffic flows and classes of traffic will indicate the streets which require higher standards of construction. Thus District or Local streets with a *public transport* route may require a paved surface, while other roads may only require a transitable surface of minimum standard. The final choice of materials will depend also on the financial resources available (see Task 3D/3, page 64).

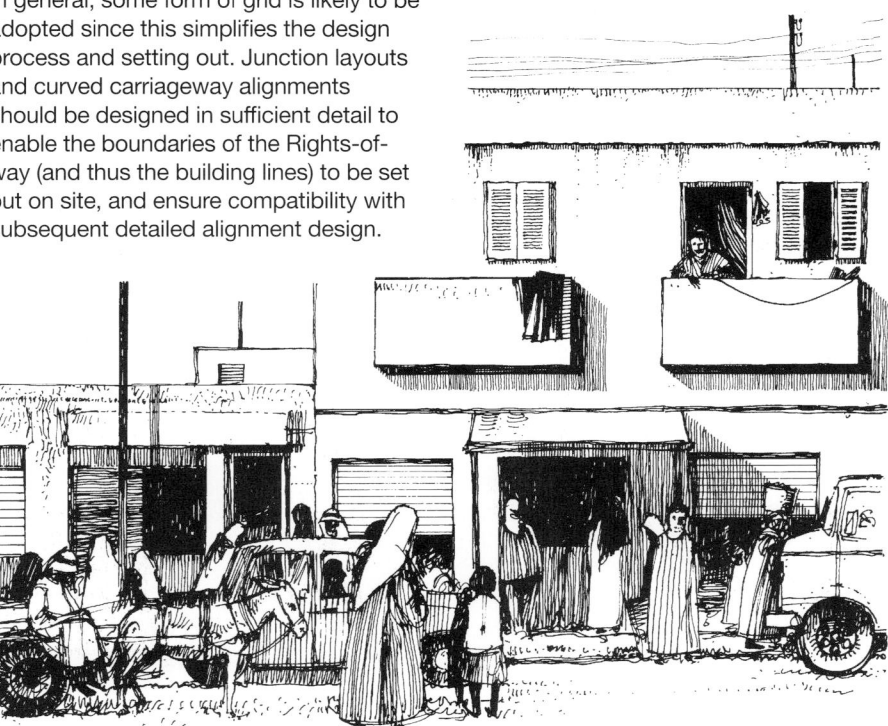

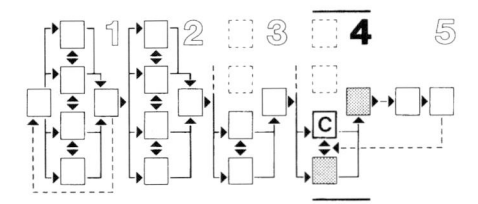

Task 4C/6
Utilities

The detailed design of each component of on-site utilities means close co-ordination with the design of circulation and housing layouts, and on-plot utilities. The design criteria, construction materials and level of service for each utility will already have been established and should be used to complete the detailed designs. The actual process of designing each utility is well documented in technical engineering literature and it is not possible or appropriate to provide this detail in the Manual. It is however, appropriate to emphasize some key factors for consideration when designing the water distribution, surface water drainage, sewage disposal and electricity distribution systems.

Staged provision

Considerable design work will be required to determine the initial level of service for each utility and the possibility of improved levels, since any subsequent upgrading must be possible with only the minimum of disturbance. This is particularly true with respect to the sewage disposal system.

Utility networks

One of the most important items of the design process is the optimisation of the utility network when applied to the whole site. This particularly concerns the drainage and sewage disposal networks, since a considerable cost saving can be achieved by minimising the extent of excavation. The layout of utilities for each neighbourhood can also be optimised by adjusting the layouts developed during Task 3C/1 (page 37) to suit each part of the site's topography and ground conditions. This process is a complex one and considerable engineering judgement and experience is required. It also involves close cooperation between specialists designing housing layouts, roads and utilities.

The outcome of this Task will be a complete set of detailed drawings showing the layout of each utility at a scale of normally 1:1000 or 1:500. Longitudinal sections of each gravity based system and construction details of each individual element of the network will also be required to scales of between 1:50 and 1:5. The choice of scale will depend on the size of the utility.

On-plot utilities

Detailed design of on-plot utilities will be determined by the selected level of provision and the ground conditions of each plot. Close coordination between those responsible for the layout of plots and any superstructure provisions will also be important, ensuring that initial development is economical and that later upgrading can be carried out easily.

A considerable amount of plot development is likely to be undertaken by the occupants themselves. It is reasonable to extend this to the provision of on-plot utilities, provided that some measure of control and supervision is exercised.

Where on-plot utilities are to be built by the implementing agency, the Task should result in a series of drawings showing the type and location of each utility on every plot at scales of not less than 1:500. Full construction details for each utility will also be required at scales between 1:50 and 1:5, depending on size. The construction details could include a series of dimensions for pit systems which would vary depending on the plot size, occupancy level and, possibly, the ground conditions. When settler organised construction is likely, it will also be advisable for the project agency to make available suitable designs for pit latrines and the like, as part of the technical advice for the project will depend on the adequacy of existing sanitation methods.

Should piped systems of sewage or surface drainage be included as part of the project, connections to the main services off the plot will be dependent on site level. This is often dealt with by providing a small manhole near the plot boundary. The possibility of sharing such connections with adjacent plots should be investigated as sharing can reduce costs.

The final details of on-plot utilities provision will probably be determined when the project is implemented (see Stage 5, page 83). The actual location of each utility should, however, be recorded as accurately as possible on plans of the site so that any future upgrading can be planned accordingly.

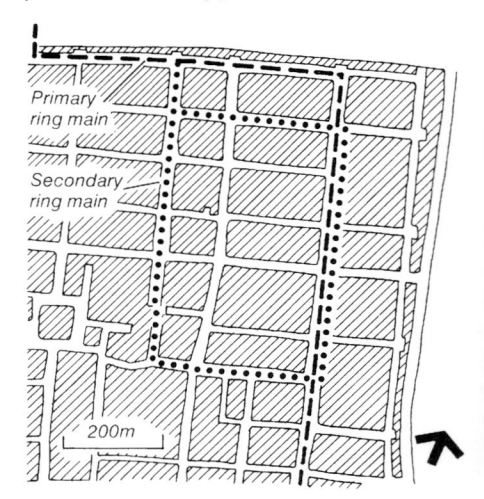

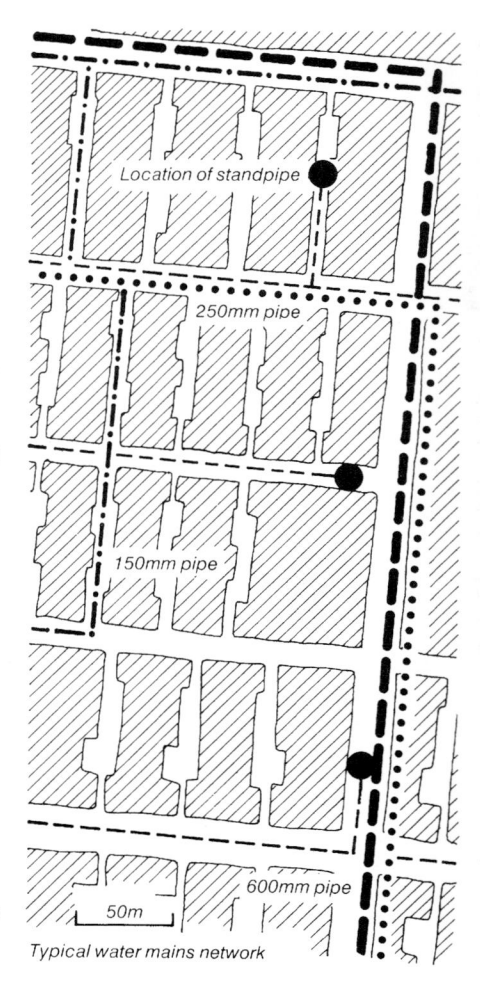

Typical water mains network

Stage 4   81

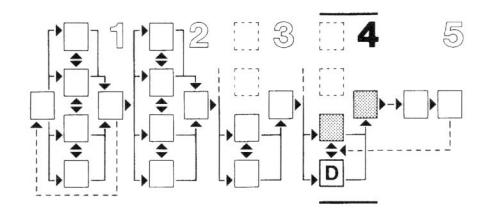

Task group 4D
Institutional and financial framework

| 4D/1 | Institutional framework | 81 |
| 4D/2 | Financial framework | 82 |

This Task group, at this Stage, does not require any specific technical descriptions or explanations. The shortness of this section should not, however, be taken as an indication that the tasks are unimportant. On the contrary, work on the details of the institutional and financial frameworks is extremely important as it forms the bridge between the detailed proposals and their implementation.

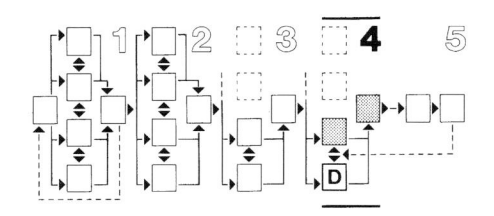

Task 4D/1
Institutional framework

This Task comprises the refinement of the Stage 3 (page 35) proposals into a carefully worded implementable form. This will require work by, or close co-operation with, a legal expert to ensure a sound basis to proposals such as:
- Establishment of a new implementing agency, if one is proposed.
- Land tenure conditions.
- Qualifications of applicants.
- Compensation.
- Exemptions from national regulations, e.g. building controls.

This is by no means an exhaustive list, but indicates the importance of this type of detailed work. In addition, it will be important to develop a capacity building strategy (see Technical note 20).

An example of the detailed proposals developed for the institutional framework of the Ismailia projects is given in Stage 5 (page 83).

Task 4D/2
Financial framework

This Task involves the refinement of the calculations prepared in Task 3D/3 (page 64) based on the detailed design work carried out in Stage 4 (page 73) tasks.

Cash flow predictions will be based both on the refined figures and on the phasing proposals outlined in Task 4E.

The quality of the work undertaken at this Stage is important, as the figures will form the basis for the charges to be made to families of the target population, and also will be the basis of applications for capital grants and/or loans to finance the project.

An example of the Detailed proposals for the financial framework of the Ismailia project is given in Stage 5 (page 83).

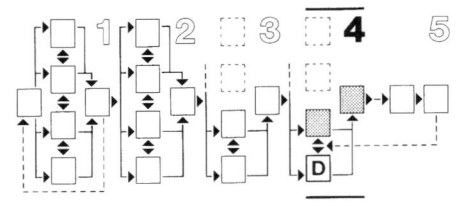

Task 4E
Phasing

Phasing of development is a very important aspect if the best use of scarce resources is to be obtained. Phasing will depend mainly on:
- *Effective demand*. This may or may not be easy to forecast, dependent on past patterns.
- *Availability of capital*. The degree of certainty of how much will be available, and when, depends entirely on the sources of capital. That obtained directly from settlers is probably the most reliable source.
- *Technical factors outside the site*. These are particularly important for upgrading and new development schemes. There are obvious advantages in linking the phasing of development of existing and new areas. This is particularly important if the existing area is tending to grow naturally into the new area.

Where a sewerage system is proposed, natural drainage areas and the location of external mains will be critical.

In terms of *utilities* the best order might be (1) basic roads (2) water mains (3) sewerage pipes (if any) (4) surfaced roads. Where money is not available for (3), then roads in a basic form should still be constructed, wherever possible, before house-building as this will prevent any problems with levels. The supply of electricity is not normally a problem for phasing.

Basically phasing is simply a matter of logic. An outline programme of phasing over the whole period of project development is desirable, but this should only be developed in financial terms for the first 5 years. Within this framework, detailed phasing will be done on an annual basis as continuous changes are likely to be necessary. This is described in Stage 5 'monitoring' (page 97).

Stage 5

Project implementation

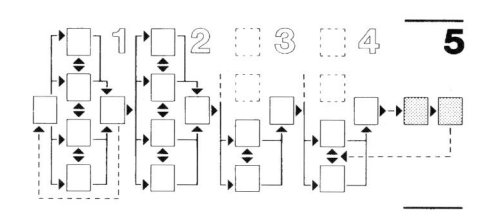

Stage 5

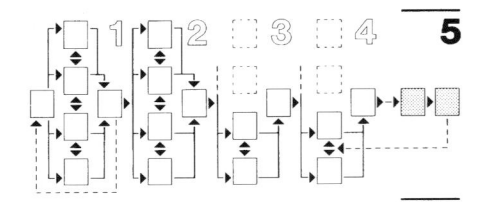

General notes

A successful project requires five main elements: 1) political will; 2) sufficient resources; 3) well prepared plans which take account of 1) and 2); 4) *effective, efficient and sensitive* implementation; and 5) will manage the operation and maintenance. 'Effective' because unless the plans are developed into a physical form on the ground they are useless; 'efficient' because unless they are cost effective, the objective of providing a low cost, low priced service to low income people is lost; and 'sensitive' because housing is one of the main preoccupations of a large section of the population, and proposals must be constantly monitored for acceptability.

The Manual is not intended to cover thoroughly the enormous subject of implementation, but to highlight certain matters which are critical to the design of the project. *It is important to see 'design' and 'implementation' as two separate activities which overlap and interrelate.* Only with implementation clearly in mind can good proposals be made. The best way to understand implementation is to implement. From this, it can be seen that an early start to implementation of a first phase, followed by detailed design of later phases is the most effective means of proceeding. This is sometimes known as 'action planning' or 'fast track planning'.

Whenever possible, the detailed design of a project should proceed in parallel with actual implementation. It is neither necessary nor desirable to complete detailed design for more than can be implemented within one or two years. It is important to have the basic framework clear, but not to complete, for example, plot layouts or detailed engineering designs, for the whole of a large project. Valuable experience will be obtained in developing the initial phases of a project and this will suggest what modifications can and should be made. A further advantage is that the project becomes more responsive to local needs, and approvals will be simpler to obtain if they are only for a limited development.

The detailed nature of implementation will depend very much on individual circumstances. The routines established by the implementing agency will usually be adaptations of those used in other local government offices for example. The Tasks which have to be carried out in this Stage do not lend themselves to presentation in a generalised form, as was possible for the previous Stages. Reference should be made to the Technical notes for information on methods of carrying out many of the operations which are required to prepare, plan and implement a successful project.

Responsibilities for operation and maintenance need to be clear, and linked to the monitoring of implementation.

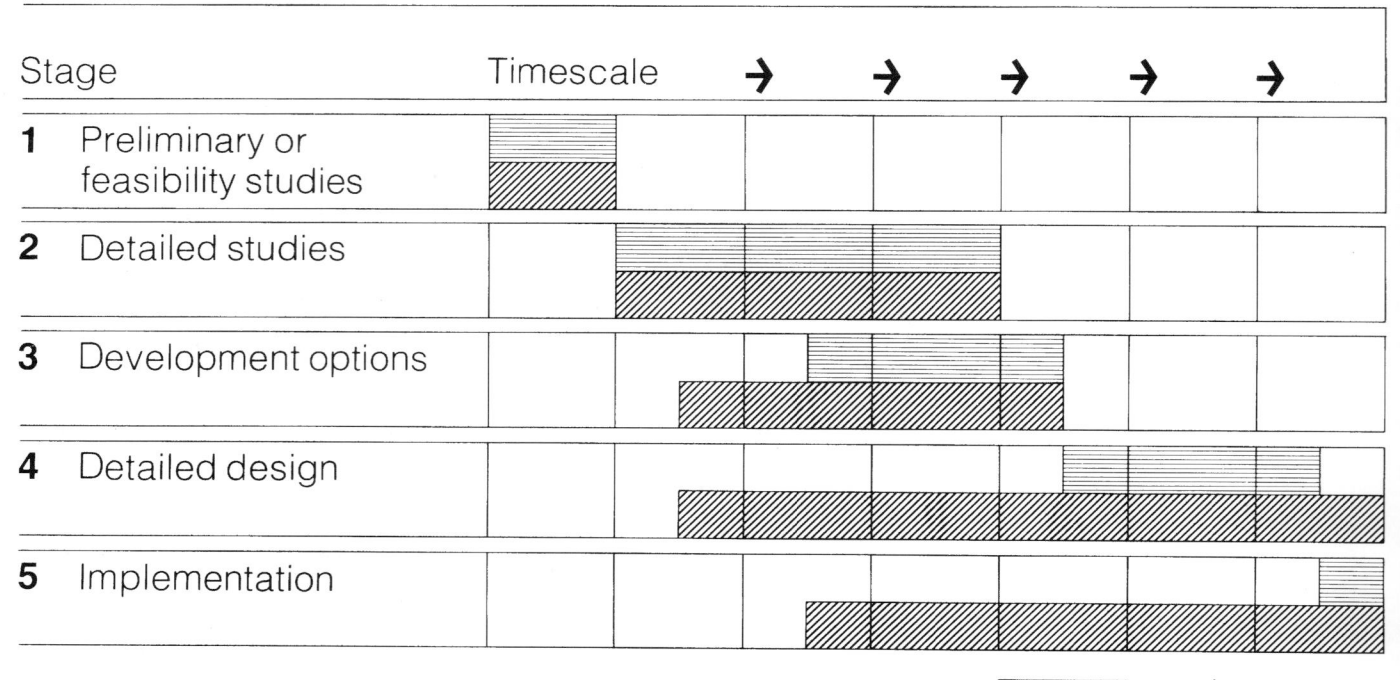

Stage	Timescale → → → → →
1 Preliminary or feasibility studies	
2 Detailed studies	
3 Development options	
4 Detailed design	
5 Implementation	

Legend: normal sequence / 'action planning'

Figure 51
Relationship between 'action planning' and normal planning process. Sequence of work showing 'action planning' or 'fast track' work in parallel with detailed studies for subsequent phases.

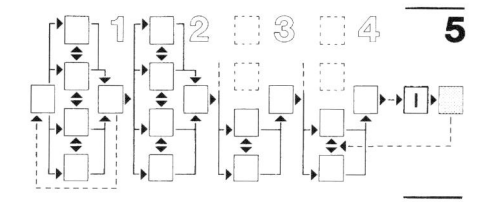

Example of proposals for administrative and financial framework for implementation

The following is an annotated, modified extract from the Ismailia Demonstration Projects Final Report, Volume 1. It provides an example of the detailed steps necessary in this particular case. In other projects there will be many local differences, for example, the relationship between the Agency and local government, actual figures quoted and the number of Agencies. The detailed proposals reproduced here, however, should provide a useful reference point and check list.

OVERVIEW

In this section the main proposals about administration, legal and institutional control, project finance, monitoring and immediate steps are presented.

PROJECT ADMINISTRATION: EL HEKR [1]

The key to implementation is the formation of an entity, hereafter called the 'Project Agency'.

A. Formation of the Project Agency

The Project Agency will be formed by Governor's [2] Administrative Order and will be, ultimately, under the control and supervision of the Secretary General of the Governorate. Thus the Project Agency will be an executive Government body charged with administration of a specific Project Area for the public benefit. The Governor's Administrable Order will be preceded by the approval of the Project (design, finance and administration) from the Governorate and District Local Councils in full session.

Responsibilities and powers of the Project Agency will be set out in the Governor's Administrative Order, and will include these specifications:

(i) The Project Agency will have the power to manage all lands within the boundaries described separately respecting all individual rights as prescribed by law. Acquisition of land, not presently in use, by the Project Agency will be automatic with promulgation of the Order. It is understood that no base land payment will be necessary for Government lands. [3]

(ii) The location of the Project Agency will be on site. [4]

(iii) The Project Agency will have the power to sell lands to the public, at prices and under conditions that it chooses, providing that such prices and conditions are approved by the Secretary General of the Governorate.

(iv) The Project Agency will have the power to enter into contract agreements with all inhabitants of the area.

(v) (This article may require a decree waiving stipulations of Law 107 of 1976). The Project Agency will have the authority to manage its own budget separate of all local budgets, on two conditions:
a) that all revenue to the budget be spent on capital or recurrent improvements in the Area, after deducting necessary administrative expenses.
b) that all financial dealings be open to the auditing and inspection of the local office of the Ministry of Finance and/or the Governorate.

(vi) The Project Agency, as an autonomous public body, may solicit and act as guarantor (with collateral) for commercial or Government loans.

(vii) The Project Agency has the authority to select applicants for land parcels, based on criteria approved (and monitored if so desired) by the appropriate Governorate Committee.

(viii) The Project Agency may enter into contract arrangements with private or public contractors or public agencies, for the construction or installation of utilities and services. It may also, for small works, enter into contract with non-registered contractors residing in the Area.

(ix) The Project Agency may, at its discretion, institute a building loan programme for the benefit of the inhabitants of the area.

(x) The Project Agency may, in coordination with the Housing Directorate, institute a programme for the sale of limited quantities of building materials at official prices. [5]

(xi) The Project Agency will have access to seconded personnel; for key positions, the Agency may directly recruit qualified persons. [6]

(xii) The Project Agency may request that the Governor institute land expropriation proceedings.

---

(1) *El Hekr is one of the two selected for upgrading/ new development, for background see Appendix 1, page 148*

(2) *The Governor is the appointed head of the Governorate or Provincial administration. He has wide delegated powers*

(3) *This is a major advantage for the project*

(4) *Important both for supervision and for access by local people*

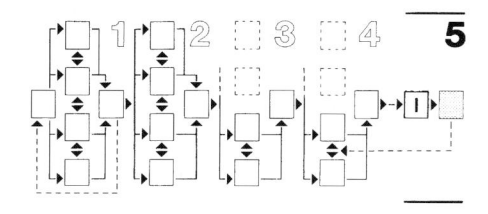

(5) *In Egypt, materials such as cement has a low controlled price to holders of building permits can obtain these materials*

(6) *Incentive payments may be made if government salaries are very low*

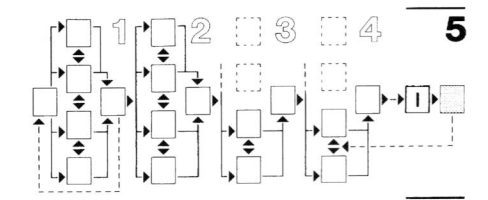

(xiii) The Project Agency of El Hekr will be governed by one Board of Directors, the members of which will include (tentatively) [7]:
– The Secretary General of the Governorate
– Representative of the Governorate and District Local Councils
– Representative of the Ismailia City Council
– Representative of the Ismailia Housing Directorate
– Representative of the Amlak Department of Ismailia
– Representative of the Executive Agency of the MHR
– Representative of the local office of the Ministry of Finance
– The Project Manager of the El Hekr Project Agency.

B. Functions of the Project Agency

In a sense, the functions of the Project Agency are outlined in the Governor's Administrative Orders as described above. To have a complete understanding of the scope of the Project Agency, however, it is necessary to enumerate its functions in detail.

(i) The management of a programme for the demarcation and registration of plots already inhabited; also the management of the designation, relocation, and compensation of a certain number of households whose removal is necessary for public improvements.

(ii) The management of a programme for the provision of marked plots to new settlers, including the processing of applications, selection of applicants, and assignment of plots.

(iii) The arranging and issuing of contracts for programmes (i) and (ii) above.

(iv) The collection of payments from contract holders.

(v) All printing, distributing and announcements of a publicity and information nature needed for programmes (i) and (ii) above.

(vi) The maintaining of an independent budget (capital and current). [8]

---

(7) It is important to include key members of agencies concerned in local development and whose assistance may be required. The present board (1980) is in fact considerably larger than this

(8) This is an extremely important feature

(vii) The ability to negotiate and enter into contract agreements with contractors or with the Water Works Department, the Electricity Board, the General Organisation for sewerage and Sanitary Drainage, the Bus Company, or the Ministry of Wire and Wireless Communications. It may also correspond and communicate with these bodies for any matters concerning the Project Area.

(viii) The borrowing of money from banks or the National Housing Fund or the Co-operative Housing Society; also for the acceptance of loans or grants from foreign sources, provided these follow the correct routines.

(ix) The assistance to inhabitants in obtaining building materials at official prices.

(x) The representation of the inhabitants of the area to national Government and other bodies, for the provision of needed community facilities, such as schools and clinics. The Project Agency will need to communicate with the Government bodies concerned. This will be in concert with the elected representatives of the Area in the District and Village Local Councils.

(xi) The setting up of a small building loan system for inhabitants of the Area in the absence of any such programme by other agencies.

(xii) The setting of prices and the preparation of specifications and documents for the future sale of certain commercial and residential plots on the open market.

(xiii) The organisation and encouragement of self-help and community improvement projects; also organisational assistance to inhabitants wishing to qualify for utilities provision under Law 259 of 1956.

(xiv) Co-ordinating with the City Council and, as part of community self-help programmes mentioned in (xiii), a capacity for small landscaping works and landscaping maintenance.

(xv) A capacity for planning and design for neighbourhood improvements, at least for the initial two years.

(xvi) The provision of technical assistance to home builders to ensure that superstructures and pit latrines are built according to clearly defined standards.

C. Staffing of the Project Agency

With the range of functions noted above, the Project Agency will need a significant administrative capacity. It is crucial to keep the costs of administration to a minimum and the following staffing profile has been calculated with these two factors in mind.

The proposed El Hekr Project Agency Organisation

General Administration   Each office of the Agency has its own chief officer. All people working in that office are responsible to their chief officer. The chief officers are responsible to the Project Manager. The Project Manager is responsible to the Project Agency Board for the implementation of the policy made by the Board. The Project Manager should have regular weekly meetings of all his chief officers to review the work done and to resolve any problems that may arise. Work programmes should be decided at such meetings.

The work of the Agency can be considered to have two major sections; the offices dealing with implementation of the physical plan, and those dealing mainly with administrative and financial matters. There must be close co-operation between all the offices. To improve efficiency, the co-ordination of the physical development offices could be undertaken directly by the Project Manager; the administrative and financial offices by his deputy, or vice versa. Overall control would remain with the Project Manager.

Project Manager's Office   The Project Manager provides overall initiation, direction and control within guidelines set by the Board. He is also responsible for relationships with government and other external agencies. It is essential that this office be dynamic, as it sets the pace for the whole Agency. The Project Manager should have a deputy who, if possible, should be of a complementary discipline. For example, if the Project Manager is an engineer, then the deputy should have a legal or financial background. This will give better control and co-ordination. Support will be by information sections which will allow monitoring of progress and feedback on problems. A social worker will conduct interviews in problem cases and will, in addition, conduct surveys to establish whether residents have problems in developing their plots, and if so, how the Agency can help. Later, this section may grow into a full community development office, if this is seen to be necessary. Information on progress in plot marking, allocation and payments will be collected monthly by a filing clerk, who will also be responsible for organising and maintaining the central filing system. It is essential that all correspondence and records of discussions are filed.

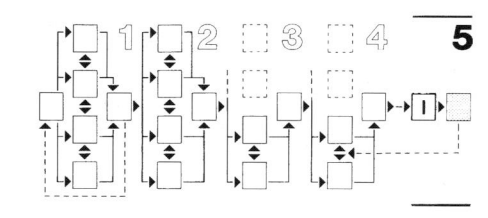

Survey Office   This office is headed by a survey engineer who is assisted in the field by assistant surveyors who are able to use basic surveying skills such as the use of a theodolite and have plan comprehension. These assistants would have tape-men (measurers) and labourers to assist them to set out plots in the new areas and measure plots in the existing areas of housing, preparing all the information required for plot registration. They will acquire over time the ability to make detailed plans for all housing areas. It is this office's responsibility to assign plots using the guidelines already approved and agreed with the Project Manager. If necessary the status of potential or existing plot holders could be verified by investigations made by the Social Worker. They will also identify illegal development in the Project area and will need to liaise closely with the Public Relations Office over the use of the police where necessary.

Civil Engineering Office   This office will have sections dealing with engineering design work and with supervision. The design section will consist initially of a qualified civil engineer and a draughtsman, and will concentrate on the detailed design and costing of the road programme, liaison with the agencies responsible for electricity, water and sewerage. As no sewerage is expected in El Hekr for at least two years, the design engineer should concentrate on the provision of standpipes. The building of the stand pipes and the necessary connections would be the responsibility of the supervision section.

A third section would deal with landscaping, and prepare detailed plans and supervise implementation and maintenance. A small staff of gardeners would be employed for this purpose under an agricultural engineer.

Building/Planning Office   This will have two main functions. First it will be responsible for preparing any detailed plans which are necessary, both for new and existing areas, and ensure that design fits within the overall planning framework. Second, it will be responsible for the provision of technical assistance to plot holders, mainly in the form of appropriate designs for the standard plot size. These will be approved by the Housing Department, and thus allow the purchase of materials at Official prices. Initially, the Architect/planner would be assisted by a draughtsman and a clerk who would handle the distribution of plans and give advice on procedures. Later the

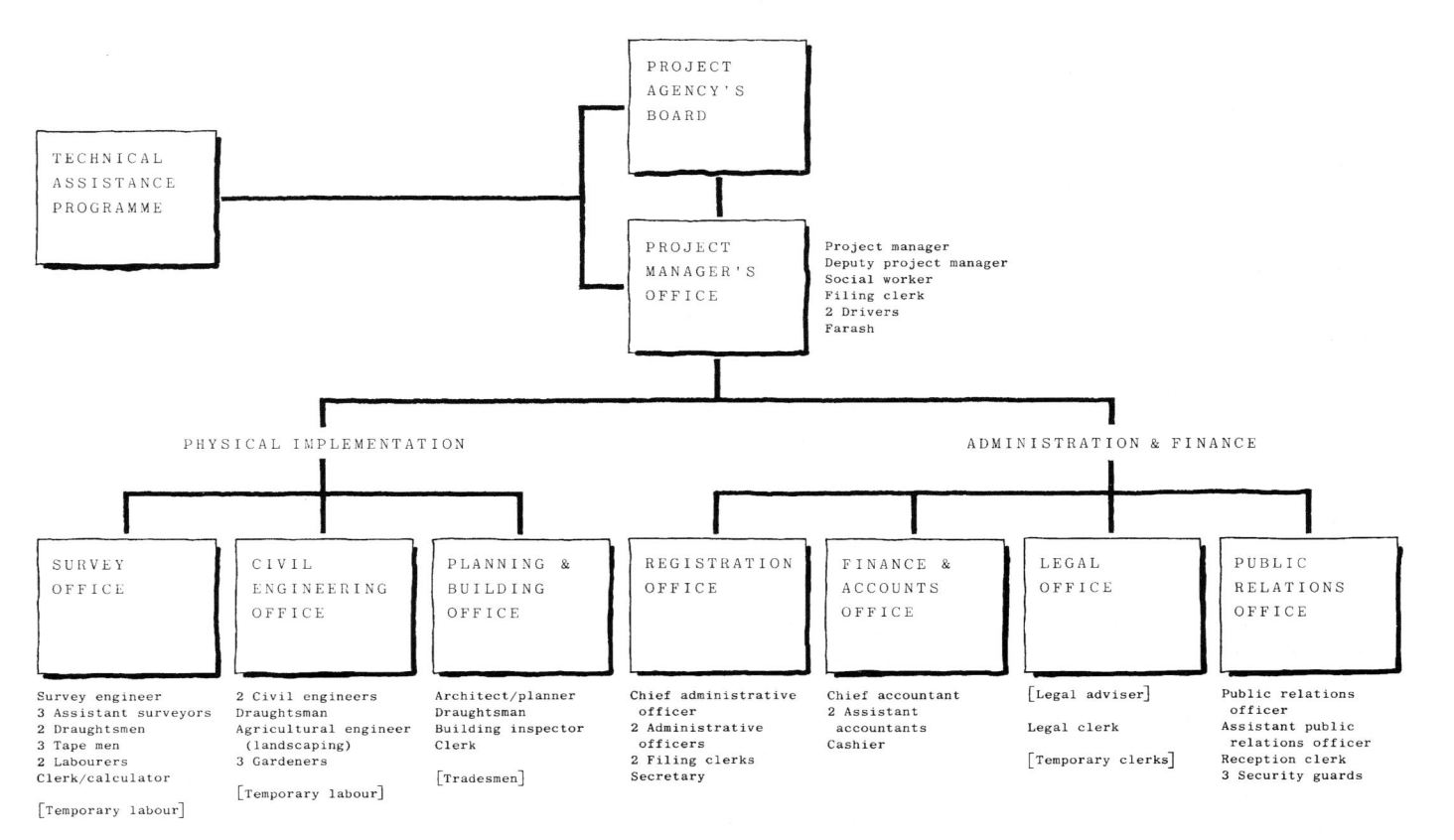

Figure 52
El Hekr Project Agency: proposed organisation

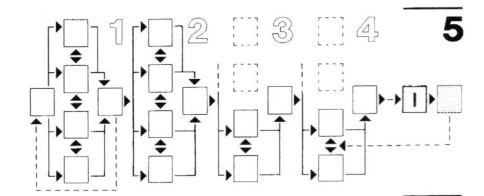

responsibility may be expanded to include the provision of advice on building techniques and materials. This would involve the employment of a small number of skilled tradesmen, who would be attached to the building office.

The Legal Office   This office, headed by the Legal Officer, will advise on all contractual and legal matters affecting the Project Agency. This will include the preparation of all contracts for plots within the Project area. Once the standard contract is agreed and the procedure established it would seem unnecessary for the Project to have a full time legal officer and this work could be done by a full time Legal Clerk in the Registration Office.

Finance Office   This office, headed by the Chief Accountant, is expected to assist the Project Manager in developing the financial plan, to negotiate loans for the Agency, and have day-to-day responsibility for the Projects finances, including receipt of payments for plots and, in 1980, the collection of amortisation payments. It will need to liaise with all the Project Offices, especially Survey and registration. Day-to-day work will include payments to staff and procurement.

Registration Office   The main functions of this office are the registration of both old and new plots and maintaining files on the plots to enable full information to be obtained on the current situation on any plot. Access to this information also means that monitoring sheets can be kept to record progress. The office works closely with the Legal and Survey offices, and after the initial period of issue of contracts, the Legal Clerk will work within this section.

Public Relations Office   This office is the 'front office' of the Project and is responsible for promoting an understanding of the aims of the Project and the services provided by the Agency. It will be responsible for preparing all publicity material and circulars to be distributed to the residents as well as the preparation of displays and signs identifying land uses in the area, for which it will require the assistance of draughtsmen from other offices. It would also be responsible for all advertising by the Project Agency. All enquiries from residents or applicants should go through this office and be directed by them to the appropriate office. The office would also be responsible for ensuring that illegal structures are not erected on the site. It would liaise closely with the local leaders in this task as well as with the police. It would be responsible for all matters of security in the office and on site.

D. Services of the Project Agency

It should be clear from previous information that it is very important for the Project Agency to operate successfully as an agent for land development and neighbourhood improvement. It is also important that the Project Agency has a capacity for the encouragement and aid of home building. Thus it is proposed that its functions include the management of a building loan programme, a mechanism for the supply of building materials at official prices and a capacity for construction advice. The nature and operation of these services is now briefly described. (It should be noted that the scope of these services depends largely on the staff available and, in the case of building loans, on funding sources.)

Building loan programme

In the absence of a national or city-level building loan programme which would be accessible to inhabitants of the Project Area, the Project Agency could set up a modest loan programme with these characteristics:

The amount of a single loan would be limited to LE400 to LE500, (the cost of reinforced concrete roofing), with payback over a medium term period (say, 3 to 6 years), charged at the Agency's own capitalisation rate (probably 7 per cent). The funds for this loan programme could come from the Agency's own revenues, from loans secured by the Agency from external sources or from a subscription programme (whereby participating inhabitants would pay into a savings fund similar to an expanded savings gama'ia[9]). Qualifications for securing such a loan would be:
(1) proof of payback ability (income test)
(2) previous subscription payments into the savings fund
(3) technical approval of the proposed construction.

It is difficult to say how extensive such a loan programme would need to be, as it would depend on the amount of capital the Agency could raise or earmark for the fund. It may be that the main constraint would be the staffing capacity of the Agency for administering such a loan programme as the paperwork involved could be burdensome.

Building materials supply

Government controlled building materials, in particular cement, could be made available at (or near) official prices through liaison by the Project Agency with the Housing Ministry and the Ismailia Housing Directorate, to promote the following arrangements:
(1) The licensing of three more official distributors of building materials
(2) The increase of the monthly materials quota for Ismailia, with a specified amount earmarked for the El Hekr Project
(3) The institution of a programme whereby settlers holding contracts in the project be allowed to buy a specified annual quantity at official prices
(4) That this routine be simplified by the Project Agency so that necessary documentation is kept to a minimum; specifically, the Agency could issue and endorse (as in the loan programme described above) a booklet, upon which the Housing Directorate can record purchases.

Technical advice

The Project Agency engineers could assist settlers in planning improvements which require structural precision (e.g. roofing). A small, fixed fee would be set by the Agency for this service. The real importance of such assistance would be that the engineers could approve the planned improvement and thus make the settler eligible for either or both of the programmes mentioned above. The Engineering Office would also provide

---

(9) *A savings system where a group pays a regular monthly amount to a fund and takes turns to withdraw money*

model plans at nominal cost to show settlers alternative ways of constructing on their plots, and could advise them on conformity with building specifications.

Besides these home-building services, the Project Agency has the opportunity to act as a vehicle for a number of community development services and self-help programmes. These services, such as adult education, birth control and nutrition information, cultural and handicraft development, and community-organization building, would be offered and run by the appropriate Government organization, but the Agency could help in promotion and organization. Since for the first time in Ismailia there would be a community level, locally based agency specifically aimed at community betterment and neighbourhood improvement, the Project Agency would provide the necessary focus and identity to the community, and may release the potential for social commitment on the part of the inhabitants, which until now has had few means of expression.

The Project Agency would also act as a representable of the community, along with Local Council members from the area, vis-à-vis the City Council to ensure that City Council services (street cleaning, garbage collection, road repair, and the emptying of pit latrines) are carried out. To the extent that these services remain substandard, after all possible pressures are applied, the Agency could, out of its own budget, improve them; perhaps by organising self-help efforts. This would be particularly important for repairing roads where, if repair is not carried out immediately, further deterioration of the road surface would result. This capacity of the Project Agency is also extremely important to ensure the regular emptying of pit latrines by suction truck. In the case of insufficient service, the possibility of 'renting' these trucks or of paying part of the daily fees should be investigated by the Project Agency.

LEGAL AND INSTITUTIONAL CONTROL

This subsection presents the proposed legal conditions and institutional processes which will control the land development activities of both the existing and new settlers. These proposals have been based on the Consultants' understanding of the existing legal context in Egypt, prevailing Government practices and capacities at the local level, and upon perceptions of desires and attitudes of the inhabitants in the Study Area.

A. New settlers: conditions of agreement for plot acquisitions – delayed freehold

The following conditions are recommended as a basis for the design of a contract for plot acquisition by new settlers.[10] The settler is the head of the household making application.

(i) The settler agrees to pay for 10, 15, 20 or 30 years, annual payments which are based upon a total value of LE, amortised at 7% annual interest. He may choose between the four time periods; at any time during this period he may change to a shorter period and payments would be adjusted accordingly. He may also choose to pay monthly, quarterly or annually.

(ii) The settler agrees to pay, upon signing, a demarcation and administration fee of LE10, and also one year's payment in advance, as deposit.

(iii) For the period chosen, the settler has the legal status of renter of the plot; if he wishes to leave at any time during this period (i.e. leaves and does not transfer the contract to another in the immediate family), he must sell his contract to another on the Waiting List[11] (see below); he is entitled to his accumulated payments and the superstructure is sold to the highest bidder, within limits set by the Project Agency. The new occupier takes on all payment obligations as if he were a new settler.

(10) These conditions do not apply to the sale of concession plots; these plots are to be sold outright following normal legal procedures

(11) In the event of there being no one on the Waiting List the contract may be transferred to another party with approval of the Project Agency

(iv) At the end of the period chosen, he or his inheritor receives freehold title for the plot, with all rights and obligations as set by law, on condition that the built superstructure meets all design specifications set out in this document or is in compliance with the building regulations. If at the end of the period, the superstructure is in violation, the settler maintains his renter status with the same restrictions of sale as described in article (iii) above.

(v) The settler agrees to occupy his plot within twelve months of signing and to continue occupying the plot with the majority of his household (see below).

(vi) The settler is not allowed, at any period or for whatever reason, to subdivide his plot (12).

(vii) The settler agrees, during the chosen period, to use his plot primarily for residential purposes. However, he is permitted to construct and operate, in addition to his habitation:
– a public place, on condition that he follows all requirements as set out by Law 371 of 1956, specifically the obtaining of a commercial permit from the Housing Directorate;
– a workshop, on condition that the workshop is not a noxious use, (Law 13 of 1904), as defined by the City Council, and that a permit is obtained as prescribed by Law 371 of 1956;
– rooms or apartments for rent.

(viii) The settler agrees, at the time of connecting his plot to public water and sewerage mains, to be assessed:
– a connection charge equal to the cost of connection;
– additional charges as may be levied by the utilities organisations.

(ix) The settler agrees that, up to the time of provision of water-borne sewerage, the construction, use, and emptying of a pit latrine by him be subject to supplementary regulations, as will be set out by the Project Agency.

(x) The settlers of Class C plots which have access to a communal space are responsible for the maintenance of that space. If the space is not maintained to the satisfaction of the Project Agency, the Agency may itself undertake the work and recoup the costs from the residents.

(12) Freehold title would include a restriction clause to this effect

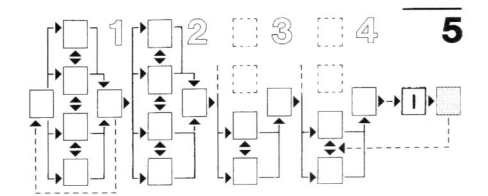

(xi) Contravention of these agreements by the settler, specifically payment default, may put the settler's plot claim in jeopardy; (delinquency conditions to be decided).

(xii) In constructing a superstructure, the settler agrees to conform with the following design regulations (or those regulations found in Law 106 of 1976 [building regulations]).
- 20% of the area of the plot shall be left unbuilt and uncovered, regardless of plot size. This open area must include at least one courtyard with a minimum width of 2.7m; additional courtyards or light wells must be at least 1m wide.
- the height of the building may not at any point exceed 1.5 times the width of the fronting street, except for stair wells and ornament. In the case of a corner plot, the width of the widest of the two streets is used for measurement. In the case of fronting streets of 9m width or less, the building may not exceed one street width. In no circumstances may a building exceed five storeys.
- the occupier is allowed to use a strip of land fronting the plot for tree-planting or a garden. This width may not exceed 1.5m on streets of 9 and 10.5m width and 2.0m on streets of 15m and 20m width. No planting is allowed on lanes of widths less than 9m. In no circumstances may walls be built around this strip, and the Project Agency may at any time acquire this strip for sidewalks, road widening or utilities installation without payment of compensation.
- enclosed balconies may be built with a maximum overhang of 1.25m, except on streets less than 9m width, in which case no balcony may be built. Balconies may not be constructed within 1m of adjoining plots.
- habitable rooms (living, dining, sleeping) must have a minimum width of 2.7m. In addition, each room (except a central sitting room) must have opening(s) of at least 0.75m^2 area giving on to the street or interior open spaces. The interior height (clearance) of these rooms may not be less than 2.7m.
- other rooms must conform to the following minimum measurements:

	Minimum width	Minimum clearance
Kitchen	1.5m	2.1m
Toilet/Lavatory	1.0m	2.1m
Corridor	1.0m	2.1m

In addition, adequate ventilation must be provided for kitchens and toilets, either by windows or roof openings of at least 0.5m^2 area.
- if stairs are constructed they must be of 1.00m width; rises may not be greater than 18cm and treads not less than 20cm.
- units for rent on upper floors must be provided with toilets (connected to the pit latrine or sewerage lines).

(xiii) The settlers of two adjoining plots may construct a common building. In this case the above design regulations apply as if the two plots are one. Before proceeding the two settlers must take the necessary steps to establish joint title to the parcels.

B. New settlers: selection of applicants and plot assignment

The Project Agency will announce, through appropriate public channels, the availability of plots and the place and date for presentation of applications. Also announced will be the following conditions[13] for screening applications:
- that the applicant be the head of the family (only one applicant per family allowed);
- that the applicant or his spouse have been a resident of the Ismailia Governorate for a minimum of 18 months[14] (this condition is waived if applicant is a current occupier of an expropriated plot in the Area);
- that the present residence of the applicant and his family be fully released upon occupying the new plot;
- that the total income of the applicant and all other members of the household does not exceed LE70 per month.[15]

In the application the following information will be requested:

(i) Applicant's name, age, identity card number, and place of employment.

(ii) Names of all members of his household who are now or will be living with him, their ages and employment, if any.

[13] These conditions should be reassessed after the first round of plot allocation

[14] This condition should be relaxed once local demand has been satisfied

[15] This type of limit is designed to avoid speculation. It may be applied to all plots but preferably only to those which are subsidised. Enforcement is difficult

(iii) Present place of residence, and proof of 18 months residence in Ismailia Governorate.

(iv) If the applicant or any member of his household has already presented an application to the Governorate for public housing, the date and number of his application.

(v) A statement of total household incomes and sources.

Applicants will be selected by Governorate committee according to these criteria and priorities:
- removal from existing plot
- household income and need
- the priorities which presently apply to selection for public housing.

Selected applicants for Round One (500 to 1000 plots) are notified; if there are more qualifying applicants than plots, the cut-offs decided by lot and others are put on a Waiting List. Notified applicants are invited to choose, within 15 days, the size of plot, whether Class A, B or C, and the repayment programme (choice of four). If a notified applicant feels he cannot build and occupy a plot within 12 months, he has the option of having his name placed at the top of the Waiting List.[16]

An applicant is allowed to submit joint preferences with other applicants for adjoining plots; in this case, as far as assignments of plots is concerned, these preferences are considered as one.

Once all selected applicants from Round One have submitted preferences as described above, the Project Agency will assign plots. In cases where certain size and class plots are over subscribed, cut-off will be decided by lot and excluded applicants will have the choice of selecting from remaining plots or being put on the Waiting List for Found Two. Settlers' preferences for plot location will be elicited on site plans; if necessary, priority for first selection will be related to the order established by lot. In all cases the Project Agency reserves the right of final say.

Once assignment is completed, the settler enters into contract agreement with the Project Agency, endorsed by the

[16] Details of the selection process are given in Technical note 12, page 120

Secretary General of the Governorate of Ismailia. The contract becomes valid upon initial payment.

In addition to the above procedure, the Agency may, if it considers it appropriate, sell up to 10% of the non-concession plots to unrestricted buyers. This would be at a higher market rate, to be decided at the time of sale. Purchasers would be required to meet full building regulations, and to complete within two years at least the ground floor of a building approved by the Agency.

C. Existing settlers: conditions of agreement – delayed freehold

The following conditions are recommended as a basis for the design of a contract for plot acquisition by existing settlers. The 'occupier' is the head of household as defined by the registration programme described below.

(i) See A(i) above.

(ii) The total amount is assessed according to the square metre area of the plot and plots Class category (see 'Project Finance' below).

(iii) The occupier agrees to pay an administrative fee of LE5 and also one years payment in advance.

(iv) See A(iii) above.

(v) If the occupier has registered his plot previously at the Amlak Department[17] or Housing Directorate his total financial obligation is reduced by the value of hekr payments he has already made.

(vi) If the occupier's plot is enlarged by street rationalisation, the total enlarged surface area is charged. If his plot is reduced by street rationalisation, he pays only for the new reduced surface area.

(vii) If his plot is reduced by street rationalisation to the extent that he must move (see third column, this page), he is given priority in new plot selection; and hekr rent he has paid up to this point can be set against his total payment obligation in the new plot. He is also compensated for the loss of his superstructure (see expropriation note below).

(viii) At the end of the chosen period, the occupier or his heir receives freehold title

(17) *Government Lands Department*

for the plot, with all rights and obligations provided that (a) the superstructure meets all building regulations let down in this document or those of the executive regulations of Law 106 of 1976 or (b) that he can prove that he is ready to meet all obligations required for Co-operative Housing loans. If conditions are not met, status is as in (iv) above.

(ix) See A(vii) above.

(x) See A(viii) above.

(xi) See A(ix) above.

(xii) See A(x) above.

(xiii) Contravention of the above agreements, specifically payment default, will result in reversion of the plot to Government leasehold, with no rights of sale of superstructure to any but the Project Agency, at compensation rates. In addition, the occupier will be unable to benefit from any of the services offered by the Project Agency.

(xiv) In expanding or rebuilding the superstructure, the settler agrees to conform with the following design regulations: (See list in A(xii) above).

D. Expropriation and compensation process

Where private (freehold) land is required it must be expropriated. If this land is unused, the expropriation routine as prescribed by Law 27 of 1956 can be applied without difficulty. This routine requires that the Governor issue and publish a declaration of expropriation in the public interest, that the owners be informed, that the Housing Directorate, through committee, assess the property value, and that the owners be given the right of appeal. This process should take two or three months.

In addition, there are certain occupied plots under hekr leasehold or simple 'hand claim' (wada' yed) which require administrative compensation for the occupier's superstructure. Such parcels must be taken for street widening, public facilities, and to allow the orderly subdivision of surrounding vacant land. These parcels are indicated on the detailed plans, but must be verified by field checking. Every attempt has been made to minimise the total amount of this form of expropriation,

and if at all possible only to take walls and out-works.

Compensation for superstructure is not required for houses built after June 1977 (date of issue of Governor's Administrative Order 402, prohibiting construction on empty land for one year), and this applies to some structures on the fringe of El Hekr.

Apart from these, the Project Agency will provide compensation for the superstructure of all needed plots, following these steps:

(i) In each block, a list of needed plots is prepared and occupiers are notified:
– that all or part of their parcel will be taken;
– that if part of their parcel is taken, and the resulting plot is less than 50m^2 or less than 5m wide, they must move;
– that if the resulting parcel is larger than these limits, the occupier may or may not choose to move;
– that if moving, the occupier is given priority in selecting a plot in the new areas;
– and that administrative compensation will be assessed for existing superstructures requiring removal.

(ii) The Project Agency will, using the compensation schedule of the Ministry of Housing and Reconstruction (a schedule used in assessing the compensation for war damage revised for inflation), calculate a simple rate (based on built m^2, type and age of structure less movable fixtures) which will be offered to occupiers. This rate should be calculated to be slightly higher than that which could be expected from a detailed assessment.

(iii) If the occupier refuses the offered amount, detailed assessment is made directly by the Housing Directorate. This process will take time, and it is hoped that most occupiers will avoid it, (it is well known that compensation by the Housing Directorate rarely reflects real value, especially for poorer structures).

Which plots will be treated first will depend upon the street widening and plot demarcation schedule. Some plots will not need to be taken for some time, and assessment of these will be left until later, though their occupiers will be informed immediately. In these operations the inspectors of the Amlak Department will be closely involved with the Project Agency.

Stage 5

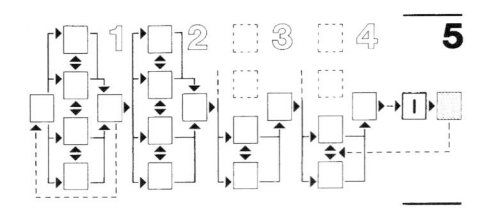

PROJECT FINANCE

It is proposed that the Project Agency be financially independent of local Government Budgets, i.e. that it will be a self-financing concern. The Agency's revenues will come from instalment payments for plot 'purchase' (both new and existing settlers), and with this revenue it will finance infrastructure improvements and also various services. In financing infrastructure improvements it will obtain loans. Supplemental income will be available in future years from the sale of certain residential and commercial plots on the open market.

In effect, the Project Agency will be undertaking infrastructure improvements to the best of its financial capabilities, and it has been assumed that it must be able to operate without any outside aid. How much of the total infrastructure needs the Agency can finance has been decided mainly on considerations of the ability to pay of the target population and also upon various practical constraints.

In the subsequent paragraphs the main features of the financing of the Project Agency's activities is proposed. It should be stressed that these proposals assume that the Project Agency has a capacity to make decisions over time and manage financing in the face of different factors which cannot be quantified at present.

Revenues and charging

The revenues of the Project Agency are derived from the available revenue generating surface area. This area is calculated to be as follows:

	El Hekr
Net area of existing plots	982,500m^2
Net area of new plots	365,700m^2
Net area of concession plots (plots reserved for future sale at market prices)	70,500m^2
TOTAL	1,418,700m^2

Both new and existing settlers will be required to 'purchase' plots through instalment payments, which when capitalised at 7% are equal to the 'price' of the plot. This price is calculated from a base plot purchase rate expressed per square metre; this base rate is proposed to be:

	El Hekr
For existing plots	1.23 LE=m^2 [18]
For new plots	1.76 LE=m^2

The 'price' of a plot is thus the base rate multiplied by the area (in m^2) of the plot, plus surcharges.

Both new and existing plots have been classified according to their commercial potential; the definition and surcharges are as follows:

In New Areas:

Class C Plots   Those plots fronting on semi-private spaces (streets of 9m width and less); no surcharge.

Class B Plots   Those plots fronting on roads of 10.5m width or more (i.e. Access, Local, and District streets); a surcharge of 0.25 LE=m^2 is added to the plot purchase rate.

Class A Plots   A small number of plots whose particular location gives them significant commercial potential; a surcharge of LE 8.00 per linear metre of frontage is added to the plot purchase rate.

In Existing Areas:

Class C Plots   The vast majority of all plots no surcharge. Class A Plots A small number of plots whose particular location gives them a significant commercial potential; a surcharge of LE 8.00 per linear metre of frontage is added to the plot purchase rate.

In existing areas of El Hekr Class A Plots have been estimated to total 6000 metres of linear frontage.

By taking the base plot-purchase rates and the surcharges for commercial potential as explained above, it is possible to calculate the actual annual charges which existing and new settlers will be faced with. For new settlers, who may choose between four different payback periods, the range of choices is quite wide, since there are also 6 different plot types and three plot 'classes'. This range of options is illustrated for El Hekr in the charging schedule shown in Table 19. For existing settlers choice is limited to four payback periods, and thus actual/annual rates will depend on the settler's plot site and the payback arrangement he prefers.

[18] LE = Egyptian Pound. 1 LE = £0.75 sterling (1977); 1 LE = £0.19 (2000).

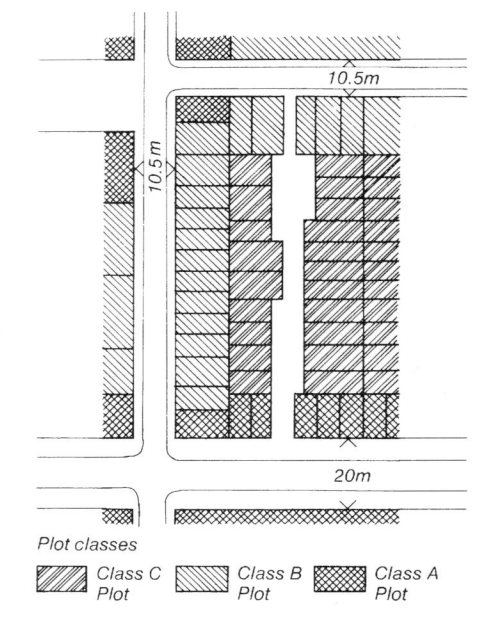

Figure 53
Plot classes

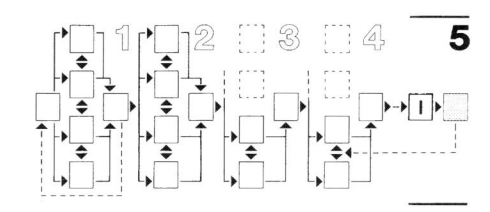

Table 19
Annual charges by plot size: El Hekr new area at 1977 prices

Plot class	Plot size	Payback period 10 years LE/Annum	15 years LE/Annum	20 years LE/Annum	30 years LE/Annum
Class C Plots	6 x 12	18.10	13.96	11.99	10.22
	6 x 15	22.62	7.44	14.99	12.78
	6 x 18	27.15	20.92	17.99	15.35
	9 x 12	28.90	22.28	19.15	16.33
	9 x 15	33.94	26.17	22.48	19.18
	12 x 12	36.21	27.90	23.99	20.44
	9 x 18	40.73	31.38	26.36	23.01
Class B Plots	6 x 12	21.26	16.38	14.08	12.01
	6 x 15	26.57	20.48	17.61	15.02
	6 x 18	31.89	24.21	21.13	18.02
	9 x 12	33.64	25.93	22.29	19.02
	9 x 15	39.85	30.71	26.41	22.52
	12 x 12	42.51	32.76	28.17	24.02
	9 x 18	47.83	36.86	31.69	27.03
Class A Plots (Except corner plots)	6 x 12	29.67	22.87	19.67	16.78
	6 x 15	34.99	26.97	23.19	19.78
	6 x 18	40.31	31.06	26.71	22.78
	9 x 12	46.26	35.66	30.60	26.14
	9 x 15	52.48	40.45	34.78	29.66
	12 x 12	59.35	45.75	39.32	33.54
	9 x 18	58.69	45.24	37.66	33.17

Note: these rates cover the 'minimum infrastructure' programme (Table 21) and additional services financed by the 'Accumulated Surplus' (see Table 22) 1LE = £0. 75 Sterling (1977). These figures are included only as a basis for comparison

Table 20
Annual charges by plot size: El Hekr existing area

Indicative plot sizes	Payback period 5 years LE/Annum	10 years LE/Annum	20 years LE/Annum	30 years LE/Annum
90m² (25th percentile plot)	27.00	15.76	10.45	8.91
128m² (median plot)	38.40	22.42	14.86	12.68
180m² (75th percentile plot)	54.00	31.54	20.90	17.83

Table 21
Capital costs of minimum infrastructure programme: El Hekr at 1977 prices

Item	Total cost (LE 1977)	Existing settlers	New settlers	Concession plots	Community facilities
1) Administration (including capitalised running costs)	94 900	55 990	34 165	4 745	—
2) Compensation	26 550	14 660	8 560	1 330	2 000
3) Markers (including surveying)	38 850	2 100	32 110	3 940	700
4) Levelling	18 400	13 060	4 780	560	—
5) Standpipes	202 165	110 000	69 000	7 500	15 665
6) Stage1 Local roads	246 810	150 500	81 310	5 000	10 000
7) Stage 1 District roads	200 290	106 370	64 905	9 015	20 000
8) Landscaping	45 000	26 550	16 200	2 250	—
Total	872 965	479 230	311 030	34 340	48 365
Share percentage	100%	54.9%	35.6%	3.9%	5.5%
Adjusted share percentage	100%	62.7%	37.3%	—	—

Expenditures

The main expenditures of the Project Agency will be investments in infrastructure elements. It is proposed that the Project Agency be responsible at least for a 'minimum infrastructure programme', the items and costs of which are shown in Table 21. In this Table all costs the Agency is likely to meet are included, and running or operating costs are capitalised. It is assumed that none of these infrastructure elements will be financed from outside sources even though most are properly the responsibility of the Governorate, City Council, and Water Authority. Also, whereas a share of total costs should be attributed to on-site community facilities and to concession plots (as shown in Table 21), it is assumed that the Project Agency must finance all costs of this 'minimum infrastructure programme'.

The Project Agency will be responsible for certain infrastructure elements and services besides those listed in the 'minimal infrastructure programme'. The costs of these items and methods of financing them are shown below in the discussion of the Project Agency's financial profiles.

In amassing the capital necessary to execute infrastructure elements it is proposed that the Project Agency take out commercial or Government loans; these loans will be serviced through the annual revenues of the Agency, as is shown below.

Stage 5

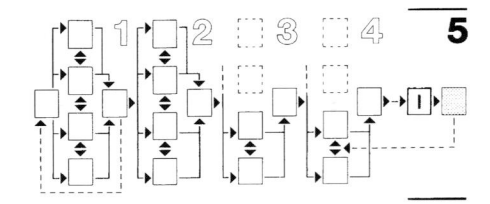

Financial profile of the Project Agency

It is important to understand how, in financial terms, the Project Agency will operate, particularly during the crucial first years. Thus five-year cash flow profiles have been constructed, even though the figures presented are only approximate; certain factors can only be known (or decided upon) after the project gets under way, for these reasons:

(1) Total annual revenues are not fixed, even assuming no arrears in repayments; since both new and existing settlers can choose different payback periods, actual revenues can be known only after the registration programme is complete. For the calculations presented here it is assumed that, on average, the 20 year payback option is chosen. It is quite possible that most settlers will pick shorter periods in order to gain freehold a little sooner, in which case the financial position (operating budget) of the Project Agency will be improved.

(2) The specific terms of any infrastructure loans to be obtained by the Project Agency are unknown at present. For the present, it is assumed that these loans will be offered at 7% for 20 years with 10% equity requirement; this is the best estimate possible, but it should be realised that more advantageous terms would increase the capital investment possibilities, and the Project Agency, as a Governorate body, should make every effort to obtain such terms.

(3) The cost of infrastructure items will inevitably vary from estimates given here; inflation will be a real problem, implying that investment in infrastructure should take place as soon as possible. On the other hand the Project Agency will be further investigating the cheapest and most acceptable solutions for infrastructure items such as standpipes and road surface treatment and there could be significant savings. Further savings could be realised by encouraging community labour contributions to infrastructure works.

(4) There is a possibility (which will be actively encouraged) that local organisations will supply or fund some elements of infrastructure during the early years of the Project. For example, the Water Authority could provide standpipes, or the City Council could provide roads and municipal services. Any such contributions would naturally affect the Project Agency's role in the first years of operation.

Taking these factors into account, likely five-year annual financial profiles of the Project Agency have been constructed and are presented in Table 22 (El Hekr). The main features are:

(i) Large revenues accruing in the first year are due to registration fees imposed on settlers (LE5 for existing plots and LE10 for new plots) and to the obligation on settlers to pay one year's installment in advance. (The registration fees are exclusive of stamp duties).

(ii) It has been assumed, for illustrative purposes, that in El Hekr a second group of new plots (667 plots of Neighbourhood 14) is sold at the start of Year Four, and that these plots are serviced in Year Three from a loan taken out at midyear.

(iii) Large infrastructure loans are raised by the middle of Year One, covering the minimum infrastructure programmes as set out in Table 21. The money obtained from these loans allows the immediate servicing of all existing plots and the new plots of Phase One (for El Hekr 964 plots).

(iv) An initial working capital of LE100 000 is assumed which is paid back, with interest, at the end of Year One.

(v) A nominal number of concession plots are assumed to be serviced in Year Four and sold in Year Five.

Referring to Table 22, it can be seen that at the end of Year One a considerable balance is obtained, of which LE20 000 is reserved for Year Two as working capital. The remainder is termed the Accumulated Surplus. In future years this Accumulated Surplus increases steadily as there is a constant excess of revenues over expenditures. This gives the Project Agency the opportunity to finance further infrastructure investments; for example, in Year Two the El Hekr Project Agency could take out and support over time an additional infrastructure loan with a

Table 22
Simplified five year cash flow: El Hekr (LE 1977)

Year	1	2	3	4	5
1) Working capital at start of year	100 000	20 000	20 000	20 000	20 000
2) Revenues					
Existing settlers:					
Fees	27 500	—	—	—	—
Year advance on plot purchase rate	108 840	—	—	—	—
Instalments on plot purchase rate (assuming to start mid year)	54 420	108 840	108 840	108 840	108 840
New settlers:					
Fees	9 640	—	—	6 770	—
Year advance on plot purchase rate	20 505	—	—	13 440	—
Instalments on plot purchase rate	10 250	20 505	20 505	33 944	33 944
Sale of concession plots	—	—	—	—	2 000
Total revenues	231 155	129 345	129 345	162 994	144 784
3) Expenses					
Administration	7 150	7 150	7 150	7 150	7 150
Other current	2 500	2 500	2 500	2 500	2 500
Infrastructure loans (starting mid year)					
Equity	71 866	—	5 880	—	—
Repayment	30 525	61 050	66 045	66 045	66 045
Project office complex	30 000	—	—	—	—
Servicing concession plots	—	—	—	1 600	—
Repayment of loan on initial working capital	7 000	—	—	—	—
Total expenses	149 041	70 700	81 654	77 295	75 695
4) Balance	82 114	58 645	47 691	85 699	69 089
5) Accumulated surplus	62 114	120 759	168 450	254 149	323 238

1 LE = £0.75 sterling (1977)

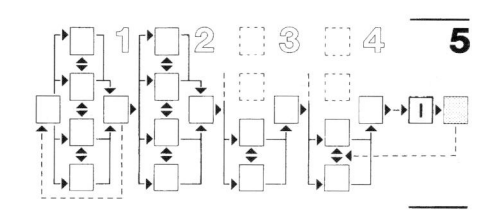

maximum value of LE678 000 which could be used for a variety of purposes, such as:
– installation of full street lighting if the Electricity Board is unwilling to undertake this (cost LE130 000);
– advance servicing of all remaining new plots (cost LE215 600);
– construction of high standard road and sidewalks over the whole site, representing 60% of the full costs of Stage 2 Local roads.

Alternatively, the loan could be used for other purposes, such as the endowment of a building loan programme, the installation of piped water to individual plots on an experimental basis, or the subsidisation of pit latrine emptying services. While the Accumulated Surplus could be set aside for the future installation of mains water and sewerage, it would only be sufficient to meet a part of such investment costs; significant subsidies would still be required. This situation is discussed in detail in subsequent paragraphs.

In conclusion, it is important to emphasise that the Accumulated Surplus when capitalised, gives the Project Agency very significant financial leverage for improvement programmes.

Future financing and the question of subsidies

As shown above, the charges imposed on settlers, and thus the revenues of the Project Agency, only cover a minimum level of infrastructure provision. They do not cover any of the costs of the waterborne sewerage system and only a small fraction of the costs of water to each plot. In addition, a portion of the costs of high level road provision is not covered. These items are assumed to be financed, at least partly, by external subsidies. It is proposed that the Project Agency explore all avenues to obtain outside financing for these elements, and the approach which should be taken is suggested in the following paragraphs.

By far the largest items requiring subsidised financing are water and sewerage serving individual plots (which must be installed together). Technical constraints mean these services can be introduced to the sites only in the future,

Table 23
Estimated network costs for water and sewerage provision (LE 1977)

	Reticulation network	On-site trunk lines	Total
El Hekr:			
Water	612 200	370 000	982 200
Sewerage	1 109 300	510 000	1 619 300
Total	1 721 500	880 000	2 601 500

1LE = £0.75 Sterling (1977)

thus the Project Agency will be aiming at encouraging their installation at an as yet undetermined future date. It can be assumed that when installed the inhabitants will be able to pay for connection charges; thus attention must be focused on network costs, and these are given for El Hekr in Table 23. As can be seen the sums are quite large, but the Project Agency could use its financial leverage to propose a sharing arrangement with outside funding sources. It is not possible to estimate just how much this leverage will amount to, since it will depend on (1) the revenues to be generated from the future sale of concession plots on the open land market, and (2) the amount of Accumulated Surplus which could be devoted to water and sewerage. The total available will probably not amount to more than 30% for El Hekr. This is not a large proportion of total costs (and total costs will inevitably rise over time due to inflation), but even the offer of contributing a small fraction gives the Project Agency leverage in contacts with funding sources.

Although the Project Agency, through its revenues, could finance full road provision, the problem is that this requires the paving of many streets that would have to be dug up in order to lay sewerage and water lines. Thus these higher-order roads could not be put down immediately, and the greater the delay in road building, the more road funds would be consumed by inflation. In effect this higher standard of roads is tied to sewerage and water provision, and the Project Agency will have to weigh the alternatives as they present themselves. If full financing for water and sewerage networks is obtained, the supplementary funds of the Agency could be fully used to finance very high standard streets and pedestrian ways. But if it must devote this

'bargaining capital' completely to obtaining water and sewerage, then the financing of these higher standard streets will have to come from its normal source, i.e. the City Council.

Decision point: future phases

As soon as Phase One new plots are taken up, the Project Agency must decide whether to carry on with the next phases under the same minimal infrastructure provision and the same charging arrangements as presented here or whether to try a different approach. If at this time sewerage and water mains have been installed in neighbouring areas, the possibility of provision of sewerage and water before plot acquisition (or within a year or two of acquisition) becomes very attractive. However, where there is ample demand for plots in the next phase and no sewerage and water can be provided immediately, then the Agency's policy will be to open up the new area for settlement with minimal provision.

Stage 5

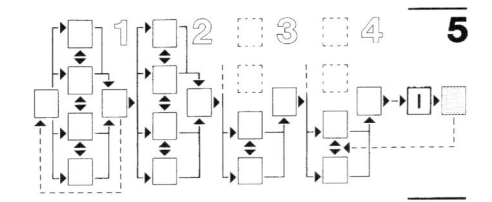

PROJECT MONITORING

The Project Agency in El Hekr will have, over time, to make decisions based on information and realities which are presently unknown. Thus, there will be a need for a monitoring function which will focus on the following areas:

(i) Each year the financial position of the Project Agency will need to be reviewed; infrastructure and utilities provision already executed will be compared with phasing and levels of provision guidelines set out in this report, and plans for the next year's executive programme will be drawn up based on: a) available funds, both from revenue and from possible loan financing b) current costs which must be met in the next year, including administration and repayment of outstanding loans, and c) realistic contractors' estimates of costs for infrastructure works.

ii) The Ismailia land market must be monitored to decide the best time, price and strategy for putting reserved residential and commercial plots on the open market for sale. Expected revenues from this sale must be considered in (i) above and (iii) below.

(iii) The Project Agency must monitor, and in fact actively encourage, the establishment of basic sewerage and water networks, and coordinate the availability of these networks with actions in (i) and (ii) above. It must also monitor national changes in the sewerage and water tariff structures, and also possible subsidy funding for water and sewerage.

(iv) The Project Agency must also be aware of changes at the national or local level with regard to new home-building loans so that the inhabitants of the Area will have every opportunity to avail themselves of these new programmes. In a similar fashion, the Project Agency must monitor changes in Government policy with regard to availability and pricing of building materials.

(v) Finally, the Project Agency must, based on preferences of settlers in the First Phase, adjust the plot size mix and also the charging schedules for later phases. Any administrative or technical problems encountered in the first phase should be recognised and avoided in later phases. In short, the Agency must learn from experience.

These monitoring functions can be termed 'internal' in that they are carried out by the Project Agency so that it can better administer the project as an on-going concern. There is also the opportunity for 'external' monitoring, i.e. the monitoring of the project in El Hekr as a basis for the repetition of the approach elsewhere in Ismailia and throughout Egypt. Much of what the Project Agency will learn through monitoring its own operations can be usefully applied in the establishment of similar projects, particularly in terms of client preferences, infrastructure costs, administration and the success of community involvement. Certainly there is a good argument for a professional monitoring capacity to be attached to these projects to collect and analyse such information.

Perhaps of all the facets of these projects it is the institutional or administrative arrangements which are most crucial, particularly since they are designed here to be straightforward, to fit in with existing local administration, and to have minimal reliance on central control. Their success, even if partial, should indicate the feasibility of this approach on a wider scale. Certainly, at least on the city level, the experience gained by the manager and staff of the El Hekr project, and also that of the various local Government offices which will be dealing with these projects, can be profitably used to start other such projects in Ismailia, using as a basic guide the Ismailia Master Plan. Since the load on the El Hekr Agency will be significantly reduced after the first few years, the transfer of personnel to new projects will be possible, with the El Hekr Agency continuing in a reduced role as a community service institution.

IMMEDIATE STEPS

The Consultants propose in this subsection the preparations and steps necessary for the early establishment of the Project Agency and commencement of project operations.

Immediate steps can be divided into two periods. Period One can be called the 'approval period', which started with the submission of the Draft Final Report on February 15, 1978. At the same time as the Draft Final Report was submitted to the Advisory Committee for Reconstruction, the preliminary Arabic summary of the main proposals was presented to the local Government bodies concerned. At the same time as the Advisory Committee prepared its comments on the Draft Final Report, the local officials responded by making suggestions which were immediately incorporated in the proposals. This was done through a series of meetings at which the project was discussed point by point, and an agreed revision arrived at. This was then put before the Governorate Local Council for approval and for the necessary enabling orders to be prepared by the Governor's Office.

At the same time as approval is being obtained at the local level it is necessary to secure the 'inception capital' for Period Two. The importance of this funding cannot be overemphasised.

One more step must be initiated during Period One, and this is the request for a Ministerial Decree waiving certain of the requirements under Law 52 of 1940, as suggested in the Advisory Committee's latter of 13 December 1977. Before the Governor of Ismailia can issue the enabling orders this Ministerial Decree must be published.

Period One will end when the 'inception capital' is available and the Governor's enabling orders are issued. How long this period will last is uncertain, but if efforts are made with a spirit of co-operation it is not unreasonable to expect it to end by May 15, 1978.

Period Two begins immediately, and under the direction of a representative of the 'inception capital' funding source working directly with the Secretary

Stage 5

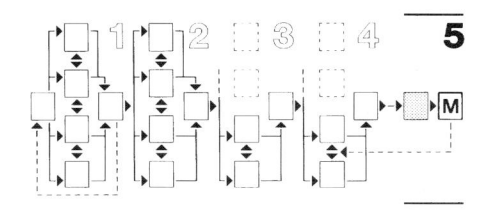

General's Office of the Governorate and the Executive Agency for Reconstruction of the MHR, the following steps should be initiated:

(i) Immediate construction and furnishing of the project office at El Hekr.

(ii) Recruitment of key personnel. The most important is the Project manager and office heads, followed by the professional staff. This will involve discussions in Ismailia with sources of secondment, and also interviews with applicants.

(iii) Production of pre-cast concrete markers and a small team of surveyors and workmen, installing these markers in the Project Area. Priority for markers should go to the community centre and social facilities reserves, followed by main streets and new plots of Phase One. In this operation inspectors of the Amlak Department will be closely involved, particularly on the fringes of El Hekr.

(iv) At the same time as (iii) above, certain levelling by bulldozer will be carried out in El Hekr, particularly at the community centre site and to make the project office easily accessible by automobile.

(v) It may be necessary to have a certain amount of preliminary publicity circulated in the Project Area which, in conjunction with the aforementioned presentations and briefings with local representatives, should make the inhabitants well aware of the meaning of the Period Two activities.

Period Two ends with the Project Agency opening its doors for business. If at all possible, this opening should be aimed for June 30, 1978, as this is the date of the expiration of the Governor's Administrative Order 402.

Technical notes for implementation

Several of the 'Technical notes' included in pages 99 to 132 at the end of the Manual are produced as a direct result of experience gained in implementing the El Hekr project in Ismailia (for background see Appendix 1, page 133). They relate to techniques and work processes which are not normally covered in technical training. They do not attempt to be comprehensive. For example, it is assumed that standard survey techniques are known, but that it is useful to describe an 'intermediate' land survey.

The Technical notes specifically concerned with implementation are as follows:

Technical note 2   Implementation: land marking in improvement/upgrading areas
Technical note 4   Implementation: measuring plots
Technical note 7   Implementation: design of layouts related to setting out
Technical note 8   Implementation: design and location of site markers (monuments)
Technical note 11   Implementation: public relations and public participation
Technical note 12   Implementation: selecting applicants
Technical note 13   Implementation: enforcement
Technical note 14   Implementation: technical assistance to plot holders
Technical note 19
Technical note 21
Technical note 22
Technical note 24

Monitoring

'Monitoring' is the process by which information on key aspects of the projects can be collected regularly to enable the project management to control effectively the running of the project. The information collected can be divided into two types:

● *Information which is easy to collect directly*, for example, the number of plots surveyed/handed over/paid for per month, or the amount of construction/layout of utilities. This enables the Project manager to compare actual progress with that planned, and to be able to define where delays occur and so to look for their causes. The production of this information should be built into the normal routines of the agency. For example, plots allocated can be entered on a summary sheet which can be totalled monthly and provide part of a regular review of progress.

● *Information which must be collected by use of specific techniques,* for example, social surveys. This type of monitoring is necessary to determine what is actually happening within the plots, for example, are the families of the type the Project is trying to help? Are they improving their houses? How fast? What materials are they using? What problems do they have? This information is important if the agency is to ensure that it meets its objectives. Monitoring allows the programme to be revised as new problems arise. Certain basic information, for example family size, occupation, income and length of residence can be obtained from application forms. Further information must be collected by means of sampling. All survey work involves time and money.

Stage 5

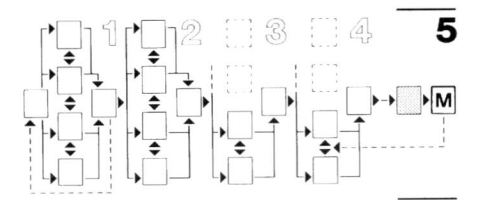

In the early stages of a project it may well appear to be a waste of time and irrelevant, or, at least a luxury. As the project progresses, however, its value will be seen and there is a great importance in having started the monitoring at the beginning of the project as this enables the situation which existed before the work started to be assessed.

It is vital, in designing the monitoring programme to ask the questions 'What information is needed?' and 'Why is it needed?' This will ensure that the information collected is relevant.

'Monitoring' and 'evaluation'

'Monitoring' is used here to mean the regular collection and analysis of information related to the development of the project, with the objective of being able to manage effectively the project. This is normally undertaken by the Project Agency itself, and will be dealt with here. 'Evaluation' normally means a broader, long term study of the project to determine how effectively it meets its objectives and how the project has affected development in the city as a whole. This would often be carried out by an outside body, for example consultants or a university department. The results may require a basic review of the project.

The two items overlap to a considerable extent, but are defined here because they often arise when dealing with international lending agencies such as the World Bank. Monitoring and evaluation can also be carried out by community based organisations and individuals.* Refer also to Technical note 19. The techniques for social survey are described in Technical note 1 (page 100). Table 24 identifies the major questions, the reasons for asking them and the means of collecting the information.

Table 24
Monitoring: information requirements

Information required	Reason	Method of collection
New plots Number of plots planned Number of plots surveyed Number of plots delivered *Improvement areas* Number of plots rationalised Number of plots marked Number of plots paid for	To be able to know the rate of work achieved, to identify areas of work which are slower and which may need more staff, to be able to forecast when the next stage of work is required.	Record on summary sheets, as work is done. Record on key plan (1: 2500, for example) to enable visual record to be made.
Consolidation of plots Time since delivery Areas walled Areas roofed Room numbers Materials Value Problems	To be able to measure the rate of construction, check on type of construction and find out what problems there are which the agency can help overcome, for example by loans for materials, simpler procedures, better information.	Sample questionnaire survey together with sketch plans (Technical note 1). Approximately six month intervals to measure progress until buildings are substantially complete
Infrastructure provision, *lengths installed by month*	To check on rate of progress.	Plot in outline the next stage of proposed work, plot on plan, work in design/in progress/ completed stages with dates.

---

* UNCHS (1994) Community Participation Training Programme, Nairobi.

Technical notes

Page	Technical note
100	1 Socio-economic surveys
114	2 Implementation: land marking in improvement/upgrading areas
116	3 Carrying out intermediate land surveys
116	4 Implementation: measuring plots
117	5 Preparing sketch plans using aerial photographs
117	6 Interpreting aerial photographs
118	7 Implementation: design of layouts related to setting out
118	8 Implementation: design and location of site markers (monuments)
118	9 Estimating land values
119	10 Pricing of plots
120	11 Implementation: public relations and public participation
120	12 Implementation: selecting applicants
122	13 Implementation: enforcement
122	14 Implementation: technical assistance to plot holders
123	15 Appropriate map and plan scales
124	16 Assessing layout efficiency
125	17 Reference tables: discount factor, present worth of an annuity factor, capital recovery factor
132	18 Standards
133	19 Participation in problem identification, planning, design and implementation
136	20 Capacity building
137	21 Land tenure policy options
140	22 Site development and design briefs
142	23 Innovative sanitation systems
144	24 Use of geographical information systems (GIS)

Technical note 1
Socio-economic surveys

Role of socio-economic surveys

The approach to project preparation out lined in this Manual depends on a good understanding of how the housing system operates. This means that it is not sufficient to know that there are a certain number of families in a certain number of houses, but rather that we should understand what function those houses have in relation to those families, how will they fit the needs of the families, what actions families can take to find housing which meets their needs and what problems stand in their way. Thus for example, a young, expanding family with an irregular income and living in expensive rented accommodation are likely to be dissatisfied because they have little security, and their problems will increase with time. They may prefer a cheap plot of land where they can build a simple shelter as this would allow them to save and improve their situation over time. Another, older family, with steady income and a pension may prefer to stay in good quality rented accommodation. The normal social surveys and statistical analysis used to simplify and help to understand the housing situation would not normally differentiate between the two families, and yet their needs, hopes and actions may be quite different. It is not possible to interview every family in order to understand their needs and problems, but it is possible to interview a sufficient number to understand the main processes and the importance of individual problems – and then to design proposals which will allow these processes to operate when they are beneficial and overcome them when they are negative. These detailed interviews are called here case studies – they allow understanding of the real situation and help ensure that proposals are relevant. At a later stage proposals can be tested against the case studies by asking the question 'are the proposals relevant to the needs of this particular family?'

Relationship between surveys

The survey methods described have validity individually, but their strength is in their use together, as described below:

1. Review of existing information *and selective meetings allows target population and likely problem areas to be identified. This is the appropriate level of survey at Feasibility study stage, though a limited number of* case studies *may also be useful if they can be carried out.*
2. Scanning surveys *are designed on the basis of (1) and allow a statistically significant sample of information to be collected.*
3. *The scanning survey forms a framework for the systematic selection of* case studies *which are the key to understanding the operation of the housing system and the priorities and wishes of the target population.*
4. *Further information may be obtained, if required, from* detailed surveys.
5. *Once the project is being implemented it is important to* monitor progress and problems. Forms of the above surveys can be used aimed specifically at identifying problems which can be tackled by the implementing agency, for example provision of small loans to allow initial construction may be necessary, if difficulty in starting is due to lack of funds. Lack of progress could also be due to shortage of materials, lack of skills or bureaucratic delays. *It is important to understand the problems before attempting solutions. Solutions must also, of course, be related to the Implementing Agency's financial and personnel capacity.*

Survey types and examples

Notes are provided on the main survey types, together with detailed examples where these are relevant.

Review of existing information

Before carrying out original surveys, it is advisable to review any existing information which may be available from census surveys, published research and government agencies. This should be checked to see that it is up-to-date and relevant to the specific conditions of the project.

Selective meetings

These usually involve meetings with people or agencies with a special understanding of the housing problems and needs of the target population. These may include local community or municipal leaders, representatives of special interest groups, long standing residents, experienced researchers or administrators. This can provide information on specific points in the project. The advantage of this method is that it requires no special preparation, does not involve laborious or expensive analysis and can be conducted as and when necessary (i.e. during Feasibility or Detailed Project Studies). Initial conclusions drawn may, however, have to be checked by other survey methods.

Public meetings

These are particularly useful in obtaining a quick, if approximate, impression of the housing problems and needs of the target population. To be successful they require efficient planning and skillful management. They also need to be planned carefully so that those attending are aware of the purpose of the meeting, its agenda and how the subject affects them. Notes should be taken of the proceedings, but individuals contributing to the discussion should not be identified in a way which may make them feel their interests could be adversely affected. In general, such meetings are useful to obtain reactions to proposals and it is hoped popular approval of them. Participatory rapid appraisal techniques can be used to aid this process (see Technical note 19).

Scanning surveys

These provide a systematic means of surveying a large population or area. Scanning surveys use a simple questionnaire to interview a selection of people. The questionnaire should be kept short and cover key questions only.

An example of the questionnaire used in the scanning survey in Ismailia is reproduced on page 104. The forms are produced in such a way that answers can be easily ticked off in the field, and easily tabulated and analysed. The descriptions of house types in question (1) should relate to local types, and use local names.

Case studies

Case studies are comprehensive, in-depth interviews with persons or households. They allow a much deeper understanding of the problems and wishes of households to be obtained than scanning surveys, and also allow important aspects such as the 'housing system' to be studied. By 'housing system' is meant the complex process of renting/sharing/moving/saving/building, by which families are housed. Only by understanding this complex process can a project be designed to fit into or remove problems in the existing housing system. For example; a family may deliberately live in crowded but cheap conditions because by doing so they can save enough to build their own house. Removal of this option may mean the family can never have their own accommodation. Case studies can also be used to identify social structures and local leadership.

Each case study takes considerable time as it must allow the interviewee to determine the pace of discussion. Skillful, independent interviewers will be needed who can understand the position and problems facing the target population and win their confidence. These interviewers will need to be carefully briefed so that they can gently steer discussion along the desired lines and focus on the most relevant information. The selection of case studies should be either random within the population being studied, or selected if a particular group, for example the lowest income group, is of most importance. The scanning survey should be the framework for the selection of case study households.

The number of cases will depend on resources, but should be sufficient so that the total number will provide a representative view. For example 15 case studies were carried out in El Hekr, Ismailia, out of a population of 40 000.

The final case studies will be in the form of narrative documents several pages long. They, or edited versions of them, should be read by designers and decision makers as a means of exposing them to sets of 'real' situations to which the project proposals must be relevant. An example of such an edited case study is included on page 111.

Detailed surveys

The need for detailed surveys will depend on the results of earlier surveys. These are carried out to provide detailed information on important aspects, such as sanitation or household income at a statistically significant level. They may concentrate on particular areas identified as having problems in earlier surveys.

As the surveys are normally longer, they require more skill on the part of the interviewers to ensure good response. See example on page 112, of part of the detailed survey carried out in a section of the low income area in Ismailia which was being studied for potential upgrading. It indicates the degree of detail which might be required when there is very little information on the subject. In this case the existing water and sanitation system needed to be understood before any proposals to improve it could be made. The provision of piped water and water borne sewerage systems is extremely expensive and a thorough understanding of existing systems and their problems may indicate alternative solutions.

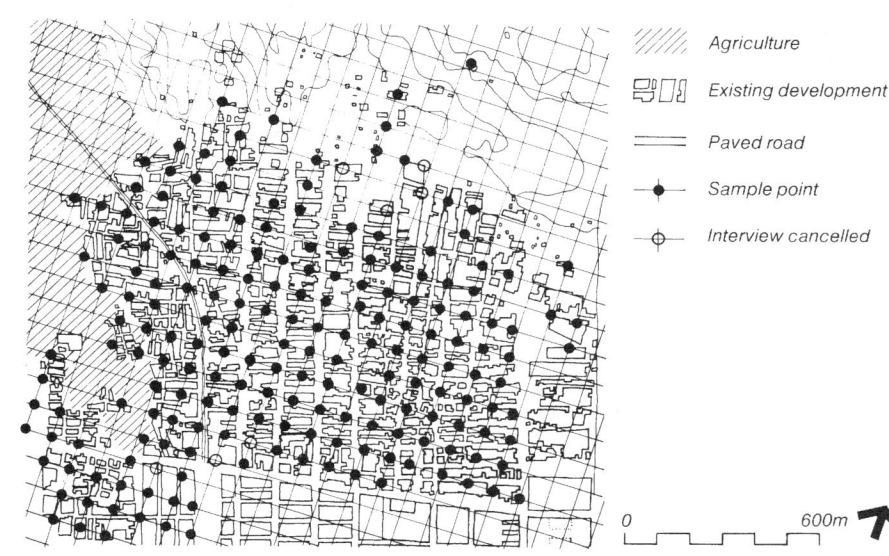

Survey practice

There are a number of important points on the conduct of surveys which are common to the different types of survey. To avoid repetition, the common elements are described.

- The objectives of the survey must be clear, i.e. for what purpose is information being collected, and from what groups is it being collected.
- The resources available in terms of time, personnel, ability to train, and capacity to analyse the material, must be known, and the scale of survey must relate to these limitations. As an example, for the scanning survey reproduced on page 104, 6 interviewers took 8 days to complete 350 interviews.
- Surveyors must be trained and tested in the field before the main survey and spot checks made during the survey. The interviewers should be trained to lead the person interviewed naturally through the questionnaire topics. The attitude and personality of the surveyors will probably be more important than their previous training.
- Material to be collected should be checked with all potential users of the survey results.
- Except for case studies, questions should be framed to allow simple, factual answers. Preferably these should be capable of being recorded on a grid or box for ease of use in the field and for later analysis (see example, page 104).
- The total number of questions should be kept to the minimum possible.
- There should be some cross checking of key information such as household income.
- The survey questionnaire or guide must be tested in use by the surveyors. Modification may be necessary in length and content depending on respondents reactions.
- Selection of respondents must be random, though there may be 'stratification' or selection of groups of particular interest. Methods of selection vary. One is to select every 10th, 20th, 40th or so house in each street, depending on the sample size. Another method is to superimpose a grid map, or air photo, on the area and to select the dwelling nearest to the intersection of the grid lines (see Figure 54). The size of the grid will depend on the size of sample required.
- Sample size should be a balance between what is possible given the resources available to collect and analyse data, and the number required for statistical significance.

Figure 54
El Hekr household scanning survey: sample distribution

Technical note 1

Analysis of social data

The system of analysis of social data will vary according to the method of collection and the purpose for which it was collected. For most analysis sophisticated techniques are not necessary and the Manual concentrates on simple, useful methods.

First, before the analysis of the data begins, checks should be carried out to ensure that the data is 'good'. By 'good' is meant that the questions have been answered correctly. Clearly, it is not always possible to know whether the truth has been told, but sometimes cross checking the answers given to particular questions, such as household income and expenditure, indicates whether the questions were understood and answered properly. Clearly a respondent who claims that the household's expenditure is regularly far greater than their income is either exaggerating their expenditure or not recording some other source of income. The person doing the analysis must decide which information to include and which to exclude.

Methods of analysing the data collected in scanning surveys and in detailed surveys are similar. However, the mechanics of sorting out the data will vary depending on the number of questions and the size of the sample. For small surveys, where the number of questions and interviewees are limited, data analysis cards can be used. Each questionnaire is placed on one card and the answers for each question are pre-coded (i.e. when the whole range of likely answers to a particular question is recorded and given a code). The person analysing the data can then sort the cards for each question according to the response. A more sophisticated variation of this can be used when the number of interviewees is large but the questions few. Then it is possible to use cards with numbers corresponding to holes which have been punched around the periphery of the card as illustrated in Figure 55. Each code (answer) for a particular question corresponds to a particular hole. When that answer is given the top of the hole is clipped away. To sort the data, then, only requires a knitting needle or some other long straight object which fits the original hole. All the cards are put onto a pack and then the needle is inserted into the particular hole. The cards are shaken, and all those which have been clipped fall out. These can then be added up and recorded in the tables showing the number of respondents giving that particular answer. This is a very simple form of card sorting and works on a similar principle to mechanised card sorters and computers.

The recommended method of sorting the answers given in larger surveys is to use analysis sheets. This is only of use for questions where answers can be coded. For example it could be applied to the household scanning survey (see page~104). However, it should be noted that some questions are subdivided into different parts. If this is the case, then each part should be treated as a separate question. Alternatively, it may be possible to aggregate all the answers and so give a total. For example, question 4 of the household scanning survey asks the number of households at that address. It then breaks down the answer both into the number of households in each tenure category as well as the number of people this represents. In that question, it is possible to have 8 answers. Alternatively, one answer could be given using simply the total number of households at that address, irrespective of their tenure. Once all the information has been recorded on the analysis sheets (Figure 56) work can begin in totalling particular sorts of responses.

When preparing the basic tables showing the numbers of respondents giving each sort of answer to a particular question, it may be decided to group certain similar responses. For example, rent levels may vary from LE 1.00 to LE 33.00 per month. The coding may include codes for 'LE 25–30' and 'over LE 30', but the number of each is so small that it may be decided to record the two categories as one.

It is advised that the tables presenting the numbers giving each type of answer should include the 'frequency' expressed as a percentage of the total possible replies. An example is given in Table 25.

To understand better the situation in the survey area and to begin to have some insight into the nature of change, comparisons between answers to different questions may be required. This is done by taking those that gave a particular answer to one question and seeing how they answered another question. Answers are divided according to the agreed (coded) range. An example is given in Table 26.

Table 26 gives the person doing the analysis a lot of information. It suggests that while the majority of households live in rented or other accommodation (61 per cent), those born in Ismailia are more likely to own their own house than to be tenants (60 to 40 per cent). It also suggests that renters, are almost twice as likely to have been born outside Ismailia than in it. Note that it only *suggests* rather than proves.

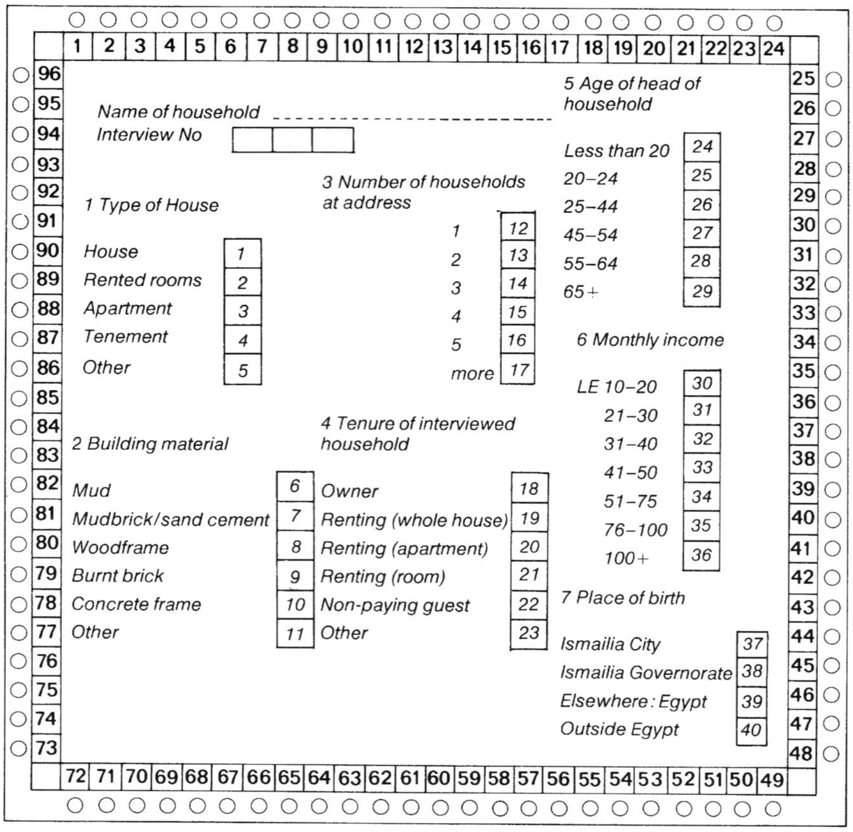

Figure 55
Analysis card: example

Technical note 1

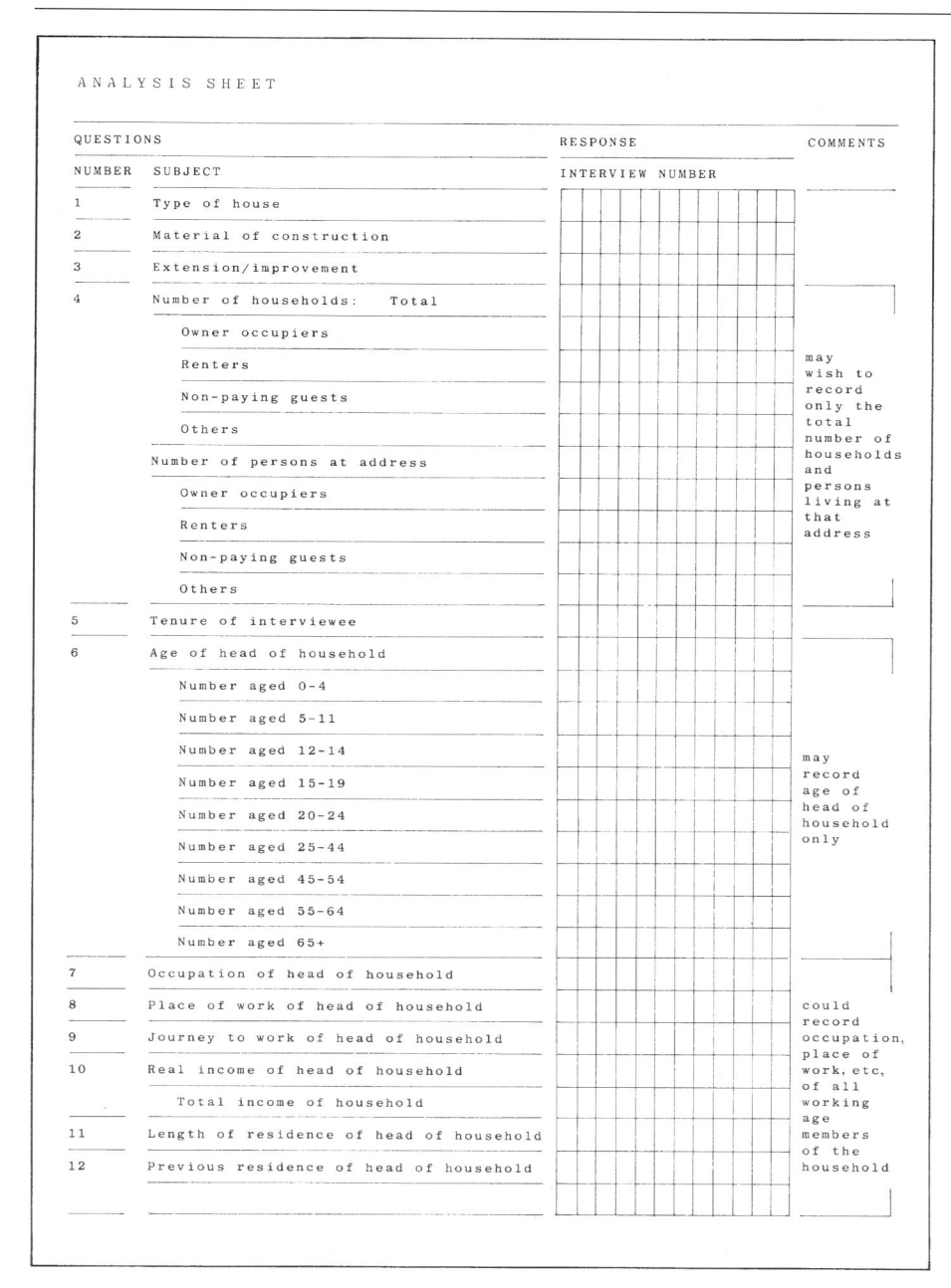

```
ANALYSIS SHEET

QUESTIONS                                         RESPONSE              COMMENTS
NUMBER  SUBJECT                                   INTERVIEW NUMBER
1       Type of house
2       Material of construction
3       Extension/improvement
4       Number of households:    Total
            Owner occupiers
            Renters                                                     may
            Non-paying guests                                            wish to
                                                                        record
            Others                                                      only the
        Number of persons at address                                    total
                                                                        number of
            Owner occupiers                                             households
            Renters                                                     and
                                                                        persons
            Non-paying guests                                            living at
            Others                                                      that
                                                                        address
5       Tenure of interviewee
6       Age of head of household
            Number aged 0-4
            Number aged 5-11
            Number aged 12-14
            Number aged 15-19                                           may
            Number aged 20-24                                           record
                                                                        age of
            Number aged 25-44                                           head of
                                                                        household
            Number aged 45-54                                           only
            Number aged 55-64
            Number aged 65+
7       Occupation of head of household
8       Place of work of head of household                              could
9       Journey to work of head of household                            record
                                                                        occupation,
10      Real income of head of household                                place of
            Total income of household                                   work, etc,
                                                                        of all
11      Length of residence of head of household                        working
12      Previous residence of head of household                         age
                                                                        members
                                                                        of the
                                                                        household
```

Figure 56
Analysis sheet: example

For most of the analysis required for the planning process, setting out as shown above, with percentage frequencies, is sufficiently clear to enable the acceptance or rejection of any hypothesis or assumption to be tested: very rarely will it be necessary to test the relationship statistically, and if it is, it is important to ensure there is sufficient understanding of the outcome.

The most frequently used statistical terms likely to be required for the analysis are 'mean' and 'median'. The 'mean' is the average and is found by the total of all the responses divided by the number of respondents. In the example given below showing the distribution of household size, the average size of those households recorded is approximately 4.8 members.

Number of respondents = 199 (Table 25)
Total number of members of
households = 958
   (assuming the number of people in the
   7–9, 10–15 and 15+ groups are 8,
   12.5 and 16 respectively)

Average size of household = $\frac{958}{199} = 4.8$

The 'median' is the mid point on the distribution of responses. Take the total number of responses being considered (in the above case 199), add one and halve total (100). Then add consecutively the number of responses given to each reply, starting with the smallest answer (in the above case, 1). Add the number given to each consecutive answer till the addition takes the total over the half total. Go back one (3) and add this answer to the proportion of the next response represented by the half total multiplied by the range covered by the response. In the example of household size.

$$M = 3 + \frac{100 - (5 + 15 + 32)}{67}$$
$$= 3 + \frac{100 - 52}{67}$$
$$= 3 + \frac{48}{67}$$
$$= 3.72$$

The difference in this example between the 'median' and the 'mean' (or average) is more than one. This difference can be very important when considering such items as earnings or expenditure. For example, it is possible that one or two very rich families living in a poor area give a false impression of the wealth of the people. On the whole, therefore, 'medians' are more useful than averages ('means') in the analysis of the survey data.

Table 25
Simple analysis: household sizes by percentage occurrence

Size of Household	Number	Percentage
1	5	2.5%
2	15	7.5%
3	32	16.0%
4	67	33.5%
5	29	14.5%
6	27	13.5%
7–9	13	6.5%
10–15	8	4.0%
15+	3	1.5%
No Reply	1	0.5%
Total	200	100.00

Table 26
Simple analysis: cross tabulation

Place of birth		Tenure					
		House owner		Renter/ other		Total	
		No.	%	No.	%	No.	%
Born in Ismailia	No.	30	67	20	29	50	43
	%	60		40		100	
Born outside Ismailia	No.	15	33	50	71	65	57
	%	23		77		100	
Total	No.	45	100	70	100	115	100
	%	39		61		100	

Technical note 1

Another less frequently used term, the 'mode', refers to the most frequently occurring response. In the example above, this would be 4 which was the answer given by 33.5 per cent of the population. It is often helpful to present the information graphically. For example, the distribution of household size could be demonstrated using columns on a graph, each of which represents a proportion of the total population or the actual number, as illustrated in Figure 57.

Alternatively, the data can be presented using a linear graph. This is especially useful if a comparison is required, for example, showing the difference in the distribution of income between the population covered by the survey and the national or city income distribution. The example from the El Hekr Project, Figure 58, shows clearly that income distribution amongst the target population was heavily biased towards incomes of less than LE 400 per annum than was found in the national urban income distribution figures.

A third way of presenting information, which is most effective for public meetings or exhibitions is to present the distribution as segments of a circle in a 'pie chart'. For example the distribution of employment could be shown as in Figure 59.

The size of each segment should be the same proportionally as the numbers in each category. The whole area of the circle represents the total population.

Finally, a word of warning to all involved in the analysis and presentation of data, it is essential that certain basic questions are kept in mind. First, who needs the information? Second, is the analysis necessary and helpful in the formulation of the plans? Third, are the conclusions drawn soundly based on sufficient information, and can they be explained by other external factors?

Example of household scanning survey form, five pages

The scanning survey forms used in Ismailia are reproduced in a reduced facsimile form. They are printed in both English and Arabic to aid analysis by consultants. Most answers can be recorded by a tick in the appropriate box which allows for greater speed of interview, and of later analysis.

The subjects included in this example relate to the purpose of the project, i.e. housing, work and income.

Figure 57
Bar graph: household size

Figure 58
Linear graph: annual household income

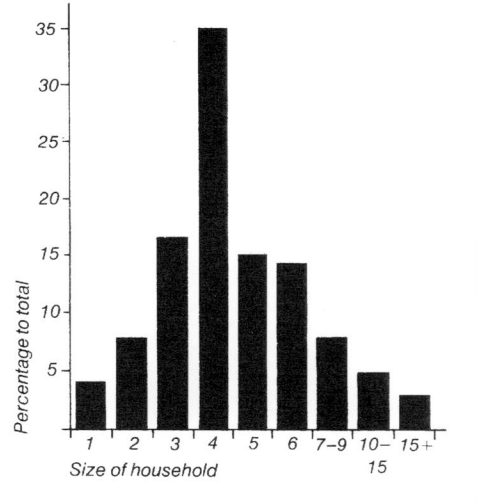

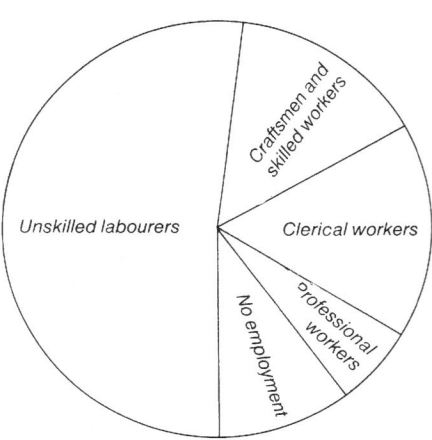

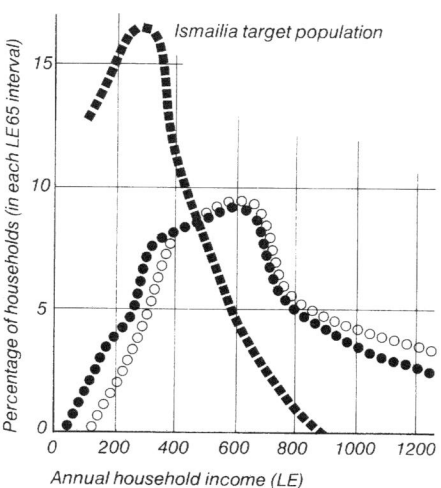

Figure 59
Pie chart: employment distribution

Technical note 1

2

4. Number of households at this address — ٤ ـ عدد الشقق فى المبنى

	No. of Code hshds leave blank	No. of Code persn leave blank		التربيز الأفراد	عدد التربيز الشقق	عدد
Number of households which are owner-occupiers					عدد الشقق التى يشغلها الملاك وعدد الافراد	
Number of households which are renting					عدد الشقق التى يشغلها المستأجرين وعدد الافراد	
Number of households which are non-paying guest type					عدد الشقق التى يشغلها أسر دون دفع أجر باعتبارهم زوار وعدد الافراد	
Other (specify)					غير ذلك (حدد)	

5. Household Interviewed — ٥ ـ الوحدة السكنية للبحوث

What type of tenure does the Household have? — ما هو نوع الوحدة السكنية التى يشغلها الساكن ؟

Ownership	1	ملك
Rental (house)	2	بيت مستأجر
Rental (apartment)	3	شقة مستأجرة
Rental (room)	4	حجرة مستأجرة
Non-paying guest	5	مكان مشغول بدون ايجار (زوار)
Other	9	غير ذلك

3

6. Personal details of members of the household interviewed — ٦ ـ بيانات اساسية عن افراد اسرة البحوث

a) Age — أ ـ السن

Head of Hsehold: 9 8 7 6 5 4 3 2 1 — رب الأسرة

0-4		اقل من ٤ سنوات
5-11		٥ ـ ١١ سنة
12-14		١٢ ـ ١٤ سنة
15-19		١٥ ـ ١٩ سنة
20-24		٢٠ ـ ٢٤ سنة
25-44		٢٥ ـ ٤٤ سنة
45-54		٤٥ ـ ٥٤ سنة
55-64		٥٥ ـ ٦٤ سنة
65+		٦٥ فأكثر

b) Relationship to head of hsehold — ب ـ العلاقة برب الأسرة

4

7. Occupation — ٧ ـ المهنة

Head of Hsehold: 9 8 7 6 5 4 3 2 1

a) Employee Government	permanent / regular temporary / irregular	أ ـ يعمل بالحكومة	دائم / موقت
b) Employee Public Sector	permanent / regular temporary / irregular	ب ـ يعمل بالقطاع العام	دائم / موقت
c) Employee Private Sector (formal)	permanent / regular temporary / irregular	ج ـ يعمل بالقطاع الخاص الرسمى	دائم / موقت
d) Employee Private Sector (informal)	permanent / regular temporary / irregular	د ـ يعمل بالقطاع الخاص الغير رسمى	دائم / موقت
e) Employee Agriculture	permanent / regular temporary / irregular	هـ ـ عامل زراعى	دائم / موقت
f) Family Business	permanent / regular temporary / irregular	و ـ يعمل لحسابه الخاص بالمنزل	دائم / موقت
g) Pedlar	permanent / regular temporary / irregular	ز ـ بائع متجول	دائم / موقت
h) Individual Craftsman	permanent / regular temporary / irregular	ح ـ عامل ماهر	دائم / موقت
i) Own Farm	permanent / regular temporary / irregular	ط ـ ملاك الاراضى الزراعية	دائم / موقت
j) Unskilled Unspecified	permanent / regular temporary / irregular	عمال غير مهرة	دائم / موقت
k) School		طلبة المدارس (حدد المرحلة)	
l) Other specify	permanent / regular temporary / irregular	غير ذلك حدد	دائم / موقت

5

Head of Hsehold: 9 8 7 6 5 4 3 2 1

8. Place of work — ٨ ـ مكان العمل

Local (El Hekr)	فى نفس المنطقة (الحكر)
Ismailia (Centre)	وسط البلد (بالاسماعيلية)
Ismailia (other, specify)	مكان آخر بالاسماعيلية
Other specify	غير ذلك (حدد)

9. Journey to work — ٩ ـ طريقة الذهاب الى العمل

Company bus	اتوبيس الشركة
Bus	اتوبيس عام
Walk	سيرا على الاقدام
Bicycle	دراجة او موتسيكل
Collective Taxi	تاكسى بالنفر

10. Real Income — ١٠ ـ دخلك كام فى الشهر

LE 25 per mth	اقل من ٢٥ جنيه
LE 26-39 per mth	٢٦ ـ ٣٩
LE 40-69 per mth	٤٠ ـ ٦٩
LE 70 per mth	٧٠ جنيها فأكثر

11. How long have you lived at this address in El Hekr? — ١١ ـ بقالك اد ايه ساكن فى العنوان ده ؟

1 yr	اقل من سنة
1 - 2 yrs	١ ـ ٢
3 - 5 yrs	٣ ـ ٥
5 - 10 yrs	٥ ـ ١٠
10 yrs	١٠ فأكثر

12. Where did you live before? — ١٢ ـ كنت ساكن فين قبل كده ؟

El Hekr (locality)	فى نفس المنطقة " الحكر "
Ismailia (city)	بالاسماعيلية (حدد)
Other (specify)	غير ذلك (حدد)

Technical note 1

Case study guide

The case study guide used in Ismailia is reproduced to show the structuring of questions and the range of information obtainable. The guide is in three parts: the first consists of a summary with basic personal information, present housing details and a brief family history; the second part relates to families originating outside the city and covers socio-economic and housing conditions outside the city, with more detail on the circumstances of arrival, including housing and employment. The third section covers all households and includes: 1) socio-economic conditions of the family 2) housing situation 3) community organisations and 4) household priorities and expectations. This structure and the detailed aspects covered need to be modified to meet the specific project requirements.

The relationships between sections of the case study are illustrated in Figure 60.

```
A   SUMMARY
    Household
    characteristics
    Personal details
    (tabulated)
    Background/history
    of household
```

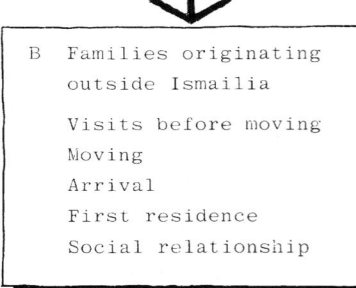

```
B   Families originating
    outside Ismailia
    Visits before moving
    Moving
    Arrival
    First residence
    Social relationship
```

```
C   All families
    Reasons for moving
    Locality description
    Building history/costs
    Social economic
      characteristics and
      changes
    Community life
    Expectations and
      priorities
    (Greatest detail
      relates to housing in
      the project area)
```

Figure 60
Structure of case studies

Comments to interviewer

The following is not a questionnaire. It is not to be used during the interviews with members of the household.

This guide can be used in three ways:
- *as a guide that the interviewer would read to prepare himself for the conversation*
- *as a check list to check the completeness of information collected during the conversation*
- *as the outline for writing the case report.*

Interviewers should encourage a free flowing conversation, while attempting to cover all the points required by the guide. The central concept of the case study is a chronological account of the social, physical and economic characteristics relating to the housing histories of the selected householders. The way in which the information is collected depends on the conversational flow, and the guide is to be used as a guide to content rather than sequence.

Residences of the household outside Ismailia can be described at a coarse level of detail, as indicated in the guide. Residences in Ismailia should be dealt with at a greater level of detail, along the lines of the Housing, Socio-Economic and Priority sections of the guide, but these sections need not be followed exhaustively. It is anyway likely that the level of remembered detail will be less than for the current residence. For residences in El Hekr the questions asked in the three sections should be asked fully. For all residences in Ismailia the three sections described in the guide should be used as a model.

Residences in the evacuation period should be dealt with at the same level of detail as residences outside Ismailia.

Questions in the section of the guide dealing with arrival in Ismailia should be dealt with fully if the initial address in Ismailia is in El Hekr. If the initial address is elsewhere in Ismailia the level of detail should be less (but still using the guide questions as a basis).

It is particularly important to encourage the members of the household to express their expectations, priorities and attitudes. It is recommended that the interviewer talks to more than one member of the family. Also more than one visit may be necessary to collect the needed information.

The guide

A   Introduction

Following is a summary of the guide, which should form the basis of a summary of the information collected, to be written on completion of the case study. The summary should follow the tabulated basic personal data, in the final writing-up of the case study.

A1.   **Summary of basic household/housing characteristics**

A1.1   Household or family type:
a. Category (nuclear, extended)
b. No. of persons in the household
c. Basic age/sex, composition.

A1.2   General character of change the family is undergoing.

A1.3   Socio-economic status of the household:
a. Occupational
b. Income
c. Educational
d. Family economy type (receiving, autonomous or contributing).

A1.4   Socio-economic mobility of the household – (including future expectations):
a. Occupational
b. Income
c. Educational.

A1.5   Residential location of the household.

A1.6   Residential itinerary of the household by localities and subsystems, beginning with migration date from rural or other area; include the anticipated future moves:
a. Tenure of each place (including current cost)
b. Shelter quality for each place.

A1.7   Brief summary of the supply/demand match/mismatch:
a. Present
b. Past.

A1.8   Principal improvement priorities:
a. Dwelling
b. Locality.

A1.9   Ability, willingness to contribute own resources for the improvements.

A2.   **Basic personal data**

This information is to be tabulated when the case study is written up. This is particularly important in areas where the selection of case studies has not had the benefit of a preceding survey.

A2.1   Place and date of birth of household head.

A2.2 Place and date of birth of his/her wife/husband.

A2.3 Present household composition:
a. Age, sex, education and occupation of all the members in the household
b. Their relationship and permanence of residence in the household.

A3. **Background history of the household** (Head of household and spouse only)

This section need not be completed in detail. It would be helpful to know something of the points listed below:

A3.1 What did his/her father do for a living (describe job/work relations/position relative to means of production and productive process)?

A3.2 If his/her father was/is in the monetary economy, how much approximately did he earn, did this change throughout life at home of respondents. Describe principal events and trends. Did he support anyone else besides his nuclear family?

A3.3 What was his/her occupational/prosperity/income/educational status at time of leaving home?

A3.4 Where are brothers and sisters now?

A3.5 Did they/do they (respondents) live in either parental home as man and wife? (For how long, principal reasons, describe accommodation, satisfaction)

A3.6 Why did he/she move from the parental home?

B. **Questions for those households with origins outside Ismailia**

The following points should be covered in the conversation, and they should be covered for each place of residence occupied by the formed household before moving to Ismailia. In writing up the sequence of residences should be organised chronologically ending with the most recent.

This section of the case study need not be emphasised, and a short paragraph summarising the information listed below is all that is required.

B1.1 Locality and Governorate (name village/town, describe characteristics, urban, rural, special economic characteristics).

B1.2 Dates of residence.

B1.3 Size, age, and sex composition of household at this address.

B1.4 Obligations to family in place of origin (or family obligations to household).

B1.5 Occupation(s) of members of household.

B1.6 Income(s) of members of household (including unearned income if any) also regularity/irregularity of income.

B1.7 Education – (all members of household).

B1.8 Housing:
Situation   Specify characteristics, for example, was it a peripheral settlement to a major city, or agricultural village.
Location   Distance from major urban area/city centre.
Tenure, cost   Details of rent paid as type, details of ownership – cost, loan cost if any, contractual arrangements, security of land tenure.
Standards   Description of the house materials, size, utilities (in house and in the vicinity of the house).

B1.9 Family expenditure distribution (food, clothing, housing, utilities, transportation, appliances, education, savings, other).

B1.10 General advantages and disadvantages of living there.

B1.11 Housing priorities at this point (location, tenure, shelter, standards, other).

B1.12 Why did they move from this place?

B2. **Visits to Ismailia before moving**

This section and each of the following four sections) is concerned with the initial move to Ismailia.

When the address is in El Hekr, full details are required, but when the initial address is elsewhere in Ismailia information is required in less detail, points to cover in less detail in these cases are marked with an asterisk (*).

B2.1 Describe for household head and spouse, whether married or not:
a. When was the first visit made here and why?
b. How many more visits were made before deciding to come and why?

B2.2* For any longer periods of stay of household head and spouse describe:
a. Work
b. Housing
c. Supported family back home
d. Or being supported by them.

B3. **Moving to Ismailia**

B3.1* Did he/she (the household head) have any contacts before coming?
a. Who were they, what relationship?
b. What did they do or where did they work?
c. Where did they live (describe place by type, rent and tenure)?

B3.2* Did any contact provide him/her with accommodation upon arrival?
a. Who was this contact?
b. Where did they provide accommodation?
c. What kind of accommodation was it (in their own dwelling, sub-rented room or dwelling, rented room or dwelling, piece of land)?
d. Did he/she pay rent, how much?

B3.3* If contact did not provide accommodation:
a. Did they help in finding any, and if so, how?
b. Did they suggest where permanent or temporary accommodation could be found?

B3.4 Did the household head have a job lined up before coming to Ismailia?:
a. What was it?
b. How did he/she find it or who helped him/her?

B3.5* Did any contacts (specify whom):
a. Find a job for household head before or after arriving?
b. Actually provide a job? If so, where, how long after arrival, and how did household head support himself/herself until then?

B3.6 Did the household head have a particular skill that he/she thought would find him/her a job easily?

B3.7 Did he/she have any other questions relative to settling down in the city and what were they?

B3.8* What were the sources of information for these questions?

B3.9 General priorities upon arrival:
a. What did he/she most hope to get out of coming to Ismailia?
b. How long did he/she expect to stay?
c. What did he/she most want to spend money on?

B4. **Arrival in Ismailia**

B4.1 Was the household head married upon arrival?
a. If so did he/she bring the family along?

B4.2* Did the household head have any obligations:
a. To his/her nuclear family back home?
b. To parents or other family members?
c. To others, and why?

B4.3* Did the household head receive any financial support:
a. From the nuclear family back home?
b. From parents or other family members?
c. From property or other investment resources?

B4.4* What was his/her attitude towards various responsibilities, such as:
a. Support of spouse and eagerness to bring him/her to the city?
b. Need to become financially independent, if supported by family?
c. Maintenance of property or other investment resource belonging or partially belonging to him/her, now or possibly in the future?

B4.5* What was the most important or the first, second and third most important thing he/she tried to do upon arriving?

B4.6* Description of job upon arriving:
a. How household head got it and how long after arriving or between jobs.
b. What and where was the job?

B4.7* If self-employed, describe in detail:
a. How the activity was chosen.
b. How household head set it up and got it started.
c. What help he/she received, from whom and under what conditions.

B4.8* Did the household head like the job?
a. If so, what did he/she like about it?
b. If not, why not?

B5. **First residence in Ismailla**

B5.1 How did the household head find a place to stay?
a. Who suggested it or other places?
b. Did he/she have a choice?
c. If so, why this place instead of others?

B5.2* Locality description:
a. Indicate population density and land use.
b. Describe utilities services and facilities of the locality.
c. Describe predominant types of dwelling and standard.

B5.3* Was the place a dwelling unit or a piece of land?
a. Number of rooms, area per person.
b. Quality of construction.
c. Was it temporary, semi-temporary or permanent?
d. Did they make any additions or modifications to the unit of land?

B5.4* Did they rent or buy or begin to buy the place?
a. How much was the monthly rent or payment?
b. Were the rent or payments a severe burden?

c. Did they try to compensate by, for example, sub-renting?

B5.5* If the family built the dwelling themselves:
a. Where did they get the materials?
b. Where or from whom did they hear about them?
c. What was the total actual cost of the dwelling unit, excluding the land value?
d. How much time did they spend building it?

B5.6* Describe the utilities (in unit, adjacent or on street) in detail, indicate on family, several families or communal use:
a. Water supply (e.g. standpipe, hand pump, well, piped tap, tanker).
b. Sewage (e.g. pit latrine, bucket/barrel, w.c. to public sewer).
c. Electricity (e.g. domestic mains supply, street lighting).

B6. **Social relations at time of arrival in Ismailia**

B6.1* With whom was the household head most friendly?
a. Relatives in Ismailia?
b. Friends made in the vicinity of the dwelling?
c. Work friends, initial contacts, others?

B6.2* When the household head moved to Ismailia:
a. Did he/she lose contact with old friends?
b. Form new relationships?

B6.3* Did he/she keep in close contact with
a. Relatives in Ismailia or back home?
b. Neighbourhood friends?
c. Did he/she want to keep in contact with them?

B6.4 Did close neighbours help or exchange favours (e.g. child care, money lending, food).
a. Did their relatives?
b. Did any other?

C. **Questions for all household**

The following four sections make up the most important part of the case study and these sections should be asked about every residence of the household in Ismailia. Again, for addresses in El Hekr the greatest possible detail is required but for the rest of Ismailia less detail is necessary, but the information collected should be on the basis of the following points. Points which can be dealt with at a lower level of detail are marked with an asterisk(*).

C1.1 Why did the family leave its previous residence?
a. Where did they move to?
b. Why did they choose this place?

c. How long did they stay there (approximate dates)?

C1.2 How did household head find a place to stay?
a. Who suggested it or other places?
b. Did he/she have a choice?
c. If so, why this place instead of other possibilities?

C1.3* Did he/she like the place?
a. If so, for what reasons?
b. If not, why not?

C1.4* Locality description:
a. Indicate population, density, general character of area i.e. predominantly residential, or commercial, industrial or a mix of these.
b. Indicate one-way distance, travel time and cost to centre of city and/or other large employment centre.
c. Indicate utilities, services and facilities of the location (describe and specify mail, police, garbage collection, characteristics of and distance to schools, sports fields).
d. Describe environmental quality and community life.
e. Describe predominant types of tenure.

C1.5* Tenure:
a. If rented, what type of contract, length of contract, frozen or unfrozen rent (rent control).
b. If owned, describe type of contract for house and land. (How and on whom registered).
c. Describe security and transferability.
d. If owner was other than occupant, who was the owner of land and house?

C1.6* Standard:
a. Was the place a dwelling unit or a piece of land?
b. Describe: number of rooms, m^2 under roof, m^2 under roof per person, m^2 of open space shared with other families (how many?).
c. Describe utilities (in unit, adjacent or on street) in detail: water (delivery and storage); sewer; streets (paved or not); street lighting; electricity.
d. Describe type and quality of construction: walls; floor; roof; windows; others.
e. Describe improvements, enlargements and other changes to the shelter.
f. Was the construction big or small? Was it temporary, semi-permanent or permanent?

C1.7* If the dwelling, including on-plot utilities and connections, was built by the family:
a. Did they build all of it by themselves? If yes:
b. Give detailed time used for different components, if no:
c. Did they have the general contractor to

do the whole work (including purchase of materials, contracting of labour) and to deliver the finished dwelling? What contractor? What conditions? Who were the workers? Details.
d. If some parts were subcontracted and the rest self-build – which parts? Who was employed, on what conditions, time? How did they find the workers?
e. What work was done by the family members themselves?
f. Did they get any unpaid help? From whom?
g. Did they get any help that was not paid in money (for example in kind, or exchanged for other services)?

C1.8* If they purchased the materials themselves:
a. Where did they get materials and hear of them?
b. What materials were easiest to find?
c. Which materials did they prefer and why?
d. Who delivered the materials? How much did it cost?
e. How much did the materials cost?
f. Was it official or black market price?
g. How long did they wait for official materials?
h. If 'black market' – what price difference?
i. Did they apply for official materials? If not, why not?

C1.9* Permits and formalities
a. What kind of permits did they need, what other formalities were necessary (for land title, for construction of dwelling and utilities, purchase of materials)?
b. How much did these formalities cost (one by one)?
c. How much time did they take?

C1.10* Problems, causes of delay, what could have been done to finish quicker?

C1.11* If the contribution was done by steps describe each stage:
a. What did it consist of?
b. How much time did it take, when was it done?
c. Repeat all the questions in C1.7, C1.8 and C1.9 above for each stage.

C1.12* The land that the dwelling was built on:
a. Was it shared with other families?
b. Was this family alone in it?
c. If they owned it, did they sub-rent a part to other families?

C1.13* Price – Investment:
a. Describe initial down payment and length and quantity of monthly payments for the land. If El Hekr: How much is paid and since when?
b. Describe initial down payment for the house. (If incremental construction, give sequence, timing and costs by stage and total).
c. Describe other investments in the house and locality improvements.

C1.14 Cost–Monthly:
a. Rent (specify for what).
b. Taxes (specify for what).
c. Utilities (specify as in Cl.6c, in detail).

C1.15 Equity:
a. Sale value at the end of residence.
b. Key money, in case of rent.

C1.16* Decision distribution pattern: How and why decisions were made? (About the choice of plot, type and sequence of construction, choice of materials, which work done by themselves, which contracted).

C1.17* Maintenance and Repairs:
a. Who was responsible for the maintenance and repairs of the dwelling house and utilities?
b. Were any repairs done, by whom, what was done?
c. How were the repairs financed?
d. Did the owner get a 'reconstruction loan'? How big, on what conditions?
e. Did he get any other loan for the repairs, improvements? How big, on what conditions?
f. How often is the sewage facility (e.g. latrine) emptied/maintained?

C1.18* Did household head borrow money to buy land, materials, to pay the labourers?
a. How much, from whom and for what?
b. At what interest rate or basis for repayment?
c. Where did he/she hear about money lending source?

C1.19* Other sources of finance used (like sale or jewellery, sale of land in the home village, sale of other property)?

C1.20* Was purchase, or construction at any point a 'joint venture' with anybody? Give details.

C1.21 Give main advantages of living in this dwelling; the main disadvantages of living in this dwelling; main problems.

C1.22 Give main advantages of living in this locality; the main disadvantages; main problems.

C2. **Social and economic characteristics of the household throughout its housing history in Ismailia**

C2.1* How many people were living in the household?
a. Who were they?
b. Employment and education of all income contributors, including: location of job; type of business; description of job; regularity (regular benefits including social security; time and cost of travel to work one-way) means of transportation.

C2.2* Did they have these jobs before moving to this location? If they found them after moving:
a. How were they found?
b. Did anyone help them find jobs? If so, who, and in what way?
c. Did household head or main contributors have a skill that helped them get a job?
d. How did the household support itself between jobs?

C2.3* Total family (household) income:
a. Distribution of family expenditures (how much for food, clothing, transportation, shelter, health, saving?).
b. Non-housing investments; appliances, utensils, tools, furniture, display, vehicles.
c. Any income generating, or expense saving, activity within the dwelling or plot area.

C2.4* Non-monetary income:
a. Did they cultivate anything or have any farm animals at this location?
b. Did they bring or receive any goods from place of origin?
c. Any other non-monetary income?

C2.5* Relatives in the city:
a. In the immediate neighbourhood or in the metropolitan area. Who and where?
b. Frequency of visits?

C2.6* Shopping:
a. Where did they do their basic shopping and with what frequency?
b. Time and cost of travel (one way) to shop. What means of transportation?
c. On a typical shopping day, how much did they spend, and on what?

C2.7* Other regular movements within the city of all household members: Who, where to, for what, time and cost, means of transportation, frequency?

C2.8* Describe forms of recreation or leisure:
a. what were they?
b. Describe cost, travel time and cost, frequency and means of transportation.

C2.9* Was anybody interested in improving housing conditions, utilities and environmental quality?
a. Local representatives; local, municipal, state or federal government; neighbours; church groups; political parties; family itself.
b. What changes and by whom?

C2.10* Describe communal life, mutual aid – organised and unorganised. Did any household members ever contribute labour or money towards improving the community?

If so, who did and in what way?

C3. Community life and organisation

C3.1 What formal and informal organisations exist (the emphasis should be on the present address and names and addresses of contacts would be very helpful to the simultaneous studies of social organisations in the project areas) in the area, what are their purposes, membership, activities?

C3.2 Who are the leaders of these organisations, formal and informal, how are the leaders selected/appointed? To whom are they accountable, can they be dismissed?

C3.3 How are the organisations, formal and informal, structured territorially and personally? What is the area covered by the group or unit? How big is the area covered by a group or unit? How big is the unit? How many members have a leader? Any hierarchy or leadership?

C3.4 Is there a hierarchy of power in the area, does a small group of families exercise control over more local organisations and leaders? (For example, it is understood that a small number of families 'control' El Hekr who are they and how do they work?).

C3.5 How have community problems been solved (i.e. provision of water/ electricity)? (In one example, revealed by the study of building materials' suppliers, a group of neighbours organised a collection of 50 piastres per household to improve a road. A second collection was attempted later for further improvements but permission for the collection was refused. What are the conditions for 'permission to collect'?).

C3.6 Are there examples of collections being made for common purposes? If so what for, who 'led' the collection~ how was it organised, and with what problems? What happened with the funds collected?

C3.7 What are the 'rules' for the common use of private facilities, for example, water pumps located on private plots, and how were the conditions agreed? Which other private facilities are used by more than one family and on what conditions?

C3.8 How were the street lines and plot limits building agreed at the settlement time, is any control attempted/exercised?

C3.9 How significant are relatives in house and environmental improvements, in physical or financial help?

C3.10 Are there ways of obtaining 'informal' loans, through relatives or others?

C4. Expectations and priorities

This information should be collected for each past residence and for the present residence. Many of the points will be difficult to cover for past residences, and the interviewer must decide in each case on the value of attempting to gather past information in this section, against concentrating on the present. It may be useful to start the conversation with the present case, and having gathered the information to try to go back to previous addresses – the points are complex and more easily understood for the present address.

Members of the household (i.e. parents and children) may differ in their priorities, and for the current address the interviewer should learn about such possible differences.

C4.1 What is the most important thing he/she would like to achieve, do, get, during this year, next five years, next ten years?

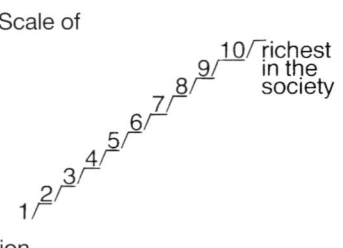

C4.2 Scale of expectation

poorest 1 / 2 / 3 / 4 / 5 / 6 / 7 / 8 / 9 / 10 richest in the society

a. Where are they now?
b. Where were you when you moved to this residence? (If recent then ask for ten years ago).
c. Where will you be in 10 years?
d. Where do you expect your eldest son to be?

C4.3 Where do you expect to live in 10 years from now?

C4.4 What do you think your dwelling will look like, tenure, type, where?

C4.5 Where do you expect your children to live? What kind of dwellings?

C4.6 Priorities for expenses and investments at the time:
a. Appliances, tools, furniture, vehicles.
b. Expenditure distribution: (food, clothing, shelter, utilities).
c. Compare actual investment patterns and ask for reasoned difference.
d. 'Other' priorities vs. housing priorities (relative priority of better housing vs. other expenses and investments).

C4.7 Reaction to possible family budget changes?
a. What would you do if your income increased by LE........................?
   (take 20%
         50%
         100%)
b. What would you do if your income reduced by LE........................?
   (take 10%
         20%)
c. What would you cut first?
d. What would you cut last?
e. What would you do if you won LE........................? on the lottery?

C4.8 Housing priorities (in general for housing type, location, cost, quality) at this time:
a. Ownership as condition for willingness to invest. (Would other than freehold form of ownership give tenure security to freehold in terms of inducing investment in improvement?).
b. Ownership vs. rental (private market and public housing). Why ownership? Why rental?
c. Ownership vs. standards vs. location. How is each priority assessed against the other?
d. Importance of private open space vs. building.
e. Importance of private open space and roofed vs. initial quality of structure.
f. Importance of private space vs. initial quality of structure vs. complete utilities in the unit.
g. Importance of improving on-plot utilities vs. improvement of dwelling.

C4.9 Specific priorities for location:
a. Distance to centre of city or other large employment centre.
b. Population density, land uses and intensity.
c. Other locality attributes: utilities (in unit or in street); services (mail, public transportation, garbage collection); facilities (schools, sports fields, cultural); commercial (including food markets, shops, pharmacies); environmental quality; community life.

C4.10 Priorities for tenure:
a. Rent, length, and type of contract.
b. Ownership and conditions.
c. Importance of security and transferability.

C4.11 Priorities for standards of building and utilities:
a. Number of rooms; square metres under roof; square metres open space (relative importance of private or shared).
b. Utilities (specify relative importance and whether in unit, adjacent or on street): water (piped, tap, truck, other); electricity (legal, illegal); gas (piped, bottled); telephone; different fittings (shower, bath, w.c., sink).
c. Type and quality of construction: walls; floor; roof; windows; other.
d. Trade offs between a, b, c above (especially utilities vs. enlargements and improved structural quality).

C4.12 Priorities for price-investment:
a. Initial down payment and monthly payments on land.
b. Initial down payment and monthly (if mortgage) payments on house.
c. If incremental construction: sequence, timing and cost.

C4.13 Costs-Monthly: For rent, taxes and utilities.

C4.14 Which of the above C4.8–12 is most important, which second, third.

C4.15 Housing and community improvement priorities:
a. General priorities for improving housing and community services and facilities.
b. Readiness to pay or contribute labour (how much, for what, under what conditions).
c. Ranking priorities for housing unit improvements vs. community improvements other investments vs. moving to other location.

C4.16 Specific improvement priorities:
a. The most important thing to be done to housing unit; who can do it; time and cost; the second and third.
b. The most important thing to improve locality; who can do it; time and cost; total and per family; the second and third.
c. The most important other family expenditure or investment; cost; the second and third.
d. Priorities and trade offs between a, b and c; willingness.

C4.17 Credit priorities (for what and how the funds will be used):
a. Mortgage long or short.
b. Long or short term loan.
c. Savings or other; explain.
d. Is the owner eligible at present to get any kind of loan for new construction or improvement?

C4.18 Priorities for assistance:
a. Technical assistance, what kind?
b. Any other assistance, specify.

Example of edited case study from Ismailia

CASE STUDY 8: EL HEKR

The most significant event in 32 year old Hussein's life was his pilgrimage to Mecca. He now lives in a small house in Ismailia with his young wife and newly born daughter, not altogether happy with his present position as a self-employed plumber.

Education and income

He started as a plumber only a year ago after spending a few years in the army and running his own grocery shop. His monthly income at present varies between LE30 and LE40. Opportunities for better jobs are limited because of his lack of education; he did not manage to get very far in primary school although his wife succeeded in reaching sixth grade.

Looking back on the days when he had his grocery shop, he says: 'I was much better off when I was trading, one can make bigger profits. I had a registered telephone and my wife was able to dress up with jewellery.' He complains that he can hardly make ends meet with the money he now earns.

Personal

Both his parents died when he was very young and he spent most of his life in El Hekr with his older brother who is married with seven children. The brother works in a store and lives in a one storey apartment consisting of three rooms but Hussein decided to live on his own after his marriage in 1975 because of the shortage of space.

First house

Their first house in Ismailia consisted of four rooms plus a large dining room and was built of mud brick and cement. They shared with the landlord, each having two rooms and Hussein made sure he paid the rent in advance, every month. But he did not enjoy sharing accommodation and decided to buy his own piece of land and build a house.

Second house

Several people were selling land in El Hekr and when Hussein heard of an available plot he made an immediate bid. The landowner refused to be paid in installments and Hussein had to pay LE230 in cash without being given a receipt to prove his ownership. Not having any formal proof of land ownership he feels doubly vulnerable and built the complete house in one stage instead of phasing it over a period so that officials would have no chance of using the excuse that the house was incomplete.

Buying the land and paying for the construction proved extremely expensive and Hussein was forced to sell his TV, recorder, his wife's jewellery and use up all his savings from the income he earned in Saudi Arabia when he went on the pilgrimage for three months. He bought all the materials himself, but hired a labourer with three assistants for the construction. He was charged LE5 per thousand bricks and the house was completed in five days using in all 7000 bricks.

Furniture

The house as it now stands consists of a medium sized room which serves as a bedroom, a smaller room (which doubles as a living room, dining room and kitchen) and a bathroom. The wife is unhappy about not having a separate kitchen. The dining room contains a butagaz stove, two tables and a few wooden chairs. The bathroom is separated from the kitchen by a nylon curtain and a wooden door connects the dining room to the bedroom and also leads out onto the road.

Advantages and disadvantages

The chief advantage of the locality is that it is quiet and not overcrowded like other parts of El Hekr. But the distance from the centre of town and all essential services makes life difficult There is a general lack of services; no post office, police station, market or mosque. There is a particular need for a police station since the rate of burglaries in the area has risen dramatically.

The distance also affects their transport costs. If a particular assignment is close to his house Hussein either goes on foot or pays 2 piastres for a bus. If he has to travel a longer distance he takes a taxi which costs about 5 piastres.

The lack of water, electricity and a proper sewerage system are regretted. There is a tap near their house and water pipes pass in front of the house but Hussein has to wait till the appropriate authorities visit him and give him the necessary permit to install water inside. He says sewerage pipes are also connected to the commercial building next door to him and believes it should be simple to extend the pipes into his own house.

But all these drawbacks do not detract from the basic satisfaction he gets from owning his own property. 'I am happy that I am tied to this house. Here I am free to do as I please. I chose this place, and constructed the house the way I wanted it.'

Technical note 1

exist. He did not leave Ismailia during the evacuation in the 1973 war but joined the home guards. According to Hussein general community relations are very good and the neighbours are allowed to use each other's private property such as water pumps and ovens.

Priorities and preferences

Among his immediate priorities Hussein lists a bicycle first to make transport much easier for his work, then household furniture, electrical appliances and domestic utensils. Regarding expenditure, they concentrate first on food and improvements to the house, then health and medical treatment followed by education and finally clothes.

In housing he has no doubt that he would rather be a landlord than a tenant. He adds: 'Given a choice I would like to live in the same area with the same conditions as far as location and population are concerned.' But he would very much like to have utilities inside the house; particularly a waterborne sewerage system in place of the pit barrel he now has. He finds the task of emptying it regularly both tiring and disgusting. 'To tell you the truth,' he says, 'the three items of location, standard and ownership cannot be separated when it comes to determining ideal housing conditions.'

Future expectations

He would like to rebuild his house in concrete and open one of the rooms onto the street and turn it into a grocery shop which he will run.

'As for my children, when they grow up I would love to build a separate house for each of them with electricity, running water and sewerage inside. I hope the area will be improved and completely changed; the streets paved, lighted and lined with trees. I would like the area to look like heaven. I want all this so that when my children grow up and reach high positions they will be living in a suitable area.'

He estimates the present value of his property at LE400 and hopes to rent it out if he can build a separate modern house in concrete with all amenities. If he does rent it out he is firm about not taking key money: 'I believe that taking key money is a sin because the person who pays will have to cut down on food and clothing expenses to save for it and that is not fair.' He has not made any improvements to the house because he considers it only temporary until he can rebuild it in concrete.

Expenditure

They do not have a fixed budget for household expenditure but buy according to their needs trying at the same time to have a little money saved at the end of the month. Hussein's wife buys the vegetables and meat from the Friday market, travelling by taxi for 5 piastres and spends from 75 piastres to one pound. She also goes to the general market four times a week. The couple only go into Ismailia on Fridays usually to visit the public gardens, taking a taxi for the twenty minute journey.

Recreation

'Our visit to the public gardens is considered the only way to add happiness to our life' says Hussein. During the rest of the week their other diversion is exchanging visits with relatives.

Community relations

There are no formal organisations in the area though Hussein was a member of a youth organisation in 1967 until he left to join the army. This group used to organise activities in El Hekr such as collecting and burning garbage from the streets. They first started a camp in a dyer's factory where they were taught public speaking and how to help those who came to them with problems. He has lost touch with the group now and does not know if they still

Example of part of detailed survey questionnaire from Ismailia

B. UTILITIES

Water

Note to interviewer: Indicate sources of water which are used, whether in dwelling, on plot, or on adjacent land on the plan where you have drawn the plan of the house.

B6.27 (Use the following symbols: Private = Pr, Shared = Sh, Public = Pu).

Location

	In dwelling	On plot	In adjacent dwelling	On adjacent plot	In land	In adjacent land	On public land	Other (specify)
Water Sources								
Standpipe								
Main connection to dwelling								
Hand pumps								
Well								
Water tank								
Canal								

Other (specify)..

Note to interviewer: Indicate, on the drawing of the house, the following: sinks, taps, where they store their water.

B6.28 Special information about different sources of water.

Different Sources of water

	Standpipe	Main connection to dwelling	Hand pump	Well	Water tank	Canal	Other (specify)
Special Information							
Use:							
Drink							
Wash							
Quality:							
Clean							
Polluted							

Restrictions on use:
What are they?..
Is water treated:

Boiling							
Filtering							

Quantity of water used:
Is water always available and at all times?
   Yes
   No

If no, when and what are the reasons?..

B6.29 Do you pay money for water?
   Yes
   No
If yes, what for? ....
Price of the water itself ....
Cost of delivery..
The resource is shared ....
Renting the source ....
Other (specify)..

The following questions B6.30 and B6.31 should be addressed only to those who have a watersource (standpipe or hand pump)

B6.30 Who constructed the facility in the dwelling?
   Owner
   Renter
   Both
How much did it cost? ....
Who contributed in the cost?
   Owner
   Renter
   Both
   Other (specify)..

B6.31 Does this facility require maintenance or repair?
   Yes
   No
If yes, what are these requirements, how much will it cost, and when?......................

B6.32 Are there public baths and laundries in this area?
   Yes
   No
If yes, did you or any member of your family use these places?
   Yes
   No   Move to B6.33
If yes, where are these places, how much does it cost for one visit, and how many times do you use it every month?

The following question should be addressed to all.

B6.33 Is the present situation satisfactory?
   Yes
   No
If not, why not? ....

Sewage disposal and drainage

Note to interviewer: Indicate position of toilet and disposal point on plan, whether in dwelling, on plot or on adjacent land (plot). (Use the following symbols Private = Pr, Shared = Sh, Public = Pu).

B6.34 Sewage disposal.

Mark the facility which you use.

Location

	In dwelling	On plot	In adjacent dwelling	On adjacent plot	In condominium	In adjacent condominium	On public land
Types							
Pit latrine							
Bucket							
Flush water closet to sewerage							

Other (specify)..

B6.35 Sullage disposal.
Location

	In dwelling	On plot	In adjacent dwelling	On adjacent plot	In condominium	In adjacent condominium	On public land
Types							
Drainage							
Pit latrine							
Flush water closet to sewerage							

Other (specify)..

B6.36 Mark position on plan, all fixtures in dwelling, on plot or adjacent plot; squatting plate, soil pipe to pit latrine, water closet.

B6.37 Indicate the dimensions (length, breadth and depth) and size of openings of:
A. Pit latrine ....
B. Drainage (if there is any) ....
Was the ground water visible when pit latrine/drainage was dug and at what level?..
In the case of drainage:
Materials used for its construction. ....
How was it constructed? ....

B6.38 How long does the pit latrine/drainage take to be filled?
No. of months..
No. of years..
Does not know   Move to B6.39
If known, how often is it emptied? ....
How is it emptied and by whom?..........
How much does it cost?..

B6.39 What are the building materials used to construct the pit latrine?
Walls: ....
Floor:..
The cover:..
Pipe material and diameter:..

B6.40 Do any of these facilities require maintenance and repair?
   Yes
   No   Move to B6.41
If yes, did you do any repair?
   Yes
   No   Move to B6.41
What are these repairs?..
How much did it cost you?..

B6.41 Are there any problems dealing with pit latrine/drainage in this area?
   Yes
   No   Move to B6.42
   Does not know   Move to B6.42

114 Technical note 2

If yes, what are these problems?
   Sewage contamination
   Polluted water
   Causes illness
   Other (specify) ....

B6.42 Does any one improve sanitary conditions?
   Yes
   No   Move to B6.43
   Does not know   Move to B6.43
   If yes, who is the one taking
   responsibility? ....
   What are the chemicals used? ....

B6.43 Who contributes to the construction of the pit latrine/drainage?
   Owner
   Renter
   Both
   Other (specify) ....
   What sort of contribution did you give?
   Money
   Work

B6.44 Are there any public toilets in this area?
   Yes
   No   Move to B6.45
   Does not know   Move to B6.45
   If yes, where are they? ....
   Do you pay for using these places?
   Yes
   No   Move to B6.45
   If yes, how much do you pay? ....

B6.45 Do you use the waste of the pit latrines (e.g. as a fertiliser?).
   Yes
   No   Move to B6.46
   If yes, give details..

B6.46 Have you or any member of your family had an illness which you think may have been caused by the sanitary conditions?
   Yes
   No   Move to B6.47
   If yes, give details..
   What was this illness?..............................

B6.47 Is the present situation satisfactory?
   Yes
   No
   If no, why? ....

Technical note 2

Implementation: land marking in improvement/upgrading areas

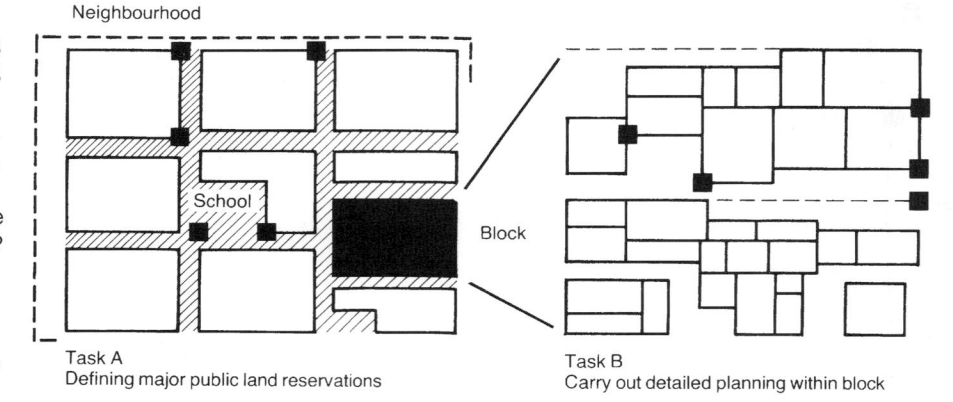

The principal Tasks in these areas are:
A Reserving the land required for public uses – such as for streets, for schools and major open spaces.
B Completing detailed planning within blocks, culminating in the defining of final property boundaries to form the basis of land holdings.

The work and time involved in Task A is much less than in Task B, and must have been completed before Task B can be commenced in any area. It is therefore preferable to have separate teams carrying out the two main tasks, so that detailed block planning does not delay the project as a whole. This also ties in directly to the process of enforcement (see page 122).

The subject of public relations and participation of the local population is dealt with separately in Technical note 11 (page 120), but it is important to make the point that the survey teams in the field are the representatives of the project that people see most, and question most. Workers should be well briefed, and preferably be accompanied by a member of the public relations staff who can give out information, explain the project, and to try to encourage local support. This has the added advantage of allowing the survey workers to get on with their work. The team carrying out task A will be particularly important as they will be the first undertaking work in any area.

Work sequence: reservation of public land (Task A)

1 As soon as possible, once the outline plan is approved, and before the stage of detailed design, the key boundaries of public land, and future development land, should be marked with numbered concrete posts (see Technical note 8, page 118). There are two situations. The first is when no reasonably accurate base maps are available of the improvement area, and the second is when there is a good surveyed base.

a *No accurate base map* Posts should be placed so as to reserve the maximum likely land necessary for roads, schools. open space, and to mark the edge of existing development. When the reservations required are specific, posts can be placed in their final locations. When locations depend on detailed design, they should be placed so as to keep options open. These points can later be plotted during the detailed survey, and after detailed design, relocated. Detailed surveys can take a considerable time, and must be phased to allow work to proceed on Tasks A and B.

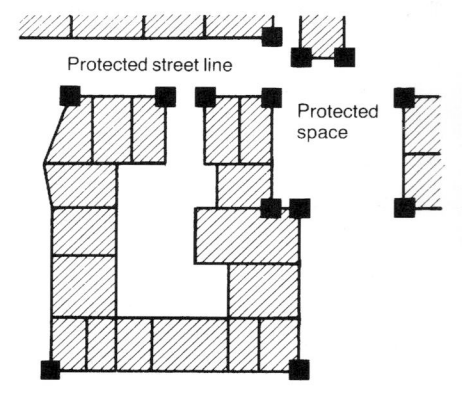

Figure 61
Land marking tasks

▨ Public reservations
■— Marker
--- New line

Task A
Defining major public land reservations

Task B
Carry out detailed planning within block

Protected street line

Protected space

Protected street line

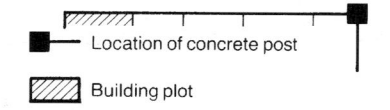

■— Location of concrete post
▨ Building plot

Figaure 62
Public-land reservation: no accurate base map

Technical note 2   115

b *Accurate base map* Where this is available, the dimensions of road and other reservations can be plotted on the plan (1:500 scale) and the posts located on the spaces in the final locations.

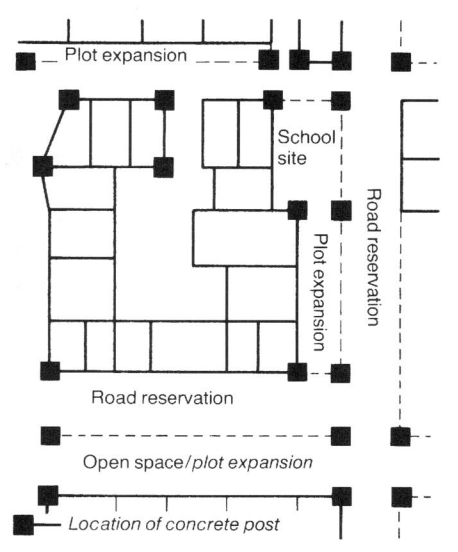

Figure 63
Public land reservation: accurate base map

In all cases posts should be painted and numbered to aid future recognition. Important public areas, such as school sites, should be reserved at this stage, rather than delayed until the detailed planning stage. They can be amended before handing over to, for example, the education authority.

2 The built up area should be accurately surveyed, if this is possible, at least along the lines proposed as through streets, and at the same time markers should be located at key points. Block corners must be tied into an accurate set of traverse lines, (see Technical note 3, page 116).

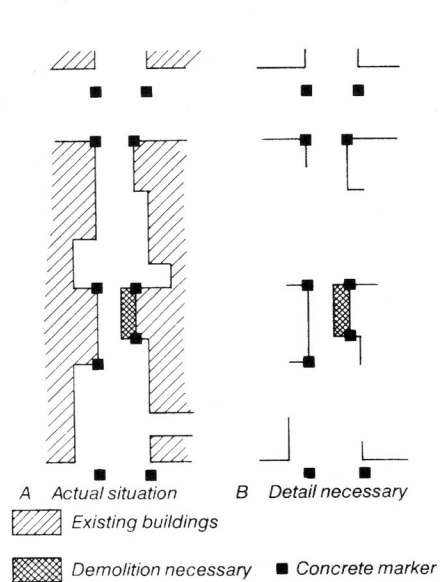

Figure 64
Survey and marketing in existing streets

Figure 64 shows the essential detail to be picked up – for example, block corners and particularly narrow points. The actual lines should be set out by the surveyors in the field, according to a set of guide lines provided by the planners – for example, minimum street width acceptable and the aim to minimise destruction.

Work sequence: detailed block plans/plot rationalisation (Task B)

1 Prepare block plan to 1:500 scale using as a basis the 1:500 scale survey frame work, and, if possible, aerial photographs enlarged to this scale (see Technical note 5, page 117).

2 Organise meeting with block residents to explain proposals.

3 Survey team measures plots (see Technical note 4, page 116), and street width, and at the same time records the identity of the owners/occupiers and numbers the plots (physically numbering the houses themselves is also an advantage for later identification).

4 Fit the measured plots to the outline plan, and draw the 'rationalised' boundaries – preserving existing buildings where possible. Final lines need not be regular, but any land surplus to public needs should be put in private use.

Figure 65
Existing plots showing rationalised lines

5 The proposed plan should be explained to, and discussed with, residents, and any reasonable modifications made.

6 The final detailed plan is drawn up, and key markers placed in the ground.

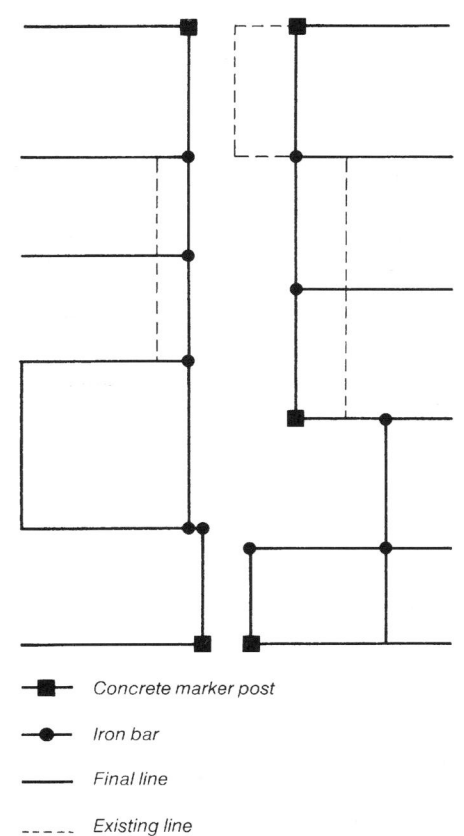

Figure 66
Rationalisation: final plan and land marking

7 Plot areas are computed, both existing and potential. These form the basis, with the location plan, for title documents and payments.

8 Arrangements for purchase of the plots are made between the occupier and the Agency. The basis of pricing is set by the Agency (see Technical note 10, page 119) and payback terms are agreed.

9 Finally, a contract is signed.

Technical note 3

Carrying out intermediate land surveys

A good land survey is one which provides the appropriate degree of detail and reliability for the task in hand. For the purposes of the Manual, two types of survey are needed. The first relates to the feasibility studies, in which information is needed about a site to ascertain its general suitability for a low income housing project. The second relates to the detailed project studies and involves information necessary for the development of detailed planning proposals.

Existing information such as mapping, aerial photographs or surveys, together with a series of short site visits, will generally be adequate for the purposes of Feasibility studies. See also Technical note 21.

For the Detailed studies, more detailed and accurate data will be required. This can either be obtained from existing sources (if accurate and up-to-date), or by undertaking some form of land survey. If a new survey is necessary it should consist of a full ground survey using a network of co-ordinated points established by primary and secondary traverses to a relative accuracy of not less than 1:20 000 and related where necessary to national survey grids.

Intermediate land survey

There will be many occasions, however, when the extent of a site or limitations on survey resources make it difficult to carry out a full survey. An alternative approach in such situations is to undertake an 'intermediate survey'. This is intended to enable the main features of a site (i.e. those which are particularly important in developing planning proposals), to be accurately fixed and secondary detail related to these main features by tape measurements, pacing, or 'line of sight'. It therefore consists of a number of different survey methods used in conjunction.

To undertake an 'intermediate survey', it is first necessary for experienced staff to assess which features are of primary and which are of secondary importance. In areas selected for new settlement, the important features will generally consist of natural features such as rivers, streams, trees or cliffs, together with any relevant manmade features such as roads, railway lines, canals, public buildings or bridges. In areas of existing development, this list can be extended to include main roads or those containing public utility networks, and key buildings.

The features to be covered by the full ground survey can then be located approximately on a plan of the site. Ideally, they will cover the main areas and form a grid to which all secondary detail can be related. If this is not the case, it may be useful to extend the full survey.

When this has been done, the survey can be undertaken in the normal way by running traverses along roads and locating all relevant detail by tacheometric survey. Data can then be plotted at scale 1:1000 or 1:2500 and used as the basis for a sketch survey using tape measures or pacing, according to the level of accuracy required. An example of this method used in an area of existing development is illustrated.

The main advantage of the 'intermediate survey' is that it only requires a small team of experienced surveyors and can produce plans of reasonable accuracy and detail very quickly. They are particularly suitable in areas of existing development where it is difficult to carry out full surveys of an entire district, but where sketch surveys alone are inadequate. Their success lies, however, in determining the appropriate balance between full and sketch surveys and this can only be developed through experience.

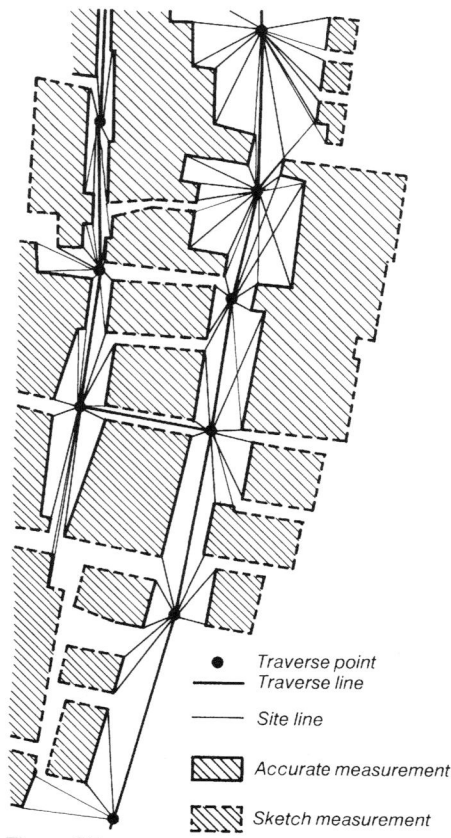

Figure 67
lIntermediate survey

Technical note 4

Implementation: measuring plots

Plot measurement is necessary when payment for plots is on the basis of area. It can be carried out in several ways, depending on the staff available and the most acceptable method to occupiers.

1 *Straightforward measuring* This is simple if the building is regular and all external walls are accessible. When this is not the case, surveyors have to climb on the houses, which is time consuming and sometimes dangerous. Measurements are then taken of external walls and diagonals, and the area calculated.

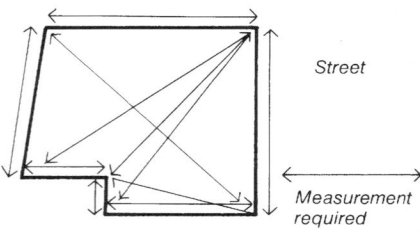

Figure 68
Plot measurement in the field

2 Aerial photographs:
a The dimensions are scaled from a 1:500 scale aerial photograph. Call the street side dimension 'X'.
b The length of the street side of the plot is measured in the field. Call this 'Y'.

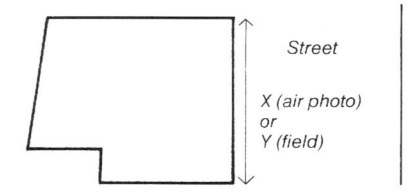

Figure 69
Plot measurement from air photographs

If X and Y differ, then multiply the dimensions from the aerial photograph by the factor Y upon X. This method saves considerable field time, and is reasonably accurate. At times, however, the plot boundaries have to be established in the field.

3 *Self measuring* Occupants may be asked to measure their own plots (a tape measure can be lent) and this can then be compared with estimated areas obtained from aerial photographs. If measurements and estimates are within 10 per cent, then they can be accepted. Otherwise the plot must be measured. This method is useful if very limited field staff are available for measuring.

Technical note 5
Preparing sketch maps using aerial photographs

Aerial photographs, if available, and especially if recent, are an extremely useful aid, both to plan preparation, and to implementation. They can be used in the following ways:

1 To form the basis of a sketch plan for the planning of existing areas.

2 In stereo pairs, (air photographs normally overlap), and when viewed in a stereoscopic viewer, the features appear in an exaggerated three-dimensional form. This means that buildings and trees appear as if in a solid model, but considerably higher than they really are. This does, however, provide a very clear picture of what is happening on the ground. See also Technical note 6.

3 Close-up photographs can be taken in a series to cover the aerial photograph, and then be enlarged to a detailed working scale such as 1: 5000. This can be done with a normal 35mm reflex camera, provided care is taken, by the following method:

a Load 35mm reflex camera with fine grain film (low ASA number).
b Fit camera with extension tubes or bellows attachment to allow close-up photography (1 to 1 image or larger required).
c Attach camera to tripod which has a reversible centre column and winding height adjuster. Use a remote shutter release cable to minimise the vibration.

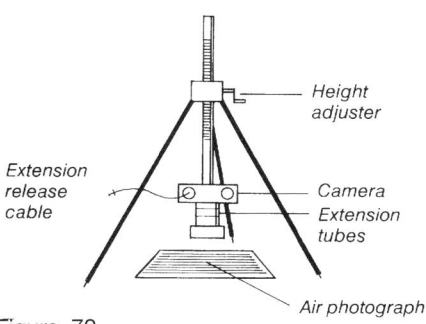

Figure 70
Camera set up

d Focus camera with the tripod adjuster, and set aperture by use of light meter (preferably internal).
e Take overlapping photographs by means of moving the original aerial photograph progressively, keeping it in a straight line by means of a reference, such as a base line on graph paper under the tripod, see sketch.

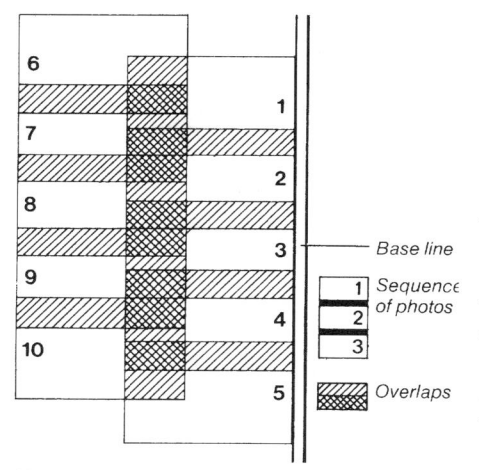

Figure 71
Sequence of photographs

f Develop film with fine grain developer.
g In the field, survey and measure one block and draw this to 1: 500 scale.
h Project the negative of the same block onto the scale drawing and adjust to obtain a good fit. With the enlarger at this setting, all negatives which were taken when the camera was at the same distance from the original photograph, will give a reasonable approximation (within one to one and a half metres) of 1: 500 scale. *The main reason for inaccuracy is that the scale will vary with height.* For greater accuracy, one dimension of each block can be measured, and the enlargement adjusted to fit this scale's dimension. Enlargements made in this manner can be very useful in the improvement/upgrading process (see Technical note 2, page 114).

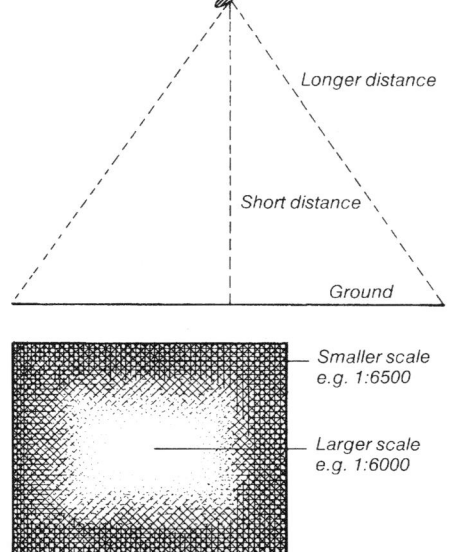

Figure 72
Distortion in air photographs

Technical note 6
Interpreting aerial photographs

This is not a subject easily covered here, but a few notes may be helpful.

The main objects of interest are buildings, walls, trees and agricultural areas. Most parts of an aerial photograph are taken at an angle, so the ground is only seen on two of the four sides of a house (see Figure 73).

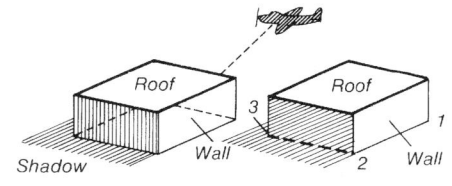

Figure 73
Appearance of building from air photographs

The problem is to know where the walls meet the ground – the line that appears on maps. Where it can be seen as in the line between 1 and 2 in Figure 73, there is no problem. Point 3 may be seen if the shadow is not too dark. If not, it can be estimated by continuing a line from 2, but parallel with the roof line as in Figure 74.

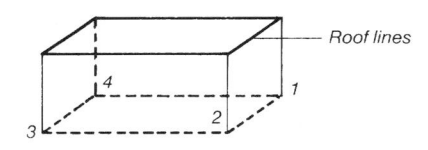

Figure 74
Visible parts of building

Point 4 is obtained by drawing 1 to 4 and 3 to 4 parallel to the roof line above. The other important aspect is to differentiate between roofed areas and walls on their own. The key again is in the shadows as Figure 75 shows.

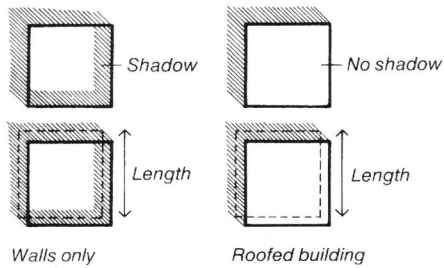

Figure 75
Differentiating walls and roofs from air photographs

In Figure 75, the lines marked on a plan would be the dotted lines – this is where the walls meet the ground.

Technical note 7
Implementation: design of layouts related to setting out

This note refers to practical aspects of layout. It is important that plot layouts be designed in such a way that setting out on the ground is reasonably simple. This does not have to mean designing a straight forward grid, but the number of lines which have to be set out using a theodolite or similar instrument should be limited.

In this example, the concrete markers shown (see Technical note 8) can be easily set out, and from these, individual plots can be set out using a tape.

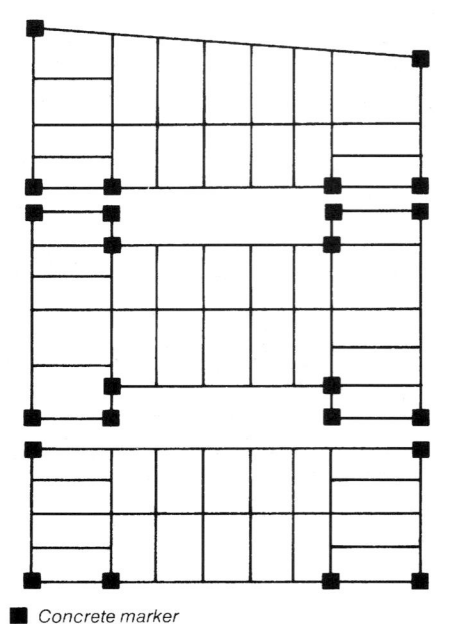

■ *Concrete marker*

Figure 76
Plot layout designed for ease of setting out

If layouts are not designed on this basis, setting out is a problem and plots are difficult to locate. Mistakes can easily be made due to the problems involved in cross checking in the field.

Figure 79
Marker location for plot setting out

Technical note 8
Implementation: design and location of site markers (monuments)

The first stage of site development is to place key markers in the ground. These should be strong and permanent, for example, reinforced concrete columns set in concrete bases.

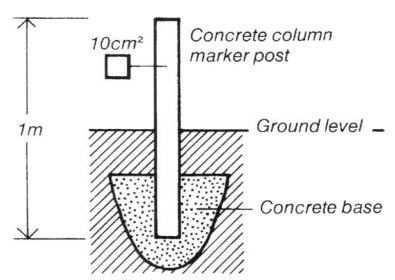

Figure 77
Concrete column maker

Locations should be at the corners of blocks, street lane entrances within a block and other points which will allow easy setting out of plots when they are being handed over.

■ *Location of posts*
▨ *Block*

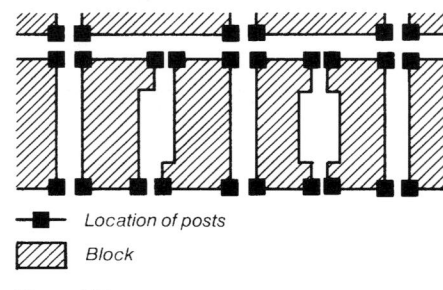

Figure 78
Location of marker posts for setting out

Smaller markers such as reinforced steel or timber posts cut to one metre lengths should be used to mark individual plots. These should be placed at the time of handing over a plot to its owner, who may then mark the plot permanently with a fence, wall, or whatever is normally used in the area.

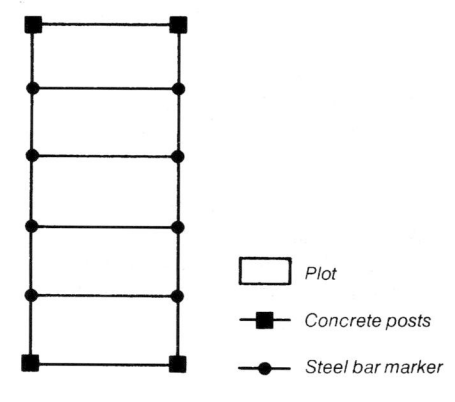

□ *Plot*
■ *Concrete posts*
● *Steel bar marker*

Technical note 9
Estimating land values

Any project means the entry, in one form or another, into the urban land market. The existing and future value of land on a given site depends above all on the context of the city-wide land market and the likely trends in land development and speculation. Since proposals involve the formalised creation of improvement of urban land, it is necessary to estimate market prices and to identify the points which are likely to influence these prices in the future. These include:
- The balance of supply and demand.
- Land tenure.
- Location.
- Services provision.

Before land values can be estimated, it will be necessary to define the various types of land and, in particular, those which are free to vary in price according to market forces. The possibility of converting land in or out of the market should also be noted.

The actual types of land present in any city will inevitably vary. In defining each type, note should be made of its degree of 'marketability' and the proportion of the total urban area which it represents. This information should be plotted on maps of the city or relevant parts.

The estimate of land values can then be carried out by surveying prices of *empty* freehold or leasehold plots in different localities and with different levels of services provision. Necessary information can usually be obtained quickly and easily from local land agents, local property tax offices and spot interviews with local residents and landowners. This will, of course, only provide a point-in-time survey and will not indicate the rate of increase in land costs due to speculation or other causes. Nonetheless, by carrying out such surveys regularly, a detailed understanding of the urban land market can be quickly acquired.

The information obtained by the informal surveys can then be plotted on maps of the urban area, and localities with different categories of land value can be identified. An example of such a map is shown in Figure 80.

A land profile can then be prepared by linking the highest and lowest areas along a series of lines, such as main roads. The extrapolated land value profile can then be obtained by noting the value of plots at intervals along each line (Figure 81).

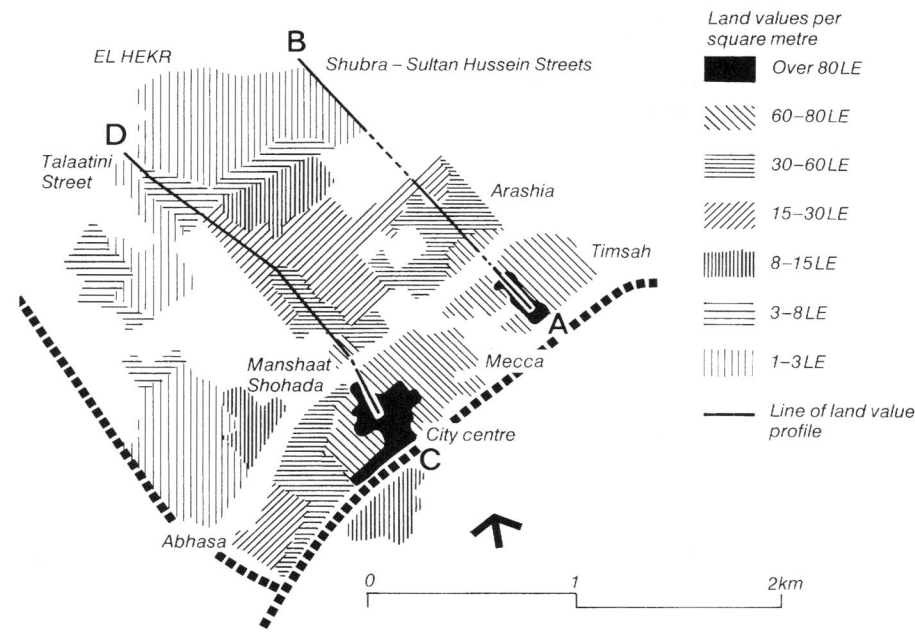

Technical note 10
Pricing of plots

Figure 80 (above)
Land value areas: Ismalia 1977

Figure 81 (below)
Land value profile examples: Ismalia 1977

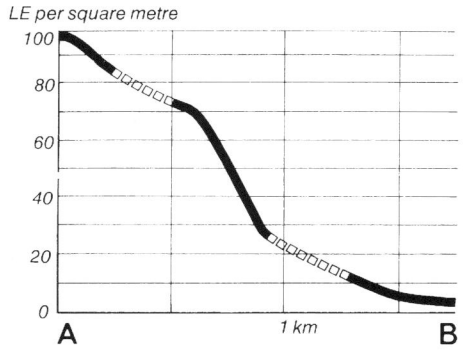

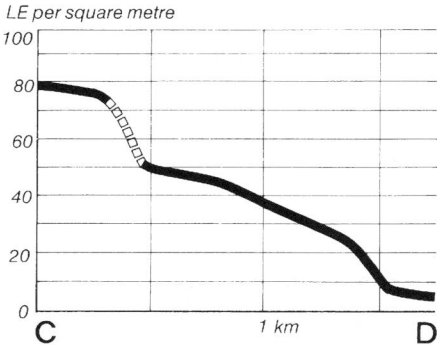

The prices charged for plots should reflect the relative advantages of different locations. Thus, a corner plot has better potential for use as a shop as it has a greater frontage, and more people pass it. Similarly, plots on main surfaced roads have a higher potential value than those on small unsurfaced roads. Charging more for these plots allows the remaining plots to be sold/leased at a lower price. This process is known as cross subsidisation.

Plots can be charged according to their locations. For example:

Class A plots   Those in areas of particular commercial value, such as street corners and important main roads.

Class B plots   Other surfaced roads and local distributor streets.

Class C plots   Plots in semi-private areas or small streets.

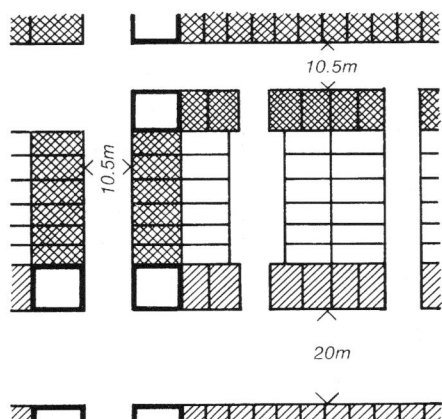

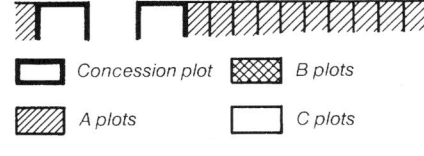

Figure 82
Plot pricing

This type of survey is only able to provide an outline of the local land market, but it can provide useful information on:
- The degree of consistency in the price of land in any given location.
- The land value range in the whole area under review.
- The main determinants of land value (such as commercial potential).
- The effect of different levels of services provision on land values.
- The influence of land tenure on prices. (In general this will have a significant impact).
- The impact of social services and social status on land prices.

For land outside the 'free' land market, a value will also exist, though it will be less likely to fluctuate with market forces, unless there is a possibility of its conversion onto the 'free' market through formal or informal channels.

Formal conversion can occur through the subdivision and servicing of new areas for sale and can be carried out either by a private developer or the local government authorities. Information should be readily available from the authorities.

Informal conversion of land into the freehold market can take place through the regularization of informal settlement to freehold status. Once again, values for this type of transaction can generally be obtained from the local authorities.

To develop an understanding of trends in land values, these surveys should be repeated at regular intervals. It will then be possible to prepare outline estimates of future land values applicable to a project by assessing changes in any of the points listed at the beginning of this Technical note. For government owned land, an inferred value will need to be determined based upon prevailing Government rates for empty unserviced land, the leasehold rent charged by government for the use of vacant lands or, finally, the rate which the local authorities have to pay to other government agencies for the use of public land.

Using these methods, it should be possible to obtain a comprehensive assessment of the local land market and arrive at an estimate of land costs which will be applicable to any given site.

In addition to the general plot grading, a number of very good locations may be kept as 'concession plots' which can be sold at the highest market price possible. This can be an important source both of cross subsidisation and also is a means of obtaining a mixture of social groups in an area.

Technical note 11

Implementation: communication and public participation

Communication and involvement of local people are not parts of the project to be considered in isolation. There may be a particular office to deal with publicity, production of information and enquiries from the public, but every member of the agency staff must play his part in the process. Communication is as much about listening as it is about sending information one way. How officials and professionals communicate with each other and with the community and private sector is very important. It forms an essential part of appraisal, planning and information. These elements are discussed further in Technical note 19.

Local social/political structure

Where local leaders or representatives exist, every effort should be made to work with them, and through them. They may be identified during the preliminary social survey work, and should be kept informed and consulted as work progresses.

Means of communication

1 *Word of mouth* This is unreliable, as information changes the more times it is repeated. It will always be, however, the main means of communication. Incorrect information can be corrected by ensuring that other means of obtaining accurate information exist. The main forms of communication by word of mouth are:
a Public meetings – these are useful in that many people can hear about the project at one time, and ask questions.
b Meetings with representatives of the public.
c Meetings with individuals. This is, in a way, the most effective – but it is not possible on a completely free basis if normal work is not to be interrupted. The need for personal enquiries can be reduced if information is made available by other means, but access of the public to officials at certain times is essential.

2 *Fact sheets* Simply written and illustrated sheets on key topics, for example, 'what is the project for', 'how to apply for a plot' or 'am I allowed to extend my house?'

3 *Newspapers*
a Information can be printed in a local newspaper. This is especially important, for example, for announcing plot distribution.
b The project may have its own monthly or bi-monthly newspaper to report progress and to answer common questions.

4 *Notices* Noticeboards explaining the proposed use of reserve sites, for example, for a school, are very important, as they inform the public and make it less likely that the land will be built on illegally. Noticeboards are also useful for explaining general points about the project.

Local commitment to the aims of the project

It is important to get commitment in principle to the aims of the project, e.g. providing water, improving streets. This then provides political and social support for the project at the stage at which individuals may be adversely affected by detailed proposals, e.g. in house removals for road widening. It is also important that anyone adversely affected is seen to be dealt with fairly.

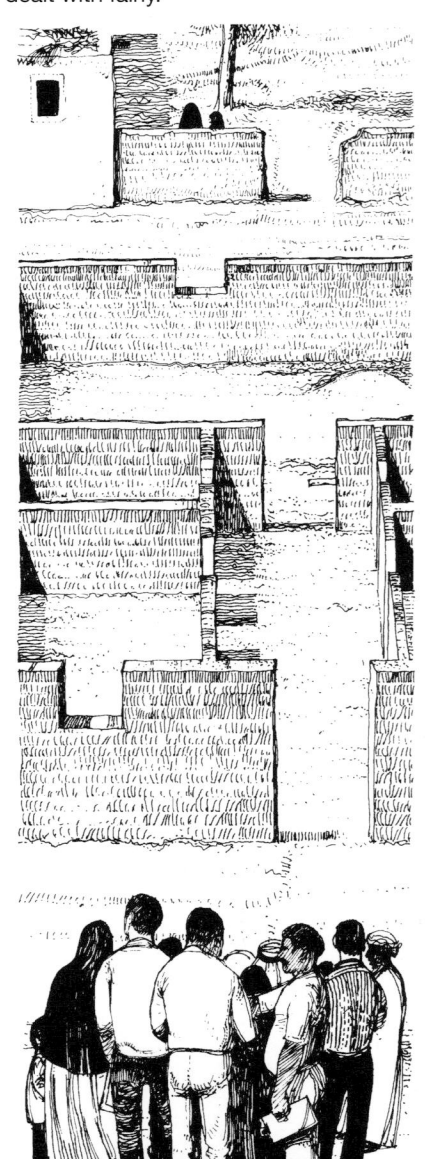

Technical note 12

Implementation: selecting applicants

The most important features of the selection procedure are:

1 It should select applicants with the characteristics aimed at in the project. For example, subsidised plots should go to families with less than a certain income per month.

2 It should be fair and not open to preferential treatment for certain individuals.

3 It should be able to be processed in as short a time as possible.

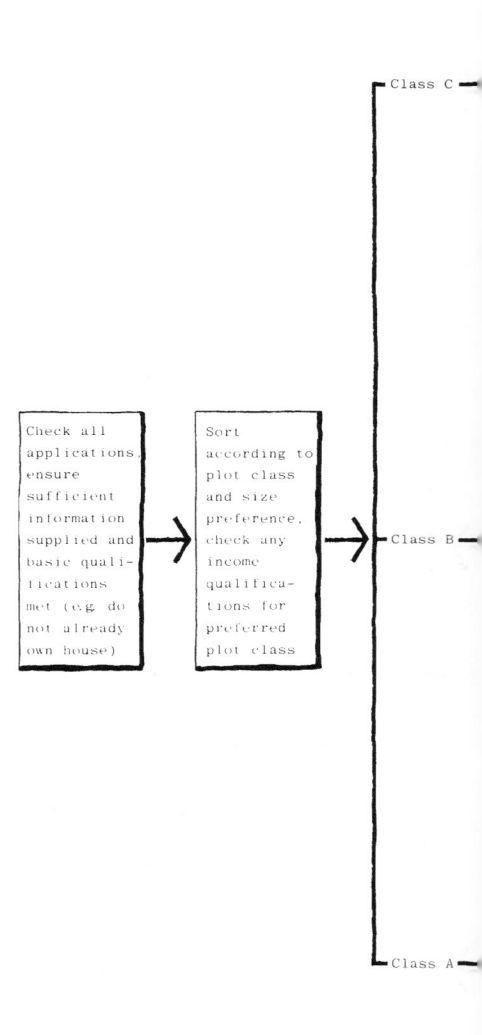

Figure 83
Selection procedure for applicants

The complexity of the process will depend on the number of options available. For example, there may be basic qualifications for applicants such as 'residence', 'ownership of property' and 'income'. Applications may be for a variety of plot classes and sizes and there may also be choices of methods of payment. There may also be second and third choices. It is feasible to sort according to this amount of information, and the flow-chart shows the process. However, it is recommended to keep the process as simple as possible. The simplest method of all may be to first select applicants by ballot, and then check those successful for eligibility.

Verification of information

This could be a very long and difficult process. It is recommended that information be taken on trust, but applicants warned that: their names will be published, or posted and that anyone who is reported as getting the plot under false pretences will be investigated and, if this is proved, will lose their plot and any monies paid. It is recommended that selection be by a full time group under the supervision of an impartial observer.

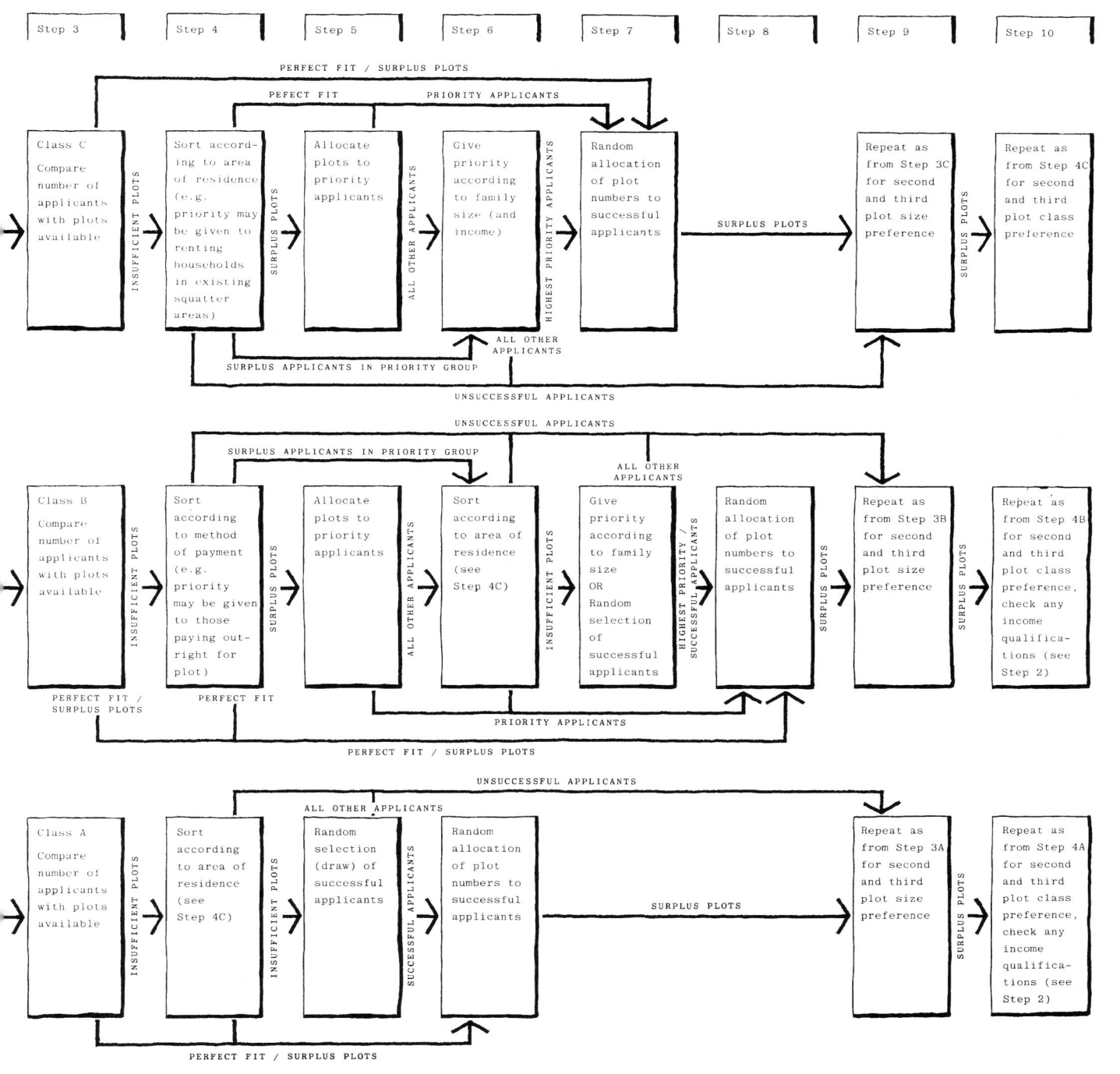

Technical note 13
Implementation: enforcement

When the project includes existing development, especially when it is on the rapidly expanding edge of town, then there will be problems of enforcement. It is quite likely that by the time plans are drawn, the empty land will be built on. It is not sufficient to have a law or order banning development, as this has possibly existed for some time. The law must be capable of enforcement. This requires:

1. A need for the enforcement.
2. Easily available proof of encroachment.
3. A means of enforcement.
4. Legal alternatives available to the persons encroaching.

The subject is particularly difficult as encroachment is likely to be partly by the people the project is designed to help – the low income groups with no alternative means of satisfying their need for housing – and partly by speculators encouraged by the project activity. The following notes represent ideas which may be useful in this difficult area:

- Enforcement through an organised community is probably the most effective means. Refer to Technical Note 19 for more discussion of participatory processes.
- As soon as it is possible (i.e. before any detailed design is carried out) the key boundaries should be marked with numbered concrete posts (see Technical note 2, page 114). These posts can be easily identified in the field, which is essential so that workers can immediately detect transgressions. When this occurs, it is important to act positively – to give a warning, so that the building can be taken down, and materials preserved. If there is no action in, say one week, then one day's notice should be given and the structure removed by force. Failure to act positively will mean that it will not be possible to control development, and much of the agency's energy will be spent in redesign and ineffective efforts at control. Land survey or aerial photographs, if up to date, are very useful in proving encroachment, but nothing is more effective than physical markers, especially if combined with lines, such as low walls, on the ground.
- If dealing with a large area, it will not be possible to control all development, nor is it desirable to stop all development. It is advisable to concentrate 'policing' on those areas, such as the margins, important road lines, and reserved land which are critical to the future of the project. It is difficult to be definitive about final lines elsewhere until detailed plans have been prepared. Enforcement is important, but it is not pleasant or popular. It is vital that the reasons for it are understood by local people and that a positive alternative, the availability of new plots, is available in as short a time as possible, and preferably prior to enforcement action.

Technical note 14
Implementation: technical assistance to plot holders

The amount of technical assistance to plot holders depends on two points:
- How much and what type of help is needed.
- What capacity the agency has to provide this help.

The help required by plot holders is likely to be in the layout of their plot, especially where layouts have to meet required building codes. It may also need to cover building techniques, if a significant number of owners are unskilled and build by them selves rather than using local tradesmen such as bricklayers and carpenters.

The implementing agency can supply layouts and sets of plans for standard plot sizes. These will help to satisfy any bureaucratic requirements. They may also devise a simplified building manual. It may also be possible to employ skilled tradesmen who could give advice and demonstrations of building techniques. This can also be a means of introducing improved building techniques.

Normally, an existing system will operate reasonably well. The agency should be sure that it can improve on the existing situation before interfering. Assistance can be provided at a number of levels:
- Simple basic information on the construction, e.g. of pit latrines, and example plans of space organisation which will allow future upgrading.
- Architectural and structural drawings and bills of quantities and/or specifications for standard plot dimension for those who can start building in permanent materials. Designs, bills of quantities or specifications should allow for construction by stages.
- Guidance for settlers reconstructing in permanent materials.
- Help in introducing improvements to local building methods.

Technical note 15
Appropriate map and plan scales

The most appropriate scale for any plan or drawing depends on its purpose and content. In practice the general rule for determining scales is 'that scale which enables all the required information to be shown clearly without confusion and which can be readily understood'. This depends also on the quality of the graphics and whether the drawing needs to be pinned up on a wall for use during committee hearings (in which case it needs to be larger than normal). The plan must also be of an appropriate size to ensure that printing costs are kept down and that the drawing is not too large to make handling difficult.

The aim is therefore to have a drawing as small as possible whilst retaining legibility and clarity of information, suitable to its purpose.

Another consideration is that of using standard paper sizes. Any printing operation requiring non-standard paper sizes becomes automatically more expensive since it requires additional manual operations, does not fit into reports and complicates graphic work in general. It is therefore a good rule to adopt a scale which may have to be smaller than originally envisaged but which fits onto standard paper. In general, 'A' sizes are now internationally recognised. These sizes are as follows:

A0	1168 x 840mm
A1	840 x 584mm
A2	584 x 420mm
A3	420 x 297mm
A4	297 x 210mm
A5	210 x 148mm

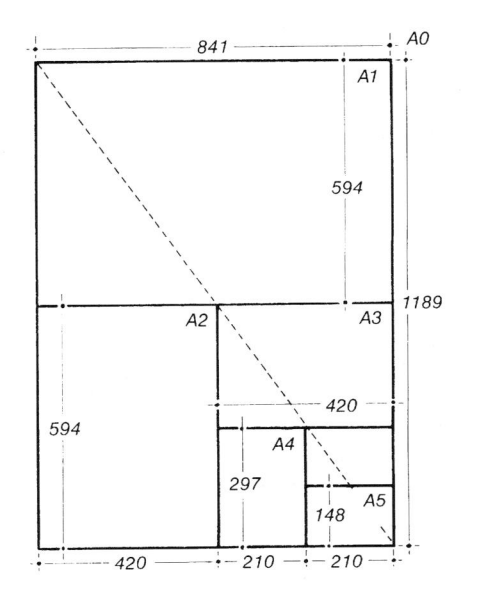

It is also important not to 'invent' scales but to use the internationally recognised scales for which scale rules exist (i.e. 1:250 000, 1:10 000, 1:2500, 1:1250, 1:500). Table 27 relates scales to their normal uses.

Figure 84
Plan scale examples
A *1:25 000*, B *1:2500*, C *1:1250*

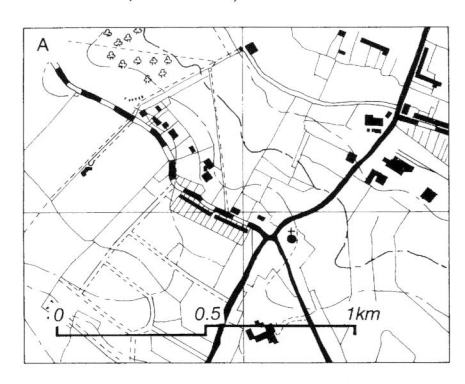

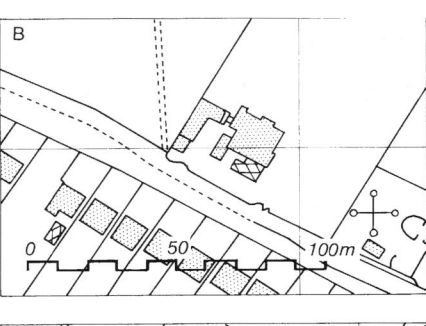

Table 27
Appropriate map and plan scales

Title of maps or plans or drawings	Purpose	Appropriate scale	Comment
Master plan of city	identify development area and monitor its growth relative to policies for growth of city	1:25 000	depending on complexity this could also be at 1:50 000 without undue loss of detail
Community plan	showing overall planning concept and policy as plot location diagram	1:10 000	useful for purposes of location programming, and monitoring, but too small for everyday detailed use
Detailed community plan	to bring together all the roads and services on one common base map	1:2500	general working map for co-ordination services and roads; found to be very useful in practice
Survey maps or layouts	setting out of blocks, roads, electricity, telephones, water, drains, street lighting etc.	1:1250 or 1:1000	smallest scale that provides sufficient accuracy pegging out, e.g. road intersections
Block/plot layouts	for setting out individual plots	1:500	this scale is useful for layouts, can be used for legal purposes; e.g. plot ownership, and is large enough to be used for monitoring on-plot development
Design drawings and working drawings of standard house-types and special community buildings	to obtain building permits	1:100 or 1:50	this depends on complexity and extent of details required for the dwelling and the size of the dwelling
Typical construction details for dwellings/ special buildings of community centre	to provide details of appropriate building construction	1:20 or 1:10 or 1:5	depending on the purpose these can be drawn at the scale required by the Government department and local practice

Technical note 16
Assessing layout efficiency

This Technical note refers to a method of evaluating either existing or proposed housing layouts to indicate the efficiency with which they use available land. Other factors, such as the ease of installing public utilities together with social, economic, cultural and climatic factors will also have to be considered in developing project proposals. The combination of these factors to produce suitable layouts will require skill and experience. The method described below is therefore intended only as a starting point.

One measure of the efficiency of a layout will be the proportion of private or revenue generating land which it provides.* To assess this, it is necessary to classify land used into three main categories. These can be defined as:
- *Public land*, including the area occupied by roads and public open spaces, the cost of which has to be borne by local residents.
- *Semi-public land*, including all schools and other specialised institutions, the cost of which is normally borne by the institution itself.
- *Private land*, including individual plots for housing, commerce and other uses, the cost of which is normally borne by the occupants. It would also include, for this analysis, communal land which is maintained by adjacent owners – e.g. a private road or cul-de-sac.

In an efficient layout, public land should ideally be 20 per cent of the total housing area. Proportions greater than this will impose an increased burden on the finances of the implementing agency.

The proportion of semi-public land will depend to some extent on the size of the area surveyed. For example, in neighbourhoods, the main need will be for a primary school, local shops, and religious buildings. For larger areas, clinics, secondary schools and other major facilities will also be needed, so that the proportion of semi-public land will need to increase. For an average neighbourhood of about 5000 people, experience suggests that 15 per cent is likely to be adequate.

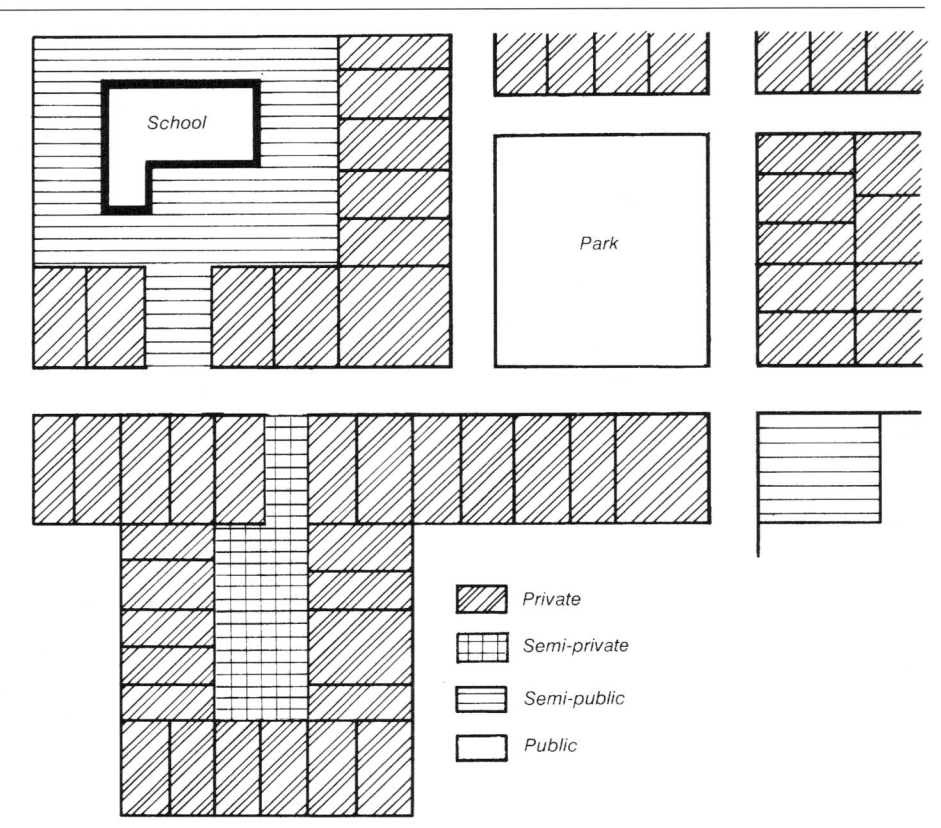

*Further details of this approach towards the efficiency of land use can be found in 'The Urbanisation Primer' by CAMINOS, H and GOETHERT, R World Bank Urban Projects Department, 1976.

Figure 85
Land control types

Efficient percentages in each category for this analysis are:
Public land   20–25%
Semi-public land   15–18%
Private land   55–62%

For purely commercial or industrial areas, the proportion of land in private (i.e. revenue generating) uses, should be higher than for housing areas since there will generally be less semi-public space.

This analysis will not guarantee that a layout is efficient in all respects, but it does provide a reference point. Local traditions and social aspirations will also play an important role in determining the final layout.

Infrastructure network efficiency

A large part of site development costs will depend on the infrastructure networks: the costs of roads, water mains and, particularly, water borne sewerage. These costs can be reduced significantly by the use of layouts which minimise total street lengths. The guidelines for layouts and plot sizes and shapes given in the Manual will tend to provide an efficient system.

The 'public land' measure, described above, reflects the proportion of road space, provided the amounts of other public land remain the same. Otherwise comparisons between layouts can be made by measuring total street lengths.

General

It is not suggested that a lot of time should be spent on the type of analysis outlined here. The methods can be applied quite crudely as a broad check on the efficiency of proposed layouts. Where tests show results far from the optimum it may be due to:
- The presence of a large area of public or semi-public land unconnected to the neighbourhood.
- Particular local customs of layout.

Departure from the optimum may not necessarily be wrong, but it will result in extra costs, and this should be taken into account by decision makers.

Technical note 17

Reference tables:
Discount factor
Present worth of an annuity factor
Capital recovery factor

The following extracts are reprinted with permission from: 'Compounding and Discounting Tables for Project Evaluation' Edited by J. Price Gittinger, Economic Development Institute, International Bank for Reconstruction and Development, Washington DC,1973, Baltimore (John Hopkins University Press).

Examples relate to how to carry out calculations, rather than being representative of calculations specific to housing projects.

Summary present worth tables

For most project purposes only the discount factor and the present worth of an annuity factor are needed and 3 decimal places are sufficient. The intervals have been selected to include the most common discount rates for benefit-cost ratio and net present worth calculations and to provide convenient intervals from which to interpolate when the internal rate of return technique is used to estimate the internal economic return or the internal financial return. Three decimal present worth calculations will permit estimating the benefit-cost ratio to the nearest tenth of a unit ratio value and permit estimating the internal economic or financial return using the internal rate of return technique to the nearest whole percentage point – as precise an estimate as is justified in a development project.

Discount factor   (Table 30, page 128)
How much 1 at future date is worth today.
(Present worth of 1)

This factor permits determining the value today of an amount received or paid out in the future. The process of finding the present worth in project preparation is generally referred to as discounting. Note that the discount factor is the reciprocal of the compounding factor for 1. Hence, it is common to hear expressions such as, 'discounted at an interest rate of 14%'.

The most common use of discounting in project evaluation is to find the present worth of future costs or future benefits.

The net benefit of the Hounslow Irrigation Scheme in Jamaica in the 14th year of the project was estimated to be J$ 173831. Discounted at an interest rate of 21%, what is the present worth at the beginning of the project (t_0)?

J$ 173 831	x	.069	=	J$ 11 994
Actual value at the future time (t_{14})		21 % discount factor for 14th year		Present worth at beginning of the project (t_0)

A cement plant will produce Tcs. 1180000 worth of cement in its first full year of operation in 1975, the 4th year of the project (t_4). Discounted at 12%, what is the present worth of that output on December 31, 1971 (t_0)?

Tcs. 1 180000	x	.636	=	Tcs. 750 480
Value of output in 1975 (t_4)		12% discount factor for 4th year		Present worth at the end of 1971 (t_0) of the 1975 output

A dam will still be in place 50 years in the future. If the value of that dam at that time is considered to be its replacement cost and this will amount to US$ 1 200 000 – and still using the convention of only 3 decimals in the discounting process – what is the present worth of the dam discounted at 17% ?

US$ 1 200 000	x	.000	=	US$ 0
Value 50 years in the future (t_{50})		17% discount factor for 50th year to 3rd decimal		Present worth at t_0

Present worth of an annuity factor   (Table 31, page 129) *How much 1 received or paid annually is worth today. (Present worth of 1 per annum; discount factor for a stream of income)*

This factor enables determination of the present worth of a constant amount received each year for some length of time in the future. It is a great time saver in the computations necessary for project evaluation. Its use is direct and simple if it is used for a constant stream of money which begins in the first year and lasts to some future year, say the 11th year of the project (from t_1 to t_{11}). But it may also be used to determine the present worth today (t_0) of a constant stream of money which begins some time other than the first year of the project – say which begins in the 7th year and continues through the 15th year (from t_7 to t_{15}), although this takes some additional manipulation.

Note that the present worth of an annuity factor for any given number of years is the total of the discount factors for all years through the last.

In Pakistan a farmer with 15 acres who invests in a tubewell is estimated, on the average, to earn an incremental net income of Rs.4415 each year over the 15 year life of the well. Discounted at 18%, what is the present worth of this stream of income to the farmer at the time of his investment (t_0) ?

Rs. 4415	x	5.092	=	Rs. 22 481
Annual amount received each year from 1st through the 15th year (t_1–t_{15})		18% present worth of an annuity factor for 15 years		Present worth of the stream of income at t_0

In the example of the cement plant below, it may be noted how the factor for the present worth of an annuity can be used when the stream of future values begins at some time other than the first year.

Once a cement factory is in full production in 1977, the 6th year of the project (t_6), it will produce cement valued at Tcs. 1 470 000 annually over the economic life of the plant, taken to be 15 years. What is the present worth of the cement production from 1977 through 1968 (t_6–t_{15}) discounted at 12% ?

In order to proceed, the factor by which to multiply the annual value of cement production must first be calculated. This involves finding that part of the factor for computing the present worth of an annuity which arises from the 6th through the 15th years. The procedure is to subtract the value of the factor for 5 years (note that it is not the factor for 6 years) from the value of the factor for 15 years.

12% present worth of an annuity factor for 15 years (t_{15})	6.811
LESS 12% present worth of an annuity factor for for 5 years (t_5)	−3.605
12% present worth of an annuity factor for the 6th year through the 15th years (t_6–t_{15}) (= sum of the discount factors for these 10 years)	3.206

Note that the value of 3.206 computed for the 10 years from the 6th year through the 15th(t_6-t_{15}) is not the same as the value of the factor for the first 10 years (t_1-t_{10}) which is 5.650. The reason is that the 10 years from the 6th through the 15th years (t_6-t_{15}) lie further off in the future than the first 10 years (t_1-t_{10}).

The computation of the factor can be checked (allowing for rounding errors) by taking advantage of the fact that the present worth of an annuity factor is simply the running subtotal of the discount factors, as noted above.

Year	Discount factor 12%	Year	Discount factor 12%
6	.507	11	.287
7	.452	12	.257
8	.404	13	.229
9	.361	14	.205
10	.322	15	.183
		Total	3.207

The factor determined by computation can then be applied to determine the present worth of the stream of future income.

Tcs. 1 475 000 × 3.206 = Tcs. 4 728 850
Annual output from 6th through 15th years (t_6-t_{15}) | 12% present worth of an annuity factor through the 15 years which we have computed | Present worth of the future stream of income at t_0

Capital recovery factor (Table 32, pages 130, 131) *Annual payment that will repay a $1 loan in X years with compound interest on the unpaid balance (Partial payment factor)*

This factor permits calculating what constant annual payments would be necessary to repay a loan over a given period of time at a stated interest rate. The total payment is a varying combination of both interest and repayment of principal.

Note this factor is the reciprocal of the present worth of an annuity factor.

The Agricultural Development Bank of Pakistan lends to farmers at 8% interest to finance tubewells. If a farmer borrows Rs. 8790 for a tubewell to be repaid in 10 years, what is the amount of his combined interest and principal payment?

Rs. 8790 × 0.149 029 = Rs. 1310
Amount initially borrowed at the beginning of the first year (t_0) | 8% capital recovery factor for a 10 year period (t_{10}) | Amount of annual payment from end of first year through end of 10th year (t_1-t_{10})

The government has agreed to make a 20 year loan of US$ 500 000 at 12% interest to a toll road authority. It will take the first 3 years of the loan period to build the road, and the government has agreed to 'capitalize' the interest until the road is complete and toll collection has begun in the 4th year. The amount to be spent on construction in the first year (t_1) is to be US$ 100 000. In both the 2nd and 3rd years (t_2 and t_3) construction expenditures are to be US$ 200 000. What is the annual amount the toll road authority must pay the government in a combined interest and principal payment if it repays the loan in the remaining 17 years of the loan period from the 4th through the 20th years (t_4-t_{20})?

By agreeing to 'capitalize' the interest during the first three years of the loan, the government has, in effect, agreed not to collect the interest which would otherwise be due but rather to add the interest due to the principal of the loan (hence the term 'to capitalize') and to charge 12% interest on the new total.

Considering the drawdown for the first year (t_1) as an example, it may be seen that the government will permit the toll road authority to continue to add the interest due to the original capital draw down for 3 years through the end of the 3rd year (t_3). Thus, the amount due at the end of the 3rd year (t_3) will be the original principal with interest compounded for 3 years. The compounding factor for 1 is used to determine that the amount due for the draw down of US$ 100 000 during the first year (t_1) by the end of the 3rd year (t_3) is US$ 100 000 × 1.404 928 = US$ 140 493. For the drawdown of the 2nd year (t_2), the capitalization process only applies to the 2nd and 3rd years (t_2 and t_3), so the compounding factor for 1 for 2 years is used. Thus, the amount due for the draw down of US$ 200 000 during the 2nd year (t_2) is US$ 200 000 × 1.254 400 = US$ 250 880. A similar process is followed for the 3rd year. These amounts are then totalled to show the amount of principal and capitalized interest due at the end of the 3rd year (t_3) as shown below.

Project year	Amount of loan drawdown (US$)	Compound interest factor to end of 3rd year(12%)	Due at end of 3rd year (US$)
t_1	100 000	1.404 928	140 493
t_2	200 000	1.254 400	250 880
t_3	200 000	1.120 000	224 000

Total principal and interest due at end of 3rd year   615 373

The 12% capital recovery factor may now be applied to the amount owed at the beginning of the 4th year (= end of t_3) to determine the level payment of principal and interest necessary for the toll road authority to be able to repay the government.

US$ 615 373 × .140 457 = US$ 86 433
Total amount including principal and capitalized interest owed at end of 3rd year (t_3) [= beginning of 4th year (t_4)] | 12% capital recovery factor for 17 years | Amount of repayment each year from 4th through 20th years (t_4-t_{20})

Discounted measures of project worth

In project preparation, the discount factor and the present worth of an annuity factor are commonly used to permit comparing the wealth generating potential of one project with that of alternative projects.

Benefit-cost comparisons. Three discounted measures of project worth are commonly used which are comparisons of benefits in relation to costs:

Benefit cost ratio = $\dfrac{\text{Present worth of benefits}}{\text{Present worth of costs}}$

Net present worth = [Present worth of benefits] − [Present worth of costs]

Internal rate of return = That discount rate such that

[Present worth of benefits] = [Present worth of costs]

These three measures are essentially the same. For any investment-type project, there exists an interest rate which is the internal rate of return and at which the benefit-cost ratio equals 1 and the net present worth is zero.

The benefit-cost ratio is commonly employed as a tool to help evaluate public sector projects, most often those of a water resource nature. Only rarely is it used for private sector projects or for such public sector investments as those contemplated by government corporations. The internal rate of return is commonly used to help evaluate both public and private investment projects. Its use is especially prevalent in larger corporations and among international lending agencies. The net present worth measure is used primarily to evaluate public sector investments and for determining the least cost combination in project optimization.

In the World Bank, the internal rate of return is the most frequently employed measure, although both the benefit-cost ratio and the net present worth are occasionally employed.

Opportunity cost of capital. All three discounted measures of project worth must be related to the opportunity cost of capital. For private enterprise the opportunity cost of capital will be a weighted average of the borrowing rate for funds and an acceptable price earnings ratio for equity shares.

For the society as a whole, the opportunity cost of capital is the return on the last (that is, marginal) investment which could be made were all the available capital fully invested in the most remunerative alternative manner. Determining the opportunity cost of capital for a society is difficult, but economists generally consider it to lie between 8% and 15% in most developing countries.

Benefit-cost ratio. In economic discussions, 'cost-benefit ratio' and 'benefit-cost ratio' are used interchangeably. In all instances, however, the computation referred to is the same. Both the benefit stream and the cost stream are discounted by an interest rate considered to be close to the opportunity cost of capital and the ratio between the present worth of the benefits divided by the present worth of the costs is determined.

The example for Trinidad and Tobago illustrates computation of a benefit-cost ratio for a population project in Trinidad and Tobago financed in part by a World Bank loan (Table 28).

Net present worth. Net present worth (often referred to as net present value) is simply the present worth of the net benefits of a project discounted at the opportunity cost of capital. In Table 28, it can be seen that the net present worth is the present worth of the benefits less the present worth of the costs, TT$ 90 462 000 − TT$ 26 004 000 = TT$ 64 458 000. Often it is computationally simpler to determine the incremental net benefit stream (generally referred to as the 'cash flow' in project evaluation) and to discount that stream. This is illustrated in columns (7), (8), and (9) of Table 29 where the incremental net benefit stream or cash flow is discounted assuming an opportunity cost of capital of 12% to find a net present worth of Ur$ 2 462 000 000.

Internal rate of return. The internal rate of return must be determined by trial and error. The measure represents the return over the life of the project to the resources engaged in the project. (Contrary to what is often stated, no reinvestment assumption need be made.) The cash flow is discounted to determine its present worth. By trial and error one discount rate is found which is too low and which leaves a positive present worth and another discount rate is found which is too high and which leaves a negative present worth of the cash flow stream. This brackets the true internal rate of return which may then be estimated by interpolation. The interpolation rule is:

Internal rate of return = Lower discount rate + Difference between the two discount rates × [Present worth of the cash flow at the lower discount rate / Absolute difference between the present worths of the cash flow streams at the two discount rates]

A present worth of an annuity factor was computed for the 6th through the 11th years to save computation. The factor in column (10) of Table 29, for example, was derived as follows:

20% present worth of an annuity factor for 11 years	4.327
LESS 20% present worth of an annuity factor for 5 years	−2.991
20% present worth of an annuity factor from the 6th through the 11th years	1.336

(It may be noted that the sum of the discount factors for all 12 years is the same as the present worth of an annuity factor for 12 years allowing for rounding errors. This provides a quick internal check).

Table 28
Computation of cost-benefit ratio: illustration from population project, Trinidad and Tobago
(in Thousand Trinidad and Tobago dollars)

(1) Year	(2) Costs[a]	(3) D.F.[c] 10%	(4) P.W.[d] 10%	(5) Benefits[b]	(6) D.F.[c] 10%	(7) P.W.[d] 10%
1974	3,206	.909	2,914	—	.909	—
1975	5,228	.826	4,318	179	.826	148
1976	4,048	.751	3,040	534	.751	401
1977	3,630	.683	2,479	1,042	.683	712
1978	2,328	.621	1,446	1,729	.621	1,074
1979	2,168			2,486	.564	1,402
1980	2,168			3,729	.513	1,913
1981	2,168			5,428	.467	2,535
1982	2,168			7,525	.424	3,191
1983	2,168			10,093	.386	3,896
1984	2,168			12,857	350	4,500
1985	2,168			15,727	.319	5,017
1986	2,168			17,912	290	5,194
1987	2,168			20,618	.263	5,423
1988	2,168			22,692	.239	5,423
1989	2,168	5.446*	11,807	24,465	.218	5,333
1990	2,168			26,145	.198	5,177
1991	2,168			27,817	.180	5,007
1992	2,168			29,456	.164	4,831
1993	2,168			31,044	.149	4,626
1994	2,168			32,585	135	4,399
1995	2,168			34,066	.123	4,190
1996	2,168			35,472	.112	3,973
1997	2,168			33,426	.102	3,409
1998	2,168			34,156	.092	3,142
1999	2,168			34,603	.084	2,907
2000	2,168			34,724	.076	2,639
Total	66,136	9.236	26,004	500,510	9.238	90,462

Source: Analysis prepared by Miss I Z Husain, Population Projects Department, IBRD.
* The present worth of an annuity factor for the 6th through 27th years was calculated following the procedure explained on page 126. The present worth of the constant stream of costs from 1979 through 2000 as given in column 2 is obtained by multiplying the costs for one year by the present worth of an annuity factor as computed (TT$2166 thousand x 5.446 = TT$11807 thousand)
a. Costs include capital and recurring costs for operating the project
b. Benefits are savings arising from births averted and include costs of food and clothing saved, education costs saved, and health costs saved
c. Discount factor
d. Present worth of an annuity factor

Benefit-cost Ratio = $\frac{90\ 462}{26\ 004}$ = 3.5

Technical note 17

Table 29
Example of net present worth and internal economic return calculation: Uruguay, third livestock development project
(in million Uruguayan pesos)

(1) Year	(2) Aggregate of ranchers incremental net cash balances	(3) Taxes [a]	(4) Subsidies [b]	(5) Technical services	(6) On-ranch investment	(7) Incremental benefits (* cash flow)	(8) D.F. [d] 12%	(9) Present worth 12%	(10) D.F. [d] 20%	(11) Present worth 20%	(12) D.F. [d] 25%	(13) Present worth 25%
1	− 438	− 120	−299	−315	−2 271	− 3 443	.893	−3 075	.833	−2 868	.800	−2 754
2	− 1 269	+ 55	− 80	− 40	—	− 1 334	.797	−1 063	.694	− 926	.640	− 854
3	+ 710	+ 114	− 80	− 40	—	+ 704	.712	+ 501	.579	+ 408	.512	+ 360
4	+ 1 133	+ 214	− 80	− 40	—	+ 1,227	.636	+ 780	.482	+ 591	.410	+ 503
5	+ 1 270	+ 286	− 80	− 40	—	+ 1 436	.567	+ 814	.402	+ 577	.328	+ 471
6-11	+ 1 230	+ 286	—	− 40	—	+ 1 476	2.333*	+3 444	1.336*	+1 972	.967*	+1 427
12	+ 3 884 [c]	+ 286	—	− 40	—	+ 4 130	.257	+1 061	.112	+ 463	.069	+ 285
Total	+12 670	+2 551	−619	−755	−2 271	+11 576	6.195	+2 462	4.438	+ 217	3.726	− 562

Source: IBRD. Third Livestock Development Project – Uruguay. Report No. PA-38a. Washington: IBRD, 1970. Annex 9, p. 1.

* The present worth of the constant stream of the cash flow from years 6 through 11 as given in column 9, for example, is obtained by multiplying the cash flow for one year by the present worth of an annuity factor as computed (Ur$1,476 million x 2.333 = Ur$3,444 million).
a. See text of original report for details of export and other taxes. The negative tax entry in year 1 is the amount of tax revenue foregone as a result of the investment program.
b. Fertiliser subsidy estimated at 33% of total cost in project year 1, 10% of total cost in project years 2 through 5, and 0 thereafter.
c. Includes $2,654 million for incremental herd value at the end of the project (= salvage value or net residual assets).
d. Discount factor.

Net Present Worth at 12% Opportunity Cost of Capital = Ur$2,462 million.

Internal Economic Return = $20 + 5 \left(\frac{217}{779} \right) = 21\%$

Table 30
Discount factor

Discount factor   How much 1 at a future date is worth today

Year	1%	3%	5%	6%	8%	10%	12%	14%	15%	16%	18%	20%	22%	24%	25%	26%	28%	30%	35%	40%	45%	50%	Year
1	.990	.971	.952	.943	.926	.909	.893	.877	.870	.862	.847	.833	.820	.806	.800	.794	.781	.769	.741	.714	.690	.667	1
2	.980	.943	.907	.890	.857	.826	.797	.769	.756	.743	.718	.694	.672	.650	.640	.630	.610	.592	.549	.510	.476	.444	2
3	.971	.915	.864	.840	.794	.751	.712	.675	.658	.641	.609	.579	.551	.524	.512	.500	.477	.455	.406	.364	.328	.296	3
4	.961	.888	.823	.792	.735	.683	.636	.592	.572	.552	.516	.482	.451	.423	.410	.397	.373	.350	.301	.260	.226	.198	4
5	.951	.863	.784	.747	.681	.621	.567	.519	.497	.476	.437	.402	.370	.341	.328	.315	.291	.269	.223	.186	.156	.132	5
6	.942	.837	.746	.705	.630	.564	.507	.456	.432	.410	.370	.335	.303	.275	.262	.250	.227	.207	.165	.133	.108	.088	6
7	.933	.813	.711	.665	.583	.513	.452	.400	.376	.354	.314	.279	.249	.222	.210	.198	.178	.159	.122	.095	.074	.059	7
8	.923	.789	.677	.627	.540	.467	.404	.351	.327	.305	.266	.233	.204	.179	.168	.157	.139	.123	.091	.068	.051	.039	8
9	.914	.766	.645	.592	.500	.424	.361	.308	.284	.263	.225	.194	.167	.144	.134	.125	.108	.094	.067	.048	.035	.026	9
10	.905	.744	.614	.558	.463	.386	.322	.270	.247	.227	.191	.162	.137	.116	.107	.099	.085	.073	.050	.035	.024	.017	10
11	.896	.722	.585	.527	.429	.350	.287	.237	.215	.195	.162	.135	.112	.094	.086	.079	.066	.056	.037	.025	.017	.012	11
12	.887	.701	.557	.497	.397	.319	.257	.208	.187	.168	.137	.112	.092	.076	.069	.062	.052	.043	.027	.018	.012	.008	12
13	.879	.681	.530	.469	.368	.290	.229	.182	.163	.145	.116	.093	.075	.061	.055	.050	.040	.033	.020	.013	.008	.005	13
14	.870	.661	.505	.442	.340	.263	.205	.160	.141	.125	.099	.078	.062	.049	.044	.039	.032	.025	.015	.009	.006	.003	14
15	.861	.642	.481	.417	.315	.239	.183	.140	.123	.108	.084	.065	.051	.040	.035	.031	.025	.020	.011	.006	.004	.002	15
16	.853	.623	.458	.394	.292	.218	.163	.123	.107	.093	.071	.054	.042	.032	.028	.025	.019	.015	.008	.005	.003	.002	16
17	.844	.605	.436	.371	.270	.198	.146	.108	.093	.080	.060	.045	.034	.026	.023	.020	.015	.012	.006	.003	.002	.001	17
18	.836	.587	.416	.350	.250	.180	.130	.095	.081	.069	.051	.038	.028	.021	.018	.016	.012	.009	.005	.002	.001	.001	18
19	.828	.570	.396	.331	.232	.164	.116	.083	.070	.060	.043	.031	.023	.017	.014	.012	.009	.007	.003	.002	.001	.000	19
20	.820	.554	.377	.312	.215	.149	.104	.073	.061	.051	.037	.026	.019	.014	.012	.010	.007	.005	.002	.001	.001	.000	20
21	.811	.538	.359	.294	.199	.135	.093	.064	.053	.044	.031	.022	.015	.011	.009	.008	.006	.004	.002	.001	.000	.000	21
22	.803	.522	.342	.278	.184	.123	.083	.056	.046	.038	.026	.018	.013	.009	.007	.006	.004	.003	.001	.001	.000	.000	22
23	.795	.507	.326	.262	.170	.112	.074	.049	.040	.033	.022	.015	.010	.007	.006	.005	.003	.002	.001	.000	.000	.000	23
24	.788	.492	.310	.247	.158	.102	.066	.043	.035	.028	.019	.013	.008	.006	.005	.004	.003	.002	.001	.000	.000	.000	24
25	.780	.478	.295	.233	.146	.092	.059	.038	.030	.024	.016	.010	.007	.005	.004	.003	.002	.001	.001	.000	.000	.000	25
26	.772	.464	.281	.220	.135	.084	.053	.033	.026	.021	.014	.009	.006	.004	.003	.002	.002	.001	.000	.000	.000	.000	26
27	.764	.450	.268	.207	.125	.076	.047	.029	.023	.018	.011	.007	.005	.003	.002	.002	.001	.001	.000	.000	.000	.000	27
28	.757	.437	.255	.196	.116	.069	.042	.026	.020	.016	.010	.006	.004	.002	.002	.002	.001	.001	.000	.000	.000	.000	28
29	.749	.424	.243	.185	.107	.063	.037	.022	.017	.014	.008	.005	.003	.002	.002	.001	.001	.000	.000	.000	.000	.000	29
30	.742	.412	.231	.174	.099	.057	.033	.020	.015	.012	.007	.004	.003	.002	.001	.001	.001	.000	.000	.000	.000	.000	30
35	.706	.355	.181	.130	.068	.036	.019	.010	.008	.006	.003	.002	.001	.001	.000	.000	.000	.000	.000	.000	.000	.000	35
40	.672	.307	.142	.097	.046	.022	.011	.005	.004	.003	.001	.001	.000	.000	.000	.000	.000	.000	.000	.000	.000	.000	40
45	.639	.264	.111	.073	.031	.014	.006	.003	.002	.001	.001	.000	.000	.000	.000	.000	.000	.000	.000	.000	.000	.000	45
50	.608	.228	.087	.054	.021	.009	.003	.001	.001	.001	.000	.000	.000	.000	.000	.000	.000	.000	.000	.000	.000	.000	50

Table 31
Present worth of an annuity factor

Present worth of an annuity factor How much 1 received or paid annually for x years is worth today.

Year	1%	3%	5%	6%	8%	10%	12%	14%	15%	16%	18%	20%	22%	24%	25%	26%	28%	30%	35%	40%	45%	50%	Year
1	.990	.971	.952	.943	.926	.909	.893	.877	.870	.862	.847	.833	.820	.806	.800	.794	.781	.769	.741	.714	.690	.667	1
2	1.970	1.913	1.859	1.833	1.783	1.736	1.690	1.647	1.626	1.605	1.566	1.528	1.492	1.457	1.440	1.424	1.392	1.361	1.289	1.224	1.165	1.111	2
3	2.941	2.829	2.723	2.673	2.577	2.487	2.402	2.322	2.283	2.246	2.174	2.106	2.042	1.981	1.952	1.923	1.868	1.816	1.696	1.589	1.493	1.407	3
4	3.902	3.717	3.546	3.465	3.312	3.170	3.037	2.914	2.855	2.798	2.690	2.589	2.494	2.404	2.362	2.320	2.241	2.166	1.997	1.849	1.720	1.605	4
5	4.853	4.580	4.329	4.212	3.993	3.791	3.605	3.433	3.352	3.274	3.127	2.991	2.864	2.745	2.689	2.635	2.532	2.436	2.220	2.035	1.876	1.737	5
6	5.795	5.417	5.076	4.917	4.623	4.355	4.111	3.889	3.784	3.685	3.498	3.326	3.167	3.020	2.951	2.885	2.759	2.643	2.385	2.168	1.983	1.824	6
7	6.728	6.230	5.786	5.582	5.206	4.868	4.564	4.288	4.160	4.039	3.812	3.605	3.416	3.242	3.161	3.083	2.937	2.802	2.508	2.263	2.057	1.883	7
8	7.652	7.020	6.463	6.210	5.747	5.335	4.968	4.639	4.487	4.344	4.078	3.837	3.619	3.421	3.329	3.241	3.076	2.925	2.598	2.331	2.108	1.922	8
9	8.566	7.786	7.108	6.802	6.247	5.759	5.328	4.946	4.772	4.607	4.303	4.031	3.786	3.566	3.463	3.366	3.184	3.019	2.665	2.379	2.144	1.948	9
10	9.471	8.530	7.722	7.360	6.710	6.145	5.650	5.216	5.019	4.833	4.494	4.192	3.923	3.682	3.571	3.465	3.269	3.092	2.715	2.414	2.168	1.965	10
11	10.368	9.253	8.306	7.887	7.139	6.495	5.938	5.453	5.234	5.029	4.656	4.327	4.035	3.776	3.656	3.543	3.335	3.147	2.752	2.438	2.185	1.977	11
12	11.255	9.954	8.863	8.384	7.536	6.814	6.194	5.660	5.421	5.197	4.793	4.439	4.127	3.851	3.725	3.606	3.387	3.190	2.779	2.456	2.196	1.985	12
13	12.134	10.635	9.394	8.853	7.904	7.103	6.424	5.842	5.583	5.342	4.910	4.533	4.203	3.912	3.780	3.656	3.427	3.223	2.799	2.469	2.204	1.990	13
14	13.004	11.296	9.899	9.295	8.244	7.367	6.628	6.002	5.724	5.468	5.008	4.611	4.265	3.962	3.824	3.695	3.459	3.249	2.814	2.478	2.210	1.993	14
15	13.865	11.938	10.380	9.712	8.559	7.606	6.811	6.142	5.847	5.575	5.092	4.675	4.315	4.001	3.859	3.726	3.483	3.268	2.825	2.484	2.214	1.995	15
16	14.718	12.561	10.838	10.106	8.851	7.824	6.974	6.262	5.954	5.668	5.162	4.730	4.357	4.033	3.887	3.751	3.503	3.283	2.834	2.489	2.216	1.997	16
17	15.562	13.166	11.274	10.477	9.122	8.022	7.120	6.373	6.047	5.749	5.222	4.775	4.391	4.059	3.910	3.771	3.518	3.295	2.840	2.492	2.218	1.998	17
18	16.398	13.754	11.690	10.828	9.372	8.201	7.250	6.467	6.128	5.818	5.273	4.812	4.419	4.080	3.928	3.786	3.529	3.304	2.844	2.494	2.219	1.999	18
19	17.226	14.324	12.085	11.158	9.604	8.365	7.366	6.550	6.198	5.877	5.316	4.843	4.442	4.097	3.942	3.799	3.539	3.311	2.848	2.496	2.220	1.999	19
20	18.046	14.877	12.462	11.470	9.818	8.514	7.469	6.623	6.259	5.929	5.353	4.870	4.460	4.110	3.954	3.808	3.546	3.316	2.850	2.497	2.221	1.999	20
21	18.857	15.415	12.821	11.764	10.017	8.649	7.562	6.687	6.312	5.973	5.384	4.891	4.476	4.121	3.963	3.816	3.551	3.320	2.852	2.498	2.221	2.000	21
22	19.660	15.937	13.163	12.042	10.201	8.772	7.645	6.743	6.359	6.011	5.410	4.909	4.488	4.130	3.970	3.822	3.556	3.323	2.853	2.498	2.222	2.000	22
23	20.456	16.444	13.489	12.303	10.371	8.883	7.718	6.792	6.399	6.044	5.432	4.925	4.499	4.137	3.976	3.827	3.559	3.325	2.854	2.499	2.222	2.000	23
24	21.243	16.936	13.799	12.550	10.529	8.985	7.784	6.835	6.434	6.073	5.451	4.937	4.507	4.143	3.981	3.831	3.562	3.327	2.855	2.499	2.222	2.000	24
25	22.023	17.413	14.094	12.783	10.675	9.077	7.843	6.873	6.464	6.097	5.467	4.948	4.514	4.147	3.985	3.834	3.564	3.329	2.856	2.499	2.222	2.000	25
26	22.795	17.877	14.375	13.003	10.810	9.161	7.896	6.906	6.491	6.118	5.480	4.956	4.520	4.151	3.988	3.837	3.566	3.330	2.856	2.500	2.222	2.000	26
27	23.560	18.327	14.643	13.211	10.935	9.237	7.943	6.935	6.514	6.136	5.492	4.964	4.524	4.154	3.990	3.839	3.567	3.331	2.856	2.500	2.222	2.000	27
28	24.316	18.764	14.898	13.406	11.051	9.307	7.984	6.961	6.534	6.152	5.502	4.970	4.528	4.157	3.992	3.840	3.568	3.331	2.857	2.500	2.222	2.000	28
29	25.066	19.188	15.141	13.591	11.158	9.370	8.022	6.983	6.551	6.166	5.510	4.975	4.531	4.159	3.994	3.841	3.569	3.332	2.857	2.500	2.222	2.000	29
30	25.808	19.600	15.372	13.765	11.258	9.427	8.055	7.003	6.566	6.177	5.517	4.979	4.534	4.160	3.995	3.842	3.569	3.332	2.857	2.500	2.222	2.000	30
35	29.409	21.487	16.374	14.498	11.655	9.644	8.176	7.070	6.617	6.215	5.539	4.992	4.541	4.164	3.998	3.845	3.571	3.333	2.857	2.500	2.222	2.000	35
40	32.835	23.115	17.159	15.046	11.925	9.779	8.244	7.105	6.642	6.233	5.548	4.997	4.544	4.166	3.999	3.846	3.571	3.333	2.857	2.500	2.222	2.000	40
45	36.095	24.519	17.774	15.456	12.108	9.863	8.283	7.123	6.654	6.242	5.552	4.999	4.545	4.166	4.000	3.846	3.571	3.333	2.857	2.500	2.222	2.000	45
50	39.196	25.730	18.256	15.762	12.233	9.915	8.304	7.133	6.661	6.246	5.554	4.999	4.545	4.166	4.000	3.846	3.571	3.333	2.857	2.500	2.222	2.000	50

Technical note 17

Table 32
Capital recovery factor

Capital recovery factor annual payment that will repay a $1 loan in X years with compound interest on the unpaid balance

Year	1%	2%	3%	4%	5%	6%	7%	8%	9%	10%	11%	12%	13%	14%	15%	Year
1	1.010 000	1.020 000	1.030 000	1.040 000	1.050 000	1.060 000	1.070 000	1.080 000	1.090 000	1.100 000	1.110 000	1.120 000	1.130 000	1.140 000	1.150 000	1
2	.507 512	.515 050	.522 611	.530 196	.537 805	.545 437	.553 092	.560 769	.568 469	.576 190	.583 934	.591 698	.599 484	.607 290	.615 116	2
3	.340 022	.346 755	.353 530	.360 349	.367 209	.374 110	.381 052	.388 034	.395 055	.402 115	.409 213	.416 349	.423 522	.430 731	.437 977	3
4	.256 281	.262 624	.269 027	.275 490	.282 012	.288 591	.295 228	.301 921	.308 669	.315 471	.322 326	.329 234	.336 194	.343 205	.350 265	4
5	.206 040	.212 158	.218 355	.224 627	.230 975	.237 396	.243 891	.250 456	.257 092	.263 797	.270 570	.277 410	.284 315	.291 284	.298 316	5
6	.172 548	.178 526	.184 598	.190 762	.197 017	.203 363	.209 796	.216 315	.222 920	.229 607	.236 377	.243 226	.250 153	.257 157	.264 237	6
7	.148 628	.154 512	.160 506	.166 610	.172 820	.179 135	.185 553	.192 072	.198 691	.205 405	.212 215	.219 118	.226 111	.233 192	.240 360	7
8	.130 690	.136 510	.142 456	.148 528	.154 722	.161 036	.167 468	.174 015	.180 674	.187 444	.194 321	.201 303	.208 387	.215 570	.222 850	8
9	.116 740	.122 515	.128 434	.134 493	.140 690	.147 022	.153 486	.160 080	.166 799	.173 641	.180 602	.187 679	.194 869	.202 168	.209 574	9
10	.105 582	.111 327	.117 231	.123 291	.129 505	.135 868	.142 378	.149 029	.155 820	.162 745	.169 801	.176 984	.184 290	.191 714	.199 252	10
11	.096 454	.102 178	.108 077	.114 149	.120 389	.126 793	.133 357	.140 076	.146 947	.153 963	.161 121	.168 415	.175 841	.183 394	.191 069	11
12	.088 849	.094 560	.100 462	.106 552	.112 825	.119 277	.125 902	.132 695	.139 651	.146 763	.154 027	.161 437	.168 986	.176 669	.184 481	12
13	.082 415	.088 118	.094 030	.100 144	.106 456	.112 960	.119 651	.126 522	.133 567	.140 779	.148 151	.155 677	.163 350	.171 164	.179 110	13
14	.076 901	.082 602	.088 526	.094 669	.101 024	.107 585	.114 345	.121 297	.128 433	.135 746	.143 228	.150 871	.158 667	.166 609	.174 688	14
15	.072 124	.077 825	.083 767	.089 941	.096 342	.102 963	.109 795	.116 830	.124 059	.131 474	.139 065	.146 824	.154 742	.162 809	.171 017	15
16	.067 945	.073 650	.079 611	.085 820	.092 270	.098 952	.105 858	.112 977	.120 300	.127 817	.135 517	.143 390	.151 426	.159 615	.167 948	16
17	.064 258	.069 970	.075 953	.082 199	.088 699	.095 445	.102 425	.109 629	.117 046	.124 664	.132 471	.140 457	.148 608	.156 915	.165 367	17
18	.060 982	.066 702	.072 709	.078 993	.085 546	.092 357	.099 413	.106 702	.114 212	.121 930	.129 843	.137 937	.146 201	.154 621	.163 186	18
19	.058 052	.063 782	.069 814	.076 139	.082 745	.089 621	.096 753	.104 128	.111 730	.119 547	.127 563	.135 763	.144 134	.152 663	.161 336	19
20	.055 415	.061 157	.067 216	.073 582	.080 243	.087 185	.094 393	.101 852	.109 546	.117 460	.125 576	.133 879	.142 354	.150 986	.159 761	20
21	.053 031	.058 785	.064 872	.071 280	.077 996	.085 005	.092 289	.099 832	.107 617	.115 624	.123 838	.132 240	.140 814	.149 545	.158 417	21
22	.050 864	.056 631	.062 747	.069 199	.075 971	.083 046	.090 406	.098 032	.105 905	.114 005	.122 313	.130 811	.139 479	.148 303	.157 266	22
23	.048 886	.054 668	.060 814	.067 309	.074 137	.081 278	.088 714	.096 422	.104 382	.112 572	.120 971	.129 560	.138 319	.147 231	.156 278	23
24	.047 073	.052 871	.059 047	.065 587	.072 471	.079 679	.087 189	.094 978	.103 023	.111 300	.119 787	.128 463	.137 308	.146 303	.155 430	24
25	.045 407	.051 220	.057 428	.064 012	.070 952	.078 227	.085 811	.093 679	.101 806	.110 168	.118 740	.127 500	.136 426	.145 498	.154 699	25
26	.043 869	.049 699	.055 938	.062 567	.069 564	.076 904	.084 561	.092 507	.100 715	.109 159	.117 813	.126 652	.135 655	.144 800	.154 070	26
27	.042 446	.048 293	.054 564	.061 239	.068 292	.075 697	.083 426	.091 448	.099 735	.108 258	.116 989	.125 904	.134 979	.144 193	.153 526	27
28	.041 124	.046 990	.053 293	.060 013	.067 123	.074 593	.082 392	.090 489	.098 852	.107 451	.116 257	.125 244	.134 387	.143 664	.153 057	28
29	.039 895	.045 778	.052 115	.058 880	.066 046	.073 580	.081 449	.089 619	.098 056	.106 728	.115 605	.124 660	.133 867	.143 204	.152 651	29
30	.038 748	.044 650	.051 019	.057 830	.065 051	.072 649	.080 586	.088 827	.097 336	.106 079	.115 025	.124 144	.133 411	.142 803	.152 300	30
31	.037 676	.043 596	.049 999	.056 855	.064 132	.071 792	.079 797	.088 107	.096 686	.105 496	.114 506	.123 686	.133 009	.142 453	.151 996	31
32	.036 671	.042 611	.049 047	.055 949	.063 280	.071 002	.079 073	.087 451	.096 096	.104 972	.114 043	.123 280	.132 656	.142 147	.151 733	32
33	.035 727	.041 687	.048 156	.055 104	.062 490	.070 273	.078 408	.086 852	.095 562	.104 499	.113 629	.122 920	.132 345	.141 880	.151 505	33
34	.034 840	.040 819	.047 322	.054 315	.061 755	.069 598	.077 797	.086 304	.095 077	.104 074	.113 259	.122 601	.132 071	.141 646	.151 307	34
35	.034 004	.040 002	.046 539	.053 577	.061 072	.068 974	.077 234	.085 803	.094 636	.103 690	.112 927	.122 317	.131 829	.141 442	.151 135	35
36	.033 214	.039 233	.045 804	.052 887	.060 434	.068 395	.076 715	.085 345	.094 235	.103 343	.112 630	.122 064	.131 616	.141 263	.150 986	36
37	.032 468	.038 507	.045 112	.052 240	.059 840	.067 857	.076 237	.084 924	.093 870	.103 030	.112 364	.121 840	.131 428	.141 107	.150 857	37
38	.031 761	.037 821	.044 459	.051 632	.059 284	.067 358	.075 795	.084 539	.093 538	.102 747	.112 125	.121 640	.131 262	.140 970	.150 744	38
39	.031 092	.037 171	.043 844	.051 061	.058 765	.066 894	.075 387	.084 185	.093 236	.102 491	.111 911	.121 462	.131 116	.140 850	.150 647	39
40	.030 456	.036 556	.043 262	.050 523	.058 278	.066 462	.075 009	.083 860	.092 960	.102 259	.111 719	.121 304	.130 986	.140 745	.150 562	40
41	.029 851	.035 972	.042 712	.050 017	.057 822	.066 059	.074 660	.083 561	.092 708	.102 050	.111 546	.121 163	.130 872	.140 653	.150 489	41
42	.029 276	.035 417	.042 192	.049 540	.057 395	.065 683	.074 336	.083 287	.092 478	.101 860	.111 391	.121 037	.130 771	.140 573	.150 425	42
43	.028 727	.034 890	.041 698	.049 090	.056 993	.065 333	.074 036	.083 034	.092 268	.101 688	.111 251	.120 925	.130 682	.140 502	.150 369	43
44	.028 204	.034 388	.041 230	.048 665	.056 616	.065 006	.073 758	.082 802	.092 077	.101 532	.111 126	.120 825	.130 603	.140 440	.150 321	44
45	.027 705	.033 910	.040 785	.048 262	.056 262	.064 700	.073 500	.082 587	.091 902	.101 391	.111 014	.120 736	.130 534	.140 386	.150 279	45
46	.027 228	.033 453	.040 363	.047 882	.055 928	.064 415	.073 260	.082 390	.091 742	.101 263	.110 912	.120 657	.130 472	.140 338	.150 242	46
47	.026 771	.033 018	.039 961	.047 522	.055 614	.064 148	.073 037	.082 208	.091 595	.101 147	.110 821	.120 586	.130 417	.140 297	.150 211	47
48	.026 334	.032 602	.039 578	.047 181	.055 318	.063 898	.072 831	.082 040	.091 461	.101 041	.110 739	.120 523	.130 369	.140 260	.150 183	48
49	.025 915	.032 204	.039 213	.046 857	.055 040	.063 664	.072 639	.081 886	.091 339	.100 946	.110 666	.120 467	.130 327	.140 228	.150 159	49
50	.025 513	.031 823	.038 865	.046 550	.054 777	.063 444	.072 460	.081 743	.091 227	.100 859	.110 599	.120 417	.130 289	.140 200	.150 139	50

Technical note 17

Table 32 continued

Year	Rate 16%	17%	18%	19%	20%	21%	22%	23%	24%	25%	26%	27%	28%	29%	30%	Rate Year
1	1.160 000	1.170 000	1.180 000	1.190 000	1.200 000	1.210 000	1.220 000	1.230 000	1.240 000	1.250 000	1.260 000	1.270 000	1.280 000	1.290 000	1.300 000	1
2	.622 963	.630 829	.638 716	.646 621	.654 545	.662 489	.670 450	.678 430	.686 429	.694 444	.702 478	.710 529	.718 596	.726 681	.734 783	2
3	.445 258	.452 574	.459 924	.467 308	.474 725	.482 175	.489 658	.497 173	.504 718	.512 295	.519 902	.527 539	.535 206	.542 902	.550 627	3
4	.357 375	.364 533	.371 739	.378 991	.386 289	.393 632	.401 020	.408 451	.415 926	.423 442	.430 999	.438 598	.446 236	.453 913	.461 629	4
5	.305 409	.313 564	.319 778	.327 050	.334 380	.341 765	.349 206	.356 700	.364 248	.371 847	.379 496	.387 196	.394 944	.402 739	.410 582	5
6	.271 390	.278 615	.285 910	.293 274	.300 706	.308 203	.315 764	.323 389	.331 074	.338 819	.346 623	.354 484	.362 400	.370 371	.378 394	6
7	.247 613	.254 947	.262 362	.269 855	.277 424	.285 067	.292 782	.300 568	.308 422	.316 342	.324 326	.332 374	.340 482	.348 649	.356 874	7
8	.230 224	.237 690	.245 244	.252 885	.260 609	.268 415	.276 299	.284 259	.292 293	.300 399	.308 573	.316 814	.325 119	.333 487	.341 915	8
9	.217 082	.224 691	.232 395	.240 192	.248 079	.256 053	.264 111	.272 249	.280 465	.288 756	.297 119	.305 551	.314 049	.322 612	.331 235	9
10	.206 901	.214 657	.222 515	.230 471	.238 523	.246 665	.254 895	.263 208	.271 602	.280 073	.288 616	.297 231	.305 912	.314 657	.323 463	10
11	.198 861	.206 765	.214 776	.222 891	.231 104	.239 411	.247 807	.256 289	.264 852	.273 493	.282 207	.290 991	.299 842	.308 755	.317 729	11
12	.192 415	.200 466	.208 628	.216 896	.225 265	.233 730	.242 285	.250 926	.259 648	.268 448	.277 319	.286 260	.295 265	.304 331	.313 454	12
13	.187 184	.195 378	.203 686	.212 102	.220 620	.229 234	.237 939	.246 728	.255 598	.264 543	.273 559	.282 641	.291 785	.300 987	.310 243	13
14	.182 898	.191 230	.199 678	.208 235	.216 893	.225 647	.234 491	.243 418	.252 423	.261 501	.270 647	.279 856	.289 123	.298 445	.307 818	14
15	.179 358	.187 822	.196 403	.205 092	.213 882	.222 766	.231 738	.240 791	.249 919	.259 117	.268 379	.277 701	.287 077	.296 504	.305 978	15
16	.176 414	.185 004	.193 710	.202 523	.211 436	.220 441	.229 530	.238 697	.247 936	.257 241	.266 606	.276 027	.285 499	.295 017	.304 577	16
17	.173 952	.182 662	.191 485	.200 414	.209 440	.218 555	.227 751	.237 021	.246 359	.255 759	.265 216	.274 723	.284 277	.293 874	.305 509	17
18	.171 885	.180 706	.189 639	.198 676	.207 805	.217 020	.226 313	.235 676	.245 102	.254 586	.264 122	.273 705	.283 331	.292 994	.302 692	18
19	.170 142	.179 067	.188 103	.197 238	.206 462	.215 769	.225 148	.234 593	.244 098	.253 656	.263 261	.272 909	.282 595	.292 316	.302 066	19
20	.168 667	.177 690	.186 820	.196 045	.205 357	.214 745	.224 202	.233 720	.243 294	.252 916	.262 581	.272 285	.282 023	.291 792	.301 587	20
21	.167 416	.176 530	.185 746	.195 054	.204 444	.213 906	.223 432	.233 016	.242 649	.252 327	.262 045	.271 796	.281 578	.291 387	.301 219	21
22	.166 353	.175 550	.184 846	.194 229	.203 690	.213 218	.222 805	.232 446	.242 132	.251 858	.261 620	.271 412	.281 232	.291 074	.300 937	22
23	.165 447	.174 721	.184 090	.193 542	.203 065	.212 652	.222 294	.231 984	.241 716	.251 485	.261 284	.271 111	.280 961	.290 832	.300 720	23
24	.164 673	.174 019	.183 454	.192 967	.202 548	.212 187	.221 877	.231 611	.241 382	.251 186	.261 018	.270 874	.280 750	.290 644	.300 554	24
25	.164 013	.173 423	.182 919	.192 487	.202 119	.211 804	.221 536	.231 308	.241 113	.250 948	.260 807	.270 688	.280 586	.290 499	.300 426	25
26	.163 447	.172 917	.182 467	.192 086	.201 762	.211 489	.221 258	.231 062	.240 897	.250 758	.260 640	.270 541	.280 458	.290 387	.300 327	26
27	.162 963	.172 487	.182 087	.191 750	.201 467	.211 229	.221 030	.230 863	.240 723	.250 606	.260 508	.270 426	.280 357	.290 300	.300 252	27
28	.162 548	.172 121	.181 765	.191 468	.201 221	.211 015	.220 843	.230 701	.240 583	.250 485	.260 403	.270 335	.280 279	.290 232	.300 194	28
29	.162 192	.171 810	.181 494	.191 232	.201 016	.210 838	.220 691	.230 570	.240 470	.250 387	.260 320	.270 264	.280 218	.290 180	.300 149	29
30	.161 886	.171 545	.181 264	.191 034	.200 846	.210 692	.220 566	.230 463	.240 379	.250 310	.260 254	.270 208	.280 170	.290 140	.300 115	30
31	.161 623	.171 318	.181 070	.190 869	.200 705	.210 572	.220 464	.230 376	.240 305	.250 248	.260 201	.270 164	.280 133	.290 108	.300 088	31
32	.161 397	.171 126	.180 906	.190 729	.200 587	.210 472	.220 380	.230 306	.240 246	.250 198	.260 160	.270 129	.280 104	.290 084	.300 068	32
33	.161 203	.170 961	.180 767	.190 612	.200 489	.210 390	.220 311	.230 249	.240 198	.250 159	.260 127	.270 101	.280 081	.290 065	.300 052	33
34	.161 036	.170 821	.180 650	.190 514	.200 407	.210 322	.220 255	.230 202	.240 160	.250 127	.260 101	.270 080	.280 063	.290 050	.300 040	34
35	.160 892	.170 701	.180 550	.190 432	.200 339	.210 266	.220 209	.230 164	.240 129	.250 101	.260 080	.270 063	.280 050	.290 039	.300 031	35
36	.160 769	.170 599	.180 466	.190 363	.200 283	.210 220	.220 171	.230 133	.240 104	.250 081	.260 063	.270 049	.280 039	.290 030	.300 024	36
37	.160 662	.170 512	.180 395	.190 305	.200 235	.210 182	.220 140	.230 109	.240 084	.250 065	.260 050	.270 039	.280 030	.290 023	.300 018	37
38	.160 571	.170 437	.180 335	.190 256	.200 196	.210 150	.220 115	.230 088	.240 068	.250 052	.260 040	.270 031	.280 024	.290 018	.300 014	38
39	.160 492	.170 373	.180 284	.190 215	.200 163	.210 124	.220 094	.230 072	.240 055	.250 042	.260 032	.270 024	.280 018	.290 014	.300 011	39
40	.160 424	.170 319	.180 240	.190 181	.200 136	.210 103	.220 077	.230 058	.240 044	.250 033	.260 025	.270 019	.280 014	.290 011	.300 008	40
41	.160 365	.170 273	.180 204	.190 152	.200 113	.210 085	.220 063	.230 047	.240 035	.250 027	.260 020	.270 015	.280 011	.290 008	.300 006	41
42	.160 315	.170 233	.180 172	.190 128	.200 095	.210 070	.220 052	.230 039	.240 029	.250 021	.260 016	.270 012	.280 009	.290 007	.300 005	42
43	.160 271	.170 199	.180 146	.190 107	.200 079	.210 058	.220 043	.230 031	.240 023	.250 017	.260 013	.270 009	.280 007	.290 005	.300 004	43
44	.160 234	.170 170	.180 124	.190 090	.200 066	.210 048	.220 035	.230 025	.240 019	.250 014	.260 010	.270 007	.280 005	.290 004	.300 003	44
45	.160 201	.170 145	.180 105	.190 076	.200 055	.210 040	.220 029	.230 021	.240 015	.250 011	.260 008	.270 006	.280 004	.290 003	.300 002	45
46	.160 174	.170 124	.180 089	.190 064	.200 046	.210 033	.220 023	.230 017	.240 012	.250 009	.260 006	.270 005	.280 003	.290 002	.300 002	46
47	.160 150	.170 106	.180 075	.190 053	.200 038	.210 027	.220 019	.230 014	.240 010	.250 007	.260 005	.270 004	.280 003	.290 002	.300 001	47
48	.160 129	.170 091	.180 064	.190 045	.200 032	.210 022	.220 016	.230 011	.240 008	.250 006	.260 004	.270 003	.280 002	.290 002	.300 001	48
49	.160 111	.170 078	.180 054	.190 038	.200 026	.210 018	.220 013	.230 009	.240 006	.250 004	.260 003	.270 002	.280 002	.290 001	.300 001	49
50	.160 096	.170 066	.180 046	.190 032	.200 022	.210 015	.220 011	.230 007	.240 005	.250 004	.260 002	.270 002	.280 001	.290 001	.300 001	50

Technical note 18
Standards

Standards, in the form of central government laws, local by-laws and regulations and government department ideals can form a considerable constraint to the provision of low priced plots because of their insistence on standards which are unnecessarily high. Building regulations have often been imported by former colonial powers, or are adapted from western standards without regard to local traditions. Health regulations may be so expensive to conform with, that in certain areas, no effective controls exist. Rules which were designed to control exploitation of poor people by landlords can also help to prevent these people from housing themselves.

To what extent a project has to conform to existing standards depends on the existing laws, the possibility of exemptions and the discretion of local officials in applying regulations. It is suggested that existing regulations be considered critically for these reasons:
- *Building regulations often do not permit or allow for traditional building materials*, such as mud brick which have many very good physical qualities, such as high thermal capacity (they help keep buildings cooler), and can reduce the cost of building a house by 50–70 per cent.
- Building regulations often specify standards of material quality or quantity which are beyond the means of low income families to meet.
- Building regulations and/or subdivision laws often impose restrictions on layout plot size limits, street widths, relationships of buildings which make development of a site considerably more expensive. They are usually designed to control speculative development where making the maximum amount of money would be the sole objective. With a government designed project, social objectives can be included in a design, which is also efficient (see Technical note 16, page 124), but which might not meet existing regulations.
- Health regulations may prohibit on-plot disposal of sewage, which may be the only way possible, economically, and which can be quite safe from a health point of view provided piped water is supplied to standpipes (see Task 3C/8, page 52).
- Space requirements of government departments are often unrealistic, e.g. areas required for schools or police offices. This is the case mainly for agencies to whom land is allocated free of charge.

Excessively large areas for schools and other public uses increases the cost of servicing plots.

Upgrading of standards

When considering appropriate standards it is important to distinguish between those characteristics of a project which can be upgraded over time and those which cannot. On this basis plot sizes and street widths are inflexible, and upgrading would involve considerable hardship and expense, as houses would have to be demolished. Standards should thus not be reduced to absolute minimums in these areas. Utilities, water, sewerage, electricity and the surfacing of roads can all be upgraded over time, as funds become available. This is also true of the buildings on the plots from houses to shops and schools.

Adopting the approach of differentiating between initial standards and standards which will be aimed at over time allows a lower cost project initially, but does not condemn people to live always with low standards. This is a considerable advantage.

Performance vs prescriptive standards

Where possible, try to use standards which specify the performance required rather than a prescriptive specification.

For example, materials can be specified in terms of bearing capacity or fire resistance rather than insisting that a specific material be used.

Technical Note 19:

Participation in problem identification, planning, design and implementation

Background and objectives of the note

What is participation?

Participation is the act of taking part in or sharing in something. In planning and managing projects it refers normally to government allowing or encouraging other actors or stakeholders to take part in identifying problems, developing solutions and taking responsibility for inputs and decisions. It can also be seen in the reverse situation – communities, or private developers allowing local government to participate in their development initiatives.

There are two main approaches. The first is based on technical considerations. That the decisions made will be better, that there will be stronger ownership of the project and that financial commitments and responsibilities for management will be honoured. This approach is typically the one used by professionals.

The second approach is from the point of view of rights. In this the right to participate is emphasised as a principle. This is an approach most often used from an advocacy or political point of view.

An essential consideration in participation is that, citizens should have at least representation in the decision making body. There is no absolute best form of participation. It is important to consider what form makes most sense in a particular situation. This note focuses on participation at the project level.

Sherry Arnstein, writing in the American Planning review in 1969[1] described participation in terms of a ladder of levels, ranging from full control at the high end through 8 levels including consultation, to manipulation by the authorities at the other. Kioe Sheng Yap[2] took this further to divide participation into 4 main groups according to who has the power and whether there is partnership. Within these groups there are also different levels.

Why participation?

Participation has many potential benefits, but also has some limitations. These are not necessarily the same for all stakeholders. Advantages and disadvantages are illustrated in Table 33.

Context of participation

There are two normal starting situations for a development project. The first is when working with an exisiting community, for example in upgrading projects. The second is when working in a situation that those benefiting are not yet known. This is common when there is new development.

Table 33
Participation: advantages and disadvantages

Stakeholder	Advantage	Disadvantage
Local government	● Creates ownership of plans and actions ● Increases chance of support for actions ● Increases potential resources ● Potentially can help develop more suitable programmes and projects ● Can provide base for local acceptance of responsibilities ● Important base for development of partnerships ● In line with officially supported policies demanding participation ● Sometimes is the only possible way to work	● Difficult to do well ● Requires skill and motivation – staff may not be familiar and may be opposed to the diminution of their own powers and expertise ● Takes increased time and effort ● Can give conflict with elected representatives ● Can be open to manipulation
Community	● Ensures community priorities are respected. ● Creates ownership of plans and actions ● Increases chance of support for actions ● Increases potential resources ● Potentially can help develop more suitable programmes and projects ● Acts as a safeguard against autocratic action ● Allows stronger input from special groups, e.g. women or ethnic minorities ● can strengthen community cohesion ● Sometimes is the only possible way to work	● Difficult to do well ● Requires skill and motivation ● Takes increased time and effort ● May conflict with existing social structures ● Can be open to manipulation ● Requires maintenance of supportive community organization ● Too little support is normally give to facilitation of community participation
Individual	● Gives individual chance to influence priorities ● Creates ownership of plans and actions ● Increases chance of support for actions ● Increases potential resources ● Potentially can help develop more suitable programmes and projects ● Acts as a safeguard against autocratic action ● Important base for development of partnerships ● Sometimes is the only possible way to work ● Can be open to manipulation	● Difficult to do well ● Requires skill and motivation ● Takes increased time and effort ● Those participating are not necessarily representative ● May still be difficult for individuals to influence ● Individuals priorities may be over-ruled ● Can be open to manipulation
Private developer	● Increases chance of support for actions ● Increases potential resources ● Potentially can help develop more suitable programmes and projects ● Important base for development of partnerships ● Can speed development by minimising objections	● Takes increased time and effort ● Difficult to do well ● Requires skill and motivation ● Can lead to conflict of views and objectives

---

[1] Arnstein, Sherry (1969) A ladder of Citizen Participation, American Institute of Planners Journal July 1969, p 217
[2] Yap Kioe Sheng, Community Participation in low income Housing Projects: problems and prospects. Community development Journal vol 25, no1 pp 56–65

Technical note 19

Working with known groups

Examples include:
- Communities being upgraded
- Communities which will be resettled
- Groups such as co-operatives, planning new development
- Communities adjacent to new development areas

In this situation, the target groups are clear, and processes and techniques are geared to the community concerned. Here a community can be fully involved in planning and decision making concerning future development. Most community participation techniques are orientated towards this.

Working with unknown groups

This situation is more difficult, as assumptions have to be made concerning the target groups. In the example of Ismailia, this applied to the new development areas. The approach taken was to assume that characteristics were the same as those in existing areas with similar profiles. Talking to groups living in similar development areas can help to understand their needs. The use of case studies can be used as a substitute for direct participation. There is little developed methodology in this area.

Who participates in what

Participation and responsibilities can and should vary over the life and different tasks of a project. It is not necessary that all participate equally and in the same way in all stages. Table 34 indicates a range of levels that can apply at different stages. It is important to emphasise that this is only an illustration of possibilities and will vary from one situation to another.

Participation is not only about communities. It also concerns individuals and the private sector.

How?

The concept of participation is attractive, but, as indicated in Table 33 there are also drawbacks. It is necessary to have staff, or access to staff, with appropriate techniques and the motivation and skills to use them. It is also necessary to have the backing of their organisations, which are often not supportive or not well set up to be able to work in a participatory manner. Official procedures may have to be modified to allow operating in a participatory manner and staff may have to be given stronger delegated powers so as to be able to make agreements with communities.

In terms of techniques, short notes are given here on participatory rapid appraisal, planning and monitoring and evaluation. References are also provided to further sources of information.

Participatory Rapid Urban Appraisal

A range of techniques have been developed, originating in Participatory Rural Appraisal. Participatory rapid urban appraisal is a process whereby key information on a town, or part of a town is collected as quickly as possible with participation of the key stakeholders involved. It is an effort to involve key actors in an important early stage of the planning process and also to improve the relevance and decrease the quantity of data collected. It is normally written about as a means to involve communities, but the principles also apply to involving officials. Much information may be held by officials in different departments or at different levels of government. Often this is not easily accessible nor is it commonly shared.

A key principle of rapid urban appraisal is 'triangulation'. Through this, information is collected on a subject by three related means – observation in the field, discussions with key informants and checking with existing reports and data. This allows the checking of data.

This can be visualised as in Figure 86.

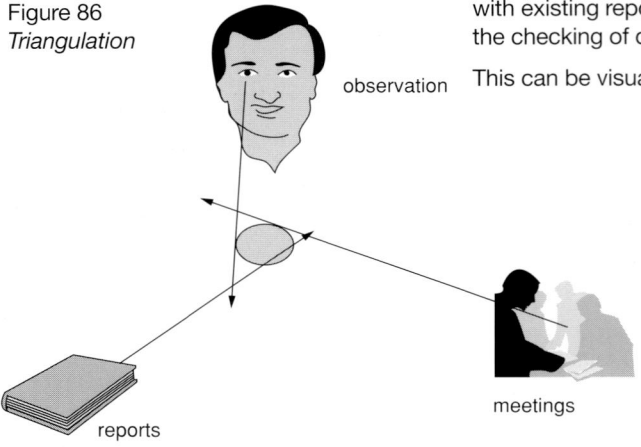

Figure 86
Triangulation

Table 34
Participation at different project stages

Stakeholder	Problem identification/ initial survey/ rapid appraisal	Planning	Detailed study, where necessary	Implementation	Operation and maintenance	Monitoring and evaluation
Local Government	●●●	●●	●●●	●●	●●●	●●
Community based organization*	●●	●●	●	●○	●●○	●●○
Private consultant	●●	●●	●●	●		●
Private developer	●	●	●●	●●	●	

Key: ●●● leading responsibility ●● co-responsibility ● may have some responsibility ○ increasing trend for this to become stronger

* Community based organisations can also be involved in new development areas where the community or part of it will be relocated. Where the future residents do not form a community, existing CBOs can be consulted as proxies.

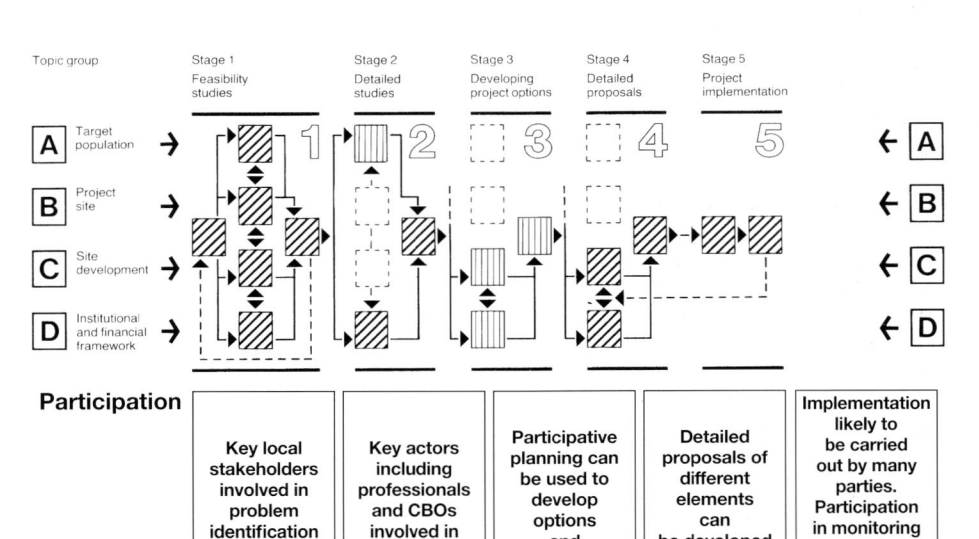

The information needs related to key strategic areas are then reviewed by groups and tables can be drawn up with indications of how to obtain the information.

It is very useful to review sources of existing information with those involved. It is rare that any one person or organisation has access to all relevant information.

This is then used a basis for observation in the field and discussion with relevant stakeholders.

There are a number of techniques that can be used for rapid appraisal. References [3] are indicated at the end of this note which can be used to support those interested in taking the concept further.

Participatory appraisal is very closely linked to participatory planning.

Participatory planning

There are a number of techniques available for participatory planning. They go under a number of names including:

Action Planning. A creative participatory process to develop actions relevant to relatively limited areas or actions. Starts with stakeholders, identifies problems, sets objectives and generates creative solutions.

Objective orientated planning and programming (OOPP) or ZOPP in the German equivalent. Similar to action planning, with a strongly structured process.

Planning for Real. Similar to action planning. Uses simple models as focus of discussion and keeps officials in advisory role.

Strategic planning. Similar to action planning, but normally dealing with city wide strategic issues.

Most of these have a similar process of working. They include processes to bring stakeholders together; to agree on common issues; to set objectives and to develop actions related to resource mobilisation and institutional roles and responsibilities.

Important elements include:
● Participatory planning techniques should ensure that all participants have the opportunity to participate and should not be influenced by inhibitions related to position, education or gender. Techniques such as having participants write their ideas on cards, which can then be discussed impersonally, can be very useful. This helps overcome normal social and power restrictions. Other techniques can be used where participants may be illiterate. An approach used in United Kingdom called "Planning for Real" uses simple models which communities can make and work with to improve communication. In these discussions professionals have a role of providing support to the community rather than dominating the discussion. For example they are only allowed to intervene if asked for information or an opinion;
● the method should encourage creative thinking and the development of ideas. Each situation is new and requires a new approach to be effective;
● the technique should be efficient in use of peoples time – it should help keep a balance between discussion and action.

A number of references that focus on participatory planning can be found in the Sources of Information.

Participatory monitoring and evaluation

Monitoring and evaluation are important tools to both manage projects and to ensure that there is learning from them. Where communities participate actively in a stronger way in planning it also makes sense that they play a strong role in monitoring and evaluating what they are doing. The approach can also be used in reviewing progress in new development projects. This allows direct feedback and learning by a community and thus facilitates the building of their capacity.

Community based monitoring and evaluation should be seen as complementary to activities in the same area by governmental or other organisations[5].

When? Relationship to the process outlined in the Manual

Figure 87 illustrates the relationship between the process outlined in the manual and the forms of participation that may be appropriate at each stage. It is important to emphasise that there is no one perfect form of participation. It will vary in each case depending on the nature of communities, individuals and contexts.

Figure 87
Participation and the process outlined in the manual

[1] Arnstein, Sherry (1969) A ladder of Citizen Participation, American Institute of Planners Journal July 1969, p217
[2] Yap Kioe Sheng, Community Participation in low income Housing Projects: problems and prospects. Community development Journal vol 25, no1 pp 56-65
[3] References on rapid appraisal include Chambers (1997) and the series of PRA notes from IIED (see Sources of Information).
[4] The following references provide detailed descriptions of participatory planning techniques: Gibson, A and Wratten E (1995) Development Planning for Real; Goethert and Hamdi Making Microplans (1988) ; Wates, N (1996) Action Planning (2000) Community Planning. See Sources of Information, page 156.
[5] UNCHS (1994) Community based Monitoring and evaluation

Technical note 20:
Capacity building

Background and objectives of the note

The Habitat II conference in Istanbul in 1996 laid a strong emphasis on the need to build capacity to develop and maintain urban development. This note has the following objectives:
- to clarify what 'capacity building' means and why it is important
- to look at who needs what capacity
- to outline how to integrate a capacity building strategy with development plans.

Figure 88
Capacity building concept

What is capacity and why is it important?

'Capacity' here means capacity to plan and manage urban development. To have effective capacity it is necessary to have trained and motivated individuals, but it is also essential that the organisations they are working in are able to use their skills effectively illustrates the idea. Individuals (1) need to be developed in terms of skills, attitude and knowledge. Their organisations (2) need development to be able to use individuals effectively. Finally, the framework (3) in which organisations work requires to be supportive. For example, it is important that that local government is allowed to create conditions that encourage staff to work full time. These include career structures and permitted salary levels.

All this takes place in a national context which it is normally not possible to influence, but which has to be taken into account. At a local level actions will mainly be working on individual capacities and the improvement of organisations. At a national level important actions may include lobbying for a more supportive national policy. This can be done, for example, through an association of local authorities, professional associations or national NGOs.

Who needs capacity, and how much?

The trend in development is for governmental and non-governmental partners to work more closely together. This implies that all the actors or stakeholders involved require to develop their capacities to work together in new ways.

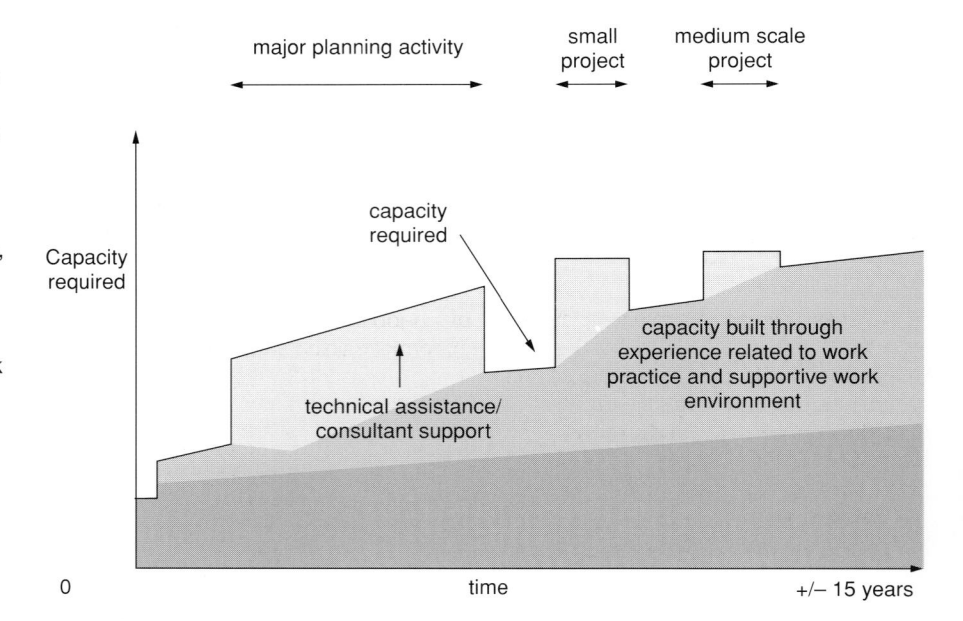

Figure 89
Relation between capacity required, means of provision and activities

It is not necessary that any one organisation should be able to carry out all activities. For example, local government may hire private consultants or an NGO to carry out the design of a project. Figure 89 illustrates how capacity needed can vary over time. There is a need to build capacity through training, on-job experience and organisational improvement, but exceptional work is often best done by specialists. However, using specialists does not remove responsibilities from local government or from communities. They have to learn to make use of outside expertise without losing sight of their own objectives.

Integration of a capacity building strategy

It is important that organisations take capacity building seriously. To do this in the most realistic way, a capacity building strategy should be integrated into the urban development strategy. Capacity building should not be isolated, or carried out without a purpose.

Linking demand with supply

The first essential is that an organisation thinks through what it wants to achieve. The second is that it can get support from capacity building organisations which are responsive to its needs. The most effective way of ensuring this is where funds are budgeted for capacity building, allowing the organisation to be a critical purchaser of services.

Figure 90 illustrates the need to link activities and funding to ensure there is a good stimulus for relevant capacity building support.

Technical Note 21
Land tenure policy options[1]

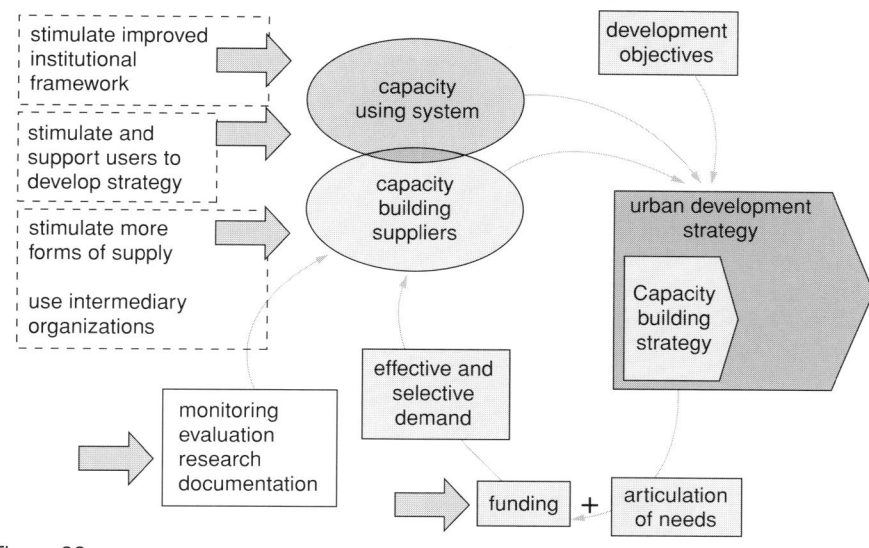

Figure 90
Capacity building system

Key steps

The key steps necessary to develop a capacity building strategy are as follows:

1 *Need assessment.* Each organization involved in development needs to be clear in terms of its responsibilities related to proposed development. It then considers the capacity it has and the capacity it needs:
a) to carry out existing functions effectively
b) to carry out proposed new work

2 An explicit *strategy* is developed together with capacity building institution comprising
a) capacity building objectives
b) on-job training
c) formal training (internal or external)
d) organisational development
e) budgeting

3 *Implementation.* The strategy requires a continuous effort. Its implementation should be monitored and reviewed annually and the strategy itself continuously adjusted.

This Technical Note expands on the text of Task 3D/2 of the Manual and places the issue of tenure options in a broader urban land market context.

Land tenure systems reflect the attitudes and priorities which each society places on land as a resource and on relationships between individuals, groups and society as a whole. Under conditions of rapid urbanisation and urban growth, competition for land becomes intense and accessibility will be increasingly influenced by the land tenure policy operating.

In formulating or implementing policies, it is important to note that a wide range of tenure categories exist in the urban areas of most developing countries. These may include statutory, customary, religious and various informal systems, each of which will be affected by a change in policy.

Before any change is made to existing tenure practices, it is therefore important to review the full range of existing categories and their relationships. For example, providing titles to one informal tenure category will influence property prices and expectations among residents in other tenure categories. In making this assessment, an estimate should be made of the extent to which lack of security has inhibited investment in housing improvements.

Characteristics of land tenure systems:

Private ownership: This is enshrined in English civil law and the French Civil Code and can be in perpetuity (freehold) or for a specific period (leasehold). It permits the unrestricted exchange of land and property and the development of land markets in which the balance between demand and supply is achieved through the pricing mechanism. Its strength is in facilitating efficient land markets, though it invariably fails to ensure equitable access to land for lower income groups.

Public ownership: Most societies apply a form of public ownership and some have nationalised all land. The demands placed on administrative systems have, however, invariably restricted their efficiency, raised the cost of land management and restricted their equity objectives.

---

[1] This Technical note draws extensively on Payne, Geoffrey 'Urban Land Tenure and Property Rights in Developing Countries: A Review' published for ODA (now DFID) by Intermediate Technology Publications, London, 1997

Customary concepts: These take many forms, but vest ownership in the group or tribe, rather than the individual. Under conditions of limited competition or change, they have proved efficient and equitable. However, they have often come under pressure in urban areas where land markets are increasingly commercialised.

Religious concepts: The Islamic concept of land ownership is perhaps the most fully developed, though extensive *waqf* land holdings have restricted the efficient and equitable development of many cities.

Informal concepts: In many cities, these are now the largest singly tenure category. As such, they form a continuum of sub-systems, from illegal squatting to the unauthorised construction of houses on land which is legally owned. Each type serves different population groups and commands different prices depending upon their perceived level of security. Terms such as *bidonville* or *favela* should be replaced with more objective criteria in assessing informal tenure systems.

Assessments of existing tenure categories should indicate the proportion of land and housing in each main category and their role in the local land and property market. Land information studies are needed which list their advantages and limitations to residents and the urban land market.

A common problem is the lack of clarity in existing tenure status. Before proposals to change the tenure status of an area are considered, it is therefore vital to identify all claims to land ownership or rights. This may require land registries and relevant agencies to be brought up to date and strengthened.

Tenure policy should seek to enhance clarity, efficiency and equity in the registration, transfer and use of land and property. The key to success is to ensure that tenure systems minimise land market distortions, balance the interests of all parties, (especially land-owners, occupiers and tenants), are familiar to local people and are simple to administer.

It is commonly assumed that the most desirable form of tenure is freehold, since this maximises the benefits of private ownership. However, this overlooks several key factors, including:
- The impact on other social groups, such as tenants, who may be forced out of their properties by higher rents
- The demand that it will stimulate from residents in other informal settlements
- The increased risk of 'downward raiding' by higher income groups
- Discrimination against other forms of tenure which may be more appropriate for large sections of the population, especially low-income households.

A common objective of tenure policy is to increase access to formal credit, since titles are widely used as collateral for loans. However, most financial institutions will determine loans primarily on the ability of the borrower to repay the loan, so that collateral is a secondary factor. Credit agencies are also increasingly willing to lend moderate amounts without requiring titles as collateral. Yet even a modest increase in tenure security may, in itself, stimulate investments in land development and house improvements.

The situation is likely to be particularly sensitive in informal settlements accommodating a significant proportion of tenants. Any major change in tenure status in such areas, may displace many tenants, through increased rent levels, or the sale of properties by their new 'owners' seeking to realise the enhanced commercial value of their properties. Modest improvements in tenure status can help to protect tenants from the risk of large rent hikes and minimise distortions in the urban land market.

In countries where more than one system operates, it may be desirable to build on existing laws and practices, rather than further complicate matters by introducing new ones.

Administrative procedures for registering land and property rights are frequently over-complex, time consuming and inefficient. Simplifying these and placing responsibility in a single local agency can achieve a marked improvement in land administration. As an interim measure, it may be desirable to maintain a land inventory to record claims and titles without having to adjudicate or guarantee them.

Difficulties in identifying and registering the variety of rights that groups and individuals have to land make it equally difficult to determine who should benefit from improved tenure – persons with original rights to land or property, tenants or sub-tenants, or those with various formal or informal documents. It may also be difficult to determine boundaries between plots, in which case two options worth considering are:

1 'Social cadastre'. This involves taking an aerial photo of a specified area, assembling all interested parties and obtaining agreement on the spot of all plot boundaries and relevant rights, for inclusion onto maps.

2 The use of GPS (Global Positioning Satellite) units to record the precise latitude and longitude of an agreed point for inclusion on to land registers.

Strengthening the administrative system can be largely financed through revenue collected from property taxes levied on households receiving increased property rights. To achieve this, it may be necessary to allow local authorities to retain all, or some of, the land and property revenues generated from their areas of responsibility. Effective management systems will also be required to ensure the efficient allocation of such revenues.

Tenure policy should be sensitive to the social, cultural and economic circumstances of the target groups and take due account of indirect ramifications. No single tenure category is capable of meeting the needs of all sections of society. The best approach may therefore be to provide a choice of tenure options, so that households can select the one most suited to their needs and be able to change easily from one to another.

For informal settlements, this need not involve formal titles. In many cases, certificates of use or official statements that settlements will not be removed, have been sufficient to encourage residents to invest in housing and environmental improvements. The determining factor is the minimum level of tenure security required *by residents*, rather than that defined by professionals. By offering this to a wide section of those exposed to insecure tenure, market distortion will be minimised and secondary investment stimulated.

Tenure policies should concentrate on forms of tenure which are sufficient to provide a sense of security and stimulate investment in house improvements. They should therefore offer residents a package of rights, with acceptable obligations, which address their needs and resources. Such 'rights-based' approaches are invariably preferable to arbitrary formal tenure categories, at least in the short term.

A step-by-step approach addressing the most critical needs first can also serve to introduce the concept of cost recovery so essential to the replicability and sustainability of land development policies.

In the case of customary lands coming under pressure for urban development, public/private sector joint ventures are an effective option, as they enable customary groups to retain a primary interest.

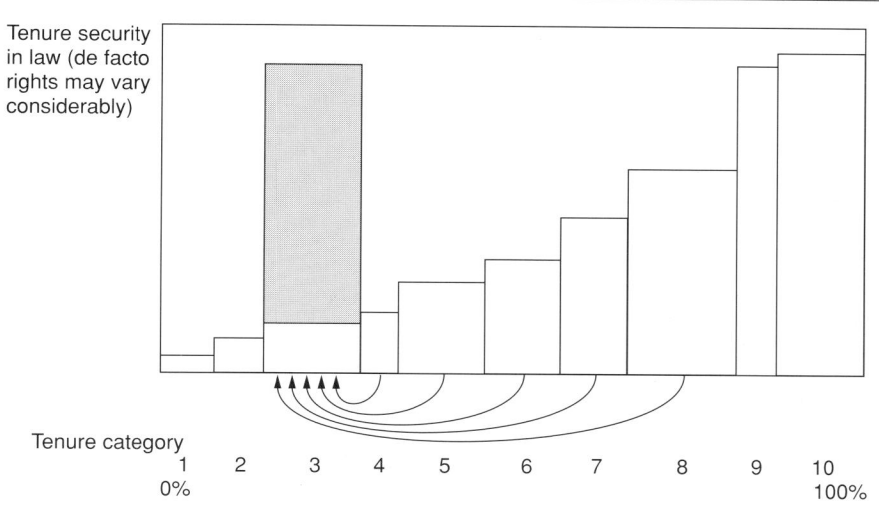

It will then be necessary to assess the capability of the financial institutions lending in the housing sector, and the terms and conditions under which they operate, to ensure that they can respond quickly and efficiently to the scale and nature of demand for loans following tenure status changes.

Since tenure registration is likely to make plot and house-holders liable for property taxes and other charges, options should be considered for deferring taxes, or establishing incremental tax rates (eg based upon property values, building types, or household incomes), so that levels are affordable to all households.

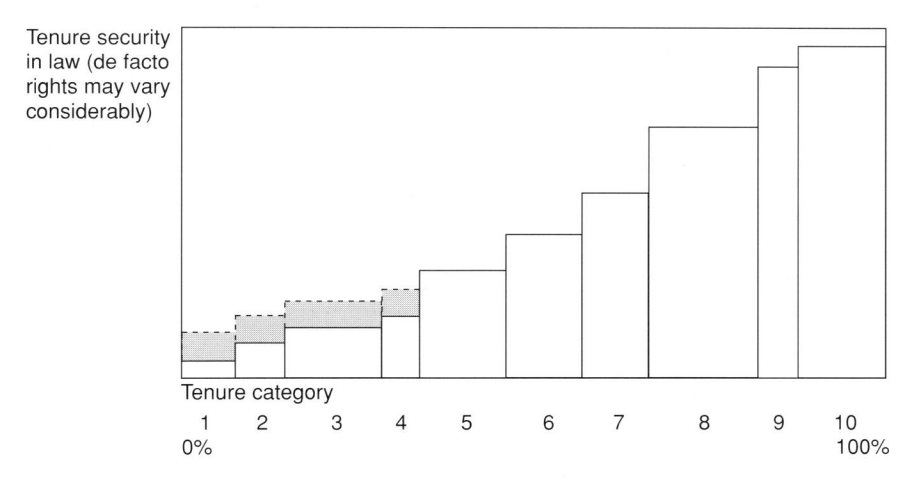

Tenure categories found in many cities:
1 Pavement dweller
2 Squatter tenant
3 Newly legalised freeholder or squatter house or plot
4 Tenant in unauthorised subdivision
5 Squatter 'owner' – regularised
6 Owner – unauthorised construction
7 Legal owner – unauthorised construction
8 Tenant with contract
9 Lease-holder
10 Free-holder

NB: for simplicity, this illustration deletes customary and Islamic tenure categories

This figure demonstrates that the provision of full, formal tenure status to informal settlements raises their commercial value and can therefore actually reduce tenure security for the most vulnerable social groups, such as squatter tenants. It also creates new, or intensifies existing, land and property market distortions because households in tenure categories with more existing security suddenly find that squatters have received full titles. This encourages 'downward raiding' as shown by the arrows.

Figure 91
Likely consequences of providing titles to 'owners' of squatter houses

Tenure categories found in many cities:
1 Pavement dweller with approval to remain
2 Squatter tenant with protection
3 Squatter 'owner' – regularised
4 Tenant in unauthorised subdivision – with protection
5 Squatter 'owner' – regularised
6 Owner – unauthorised subdivision
7 Legal owner – unauthorised construction
8 Tenant with contract
9 Lease-holder
10 Free-holder

NB: for simplicity, this illustration deletes customary and Islamic tenure categories

This figure suggests that a rights base approach increases tenure security for the most vulnerable social groups. It also increases social equity without distorting land or property markets

Figure 92
Likely consequences of improving tenure rights in unauthorised settlements

Technical note 22
Site development and design briefs

The City Summit in Istanbul in 1996 endorsed the Habitat Agenda, in which all countries agreed to the active participation of private sector developers, NGOs and local communities in decisions on urban development and the formulation of shelter policies.

This new strategy will have far reaching implications for the role of the public sector in urban development. At present, many urban development authorities develop land themselves for allocation according to various social and financial criteria. This may involve the development of public land, or the acquisition and development of land held under private or customary tenure.

In future, this direct approach is likely to be replaced by more indirect methods, in which public sector agencies prepare site development and design briefs and invite a range of groups to respond with proposals. This should encourage more market sensitive and demand led approaches, whilst reducing the burden on scarce public sector resources.

So how can such briefs be prepared and implemented? Experience varies widely from country to country, but all have a common theme – to specify the minimum social, financial and environmental requirements which need to be included in a proposal in order to obtain planning approval.

A good brief will be just that – brief. It should also be *clear* and based on criteria that are *realistic* in terms of yielding an acceptable return on investment by developers, in return for the reduction of risk involved. After all, the benefit of this approach to a developer (whether a commercial developer, NGO or community group), is that it eliminates risk by specifying *in advance* the conditions which need to be met in order to proceed.

This Technical Note covers the factors to consider in preparing site development and urban design briefs. The former can be considered synonymous with economic feasibility studies, whilst the latter covers the design of the physical environment.

Site development briefs

A method for undertaking feasibility studies is presented in Stage One of this manual. However, preparing a *brief* for a feasibility study requires the ability to place oneself in the mind of a reader who may not share the same assumptions or objectives. It is therefore important that a site development brief should:
- Be based on a realistic assessment of the likely development costs (including short term finance), selling prices and potential profit margins for each project component.
- Specify social and environmental requirements which maximise the public benefit of a development without deterring potential developers.
- Concentrate on aspects of particular public concern.
- Distinguish between those elements which are mandatory and those which are preferred, but optional.
- Be clear, concise and unambiguous. Provide only that information which a potential developer needs to know in preparing proposals.

Initially, at least, it will be necessary to undertake a feasibility study in order to obtain the information necessary in order to prepare a site development brief.

Options for increasing the proportion of non-profitable elements, such as housing for low-income groups, or communal facilities, will be increased if provision is permitted for a proportion of more profitable components. The balance between these will vary according to the specific characteristics of each site and the extent to which a mixture of activities and social groups is acceptable locally. Assessments of costs should be based on current commercial rates of interest.

Whereas a feasibility study may begin with an assessment of a target population (see Stage 1), a site development brief will usually be based on the constraints and opportunities presented by a specific site. These will exert a strong influence on the target population which is most likely to want and be able to afford to live and work there and the range of appropriate activities.

Once a feasibility study has confirmed an appropriate range of development options for the site, steps can be taken to prepare the site development brief.

This should contain information on the following:

The site:
- The site location and address, plus boundaries and access points, together with a site location and layout plan.
- Land area and topographic details.
- Existing uses, if any.
- Details of ownership and rights.
- The history of the site and the reasons for its being available for development.

Site development:
- Any restrictions on permitted uses and their location.
- Requirements regarding public open space, road reservations, landscaping and public amenities.
- Requirements regarding minimum plot size, set-backs or floor area ratios and initial density levels.
- Requirements regarding building materials and construction systems for initial development, together with levels of initial services provision.
- Requirements regarding the extent and nature of any non-profitable, social, or environmental components to be included in the development. These may include social housing, car parking requirements and children's play areas, etc.
- Details of any financial or other contribution by the public sector.
- Any requirements regarding phasing, especially the provision of less profitable project components.
- Other factors which would generate a public benefit and encourage the development authority to approve one proposal in preference to another.

Special care is required when selecting tenure options for upgrading projects in informal settlements. The aim should be to provide the minimum level of security required to encourage investment, without increasing costs or rents.

The target population:
- The proportion or number of lower income households to be included in the development.
- The nature and extent of any external subsidy available to assist such households, or contribute towards the costs of on- and off-site infrastructure and public amenities, such as schools, health clinics and other facilities.
- Identify local groups or organisations.

Urban design briefs

Urban design briefs have an additional objective to site development briefs: They seek to ensure the achievement of appropriate, good quality environments. Unlike planning, which is primarily concerned with two dimensions, urban design is concerned with three dimensions – the creation of urban form and the spaces between buildings. It is particularly concerned with the form and design of the public realm.

Urban design has two means of achieving policy objectives – design guides and design briefs. The former are general documents which specify the range of architectural forms and treatments which will be acceptable to a planning authority over a wide area, whereas design briefs apply to specific sites or well defined areas ensuring that the urban design potential of that site is maximised, while controlling the architecture as little as possible.

In central urban areas, a considerable degree of control may be required over development proposals, especially if the site is in an area of historic, touristic or economic importance. In primarily residential neighbourhoods, development control requirements can be restricted to key areas of the public domain, leaving residents to decide on the use of their plots and the form of their immediate environment.

Briefs therefore need to be sensitive to specific site conditions and identify the key factors of concern to the wider public. They will need to be based on a feasibility, or site development study to ensure that they are economically viable.

It is vital that briefs contain a clear and concise summary of development policies applicable to the site. All conditions to which development proposals should conform need to be specified. At the same time, any aspects which are open to negotiation, or on which requirements may be optional, rather than mandatory, should also be specified. The views of all key stakeholders should be sought before finalising individual briefs and comments incorporated as appropriate to ensure widespread public acceptance.

A good brief should contain the following sections:
- An analysis of the site, indicating the reasons for the brief, the character of any existing development and the pressures for change which proposals should address. Connections and links to surrounding streets, land uses and buildings should be shown in detail, together with any site conditions which will influence development options. Any transport or parking requirements should also be specified.
- A statement of design objectives which lists the qualities to be encouraged and those which will not be acceptable. These may include reference to the scale and form of new buildings, their relationship to communal and public spaces and landscaping requirements. In many cases, the character, form and morphology of existing settlements can suggest options for future development. Any restrictions on building heights, set-backs, or floor area ratios should be specified. Plans and drawings should be used wherever appropriate.
- Controls to be exerted over proposed developments and the sanctions to be imposed in the event of non-conformity.

Key elements in proposals will be the size and shape of plots. Invariably, these will be smaller for low income households, though it is important that briefs permit a range, so that households can choose the combination of plot size, levels of infrastructure and type of initial building which reflect their needs and priorities.

Requirements regarding the form in which proposals are to be submitted for consideration, and the level of detail required, need to be specified clearly. As with site development briefs, any requirements regarding the phasing of development proposals should be clearly stipulated.

Any loopholes in the brief can be easily identified by inviting a professional colleague or developer to prepare proposals which seek to undermine policy objectives while conforming to the terms and conditions of the brief.

It should always be remembered that an effective brief is one that concentrates attention on the key elements of general public interest and stimulates creativity in other areas by adopting as relaxed an approach as site conditions permit. Care should therefore be taken not to be over restrictive.

It is important to invite a wide range of stake-holders to assess proposals based on the brief. This will increase support for the decisions reached and promote a transparent administrative process. Time taken at this stage can also result in considerable savings later, by reducing the risk of local hostility to new development proposals.

Design briefs provide an opportunity for local development authorities to initiate proposals without having to seek recourse to unpopular, time consuming and inefficient land acquisition and development procedures. They are cost effective means of increasing public control over urban development and increasing the participation of key stake-holders.

They also have major advantages to potential developers in eliminating risk and reducing the time required for processing development proposals. Once the brief has been published, interested parties can be given a reasonable time to prepare and submit proposals. Once the decision has been taken on the successful proposal, the developer can begin on site as soon as convenient. Project costs can be reduced considerably as a result, with benefits passed onto consumers in the form of lower prices. The rate of planned urban development can also be enhanced without increasing the burden on scarce public sector staff and other resources.

Despite their many advantages, even a good brief cannot guarantee a good environment. However, it should reduce the risk of an inappropriate or unattractive development taking place.

For suggestions on further reading concerning urban design and briefs, see Sources of Information.

Technical note 23
Innovative sanitation systems

Most countries in the world either provide, or aspire to, systems of sanitation which involve individual connections of a water closet into a public sewer system. These mix urine and excreta and transport the resulting sludge across the urban area to a central treatment plant, or point for disposal untreated into the sea, or local rivers.

The technology on which these systems are based was developed in the mid-nineteenth century in Britain and other European countries to counter the spread of cholera and other environmentally borne infectious diseases. As such, it has only been in general use for about a century, during which cities have grown larger and more complex than ever before.

A major reason for the popularity of conventional sewerage systems is that by pulling a handle or lever, the wastes vanish from sight without leaving any smell. However, this does not remove the problem of human wastes; it simply passes it elsewhere. Among the limitations of conventional public sewer systems are the following:
- They are completely dependent upon large quantities of treated water, even though data suggest that 280 million people in urban areas lack access to safe water, even for drinking and nearly half of urban populations in the South lacked a water supply into their home[1].
- The capital and operating costs of public sewer systems are beyond the reach of all but the most affluent households in many cities of the South, yet according to one study[2], the choice of sanitation technology has the greatest potential to reduce infrastructure costs.
- The mixing of solid and liquid wastes results in effluents which require expensive treatment if they are not to cause serious pollution when discharged into water courses. The former may cause disease if people come into contact with the sewage, while the latter may deplete oxygen in receiving water courses, killing fish and causing smells. It is therefore important that cost comparisons between sewers and other sanitation technologies make an appropriate allowance for the cost of sewage treatment.[3]
- The mixing of solid and liquid wastes pollutes a large quantity of water and creates toxic solutions which then require expensive chemical treatment, or cause pollution to the natural environment if discharged untreated into water courses.
- Leakage, which can be extensive in poorly maintained systems, compounds pollution of the water table, creating major health risks.
- Cities are simply growing too fast for conventional sewerage systems to keep pace. As a result, only a third of urban populations in Asia are connected to public sewers, though this figure is about two thirds in Latin America, though some cities in Africa have no sewers at all[4]. The low level of existing provision and treatment capacity would require massive capital investment to increase connections in line with potential demand, which may be unavailable due to frequently low levels of cost recovery. It is therefore not a feasible prospect for general application, even where it is wanted.

Given these limitations, it is perhaps surprising that they are still regarded as the ultimate solution by many professionals working in the field of municipal engineering and public health. It is certainly unrealistic to expect that these systems can be extended to serve a large proportion of urban populations, let alone all households.

Alternative systems, which are more affordable, flexible and ecologically efficient therefore need to be considered for general application, but particularly for any project intended to benefit lower income groups. At the same time, it will be necessary to win popular acceptance by retaining the main advantage of what has become widely known, for good reasons, as 'the convenience'.

Alternative systems

Task 3C/8 of the Manual identifies the most common technical alternative options. However, a number of additional systems have been developed and applied in many countries during the last fifteen years which deserve mention. Among these are the following:

Shallow sewers:

These work in the same way as conventional sewer systems, but are cheaper because sewers are laid at shallow depths, reducing the cost of excavation and allowing small chambers to be used instead of much more expensive conventional manholes.

They are appropriate where rights of way are narrow, so that there is no possibility of traffic loading and where sewers can be laid under pedestrian pavements and through gardens and yards. A good example of the latter is in the Brazilian condominial sewer system. (See Watson, G. 'Good sewers Cheap: Agency-Customer Interactions in Low-Cost Urban Sanitation in Brazil', World Bank Water and Sanitation Division, 1995, World Bank, Washington DC, 1995)

Sewered interceptor tank systems:

These are also known as Settled Sewerage systems. They are designed on the assumption that there will be an interceptor tank, normally some form of small septic tank, on every connection to the sewer. Solids settle in the interceptor tanks, provided that the latter are periodically desludged. The sewers thus need to be designed to transport liquids only and this means that they can in theory be smaller and laid to flatter slopes than conventional sewers. Some caution is appropriate, since there is a possibility that the interceptor tanks will cease to function if they are not desludged when they are full. Care also needs to be taken to select the minimum diameter pipe and gradient to be used.

In one example in Madras, India, interceptor tanks measured about 800mm x 600mm in plan, with an effective depth of only 500mm. These connected to 100mm diameter pipes and were still working satisfactorily more than two years after they were installed even though the interceptor tanks had not been desludged[5]. Another example in Peshawar, Pakistan was designed with circular tanks of 900mm diameter and 2m depth and have been working well for the last four years.

Sewer connections to septic tanks

A variation on the basic interceptor tank system is to provide shared septic tanks

---

NB The editors wish to acknowledge the advice, material and comments on drafts of this technical note provided by Kevin Tayler of Gilmore Hankey Kirke International, London and Professor Duncan Mara of Leeds University.
[1] United Nations 'An Urbanizing World' UNCHS, 1996, p. 264
[2] Cotton, Andrew and Franceys, Richard 'Services for Shelter' Liverpool University Press, 1991, p. 4

[3] Taylor, Kevin "Planning and design of sanitation facilities: Handout 4 – sewered options" Mimeo Gilmore Hankey Kirke International, St James Hall, Moor Park Road, London SW6 2JW
[4] United Nations, 1996 op cit p. 268

[5] Taylor, Kevin op cit

serving 5–20 houses, from which the effluent is discharged to the sewers. In this system, the connections from houses to septic tanks are designed as conventional sewers and the sewers downstream from the septic tanks to sewered interceptor tank system standards. Interceptor tanks at the end of community built systems will protect the main sewers from any solid materials carried in the branch systems and the approach may therefore be attractive to sewerage authorities which are concerned by the prospect of direct discharges from community built sewers into their own sewers.

Communal toilets

These take two forms: Public toilets, which are open to everyone and communal toilets that are reserved for a number of families. In India, the former work best when someone charges for their use, while the latter can work well where the user group can be defined.

One of the best known of the former types is the Sulabh system in which toilets are developed and maintained by an NGO (Sulabh International, based in India). These offer clean toilets for a very modest cost and employ local staff. Wastes are either connected into public sewers or treated locally. Sulabh also provide advice and help in the construction of community and family facilities.

Another option was developed in Bombay by another group of NGOs, including SPARC, the National Slum Dwellers federation and Mahila Milan.[6] These provided separate toilets for men and women and included communal taps, washing areas and refuse collection points. Local residents were employed in constructing and maintaining the toilets and acquired skills in the process which increased incomes by up to 200%.

Communal toilets work best when the families allowed to use the toilet are clearly defined and access is restricted, perhaps by issuing a key to the intended users.

Treatment options

Sewered disposal systems must incorporate treatment if they are not to pollute the environment. Conventional treatment systems have proved problematic in many low income countries, in some cases because of high running costs and in others because of the lack of skilled operators. Another problem with conventional systems is that treatment tends to be centralised, so that expensive trunk sewers are needed to bring sewage to them. In recent years, there has been considerable interest in low cost decentralised treatment systems which can overcome these problems.

Waste stabilisation ponds are one option. In essence, they consist of a series of ponds through which the sewage flow is passed. Natural biological processes in the ponds reduce the organic load of the sewage to a point at which it can be discharged without harming the receiving water course. The advantages of stabilisation ponds are that they require relatively little maintenance and can operate without power, so that they are cheap to run. Their disadvantage is that they need a lot of land, which can increase their capital cost in urban areas where land values are high. It also affects their suitability for decentralised systems, since these are likely to need treatment facilities in areas which are already built-up and where land availability is a major constraint.

In recent years, so called 'small footprint' treatment systems which require little land have been developed, mainly in industrialised countries. Some, such as the Australian Memtec system rely on membrane technology and are claimed to be able to remove 97–99% of all contaminants, including human wastes, bacteria, viruses, heavy metal and oil. Their suitability for use in developing countries has still to be established.

Other systems depend on anaerobic processes to reduce the organic load of the sewage. Anaerobic waste stabilisation ponds are the simplest option in this category and can remove 50–75% of the organic load in the right conditions. This means that they will normally have to be followed by secondary aerobic ponds which, as already noted, have a relatively large land take. Another aerobic system which is attracting interest is the up-flow anaerobic sludge blanket reactor system (UASB). The UASB system was developed in the Netherlands, but a few reactors have been built in India. Preliminary evaluation suggest that small UASB reactors may be available option for decentralised treatment.

In some countries (eg. El Salvador, Guatamala and Mexico) experiments are taking place with solar heated toilets. These may consist of a unit installed in the vault to increase evaporation, or a collector (such as a blackened piece of aluminium sheet) placed on top of the pit and exposed to the sun. The benefits of these systems for wider application has yet to be established.

Selecting the preferred option

The choice of technology most appropriate for specific situations will be influenced by several factors, including:
- Social attitudes and practices. They can be divided basically into two types: washers or wipers. In the former, people use water to clean themselves, while in the latter, paper, stones, reeds, grass etc are widely used.
- Costs and levels of affordability. The capital and operational costs of on-plot and off-plot methods of disposal and treatment vary considerably according to the level of provision involved. Involving local residents in the provision and operation of sanitation systems will invariably reduce costs and ensure that they are well maintained.
- Density levels. Where these are high, on-plot options are less appropriate, since plot sizes tend to be too small and the unit costs of public sewerage systems become more affordable.
- The layout of the settlement will also influence options, since the cost of installing public sewers or gaining access for tankers may be very high in areas with narrow, winding lanes, unless appropriate standards are applied. In such cases, sewer installation costs can be reduced.
- Environmental considerations. In El Salvador, Vietnam and Guatamala, experiments are also being made with toilets which separate urine and faeces, to reduce environmental pollution, though it is too early to assess their performance.

NB. The editors wish to acknowledge the advice, material and comments on drafts of this technical note provided by Kevin Tayler of Gilmore Hankey Kirke International, London and Professor Duncan Mara of Leeds University.

---

[6] UNCHS, 1996, op cit p385

Technical note 24
Use of Geographical Information Systems (GIS)

A Geographic Information systems or GIS is a tool to store, organize and use information linked to location.

The technology of storing, retrieving and working with land based information using computers has become increasingly easy to use and affordable in recent years and offers a useful set of tools to practitioners working on settlement upgrading and new development projects.

This note outlines some of the main features of GIS and the potential advantages in its use. It also draws attention to the implications of using the technology in terms of the demands it places on institutions and their ways of working.

Urban development, and especially upgrading, implies a close interaction between many actors, including planners, project officers, policy makers and residents. The information needed for management and planning purposes needs to be easily accessible, updated and shared among them.

The start of an upgrading or new urban development process requires good knowledge of the physical conditions of the settlement and the profile of its inhabitants. Information about the physical features of the built-up space is normally collected together with social and economic data during the process of settlement plan making. The data assembled should then be continuously updated via field surveys and be able to be retrieved to become a key support decision. The use of computers simply facilitates this work by using tools and other instruments that facilitate data storage, retrieval, manipulation and display.

How does GIS work?

GIS facilitates the working with information by organizing it together with the exact location. This is known as spatially referenced information. The basic rule is that all relevant information must be linked to a coordinate point (x,y), a coordinate referenced area or a set of two or more coordinates (in case of a line).

The other aspects of information relate to what happens in a particular location. This data can also be organized in different thematic layers that can be superimposed to each other. This allows the establishing and clarifying of the relationships between different types of data e.g. house location and ownership and income status. It is like superimposing transparent maps, but is more powerful and flexible. Users can turn on and off combinations of layers to explore relationships.

Thematic maps can be generated and be made accessible in printed or electronic formats for different users.

In practical terms, when designing the settlement layout, planners must have at hand the precise location of buildings as well as the boundaries of land parcels. This is essential for an efficient process of 'reblocking' and the planning of new accesses and roads. Data on income of the inhabitants and economic activities taking place within the settlement also allow scenario building and forecasting about the future development of the settlement providing trends are properly monitored. For example, the decision about the relocation of buildings and families and the subsequent payment of compensation for demolition depends on the availability of the basic information about the land parcel, the building unit and their occupants. Also important are the location of the plot, the situation of the building unit, its address, its size, building quality, ownership status, services available, family size of the occupants, name of owner, employment status, age, and time of residence.

Geographical information systems make the access to this set of information a lot easier and offer additional advantages in comparison to manual systems. GIS allows decision-makers to find rapid answers to their questions and communicate with graphic outputs.

The identification of who lives where is an important step during the preparatory phase of the upgrading program. The result of this step is often registered into a manual cadastre of the settlement and the residents. The difficulties derived from the lack of accurate maps is commonly overcome by the use of aerial photographs which together form the basis for launching the process of infrastructure improvement, service provision and the registration of land ownership. These may be used to produce new maps. Field checks and on-site measurements help to bring accuracy to the cartographic basis of upgrading plans. Many GIS software programs are equipped with embedded tools to work with raster maps originated from photographs. Orthophotos, which combine attributes of air photographs and maps are also a type of solution that eliminates differences commonly found in aerial photos. They can be used as the basis of thematic layers produced to form new sets of spatial data. This procedure is called map overlay.

As described elsewhere in the Manual, there are different types of surveys intended to provide the basic set of information to support the design and project preparation of the upgrading process. The result of these field surveys is commonly organized in an information system handled manually by project teams. This can form the embryo of a GIS at the settlement level.

The advantage from using GIS is that a database containing all sorts of non-graphic information such as ownership (attributes) can be organized in an automated format. GIS makes the linking with the graphic elements represented in the thematic maps a lot easier. This linkage allows not only data manipulation within the database management structure but also permits spatial implications from data manipulation to be visualized immediately in map formats.

Potential benefits of using GIS

A fundamental question is 'is it worth the effort to use GIS in upgrading and new development programmes?'. It is not a simple question to answer. In the end it is necessary to balance the advantages and the costs in each case. First, the potential benefits:

● The establishment of a GIS can provide the means to establish the embryo of a land information system and a basic computerised cadastre of the area. Feasibility depends on the capability of field checks to provide accurate topographic coordinates and measurements and on the ability of follow-up household surveys to collect data on land ownership. The database developed from land ownership survey and data input in terms of digital mapping can be combined via a GIS program. Once these steps are undertaken, the use of GIS will make possible a continuous monitoring of the changes in the settlement both in physical terms and in land ownership transaction provided that updating mechanisms are put into place. Trends in land and housing markets can be monitored and scenarios can be drawn in order to assess opportunities and constraints relevant to the settlement.
● Information linking location and development potentials also allows local tax assessment collection to be carried out in

a more transparent and effective manner. In many cases, this has been a very strong benefit.
- Infrastructure improvement requires a proper registration and location of the networks within the settlement. GIS can support this by allowing sharing of key information between different agencies involved. GIS is then likely to become a strategic support tool in the establishment of a common utility information system.
- The maintenance of infrastructure networks depends on reliable information regarding the type of pipes and cables, dimensions, capacity, length, depth, location, etc. The larger the network in place, the more coordination is required when malfunctioning or leakage is detected and repair needs to be undertaken in very precise locations under the ground.
- GIS can also provide a good base for establishment of transparent information systems as it makes data more systematic and accessible. Provided there is access to data, this can be a major factor for improving governance.

Implications in terms of finance and organisation

The financial resources needed to purchase the software and hardware and to train users of the system are significant, though on balance the benefits are normally considered to far outweigh them. For example, improvement in tax revenue or better coordination of infrastructure can recover many times the investment in the GIS system.

Prices of hardware and software tend to decrease over time for the same power, but new, more powerful equipment tends to remain at a similar price over time. In 1999, a GIS unit composed of a powerful desktop PC computer, a digitizer (A0 size), a plotter, a scanner and a colour printer can be purchased for about US$ 7 500. A commercially available GIS software lab composed of a core GIS program plus network analysis, overlay and additional issues would cost an additional US$ 7 000. Training of personnel to operate and maintain the system requires time and continuous investment to keep updated with the rapid developments that take place in this field. Training and up-gradation of the system is recommended, and therefore a budget line must be created to keep the system and its prerequisites operational.

The implementation of GIS in a local government institution requires development of staff, but normally not redundancy. It demands capacity building in order to understand the technology and its use in the daily performance of tasks. However, resistance to learn to use new tools and to deal with new technologies may hinder the establishment of a Geographical Information System. Senior level managers may fear that greater transparency in information management and accessibility to data will threat their power and control on information. Furthermore, they may resist the ascent of junior staff – who are normally more literate with computers – and who may create another layer of power in the information management cycle within the organization. One of the most important hurdles to be overcome is likely to be institutional and individual attitudes towards sharing information. GIS requires that information be collected from different sources to be able to be worked on later. For these reasons, there needs to be a strong will from top decision-makers to make the system work and to keep it going.

Steps to implementaton

First, the advantages to management of the agencies concerned must be clear so that there is a commitment to implement and support the system. GIS is not only a computer based system. In addition to looking at the technological parts of the system, it is necessary to pay attention to the human resources, the organisational setting and the arrangements for decision making regarding the management of the information which is required to have an information system operational.

There are a number of user-friendly and easy-to-learn packages in PC formats that are available in the market. These include ArcInfo, ArcView, AtlasGIS, and MapInfo. Before a decision is made about the technology choice one should look carefully at the type of software support that exists in the country/city and pursue professional advice about the specific properties and capabilities of the systems available in the local market. A comparison between systems capabilities and the main purpose to establish GIS should be made.

Possibilities for training personnel and managing the system, including options for data collection, storage and display should be considered at the outset. This is an important phase. Care in purchase can save local governments and institutions the headache of investing in something that could be difficult to use.

Normally the existing manual system in data collection and storage should provide the basis for establishing a GIS.

Once a choice is made regarding the software and the organisational setting and human resources development, the next step is data entry. That means the organisation of graphic information and data related to it (e.g. road lines can be linked with data on width, type of pavement, addresses, coordinates). This implies the transformation (digitalisation) of basic maps, cartographic maps and aerial photographs via a digitizer (available in the market in different formats) as well as physical, social and economic data about the inhabitants into computer data via database management systems or embedded capabilities of GIS programs.

Finally, GIS is only a tool. As with any tool, it is what it is used for that matters. The benefits, which are potentially considerable, have to outweigh the significant costs involved.

References

Those considering this option can find a wide range of publications on the topic. A classic work recommended is D. Maguire, M. F. R. Goodchild and D. W. Rhind (eds), *Geographical Information Systems: principles and applications*, Longman Scientific & Technical, John Wiley & Sons, USA, Volumes I & II. The reader will get a comprehensive overview of the history of GIS, the concepts and theories involved, different applications, concrete experiences and assessment of the results in different contexts.

Technical note 25
Gender sensitivity in urban projects

This technical note stresses the importance of gender sensitivity in urban planning and development. It also highlights how to prepare and develop projects in a gender sensitive manner.

Gender refers to the relationship and differences between men and women. More specifically, gender refers to the social, economic and political relations, and not to the biological differences. Relations between men and women form one of the foundations on which any society organises itself. Gender relations therefore also have an impact on urban development. Being open to, aware of and responsive to issues having to do with these relations between women and men, is called gender sensitivity.

The issue of gender should not be seen as separate from the project process. Gender is not something to add on to a project, it should be part and parcel of the project. It cuts across all the stages of urban project development as described in this manual. The process of studying, developing, planning, implementing and monitoring the urban projects may have a different impact on the lives and roles of men compared to women. It can result in changes in gender roles, relations and inequalities. The other way round, gender roles also influence the urbanisation process itself. It is therefore of utmost importance to be gender sensitive in every phase of the project, and involve both women and men in all project stages; of thinking, planning and implementation. In other words, to mainstream gender in urban development.

Mainstreaming gender in urban projects is not complicated. It basically demands commitment to do it. It implies the following actions in the various stages of the process:

Stages 1 and 2: Feasibility and detailed studies

Broadly speaking, there are two options to ensure that the studies will be gender sensitive: to include experts with gender expertise in the study team doing the feasibility and detailed studies. The expert should ensure that gender sensitive indicators are included in both the feasibility and detailed studies; to train all members of the study team in gender issues before the study takes off.

Target population

Women and female-headed households usually form a large proportion of the urban poor in developing countries. Various studies and international reports have emphasised the feminisation of poverty and the increase of female-headed households. Even within households, poverty levels may differ, with women and children usually belonging to the poorer segment of the household. To reveal the different views, needs and priorities of the target population, the feasibility and detailed studies should look beyond the level of household, or head of household and provide a breakdown in male and female responses. Collection and analysis of data on women and men will provide insight in the complexity of the target population. The importance of collecting and analysing data on women stems from their triple roles: in production, caring and the household. Their economic activities usually take place at the lower end of the informal and formal sectors, incomes are small and on an irregular basis. Income generating activities will have to be combined with their other roles. Questions to be answered on the target population include:
- Does the target population consist of predominantly men or women?
- Are there many female-headed households among the target population?

Economic characteristics of the target group should include information on:
- What are the sources of income of women and men?
- Are they wage earners, informal sector workers, traders, etc.?
- Who are major contributors to the fixed expenditures, e.g. rent, loan repayment?
- Do women earn a major share of the family or household income?
- Can women survive on their own incomes, or are they depending on relief, subsidies and remittances?

Household characteristics should give an insight in the gender breakdown of households. Information should be obtained on:
- Do husband and wife live in the same household?
- Who is heading the household in day-to-day life?
- Does the household cater for relatives, or dependent family members?
- Does the household include temporary members, such as relatives from rural areas?

Involvement of women in the consultation process will provide another very important contribution towards gender sensitivity. Women, just as men, should participate in and be consulted at all stages of urban projects. To ensure adequate participation of women in the process, it is recommended that meetings be organised close to the target group, at the project or the employment site. It is also recommended that childcare facilities be provided, for instance by hiring a local childminder for the duration of the meetings and surveys. Thirdly, more women will be attracted if they receive some economic benefit, for instance by providing food and drinks for the meeting.

Project site

The main issue here is accessibility of the site. Access to employment opportunities, public facilities and transport links are especially important for women due to their triple role in the household, care and production process.

The land tenure system might form the major obstacle for women to access a plot or site. In many countries the land tenure system is organised in a way which denies women access to land or housing. The land tenure system should make it possible for women to own land, get title deeds, ownership rights and financing in their own names on equal terms with men. A change in the legal system might be needed to facilitate this.

Site development options

The special needs of both women and men should be taken into consideration during all stages of site development. Women might emphasise different priorities than their male companions with regard to housing layouts and densities, e.g. safety (street lightning), food security (urban agriculture). Plot development will have to take into consideration women's roles in:
- Production; e.g. home-based informal sector, easy access to (formal) employment site
- Care; e.g. children, husband, (sick) relatives, and
- Household; e.g. food, water, fuel.

Access to commerce and industry, public facilities and recreation, circulation and transportation and utilities are crucial for poor women's survival strategies.

Institutional and financial framework

The agency responsible for a project should possess the necessary capacity and skills to mainstream gender issues in the project process. Hiring expertise or obtaining training can enhance this capacity. The financial framework should include all additional costs of full participation of women in the process; e.g. childcare, meetings on-the-spot, transport costs, food and beverages. The feasibility study checklist should include relevant measures to analyse the involvement of women, as well as their benefits.

Attitudes to locality, plot characteristics and dwellings.

The attitudes of men and women to the locality, plot characteristics and dwellings may differ. It is recommended that the views and priorities of men and women be analysed separately, rather than obtaining the views of the household only.

Potential for community involvement

As mentioned before, adequate community involvement, both of women and men, is a key to the success of any urban project. Women's participation may be enhanced through involvement of their clubs, groups and organisations in the project process. This is particularly the case in countries where women's participation is limited by social norms.

Nature of housing demand

Looking at the nature of housing demand, information will be required on:
- Type of household; e.g. female-headed;
- Tenure category, do women have ownership rights, access to rental?
- Means of obtaining dwelling, e.g. access of women to financing, to building co-operatives;
- Preferred locations; e.g. close to schools, clinics, water points and other facilities.

Stage 3: Site development

Formulating site development options

The information collected on gender issues during the study phases should be taken into account during the site development process. Involvement and participation of women during the process of deciding on housing layout, and plot development will add to the success of the project.

Environmental and health issues, such as contaminated water, pollution, epidemics and spreading of AIDS and related diseases, will have the strongest impact on those spending more time at home, usually women and their dependants. Considering and working on reduction of environmental and health risks will especially benefit women.

The planning of sites for commerce and industry will have more advantage for women if they are close to utilities and public facilities, such as schools, clinics, crèches, etc. It will be more convenient for women to combine their triple roles. The same counts for safe and easy access to transportation at affordable prices.

Institutional and financial framework

One of the criteria in selecting the institutional framework should be the gender planning and management capacity in the implementing agency. High political backing of gender sensitive politicians is an added advantage. Active involvement of the target group through their civil society organisations might bring a stronger female voice, as well as female views on the project impact on gender relations.

Land tenure is an issue which needs special attention. In many societies land title and land rights are available exclusively for men. In these countries it is very diffficult, or even impossible, for single women, female heads of households and married women to obtain land rights or title deeds. As these categories usually represent a high percentage of the urban poor, they can easily be missed out. There might be a need to review the by-laws on land tenure.

When developing the financial options, and calculating the ability to pay for project costs, it is important to relate the income to the person paying the rent or repaying the loan. If the woman is the one paying, her income should be considered. Access to financing for both men and women should be available. Most women have problems providing collateral. However, experiences with microfinance institutions prove that women generally reach high levels of repayment, also without having provided collateral.

Stage 4: Designing site development, project implementation and monitoring

At these stages the process should continue paying attention to all the gender issues mentioned in the study and site development stages. The process should continue to consult men and women, addressing their priority needs, and may make a special effort to also hire women as well as men in the implementation of the project. In many countries, women are skilled builders in rural areas. This is often overlooked once it comes to urban areas.

Gender sensitivity among men and women can be strengthened through gender training and dialogue on gender issues throughout the process.

For the monitoring process, indicators should be developed to measure the actual project impact on the lives, well-being, and poverty situation of both men and women. This is the only way to prove if the project is gender sensitive and really making an impact.

Appendix 1

Profile of El Hekr (Hai El Salam) Project, Egypt

This section of the Manual provides a brief review of the stages which led up to the implementation of the El Hekr (Hai El Salam)* project, a description of the project and its current progress.

Background

In December 1974, Clifford Culpin and Partners were appointed Lead Consultants to undertake the Ismailia Master Plan Study. This Study was part of the reconstruction programme, following the cession of hostilities, initiated by the Ministry of Housing and Reconstruction, Egypt, and funded by the United Nations Development Programme.

The October War of 1973 and the subsequent re-opening, in June 1975, of the Suez Canal restored to Egypt a valuable national asset. The primary objective of the Ismailia Master Plan, the positive development of the city, arose directly from President Sadat's reaffirmation of the importance of planning as a means of providing for progress in the Suez Canal Zone.

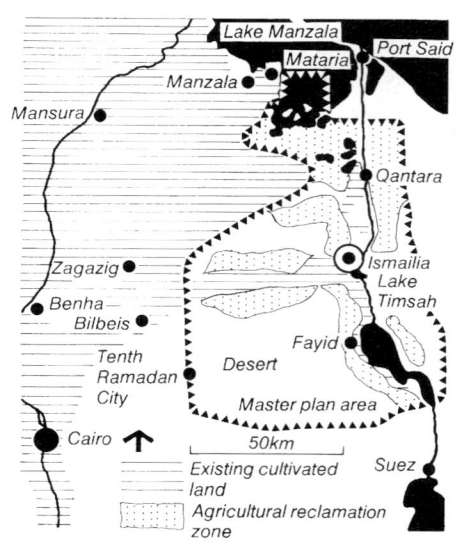

Figure 93
Ismailia area master plan

The Master Plan provides for a future total population of approximately 1.3 million, of which 600 000 will be accommodated in Ismailia.

One of the most significant Master Plan proposals recommended a new approach to housing provision which potentially has wide application nationally as well as regionally. The Master Plan recommended that the Egyptian Government should initiate innovative policies and move away from direct housing provision towards a more flexible system of government aid and support for different agencies whether public or private, including the informal sector.

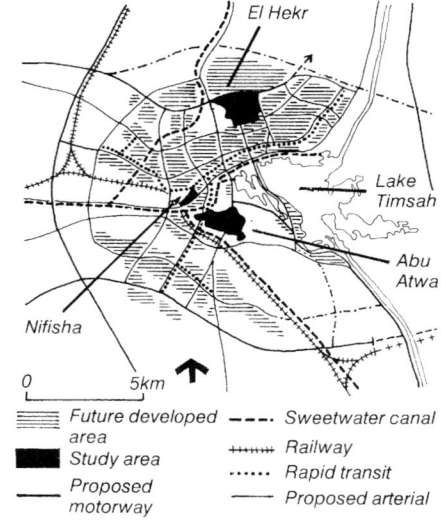

Figure 94
Ismailia master plan

The Master Plan housing recommendations were based on the fact that the informal private housing sector adds more units to the national housing stock than all public efforts combined, even though it receives no government support. In addition to providing dwellings, at costs considerably below those achieved by the formal public and private sectors, the informal sector also allows households to match their priorities and needs with their ability to pay. It is also more likely to use local materials, labour and appropriate technologies than is the formal sector. The most important advantage, however, is that the informal sector process is economically accessible to low and to very low income families.

Following the consultants recommendations the Ismailia Demonstration Projects were commissioned in May 1977 by the Ministry of Housing and Reconstruction, Egypt, and the British Ministry of Overseas Development. The purpose of the Projects was to illustrate in detail the principal policies initially developed in the Master Plan, in particular the housing policies for Ismailia, and in effect to pave the way for their early implementation.

The Ismailia Demonstration Projects developed in detail the principal Master Plan recommendations, in particular for housing, and established policies and guidelines for implementing the first sites and services project in Egypt.

The Demonstration Projects, which were completed in May 1978, concentrated on three main issues: first, to maintain the momentum achieved by the preparation of the Master Plan; second, to focus on problems requiring immediate action in Ismailia and third, to formulate appropriate proposals capable of easy implementation, with minimum subsidy, at the earliest opportunity.

The El Hekr (Hai El Salam) Project proposals

The El Hekr (Hai El Salam) project was one of three selected and included uncontrolled low income housing on the northern perimeter of the city, and adjacent empty desert land.

Although in the Master Plan Study the housing needs for all income groups were considered, more attention was devoted to low income groups since these were least served by existing housing systems.

To reach these groups it was clear that either subsidies must be given, which restricts the amount of provision to the budgets likely to be available, or limitations must be made on the standards of provision in terms of space, infrastructure and/or superstructure. These possibilities were examined, rather than assuming an *a priori* minimum standard of provision, so that a full range of options could be developed and implications understood.

During the preparation of the Demonstration Projects a comprehensive series of social surveys and studies of low income areas was undertaken to understand properly the existing situation, social characteristics, incomes, affordability and priorities with regard to housing need. Also, extensive work was carried out to understand the mechanism and costraints of the existing housing system.

The success of housing or 'sites and services' proposals depends not only on a theoretical analysis of ability to pay set against levels of provision, but also upon the practical realities of costs and means of execution, potential revenues, and assurances of subsidies. Proposals were prepared which tried to anticipate actual conditions, but which were flexible enough to be able to adjust levels of provision to future financial conditions.

Dominating the proposals was the overriding objective that any new development, improvement or upgrading must be within the 'target' population's ability to pay for it.

The 'target' population consists of low to very low income households, and is based on socio-economic characteristics

---

* The El Hekr project has been renamed 'Hai El Salam' or 'Peace District' by the Local Council.

Appendix 1   149

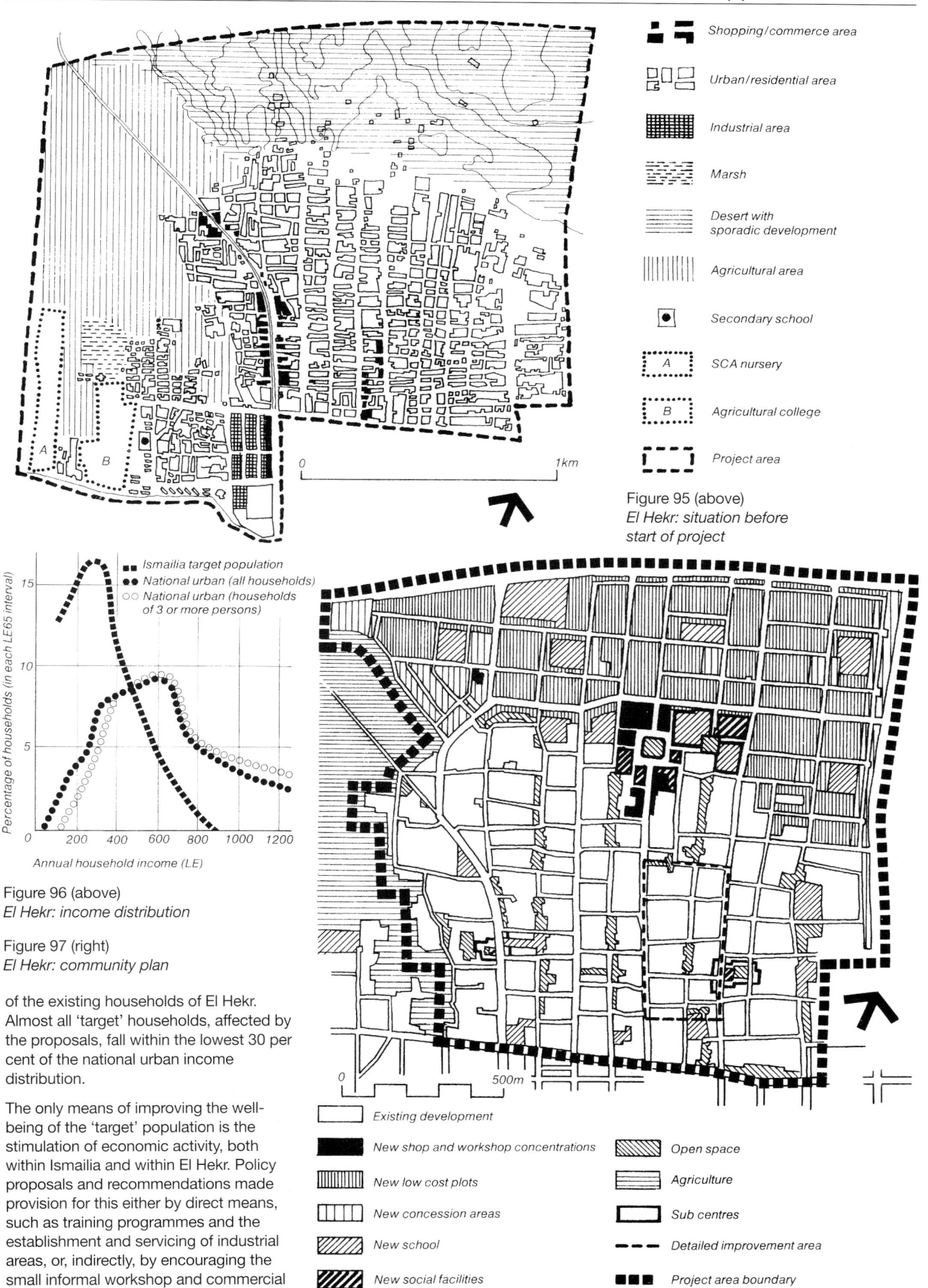

Legend (Figure 95):
- Shopping/commerce area
- Urban/residential area
- Industrial area
- Marsh
- Desert with sporadic development
- Agricultural area
- Secondary school
- A SCA nursery
- B Agricultural college
- Project area

Figure 95 (above)
El Hekr: situation before start of project

Figure 96 legend:
- Ismailia target population
- National urban (all households)
- National urban (households of 3 or more persons)

Y-axis: Percentage of households (in each LE65 interval)
X-axis: Annual household income (LE)

Figure 96 (above)
El Hekr: income distribution

Figure 97 (right)
El Hekr: community plan

of the existing households of El Hekr. Almost all 'target' households, affected by the proposals, fall within the lowest 30 per cent of the national urban income distribution.

The only means of improving the well-being of the 'target' population is the stimulation of economic activity, both within Ismailia and within El Hekr. Policy proposals and recommendations made provision for this either by direct means, such as training programmes and the establishment and servicing of industrial areas, or, indirectly, by encouraging the small informal workshop and commercial sector.

Legend (Figure 97):
- Existing development
- New shop and workshop concentrations
- New low cost plots
- New concession areas
- New school
- New social facilities
- Open space
- Agriculture
- Sub centres
- Detailed improvement area
- Project area boundary

El Hekr is not to become exclusively a low income area, isolated from the general economic and social life of the city. Proposals allow for a proportion of higher income households and opportunities for business investment so that the areas can absorb more urban activities and, in time, through the process of incremental upgrading, display the characteristics of established areas of Ismailia.

In addition to using the Master Plan as a basic framework in developing land use proposals for El Hekr, proposals have been influenced by the following three policies: first, that development of new areas of the city be integrated with adjoining older neighbourhoods and that the improvement of existing older communities should not be carried out in isolation; second, that progressive intensification of land use, such as increased density of habitation and increased concentration of commercial activities, already a natural feature of urban development in Egypt, be allowed for in space standards for residential, commercial and public facilities; third, as the maintenance of public land is a considerable financial burden on local administration, that public land be minimised by introducing the concept of semi-private land, its maintenance to be the collective responsibility of the users.

By the year 2000, the population of El Hekr is planned to rise from its existing level of 37 000 to 90 000. To accommodate this increase in population, proposals include improvement of 132 hectares of existing area and development of 94 hectares of sporadically developed land. Sub division plans provide for 3527 plots.

In the new areas and, where possible in existing areas, a hierarchy of residential groupings was proposed which minimised infrastructure layout costs and produced layouts which reflected existing social preferences. The hierarchy is made up of clusters, blocks and neighbourhoods. A cluster is a grouping of 20 to 30 plots giving onto communal space; a block comprises 4 to 5 cluster groups containing 120 to 180 plots, bounded by Access or Local roads. Neighbourhoods comprise up to 6 blocks of 700 to 900 plots accommodating 5000 people. The neighbourhood provides an appropriate catchment area for the provision of social services. Within the Project Area a main Community Centre is proposed providing a wide range of activities and services, such as public facilities, communal, workshop and entertainment establishments. A mosque and the offices of the Project Agency are also included.

Detailed proposals and guidelines were developed to achieve the Project objectives.

The status of land in El Hekr is Government leasehold, and the rights of this form of tenure are confused and unclear. An important initial consideration was the need to rationalise land tenure. Well defined plots with secure land tenure should be offered to all plot occupiers. This would be achieved through the mechanism of *delayed freehold* title thereby removing uncertainties and giving incentive for maximum investment in home building and improvement. For the benefit of new settlers an appropriate range of plot sizes would be provided to allow for progressive development of all plots and efficient provision of infrastructure. Limited economic activities would be permitted on all plots including the provision of rental accommodation.

It was proposed that various institutional controls should be established to ensure that new plots are rapidly built on and occupied and not held for speculative exploitation.

A basic principle of the financing policy was that, as far as possible, development should pay for itself. Therefore for the projects to start immediately a policy of self-financing was adopted so that, in the event of national funds not being available, it would still be possible to implement the projects at a basic level. New and existing settlers would be required to purchase plots, classified according to their commercial potential, through instalment payments. The 'plot purchase rate' would reflect future potential and plot size and would also finance a minimum level of provision of infrastructure and other programmes. The 'plot purchase rate' would be amortised over different periods and payment linked with the eventual acquisition of freehold title.

In accordance with Master Plan recommendations, full infrastructure provision was proposed as a long term goal. In view of the target population's limited ability to pay, the practical limitations imposed by existing major networks and the financial capabilities of the executing authorities, the provision of facilities will be staged and capable of progressive upgrading to full standards.

Tables 35 and 36 show the levels of infrastructure provision. They clearly show the options available and were the basis on which recommendations were made.

The initial level, as defined in terms of minimum public health benefits, is the provision of potable water from public standpipes at 150 metre spacing and on-plot pit latrines. The final level is the installation of multi-tap metered water connections to each plot and a full water borne sewerage system. Other priorities are a collection service for domestic refuse and domestic electricity supply. Public telephones will be installed within 500 metres of every house and provided within business and commercial establishments.

Institutional proposals were prepared that required no legal or administrative reform at national level. The proposals drafted for legal and administrative control fitted existing practices and routines and aimed to make full use of the advantages of local control and of the powers of local government. The form of administration proposed was directly linked to the Governorate, the provincial government which has delegated powers from central government, but limited financial resources. In El Hekr it was recommended that a financially independent Project Agency be set up with powers and obligations established by enabling legislation in the form of Governor's orders.

It was proposed that the Project Agency, for implementing the Demonstration Project area, should be responsible for phasing, charges and the provision of improvements to maintain financial viability. Procedures for obtaining necessary permits and permissions were to be kept simple and to a minimum.

The Agency's functions are designed to encourage the home building systems. They include the provision when found necessary, of building materials at official prices and in quantities to match the incremental building process, and making credit in the form of small loans available to facilitate home improvement and progressive additions to basic structure.

Through the continuous process of monitoring, the Project Agency should build up a body of knowledge and experience so that similar projects may be set up elsewhere in Ismailia and Egypt as a whole.

The Project Agency is the key to implementation.

The implementation stage: position at 18 months

The above proposals were developed with the local authorities, and approved by the local councils in June 1978.

El Hekr (Hai El Salam) Project Agency was established by an executive order of the Governorate in October 1978 which gave the Agency complete control over the planning and development of the area and the sale of any land. The Managing Board includes representatives of the various agencies and departments concerned with the provision of basic services, representatives of the City Council, local political party organisations, the Governorate, and the Project Manager.

As proposed, the El Hekr (Hai El Salam) Project Agency has its own development, administrative and finance departments. These departments are divided into offices dealing with engineering, surveying, architecture and building, landscaping, registration, finance, legal and public relations work.

The Agency is assisted in all aspects of its work by Clifford Culpin and Partners, under the Ismailia Technical Assistance Programme. The Technical Assistance Programme gives advice to the Governorate on the implementation of the Master Plan as well as guidance on all technical and administrative matters to the Project Agency and its Board.

The aim of the Ismailia Technical Assistance Programme is not only to help ensure the development of Hai El Salam (El Hekr) as planned but to help the local staff to develop the experience required to undertake, in the future, similar projects without outside assistance.

Table 35
El Hekr: costs per plot of options for different levels of infrastructure provision in new areas

Level of infrastructure provision	Costs per plot (1977 LE)**		
	72m² plot	108m² plot	135m² plot
Level I			
– administration, markers, compensation, registration	17	25	31
– pit latrines (includes capitalised running costs)	105	105	105
– standpipes	14	21	26
– stage I local roads	17	26	32
Total	153	177	194
Level II			
– Level I plus:	153	177	194
– electricity	53	53	53
– landscaping	3	5	6
Total	209	235	253
Level III			
– Level II plus:	209	235	253
– paved district streets	11	16	20
– stage II local roads	27	41	51
Total	247	292	324
Level IV			
– Level II (less pit latrines) plus:	104	130	148
– reticulated water network*	34	50	62
– water connections	65	65	65
– reticulated sewerage network	53	79	79
– sewerage connections	95	95	95
Total	351	419	469
Level V			
– Level IV plus:	351	419	469
– paved district streets	11	16	20
– stage II local roads	27	41	51
Total	389	476	540
Level VI			
– Level V plus:	389	476	540
– trunk sewers	36	54	68
– trunk water mains	36	54	67
– paved access roads	41	61	76
Total	502	645	751
Level VII			
– Level VI plus:	502	645	751
– service core	163	163	163
Total	665	808	914

* (excludes standpipe provision) ** (In 1977 1LE = £0.75 Sterling)

Table 36
El Hekr: ability to pay for different levels of infrastructure

Level of infrastructure provision	Percentage of households affording each level		
	72m² plot	108m² plot	135m² plot
Level I	96	93	87
Level II	87	81	78
Level III	79	72	66
Level IV	41	30	23
Level V	35	21	15
Level VI	17	11	6
Level VII	10	4	1

Work began on the implementation in October 1978. To help the start of work the British Government gave £65 000 as inception capital for urgent preliminary work such as the building of a project office, surveying and legal work. In the first two and a half months most of the Agency staff were recruited. The Agency now has a Project Manager and 27 staff covering legal, financial, surveying, registration, public relations and monitoring work.

The initial task undertaken by the Ismailia Technical Assistance Programme with Agency assistance was the preparation of a master survey of the project area. This included setting out all roads, housing blocks and major open space uses in the new areas as well as key points in the existing areas. Plots were then prepared and made available to households affected by major roadworks and the Community Centre. Work on the Community Centre has begun.

The Social Centre has been built and is in use, as are the Polyclinic and the Project Agency office. The Square has been levelled. The Primary School, which is part of the Community Centre development, has been built and is now in use, and other school sites have been agreed and construction started.

Work on the first stage road construction programme of 3.4 kilometres is complete. A further 2.5 kilometres of road provided by the Governorate is approximately 50 per cent complete. One kilometre of water pipe has been laid, 16 new standpipes have been connected and 4 old

Appendix 1

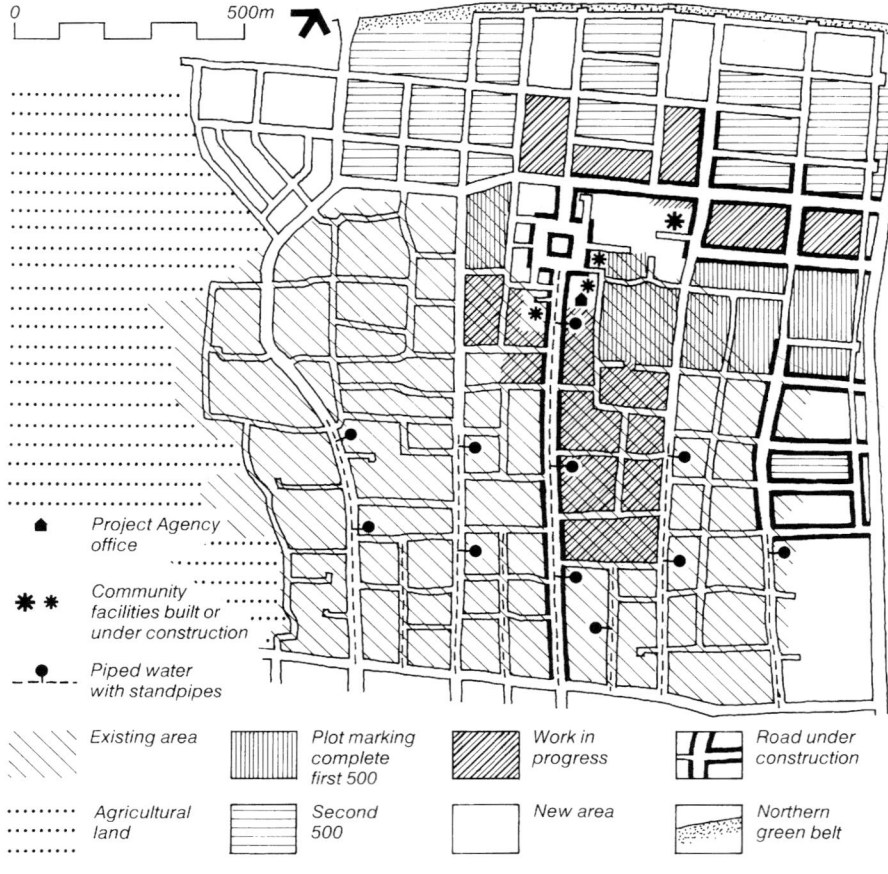

Figure 98
El Hekr project: progress to March 1980

standpipes renewed. Electricity to a water pump, to irrigate the northern tree belt, has been provided and planting started.

In April 1979 the first 500 new plots were advertised. The successful applicants were selected after careful screening in July. 493 allottees have paid for their plots and 464 new plots have been delivered. Building work has started on 103 new plots and 34 houses have been completed on these new plots. In addition to new plots, 148 plots have been provided for those affected by the plan within the area as well as approximately 183 households living on land required by the Governorate for other projects elsewhere in Ismailia. A further 1046 existing or adjusted plots have been surveyed and of these 927 have been paid for and delivered. All survey work is complete in 19 blocks and is under way in a further six.

The sale of the second 500 plots, of which 200 have already been allocated to applicants to the initial sale of plots, was advertised in March 1980 and 2215 applications were received. The Project Agency Board expects to select applicants for the available plots by May 1980. For house owners, in areas not yet being surveyed, who wish to have their plot registered so that they can extend or rebuild their existing houses, an express survey service is offered at a small extra charge to the applicant. To date, 340 applicants have benefitted from this service.

The Agency has recently taken on wider responsibilities and offers technical assistance to plot allottees. Detailed architectural drawings and specifications have been prepared. These will be sold to plot holders at a small cost and be used by them in making application for government-priced building materials. Assistance is also given to plot holders to process their applications for these materials. In addition, the first loans have been given to households affected by roadworks, to enable them to build houses on their own plots.

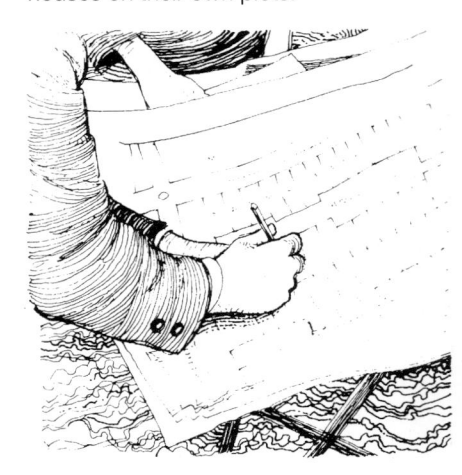

Work has begun on the first landscaping project, a one-kilometre forest belt along the northern boundary of the site, and proposals are under way for further local tree planting schemes along the completed roads and in the open spaces.

The Agency's income to December 1979 was approximately LE 665 000 from the sale of plots, down-payments and instalments, and administrative charges on the land. The approved Agency budget for 1980 includes a capital works programme of LE 485 000. In addition, the City Council has budgeted LE 164 000 for additional improvement to roads, street lighting and community buildings.

The Project Agency has also begun a monitoring programme. This work includes not only a monthly summary of survey work and the progress of civil works but also the analysis of plot applicants, allottees and those failing to get plots. The Agency has already undertaken an initial analysis of the problems experienced by those in adjacent plots and those affected by the plan who were given new plots. Further survey work, including routine field inspections, has been carried out to monitor the progress of construction activity on new plots. The findings of these surveys will help the Project Agency to assess the effects of allocation procedures as well as the assistance given to plot allottees.

It has been demonstrated during the first 18 months that the El Hekr (Hai El Salam) Project Agency is fast developing as an agency capable of undertaking all aspects and functions of this type of development project with limited external assistance.

It has also been shown that considerable development can take place with only minimal external funding by building on the resources of the local population.

Useful figures relating to El Hekr (Hai El Salam) are reproduced here. They relate to proposals and progress between October 1978 and March 1980.

Table 37
El Hekr (Hai El Salam) project: useful figures March 1980

Project area

Population 1978	37 000
Population 2000	90 000
Improvement area	132 hectares
New development area	94 hectares
Total area	226 hectares
Plots (Total, new areas)	3527

Plot sizes

Low cost (new areas)
Small   25% provision
  Dimensions (m)   6×12   6×15   7.5×12
  Area (m²)   72   90   90
Medium   65% provision
  Dimensions (m)   6×18   7.5×15   7.5×18   9×12   9×15
  Area (m²)   108   112.5   135   108   135
Large   10% provision
  Dimensions (m)   9×18   12×12
  Area (m²)   162   144

Concession plots
  Dimensions (m)   15×24   18×24   24×24
  Area (m²)   360   432   576

Plot costs (LE/m²)

Class	Ordinary	Corner
A	10.00	12.00
B	4.00	4.50
C	2.25	2.50
Concession	Open market price	

Payment terms

Class	Down payment	Repayment period (years)
A	100%	—
B	50%	15, 25
C	25%	10, 15, 25
Concession	100%	—

Infrastructure

	Initial provision	Final provision
Water supply	Public standpipes at 150–200m intervals	Individual connections
Sewerage	Pit latrines	Full sewerage system
Electricity	Individual connection (optional)	No change
	Street lighting	No change
Roads: (ROW)		
Arterial – 20m	Surfaced (DBST)	Paved (Asphaltic concrete)
District – 15m	Surfaced	Paved (Asphaltic concrete)
Local – 10/15m	Gravel	Surfaced
Access – 6/10m	Earth	Gravel/earth

Plot preparation: October 1978 to March 1980

	Planned	Surveyed	Paid for	Delivered
Existing areas	1123	1046	927	927
New areas	1940	575	525	508
Total	3063	1621	1452	1435

Infrastructure

	Planned	Tendered	Work in progress	Complete
Water pipe (km)	4			1
standpipes	30			20
Roads (km)	7.75	6.55	5.86	3.65

Finances: October 1978 to 31 December 1979

Income	LE Received	LE Outstanding	LE Total
Sale of plots	281 747	205 938	
Interest	1 143	72 611	
Administration/regional fees	15 091	974	577 504
Bank interest			5 829
Other sources			7 199
Inception capital (ODA)			74 387
Total			664 919

Approved 1980 Budget

Income	LE	Expenditure	LE
Current assets	303 779	Infrastructure:	
Instalments	30 000	roads	105 000
New plots (600)	123 000	electricity	180 000
Emergency relocation (100)	7 400	Water	85 000
Existing plots (1000)	67 500	Other development works including equipment	115 000
Administration/ regional fees	18 000	Administration etc.	25 100
Bank interest	5 000	Depreciation	4 579
		Contingency	40 000
Total	554 679		554 679

LE = Egyptian Pounds   1LE = £0.75 Sterling (1980)

Appendix 1

Table 38
Hai el Salam project: summary

Aspect	Experience	Lessons
Participation	The project was planned to be developed in a strongly participative manner. In practice this was hard to implement in Hai el Salam, though an 'open door' policy allowed the community to express views and the project was flexible in implementation, allowing changes to be made. A second project in Abu Atwa had a different combination of project staff and local community. Here the planning and implementation was carried out in a more participative manner.	There are many forms of participation, many different actors and no two areas, even in the same city, are the same. It is important not to take a rigid standard approach. This makes demands on the flexibilty of staff concerned.
Standard land pricing in upgrading areas	Land was priced at a standard fixed price, aimed to be affordable to low income groups. This meant that those on good commercial locations were at a considerable advantage. It was difficult later to raise prices in line with inflation. As a result income to pay for infrastructure was progressively reduced.	Land prices should be fixed relative either to a market based index or to something else which does not require a difficult or unpopular political decision. Land in prime locations could be sold or leased at higher prices, ensuring greater potential for cross subsidy.
Land pricing in new areas Targeting of low income groups	Land prices in new areas were fixed to balance market value and affordability. The selection process and rules were fixed to try to ensure that low income families could access land. In upgrading areas this was largely successful. In new areas, after the initial rounds of allocations, fewer low income families managed to access plots.	As with upgrading areas, it was difficult to later raise prices in line with inflation. It is very difficult to enforce rules to ensure that low income families have access to land. Stronger management practices would include working more with the market and greater use of community controls.
Progressive upgrading of infrastructure	Infrastructure was planned and developed incrementally. Later funding from USAID allowed full water borne sewerage.	An incremental approach to infrastructure is realistic and politically acceptable. It is possible to focus on eventual high standards rather than tie programmes down to permanent low standards.
Employment generation	It was allowed to have small shops or workshops. Many flats were built for rental accommodation.	Flexible land use helps to ensure there are work opportunities. There should, however, be local safeguards against excessive noise and other pollution.
Setting up a self financing land development agency	The self financing mechanism worked very well in the early years. Later it became more difficult as fixed land prices, together with inflation, reduced income. Later funds for operation and maintenance became limited and income was diverted to other areas. Some land was auctioned. This attracted much interest and income, but tended to inflate expectations.	A self financing project, if location is good, can work very well. However, a formula needs to be developed whereby it is possible to achieve a wider redistribution and at the same time time provide incentives for prudent management.
Capacity building	Capacity laws built by involving staff in on-job training supported by formal training. This worked very well, but basic conditions did not change much in local government, so that capacity building was not fully satisfied.	Capacity building can benefit from team work on site, linked closely to implementation. However, it is still essential that either central or local government should provide good working conditions and organisational back-up.

The Hai el Salam project has been the subject of several studies. A number of these are included in the reference materials section. Here, a few key lessons are highlighted.

Sources of information

This section provides some selected sources of information. The list aims to provide some pointers to sources, rather than trying to be complete.

BOOKS

Books may be difficult to obtain and expensive but can provide a more general view of housing than is possible in the Manual or go into considerably greater detail. A very brief selection is given below.

General

Charles Abrams
'Housing in the Modern World'
(paperback, Faber, London, 1964)
Now slightly dated, but still one of the best general books on housing.

Orville Grimes
'Housing for Low Income Urban Families'
(paperback, John Hopkins University Press, London, 1976)
An assessment of housing economics and ways of relating policies to available resources.

John F C Turner
'Housing by People'
(paperback, Marion Boyars, London, 1 976)
A plea for locally controlled rather than centrally administered housing. Now translated into several languages.

Barbara Ward
'The Home of Man'
(paperback, Pelican, London, 1976)
Written for the Vancouver Habitat Conference and endorsed by the United Nations. A comprehensive review of development problems which argues the need for access to basic services for all.

Peter M Ward (editor)
'Self-Help Housing: A Critique'
(hardback, Alexandrine Press Book, Mansell Publishing Ltd, London, 1982)
A review of the emergence of self-help processes including a theoretical critique of the proposition of self-help and an evaluation of the impact and contribution of self-help housing in different contexts.

Bentley, I Alcock, A Murrain, P McGlynn, S and Smith, G
'Responsive Environments: A Manual for Designers'
The Architectural Press, London 1985

Chambers, R (1997)
'Whose reality counts?: putting the first last'
Intermediate Technology Publications London
This book discusses participatory rapid appraisal applications.

Charles Correa (1985)
'The New Landscape'
Book Society of India
A concise exploration of how designers can create decent and affordable settlements in the expanding cities of the Third World, with examples from Bombay.

Forbes Davidson, Mirjam Zaaijer, Monique Peltenburg, Mike Rodell. (1993)
'Manual for urban relocation and resettlement'
Institute for Housing and Urban Development Studies Rotterdam.
A guide to planning for relocation and resettlement when it is not avoidable.

Hayward, R and McGlynn, S
'Making better places: Urban design now'
Butterworth Heinemann, Oxford 1993.

Herbert Girardet (1996)
'The Gaia Atlas of Cities'
Gaia books, London
A resource book for the Habitat II City Summit, arguing the case for an ecological approach to urban planning and management.

Percy Johnson-Marshall and Associates
'Designing briefing in towns' mimeo 1979.
John Punter, Matthew Carmona and Adam Platts (July 1994)
'Design Policies in Development Plans'
Urban Design Quarterly Issue 51.

Reinhart Goethert and Nabeel Hamdi
'Making Microplans: A community based process in programming and development' (1988)
IT Publications
Discusses ways of involving local communities in settlement upgrading.

Anthony Gibson and E Wratten
Development Planning for Real
(1995) Neighbourhood Initiatives Foundation, The Poplars, Lightmoor, Telford, Salop, TF4 3QN, UK

Moser, Caroline ON
Institute of Development Studies, University of Sussex: Towards Gender-Aware Housing Policy and Practice. 1996

Nabeel Hamdi (1991)
'Housing without Houses'
Van Nostrand Reinhold
The book is a plea for professionals to develop practical methods of working more closely with local people in the design of housing projects and offers examples from several countries.

Nabeel Hamdi and Reinhard Goethert (1997) 'Action Planning for Cities: A Guide for Community Based Interventions' John Wiley, Chichester, UK. pp 252.
A practical review of action planning methodologies for community action, the book deals with theory, tools and training.

Home, R and Jackson, J (1997)
'Land rights for informal settlements: Community control and the single point cadastre in South Africa' RICS London
This paper investigates the possibility of applying new spatial techniques, especially GIS and GPS to the provision of progressive land rights for informal settlements at the level of community controlled land offices.

ICLEI, (1996)
'The Local Agenda 21 Planning Guide. An introduction to sustainable development planning'
ICLEI – International Council for Local Environmental Initiatives Toronto
A practical guide with worksheets and cases of developing local Agenda 21 plans.

Joseph Leitman, (1993)
'Rapid urban environmental assessment lessons from cities in the developing world, vol. I : methodology and preliminary findings'
Urban Management Programme/ World Bank Washington,
Description of approach and tools (Vol. 2) to be used as a basis for developing environmental management plans following the approach of Agenda 21. It builds on the approach developed in participatory rural appraisals.

Joseph Leitman(1993)
'Rapid urban environmental assessment lessons from cities in the developing world, vol. 2 Tools and outputs'
Urban Management Programme/ World Bank Washington
Description of approach and tools (Vol. 2) This volume focuses on practical instruments to use in the field including stakeholder analysis and sample terms of reference.

Jan van der Linden (1986)
'The Sites and Services Approach Reviewed'
Gower
An assessment of achievements and limitations of the approach with examples.

Kevin Lynch and Gary Hack
'Site Planning' (1984)
MIT Press (6th printing 1989)
An application of Lynch's well known design theories to the practical challenge of site planning, with informative appendices.

Sources of information

Geoffrey Payne (Editor) (1999)
'Making Common Ground: Public-private partnerships in land for housing'
Intermediate Technology Publications, London
A review of international experiences in developing innovative partnerships in providing affordable land for housing.

Geoffrey Payne (Editor) (1984)
'Low-Income Housing in the Developing World: The Role of Sites and Services and Settlement Upgrading'
John Wiley
A review of key issues and examples.

Monique Peltenburg, Forbes Davidson, Pat Wakely, and Hans Teerlink, (1996)
'Building Capacity for Better Cities'
Institute for Housing and Urban Develoment Studies Rotterdam
Strategic approach developed for Habitat II to develop a more effective approach to capacity building. It includes discussion of capacity building concepts and is based on the experience of a number of capacity building institutions and also of user organisations. Has companion volume of cases.

Lloyd Rodwin (Editor) (1987)
'Shelter, Settlement and Development'
Allen and Unwin
Dated, but comprehensive overview of policy issues and options for practice.

Reinhard Skinner, et al (1987)
'Shelter Upgrading for the Urban Poor: An Evaluation of Third World Experience'
Island Publishing House, Manila
A comprehensive review of experience with several case studies.

Beth Turner (Editor) (1988)
'Building Community'
Building Community Books London
Twenty five case studies from various countries illustrating the achievements of community groups in meeting their shelter needs.

UNCHS/UNEP (1997)
'Implementing the Urban Environment Agenda' (3 vols)
United Nations, Nairobi
A practical guide illustrating principles and case studies of innovative approaches to integrating urban development and environmental policy objectives.

UNCHS (various dates)
Community participation training programme
This programme has a number of useful and practical publications relating to community participation in planning, implementation and monitoring and evaluation.

UNCHS, (1988) Community participation: A trainers manual
United Nations Centre for Human Settlements Nairobi, pp.65.
Suitable for use related to training for community participation. Links also to video on the subject.

UNCHS (1996)
'An Urbanizing World'
Oxford University Press
The resource document produced for the City Summit (Habitat II), this is the most comprehensive source book on the subject available.

UNCHS (1989)
'Guide for managing change for urban managers and trainers'

UNCHS 1989
Excellent source book for introductions/exercises in problem analysis, organisational, change action planning. Can be used also for stand alone training.

UNCHS (1993)
'Public/Private Partnerships in Enabling Shelter Strategies'

UNDP
A review of innovative approaches involving new relationships between public, private and community sectors in shelter provision and improvement.

UNDP (1991)
'Cities, People and Poverty: Urban Development Co-operation for the 1990's'

UNDP
An overview of urban development issues and the role of international assistance agencies.

Nick Wates (1996)
'Action Planning'
The Prince of Wales's Institute of Architecture, London
This short book reviews the extensive experience of organising action planning and shows how to make it work.

Nick Wates (2000)
'The Community Planning Handbook'
Earthscan Publications, London
A well-designed, accessible handbook of ideas and tools for participative planning at the local level.

World Bank (1993)
'Housing: Enabling Markets to Work'
The World Bank
The Bank's sector policy paper provides an overview of housing markets and discusses ways of matching demand and supply.

Building

Paul Gut and Dieter Ackerknecht (1993)
'Climate Responsive Building: Appropriate building construction in tropical and sub-tropical regions'
SKAT – available from IT Publications

Building Issues series
Lund Centre for Habitat Studies, (LCHS)
Lund University, Lund, Sweden
A useful series of practical materials on building and project design issues.

D L Jayaneti and P R Follett (1998)
'Bamboo in construction: An introduction'
TRADA Technology Limited, INBAR and DFID, London
A practical guide to the potential applications of bamboo in building construction.

Roland Stulz and Kiran Mukerji (1993)
'Appropriate Building Materials'
IT Publications, London
Now in its third edition, this is a standard source-book on the subject.

Infrastructure

Mara D D, Alabaster, G P, Pearson H W and Mills, S W (1992)
'Stabilisation Ponds: A design manual for eastern Africa'
Lagoon Technology International, Leeds, UK

Sandy Cairncross and Richard Feachem (1979)
'Environmental Health Engineering in the Tropics: An Introductory Text' -2nd edition
John Wiley
Despite its age, still a standard text.

Andrew Cotton and Richard Franceys (1991)
'Services for Shelter'
Liverpool University Press
Comprehensive and well illustrated manual covering infrastructure options for housing projects in developing countries.

Richard Franceys, with J Pickford and R Reed (1992)
'A guide to the Development of On-Site Sanitation'
World Health Organisation
In depth information on technical, design and operational aspects of major systems.

Duncan Mara (Editor)(1996)
'Low-Cost Sewerage'
John Wiley
Reviews low-cost alternatives to conventional sanitation systems, based on experience in Africa.

George McRobie (1996)
'Services for the Urban Poor: A People Centred Approach'
Lund University, Sweden, Building Issues Vol. 8 No1
A concise review of how to involve local communities in servicing settlements.

John Pickford
'Low-cost Sanitation: A survey of practical experience'
Intermediate Technology Publications
Reviews systems applicable in both rural and urban areas.

R A Reed (1995)
'Sustainable Sewerage: Guidelines for community schemes'
IT Publications
This handbook describes how conventional sewerage systems can be modified to reduce construction and maintenance costs.

Peter Schubeler (1996)
'Urban sanitation management in developing countries: three conceptual tools'
Swiss Centre for Development Co-operation in Technology and Development
This short book addresses three questions: Why are tools required? What are their main features? How are they applied in practice? Examples are given.

UNDP–World Bank (1996)
'Proceedings of Workshop on Sanitation for Poor People in Urban Areas'
London
Papers review the technical, social, institutional and economic aspects of alternative approaches.

Uno Winblad and Wen Kilama (1985)
'Sanitation Without Water'
MacMillan
A detailed and balanced account of different systems for ecologically sustainable sanitation systems with examples from all parts of the world.

References on Ismailia

Davidson, Forbes, (1991) 'Gearing up for effective management of urban development' Cities, May 1991, Butterworth–Heinneman pp. 120-134 Oxford, pp.13.
An examination of the institutional development aspects of the Ismailia Demonstration projects and the later technical assistance programme. It discusses the relationship between opportunities for practical experience given by projects and the complementary supports possible.

UNCHS, (1995) Hai el Salam Project - an Upgrading and Sites-and Services Project, Ismailia, Egypt UNCHS Nairobi, p. 81.
Review of the project after 15 years. It discusses finance, community participation and project agency development.

Organisations active in housing and settlements

Centre for Alternative Technology
Machinlyth Wells
Dyfed Wales UK

Co-operative Housing Foundation
2501 M Street NW
Washington DC 200037 USA

Department for International Development (previously ODA),
94 Victoria Street
London SW1E 5JL
The Department supports a range of activities in the field of housing and urban development, including projects, research and publications.

DGIS (Netherlands Development Co-operation)
PO Box 20061
The Hague 2500 EB
The Netherlands

Homeless International
Guildford House
20 Queens Road
Coventry CV1 4RG UK

Intermediate Technology Development Group
103–105 Southampton Row
London WC18 4HH

IIED-America Latina
Piso 6, Cuerpo A
Corrientes 2835
1193 Buenos Aires
Argentina

International Capacity Building Network
This is a network to support a more effective capacity building for urban development.
Support group members include:

DPU Development Planning Unit
University College London
9 Endsleigh Gardens
London WC1H 0ED
United Kingdom
http:/www.ucl.ac.uk

HSD Human Settlements Development Programme
Asian Institute of Technology
PO Box 4
Klong Luang, Pathum Thani 12120
Thailand
http:/www.hsd.ac.th

IBAM Instituto Brasileiro de Administracao Municipal
Largo IBAM 1, Humaita
22271-070 Rio de Janeiro - RJ
Brazil
http:/www.ibam.org.br

Institute for Housing and Urban Development Studies
PO Box 1935
3000 BX Rotterdam, The Netherlands
http://www.ihs.nl

LCHS Lund Centre for Habitat Studies
Lund University
Box 118
SE-221 00 Lund,
Sweden
http:/www.lchs.lth.se

UNCHS Capacity Building Section
Nairobi, Kenya

International Institute for Environment and Development (IIED)
3 Endsleigh Street
London WC1H 0DD UK

Inter-American Development Bank
1300 New York Avenue, N.W.
Washington D.C. USA
http://www.iadb.org

Max Lock Centre
Westminster University
35 Marylebone Road
London NW1 5LS
Email: maxlock@wmin.ac.uk
http://www.wmin.ac.uk

Network-Association for European Researchers on Urbanization in the South (NAERUS)
Alain Durand-Lasserve
Centre d'Etudes de Geographie Tropicale
Domaine Universitaire Bordeaux
33405 Talance-Ceget France
Email: adl@rr15.cnrs.fr

PACT
777 UN Plaza
New York 10017 USA
A good source of relevant 'how to do it' materials.

SIDA
S105 25 Stockholm Sweden

SKAT (Swiss Centre for Technical Co-operation in Technology and Management)
Vadianstrasse 42
CH-9000 St Gallen
Switzerland
http://www.skat.ch
Email: info@skat.ch

UNCHS
PO Box 30030 Nairobi Kenya
http://www.unhabitat.org

UNDP
304 E 45th Street
New York 10017 USA
UNDP has a number of programmes supporting urban management and housing.

US Agency for International Development (USAID)
Office of Housing and Urban Programs
Washington DC 20523 USA

World Bank
1818H Street NW
Washington DC 20433 USA
The Bank produces reports on individual countries and sectors, together with a series of research and sector working papers, many of which are free. Some are published directly by the Bank and others through the Urban Management Programme, sponsored by the Bank and the United Nations. A catalogue of publications is issued annually by the Publica-

Sources of information

tions Department. Among the most useful are:
'Housing: Enabling Markets to Work'
The World Bank 1993
'Urban Policy and Economic Development: An Agenda for the 1990's'
The World Bank 1991

Internet and World Wide Web Sites

The Internet provides a wealth of useful, and useless, material. A recent search for references under the heading of urban development in developing countries produced over 35,000 items! Some of these may be old, but others list upcoming conferences, books, lectures and reports.

To reduce the list of responses to a manageable level, it is important to specify exactly the subject of interest. Web sites and discussion groups are always being formed, so it is also important to monitor changes.

The following is a partial list of useful sites which may be used as a starting point. Note that sites also change names and are closed down, so don't be disappointed if a site is no longer there.

CENDEP participatory source book
http://www.brookes.ac.uk/~e0191751/home.html
A very useful source of material on participatory planning and rapid appraisal also available in Spanish.

Centre for Alternative Technology
http://www.foe.co.uk/CAT

Composting toilet systems
http://www.composter.com

Environmental management & related topics
dev-habitat@ihnet.it

Europe's Forum on resources for international co-operation (EUFORIC)
http://www.oneworld.org/euforic/

Forum on developing countries (news, events, help needed/offered, links, etc)
forum@araxp.polito.it

Garnet (Network in Water Supply and Sanitation)
http://info.lboro.ac.uk/cv/wedc/garnet/grntover.html

Greener environmental management
greenleaf@worldscope.co.uk

Intermediate Technology Development Group
http://www.oneworld.org/itdg/publications.html

Low cost sewerage network
lcsewerage@mailbase.ac.uk

Local government forum organised by University of Birmingham, UK including Latin American linkages
logov@bham.ac.uk

N-AERUS (Network-Association of European Researchers on Urbanization in the South)
naerus_list araxp.polito.it and
http://obelix.polito.it/forum/naerus

Solid waste management & related topics
ecoct-p@segate.sunet.se

United Nations Centre for Human Settlements (Habitat). Base address:
http://www.unhabitat.org or
http://www.undp.org/un/habitat

Urban design resource network (RUDI)
http://rudi.herts.ac.uk

World Bank
http://www.worldbank.org/

World Bank Participation Sourcebook
http://www.worldbank.org/html/edi/sourcebook/sbhome.htm

Journals

Cities
Elsevier Science Ltd
The Boulevard
Langford Lane
Kidlington
Oxon OX5 1GB UK

Environment and Urbanization
IIED 3 Endsleigh Street
London WC1H 0DD
This is a particularly affordable publication see also its Latin American sister publication Medio Ambiente y Urbanizacion.

Habitat International
Dept of Urban & Regional Planning
University of Illinois
Room 111 Temple Buell Hall
611 Taft Drive
Champaign IL 61820 USA

Habitat News
UNCHS,
PO Box 30030 Nairobi Kenya

Open House International
Nick Wilkinson, Editor and publisher,
University College London, The Bartlett,
Development Planning Unit
9 Endsleigh Gardens, London WC1E 0ED
Email: nicho@sinan.arch.emu.edu.tr

Medio Ambiente y Urbanizacion
IIED-America Latina
Piso 6, Cuerpo A
Corrientes 2835
1193 Buenos Aires
Argentina

Third World Planning Review
Liverpool University Press
4 Cambridge Street
Liverpool L69 7ZU

Urban Age
The World Bank
1818H Street NW
Washington DC 20433 USA
Email: mbergen@worldbank.org

Urban Studies
University of Glasgow
Adam Smith Building
Glasgow G12 8RT   UK

Glossary

A brief glossary is presented here of technical terms which may be unfamiliar or which are used with a particular meaning in this Manual. Entries are in alphabetical order from the first letter of the word or group of words.

Ability to pay (for housing) The amount that a person or household can pay for housing after other essential expenditure is subtracted from income.

Access Street Providing direct access to plots with no through traffic function.

Action planning Term for the process of beginning implementation after only a brief reconnaissance survey and in parallel with continuing longer term planning.

Affordability See 'ability to pay'.

Arterial road Main traffic route for motor vehicles travelling between different parts of the city.

Attainable standards The level of achievement possible within a given economic framework.

Bi-lateral An agreement made between two parties.

Block Smallest developed area surrounded by local or higher order streets.

Capitalisation The present monetary value of a series of future payments or receipts given a time period and the rate of interest.

Case study (in social survey) Detailed study through interviews of a household's characteristics, housing history and priorities. Interviews are usually fairly informal and of several hours duration.

Circulation (referring to space) The land area used primarily for movement, both on foot (pedestrian movement) and by vehicle.

Cluster (housing) A group of plots round a communal space.

Communal space Unbuilt land used for access, recreation and domestic uses, maintained by the surrounding residences. Responsibility for maintenance may be written into agreements for plots fronting onto the communal space.

Concession plot/area A plot or area which is sold or leased at a market rate for development.

Consolidated development Final stage in the development process of plots.

Core unit Development on a plot prior to sale/lease, comprising at a minimum a connection point to utilities systems (service slab) and at the maximum built accommodation designed to be the first part of a larger house.

CBO Community Based Organisation.

Criteria Factors taken into account in reaching a decision or in establishing standards.

Cross-subsidy See 'internal cross-subsidy'.

District street Street providing for the main vehicular movement within an area surrounded by arterial streets.

Dwelling A house or habitable unit or form of shelter; residential accommodation.

Efficient land use Making maximum use of land at minimum cost while respecting certain standards.

External subsidy A subsidy generated from outside a project usually in the form of a government grant or waiver.

Facilities (social) Buildings and land for social, recreational or service activities.

Fast track planning A method of planning enabling implementation to be commenced prior to the completion of overall plans.

Feasibility studies Preliminary investigations or studies to assess whether projects are capable of realisation within a specific budget. World Bank definition identification and preparation of preliminary design of technical and institutional alternatives, and comparison of respective costs and benefits inclusive of detailed investigation, (equivalent of Stages 1–3 of Manual).

Formal recreation Recreation having organised games on specifically designated areas.

General urban area An area of urban development, primarily residential, but including shops, workshops and other small land uses.

Gross Total, without any deduction.

Gross density (housing) The number of units per unit area in residential areas including schools, public open space, roads and other facilities.

Household All people living in one house who share food on a regular basis.

Housing system A set of complex inter-relationships including people's needs for housing, people's ability to pay, the legal framework, market values, resources available and the state of the construction industry.

Improvement area An area of existing development for which proposals are made for improving infrastructure, land tenure security and social facilities.

Infill plots Plots of land developed on vacant or underused land within existing built up areas.

Informal building Building which is carried out by individuals or very small, unregistered firms, involving varying degrees of self-help from the household involved and/or direct local labour.

Informal development (of an urban area) Area which has been developed outside the formal (legal) planning and sub-division systems. Most traditional urban development has been by this means, as is squatting.

Informal recreation General recreation not requiring special provision.

Infrastructure Basic installations on which urban development depends. Here means roads, water, sewerage, solid waste disposal system, electricity, telephones.

Initial/basic development Preparing land for development by provision of the minimum infrastructure levels decided, such as, access roads with base course and water to standpipes.

Internal cross-subsidy A form of subsidy generated within a project, usually by differential pricing of plots of land so that profits from selling expensive land can subsidise sales to low income groups.

Land Tenure The mode by which land is held or owned, or the set of relationships among people concerning the use of land and its product.

Landscaping: hard The provision of pavings, trims, parking surface, retaining walls, boundary walls.

Landscaping: soft The provision of trees, shrubs, plants and related irrigation.

Local street Lowest level of street carrying through local traffic. Pedestrian use would predominate at this level.

Mark up rate An amount by which a wholesale price is increased to obtain a retail selling price.

Monitoring The process by which information on key aspects of the project is collected regularly in order to assess progress relative to plans, and to form a basis for the review of plans.

Multi-lateral An agreement made between more than two parties.

Neighbourhood An area whose inhabitants share certain social services such as a primary school. They are usually designed to minimise walking distances to school and avoid the crossing of major roads by children.

Net Amount after deduction, such as, income after tax is deducted.

Net density (housing) The number of units per acre in residential areas exclusive of schools, public open space and other facilities; pertaining to residential land use internal access roads and 50 per cent width of 'distributor road'.

NGO Non Governmental Organisation

Objectives Primary aims of project.

Opportunity cost (of land) An amount of money which a piece of land would command if sold on the open market. This amount represents a lost 'opportunity' and is therefore a cost to the project.

Parameter A figure or quantity used as a limit which is constant in a particular situation, but which may change if that situation is altered.

Percentile (for housing) Value below which a certain percentage (of households) falls. e.g. 10 pounds per month as the 5th percentile means that 5 per cent of families earn less than this.

Pit latrine Latrine comprising a hole in the ground usually hand dug, for the collection of excreta. The hole is generally located beneath the squatting plate and is protected by a superstructure.

Plot coverage ratio The proportion of a plot's area occupied by buildings.

Plot development The carrying out of construction work within plot boundaries.

Plot occupancy level The number of people normally resident on an individual plot.

Private open space Open space available exclusively for the use of occupants on a plot.

Progressive development A form of development in which buildings and services are gradually improved as funds become available.

Project agency An administrative unit responsible for project implementation.

Public facilities Services, such as, schools, health clinics, places of worship, community centres, required by the community.

Public space Land not in private, revenue generating, use. Includes all roads and public recreational spaces.

Resources Public and private finance, land, labour and materials available for the implementation of the plan.

Reticulation (of utilities) The network of public mains used to serve an area of settlement.

Right-of-way (ROW) The total width of a road and its associated pavements or sidewalks and reservations.

Sanitation Measures for the promotion of health in particular drainage and sewage disposal.

Sanitary or wet core Core unit comprising a services slab only.

Scanning survey A form of social survey intended to obtain quickly general information on the study areas.

Semi-private space See 'communal space'.

Semi-public space Land designated for use by specialist agencies or groups (i.e. schools or sports clubs), but which is normally accessible for public use.

Serviced areas Areas of an urban area provided with public utilities and facilities. They include housing areas and associated commercial, industrial and other areas.

Service slab A floor slab containing plot connections to public utilities.

Sewage Human waste and waste water, usually carried along a sewer pipe or stored in a septic tank or pit latrine.

Sewerage A system of sewer pipes.

Sites and services A method of land sub-division in which individual plots are provided together with a certain level of infrastructure provision. Subdivisions include opportunities for employment and social facilities.

Stakeholder A person or organisation to whom or to which the outcome of a situation is important enough to commit effort to attempting to ensure a positive outcome.

Standpipe A vertical pipe with a tap connected to the mains water supply system, where drinking water may be obtained by the community. Also known as 'public tap' or 'fountain'.

Statistically significant (of results of a sample survey) A relationship between the number of replies and the number of (households) questioned which indicates whether the results are applicable to the total population from which the sample was drawn.

Superstructure All building works above ground.

Target population The section of a city's present and future population whose housing needs and resources the project is intended to match.

Transitable (roads) Capable of permitting the safe and regular passage of vehicles.

Urban management is the activity of mobilising diverse resources to work in a co-operative and co-ordinated manner to achieve city operational and development objectives.

Utilities (public) Physical services, such as, water, sewerage and electricity, but excluding roads.

Index

A

Ability, to pay for housing   3, 18, 159
access
   to commercial development   77
   to industrial development   77
accessibility
   of employment opportunities   6
   of site locations   6, 22
accommodation
   rental   3
   see also housing
action planning   84, 140, 159
activity
   commercial see commercial activity
   industrial see industrial activity
administration
   land/property rights   138
   project, example (Project Agency)   85–9
administration framework, example (Project Agency)   85–97
administrative units   61
aerial photogrammetric plans   24
aerial photographs   5, 8, 10, 22, 23, 26, 31, 76
   and Geographical Information Systems (GIS)   144, 145
   interpreting   117
   measuring plots   116
   plot boundary identification   138
   preparing sketch plans   117
affordability   13, 32, 64–71, 82, 159
   detailed proposals   74
   monthly payments, housing   33
   and sewage disposal options   143
agency-built housing   76–77
amortisation   67
analysis
   cash flow sensitivity   71
   cost recovery   68–69
   data
      graphic presentation (examples)   104
      ranking system   34
      rating methods   34
   financial   65–71
      annuity factors   125–29
   master-sheet   33–34, 34
   project site, detailed   22–25
   sheets (example)   34, 103
   site development   26–31
   social data   34, 102–5
      basic tables (example)   102–3
      coded range of answers (example)   102
      cross-checking answers   102
      pre-coded questions   102
   statistical terms   103–4
   studies
      detailed   33–34

feasibility   14–15
   physical   33–34
   socio-economic   33, 34
annuity factors
   present worth calculations   125–26
      internal rate of return   127–28
      net worth   127
      table   129
apartments, private   28
applicant selection   120–21
   new settlers (example)   90
appraisal, participatory urban rapid   134–35
approval
   outline   17
   project options   14, 73
aqua privies   31
areas
   higher income   41
   serviced   160
   site   23
   typical neighbourhoods   40
assessment
   ability to pay   33
   building options   45
   costs and their allocation   13, 32–33
   density options   37–38
   housing demand   21
   housing layout   37, 38–39
   initial
      circulation   11
      commerce   10
      development options   9
      ground conditions   8
      housing density   9–10
      housing layout   9
      industry   10
      institutional framework   12
      plot development   10
      project   1, 2
      public facilities   11
      transportation   11
      utility networks   11
   layout efficiency   124
   of options   35
   outline project site   5–8
   tenure preferences   21
   type of demand   21
assistance, technical   76, 122
attitudes
   household
      gender sensitivity   147
      to housing   21

B

benefit-cost ratio   126–27
bi-lateral, definition   159
bicycles
   circulation   50
   routes   52
block plans
   land markings   114
   marking, work sequence   115
   plan scales   115
blocks   159
   layout   38, 75, 79, 118
   size   40
borehole information   8

boundaries
   administrative   24
   housing layout   75
   land tenure zones   23
   neighbourhoods   75
   political   24
   site   7
briefs
   site development   140–41
   urban design   140–41
building
   costs   13
   existing   9, 10
   informal   159
   options   45
   owner-managed   76
   regulations   45, 132
   for short-term household needs   10
   unit costs   45
   see also housing
building materials   29
   loans for   45, 88
   supply   88
   surveys   29
building workers, training   45

C

capacity
   building strategy   136–37
   building system   137
   importance   136
capital, availability   82
capital recovery factor
   benefit-cost comparisons   126–27
   calculation
      example   126–27
      table   129–30
   opportunity costs   127
capitalisation   159
case studies   3, 18, 101, 159
   edited, Ismailia (example)   111–12
   guide   106–11, 159
cash flow
   applications   70
   calculating   70
   elements   70–71
   example (Ismailia)   94
   predictions   82
   sensitivity analysis   71
CBOs (Community Based Organisations)   134, 135, 159
charging, project finance, example (Ismailia)   92
checklists
   circulation options, selection   52
   evaluation   72
   information
      ranking   14–15, 71
      rating   14–15
      tabulation   14–15
   task sequence   14
   transportation options, selection   52
circulation   41, 159
   bicycles   50, 52
   initial assessment   11, 31
   new settlement projects   11, 31, 50
   options   31, 50–52
      operational efficiency   51

Index

selection checklist 52
upgrading projects 11, 31, 50, 51
pedestrian 50, 52
requirements 50
climate, local 25
climatic conditions 25, 28
clusters
definition 159
see also plots, clusters
co-operative building 21
co-operative group 63
commerce 10, 30, 46, 77
detailed plans 30, 77
initial assessment 10
plan scales 77
site development 10, 30, 77
commercial activity
cross-subsidies from 46, 70
definition 30
estimating potential increase 30
large-scale 47
layout options 46, 47
location 46
new settlement projects 46
range 46
selection of options 47
small-scale 47
upgrading projects 46
commercial plots, land tenure form 63
communal space 159
semi-private 160
communal toilets 143
communication
importance of 120
means of 120
Community Based Organisations (CBOs) 134, 135, 159
community facilities 29, 47–48, 78
community involvement 100, 120, 147
community organisations, assessment 19
community participation 133–35
compensation process, example (Ismailia) 91
consolidation, plot 28, 159
core units 159
assessing need for 45
cost-benefit ratio 126–27
costs
ability to pay 3, 13, 18, 33, 66
administrative 62
agreement on 62
allocation of 13, 32, 65, 66
allowances
default of payments 65
depreciation of assets 65
assessment of 13, 140
building 13
construction
estimates 11
phased 71
of detailed proposals 74
development 1, 7, 32, 67, 69
dwellings 64
estimation 13
factors affecting 67
of financing 64
infrastructure 64, 65, 66

land 1, 2, 7, 13, 32, 64, 66, 67
land acquisition 65, 71
on-plot development 66
operational 65
opportunity 33, 127, 160
planning and supervision of contracts 65
plot development 68
plot options 42, 43
plots, price differentials 68
public facilities 65
public land 40
recovery 13, 64, 68
analysis 68–69
means of determining 68
roads 28
schedule of component costs 66
sewage/sewerage treatment 142
superstructures 66
total project 13, 32, 40
unit, building 45
utilities 28, 51, 52, 60
provision 40
utility networks 41, 59
cross-subsidy see subsidy

D

data
Geographical Information Systems (GIS) 144, 145
see also analysis
delayed freehold
existing settlers 91, 150
new settlers 89
demand see housing demand
demographic profile 19, 20
see also target population
densities
existing, initial assessment 9, 26
future estimates 10
household numbers 10
project population 10, 27
new settlement projects 9, 10, 26, 37, 40
upgrading projects 9, 10, 26, 37, 40
density
intensification of use 37
levels 37–8
options
gross housing 37–38, 40, 159
net housing 37, 40, 160
selection 40
see also housing, density
design
co-ordination
housing layouts 38–39
infrastructure 39
detailed, initial levels of development 73, 159
and implementation 84
pre-built housing 77
site development 74–80
detailed plans 74
urban briefs 140–41
detailed studies
analysis 33–34
financial framework 32–33
housing 45

institutional framework 32
land 23
new settlement projects 17
project preparation 17
project site 26–31
purpose of 17
site development 26–31
upgrading projects 17
development
commercial, detailed plans for 77
industrial, detailed plans for 77
informal 159
initial 159
plots see plots
progressive 28, 45, 76, 160
sites see sites
development costs see costs
development plans 5, 6
discount factors
calculations (*example*) 125, 128
tables 128
discussions
agencies 66
government agencies 5
government departments 12, 17, 20
local people 120
drainage 24, 25, 59, 80
dwellings 159
household attitudes to 21
layout
climatic factors 29
cultural factors 29
new settlement projects 21
options 45
tenure status 21

E

economic characteristics of population 3–4, 19
education, location options, school sites 47
educational facilities 11, 29
see also public facilities; schools
El Hekr (Hai el Salam) project 2, 85, 148–53
background 148, 149
community plan 149
income distribution 149
Master Plan 148, 150
position at 18 months 150–53
and Project Agency 150, 151, 152–53
proposals 148–50
statistical table 153
summary 154
electricity supply 31, 57–58, 59, 82
employment opportunities
commerce 10
creation of 67
existing 6, 22
industry 10
potential 6, 22, 30
enforcement, implementation 122
evaluation
checklists 72
and monitoring 98
participatory 135
expectations, household 19

Index

expenditure, household 4, 19
expropriation process 91

F
facilities
  definition 159
  public *see* public facilities
fast-track planning 84, 159
feasibility studies 1–16, 26, 69, 159
  analysis 14–15
  briefs 140
  financial framework 13
  gender sensitivity 146
  institutional framework 12–13
  land 7
  project feasibility 9, 10, 12, 14
  purpose 1
  sites
    development 9–12
    project 5–12
  statement of objectives 2
  target population 3–4
field surveys, methods 4, 100–14, 116
finance, sources of 65
financial framework 12, 13, 60
  appraisal 65
  cash flow predictions 82
  cost allocation 65
  costs of development 64
  detailed proposals 84
  detailed studies 32–33
  feasibility studies 13
  gender sensitivity 147
  identification 13
  Ismailia
    building loan programme 88
    delayed freehold 89, 91
    expenditure 93
    expropriation and compensation 91
    future financing 95
    Project Agency profile 94–95
    revenues and charging 92–93
    subsidies question 95
  option development 64–71
  refinement of calculations 82
  selection 64–65
  self-financing 2, 70, 92
  sources of finance 70
  terms
    mark-up rate 159
    net 160
    resources 160
freehold ownership *see* land, tenure
frontages 27, 28, 41, 42, 47

G
gender sensitivity 146–47
Geographical Information Systems (GIS) 144–45
  advantages 144
  financial implications 145
  implementation 145
  and infrastructure 145
  organisational implications 145
  potential benefits 144–45
geological structure 8, 24
gross housing density 159

ground conditions 8, 11, 24–25, 59
  aerial photographs 8
  aggressive chemicals 24–25
  bearing capacities 25
  ground water 24, 25
  initial assessment 8
  salts 25
  site visits
    observations
      aggressive chemicals 8
      cracking of buildings 8
      earthquakes 8
      flooding 8
      geological structure 8
      ground water 8
      salts 8
  soil surveys
    boreholes 8
    hand probing 24
    results 25
    trial pits 8, 24, 25
  water table 25

H
Habitat Agenda 136, 140
health, public 52
health facilities 11, 29, 48
  see also public facilities
high income housing layout 41
higher income areas 41
higher income plots, layouts 76
households 159
  ability to pay 36, 37
  attitudes to dwellings 21
  characteristics 4, 19–20
    demographic profile 19
    health 19
    migration patterns 20
    occupation 19
    residence 20
    scanning survey forms (*examples*) 104–5
    size 20
    social profile 20
  economic characteristics
    economic status 19
    expectations 19
    expenditure 4, 18, 19
    loans 19
    savings 19
    sources of income 19
  income 3, 4, 18, 19, 66
    allocation 33
  low income *see* low income households
  needs 3–4, 18–21, 72
  plot option selection 43
  size 4, 18, 19
  structure 4
  surveys 100–14
  target population 3, 4, 18, 19, 20–21, 160
houses
  individual, existing 28
  rooming, existing 28
  see also buildings; dwellings
housing
  ability to pay for 3, 18, 159
  agency-built 76–77

building 45, 76–77
  selection options 45
  self-help 21
demand 4, 18–21, 147
  categories 21
  definition 21
  effective 4
  estimation of 4
  identification 4
  level 4
  nature 4, 21
  new settlement projects 21
  potential 4
  types 4, 21
  upgrading projects 21
density
  developing project options 37–41
  initial assessment 9–10
  levels 26, 37–38
  and sewage disposal options 143
detailed studies 45
existing 18, 21, 26, 28, 29
finance 64–70
high income 41
individual, types of provision 44
initial assessment 9–10
layouts 9, 26, 27
  blocks 38, 75, 79, 118
  design 38–39
  detailed proposals 75–76
  development project options 37–41
  efficiency 23, 37, 38, 39, 124
  existing 26
  hierarchy of plots 38, 40, 41, 75
  high income 41
  middle income 41
  proposals 75–76
  surveys 27–28
middle income 41
needs 1, 3–4, 18–21
neighbourhood areas 27
new settlement projects 9, 38, 76
options
  alternatives 37–9
  selection 40–45
percentile 160
plots 20, 27, 28, 41–43
pre-built, designs 77
preferences 18
public 28
subsidies 2
surveys 9, 27, 38, 76
system 18, 101, 159
types
  ability to pay for 18
  arrangement of rooms 29
  private open space 29
  public 28
  range 28
  willingness to pay for 18
humidity, relative 25

I
implementation 84–98
  and design 84
  design
    layouts 118, 124

site markers   118
enforcement   122
example (Ismailia)
  Agency establishment   97
  commencement of operations   96–97
  legal and institutional control   89–91
  project administration   85–89
  project finance   92–95
land marking   114–15
measuring plots   116
monitoring   96, 97–98
project   83–98, 147
  general notes   84
proposals   72
public participation   120
public relations   120
selecting applicants   120–22
technical assistance to plot holders   122
  layouts and building codes   122
technical notes   97
see also El Hekr (Hai el Salam) project
implementation agencies   61, 62
see also Project Agency
improvement area   159
incomes
  distribution   3, 4
  El Hekr (Hai el Salam) project   149
  gross   19
  household   3, 4, 19
  individual   4
  net   19
  regularity   4
  sources   19
  target population   36
industrial activity
  cross-subsidies from   46, 70
  employment potential   30
  large/small scale   30, 47
  layout options   46, 47
  location   47
  new settlement projects   46
  range   46
  selection of options   47
  upgrading projects   46
industrial plots, land tenure form   63
industry
  detailed plans   30
  initial assessment   10
  site development   10, 46, 47, 63
infill plots   159
informal development   159
informal recreation   159
information, borehole/trial-pit   8
infrastructure   159
  costs   64, 65, 66
  design   39
  and Geographical Information Systems (GIS)   145
  layout efficiency   40
  level of investment   67
  minimum level   60
  network efficiency   124
  phasing networks   41
  provision
    levels   13, 50–60, 150, 151

    types   13, 50–60
    standards   70
  see also utilities
initial proposals   1
institutional control (examples)
  existing settlers   91
  new settlers   89–91
institutional framework   12–13, 32, 60–62
  capacity   12, 13, 60, 61
  detailed studies   32
  executive function   60
  existing institutions   32
  feasibility studies   12–13
  gender sensitivity   147
  housing   12
  liaison   61–62
  new settlement projects   12
  powers   60
  selection   60–62
  sound basis for proposals   81
  types of organisation   61
interceptor tanks   142
Ismailia, demonstration project see El Hekr (Hai el Salam) project

L

land
  acquisition costs   70, 71
  area, typical neighbourhood   40
  categories, and layout efficiency   124
  commercial plots   63
  costs   1, 2, 7, 13, 32, 118, 119
  detailed studies   23
  existing types   7
  feasibility studies   7
  identifying features   7
  information   23
  marking   114–15
    work sequence   115
  public   7, 23
  semi-private   160
  semi-public   160
  speculation   63, 118
  status   23
  surveys   23, 76, 116, 117
    intermediate   116
  tenure   7, 23, 63, 159
    characteristics   62, 137–38, 139
    co-operative   23
    delayed freehold   63, 89–90, 91, 150
    freehold   7, 23, 33, 63, 138
    industrial plots   63
    leasehold   23, 63
    and plot development   63
    policy options   137–39, 140
    regulations
      compliance with   63
      enforcement   63
    rental   23
    residential plots   63
    rights   62
    security   138, 139
    selection of preferred options   62, 63
    squatters   23

    status   13
    title   62
    types   23
  use   9, 26–31
    efficient   159
    limitations on   49
    military   11
    options for   49
    planning of site   36
    polluting   11
  values see values
landscape, existing features   24
landscaping   49, 78, 159
  design proposals   49
  options   49
latrines   2
see also pit-latrines
layouts
  commercial   47
  design for setting out   118
  efficiency
    housing   23, 37, 38, 39, 124
    infrastructure   40, 124
    streets   11, 51
  higher income plots   76
  industrial   47
  options   37
  plots   37, 38, 75, 76
  roads   38, 39, 50, 79
  and sewage disposal options   143
  streets, surface water drainage   57
  upgrading projects   76
see also housing, layouts
legal control, example (Project Agency)   89–91
liaison   61–2
loans
  and ability to pay   138
  bi-lateral   65, 67, 70–71
  for building materials   45, 88
  multi-lateral   65, 67, 70–71
  repayments   68, 69
local climate   25
locality, household attitudes to   20
low income households   2, 3, 4, 6, 21, 64
  economic characteristics   19
  and forms of tenure   138
  new settlement projects, ability to participate   22

M

map overlay   144
mapping   31
  base   23
maps
  base   114, 115
  Geographical Information Systems (GIS)   144, 145
  scaled   23
  scales   5, 123
  and superimposed grids   26
mark-up rate   159
materials, building see building materials
meetings
  public   100
  selective   100
middle income housing layouts   41

Index

modular design system 42
monitoring 97–98, 147, 159
   and evaluation 98
   example (Project Agency) 96
   participatory 135
multi-lateral, definition 160

N

needs, household 3, 18, 72
neighbourhood 37, 38, 160
   area calculation (*example*) 40
   study of existing 26–27
net housing density 160
   options 37, 40

O

objectives 2, 35, 160
   example (Ismailia demonstration project) 2
   housing project 36
on-plot utilities *see* utilities
opportunity costs 33, 127, 160
options
   building 45
      selection 45
   circulation and transport 31, 50–52
      checklist 52
      costs 51
      layout 52
      parking 51, 52
      road construction costs 57
   commerce
      design 46
      layout 46
      selection 47
   density *see* density
   detailed proposals, approved 73
   developing project 35–72
   financial framework 64, 65
   housing layout 38–39
      selection 40, 41–42
   industry
      design 46
      layout 46
      selection 47
   institutional framework 61
      selection 62
   land tenure 62
      selection 62–63
   landscaping 49
   on-plot sewage disposal 59–60
   physical planning 37
   plot size and shape 41–44
      costs 42
      frontages 42
      selection 43
   project *see* project
   public facilities 47–48
   recreation 48
   site development 36, 37
   utilities 52–60
   utilities networks 59
organisation, example (Project Agency) 86–89
orientation of plots 28
owner-builders
   loans 76
   technical assistance 76, 122

P

paper sizes, standard 123
parameter 160
parking 31
   options 51, 52
parks 48, 78
participation
   advantages and disadvantages 133
   approaches to 133
   community 133–35
   with known/unknown groups 133–34
   public 120
   staffing 134
   techniques 134–35
payments, ability to meet 3, 18, 159
pedestrian circulation 50, 52
pedestrian routes 31
phasing
   detailed proposals 82
   infrastructure networks 41
   site development 36
photographs *see* aerial photographs
physical studies 7, 8, 9, 22–29, 33–34
pit-latrines 31, 55, 59, 66, 80, 160
planning
   action 84, 135, 140, 159
   fast-track 84, 159
   participatory 135
   physical 37, 72
   process 2
   proposals 5
plans
   aerial photography 24, 117
   block 114, 115
   commerce 30, 77
   industry 30
   scales *see* scales
   site development design 74
plots
   acquisition agreement conditions
      bilateral 159
      example (Project Agency)
         existing settlers 91
         new settlers 89
   applicant selection
      procedure 120–21
      verification of information 121
   blocks 38, 41, 75
   boundaries, identification 138
   characteristics
      consolidation 28, 159
      coverage 27, 160
      household attitudes 20
      new settlement projects 20, 27, 28
      orientation 28
      shape 27, 28, 41, 42, 43
      shape/size 20
      upgrading projects 20, 28
   clusters 37–39, 40, 41–42, 75, 124, 159
      access 75
      layout 40, 41–42, 75
      new settlement projects 75
      open spaces 40
      sizes 40, 41–42
      upgrading projects 75
   concession 159
   coverage ratio 160
   design module 42
   development 10, 27, 28, 29, 37, 160
      ability to pay 37
      costs 68
      cultural aspects 77
      initial assessment 10
      limits of provision 37
      new settlement projects 37
      occupancy level 160
      options 10, 37
      phasing 37
      social aspects 77
      upgrading projects 37
   existing, calculation of numbers 27
   holders
      example (Project Agency) 88–89
      technical assistance 122
   internal cross-subsidies 68, 160
   layouts 37, 38, 75, 76
   measuring 116
   neighbourhoods 38, 40
   occupancy level 160
   options
      area 42
      costs 42
      depth 28, 42
      frontages 27, 28, 41, 42, 47
      selection 43
   pricing differentials 68, 119
   range 42
   rationalisation 115
   selection, land tenure form 63
   shapes 42, 140
   size 140
      maximum 41, 43
      minimum 41, 43
      new settlement projects 41
      upgrading projects 41
   tenure status 20
   views of target population 41
political framework 61
pollution 8, 11, 142
population
   density 37, 38, 40
   economic characteristics of 3–4, 19
   neighbourhood, calculation of 27, 40
   total existing, calculation of 4, 27
   see also target population
pricing, of plots 68, 119
priorities
   new settlement projects 20
   project 29
private open space 38, 39, 124, 160
progressive development 28, 45, 76, 160
project
   agency 160
   appropriate options 36
   costs 13, 32, 40, 65–66
   evaluation 98
   feasibility 9, 10, 12, 14
   funding 64
   implementation 83–98
      general notes 84
      timescale 84

Index

objectives 36
options
   political support 72
   selection 71
preparation 2, 17
sites *see* sites, project
technical advice 76
Project Agency 85–97
  administration
    formation 85
    functions 86
  commencement of operations 96–97
  decision point, future phases 95
  early establishment 96
  finance 92–95
    financial profile 94–95
    future financing 95
      subsidies question 95
    future phases 95
  legal and institutional control 89–91
    existing settlers, delayed freehold agreement conditions 91
    expropriation and compensation process 91
    new settlers
      delayed freehold agreement conditions 89–90
      plot assignment 90–91
      selection of applicants 90
  monitoring 96
  project administration 85–89
  services of 88–89
    building loan programme 88
    building materials supply 88
    technical advice 88–89, 89
  staffing 86–8
project team, access to information 34
projects
  Ismailia demonstration 2, 85, 106–14
  self-financing 2, 70, 92
proposals
  affordability 74
  detailed design, initial levels of development 73–82
  El Hekr (Hai el Salam) project, implementation 148–50
  housing layouts 75–76
  initial 1, 159
  phasing 82
  planning 5
  site development plans 74
  see also financial framework
public facilities 11, 28, 29, 47–49, 160
  costs 65
  design options 47
  distance to 22
  initial assessment 11
  new settlement projects 11
  provision 78
    extent 47–48
    range 47–48
public space 38, 39, 160

Q

questionnaires, survey, detailed (*example*) 112–14

R

rainfall 25
recreation 11, 78, 160
  formal 159
  informal 159
  official standards 48
  provision 29
  space options
    formal 48
    informal 48
refuse disposal 31, 58
regulations
  building 132
  health 132
research
  co-ordination 18
  methods 18
  original 18
    formal 18
    informal 18
  social 18, 100–14
roads
  arterial 159
  construction standards 51, 52, 79
  costs 28
  definition of lines 79
  design standards 50–52, 79
  layouts 38, 39, 50, 51, 52, 79
  Rights of way 51, 52, 160
  and site levels 79
  and site regrading 79
  transitable 160
  see also circulation; streets; transportation
rooms, size 28, 42
rubbish disposal 31, 58

S

sanitation 12, 31, 52, 54–57, 59, 80, 160
  innovative systems 142–43
scales
  block plans 115
  commerce plans 77
  map, appropriate 123
  maps 5, 23, 123
  plans 5, 123
  utilities design drawings 80
schools 11, 29, 37
self-financing projects 2, 70, 92
self-help building 21
semi-private land 160
semi-public land 160
septic tanks 31, 56, 142–43
service slab 160
serviced areas 160
services, Project Agency 88–89
servicing options 51
sewage/sewerage 160
  disposal 12, 52, 54–57
    innovative systems 142–43
    on-plot 42
    selection of options 143
  levels of service 59
  pit-latrines 31, 55, 59, 66, 80, 160
  treatment
    costs 142
    decentralised 143

sewers, shallow 142
sites
  area and shape 6, 7, 23
  availability 5
  boundaries, identification 7, 24
  characteristics 26–31
  detailed analysis 22–3
  development
    access, initial options 9–12, 160
    briefs 140–41
    design 74, 147
    formulating site options 36–60
    and gender sensitivity 146, 147
    new settlement projects 9, 26
    options 36, 146
    phasing 36
    plan proposals 74
    survey and analysis 26–31
    target population 9
    upgrading projects 9, 26
  and gender sensitivity 146
  ground conditions 8, 24–25
  location 6, 22
  markers 118
  militarily sensitive 6
  new settlement projects 1
  politically sensitive 6
  project
    detailed analysis 22–25
    feasibility studies 5–12
    outline assessment and selection 5–8
  suitability 1, 2, 6–12, 22–31
  topography and landscape 7, 24
  upgrading projects 1, 6
  visits 8, 10, 11
sites and services 160
social balance 3
social facilities 11, 29, 160
social profile 19–20
social surveys 26, 27, 31, 34, 100–14
  analysis of data 34, 102–5
socio-economic studies, analysis 33, 34
socio-economic surveys 1–4, 18, 21, 100–14
  analysis of data 102–5
  case study guide (*example*) 106–11
  detailed questionnaire (*example*) 112–14
    sewage disposal and drainage 113–14
    utilities 112–14
    water 112–13
  edited case study (*example*) 111–12
  household scanning survey forms (*examples*) 104–5
  relationships between surveys 100
  role of 100
  sample size 101
    statistically significant 160
  survey practice 101
  types and examples 100–1
  utilities (*example*) 112–14
soil studies 8, 24, 25
space
  communal 159
    semi-private 160

options, recreation   48
private open   29, 38, 39, 124, 160
public   38, 39, 160
staffing
   participation   134
   Project Agency   86–88
stakeholders   134, 136, 140, 160
standards   132
   attainable   159
   criteria   159
   existing   12
   infrastructure   70
   official government   11
   upgrading   59, 60, 132
standpipes   2, 160
   public   53
streets
   access   50, 52, 159
   district   50, 52, 159
   functional requirements   51
   inventory   31
   layouts   50–52, 79
      efficiency   11, 51
      surface water drainage   57
   local   159
   options   31, 50–52
      Rights of way   51, 52, 160
      upgrading projects   52
   see also circulation; roads; transportation
studies
   detailed see detailed studies
   feasibility see feasibility studies
subsidies
   developing financial options   64
   external   159
      determining   70
   external sources   64, 160
   indirect   67
   internal cross-   2, 41, 42, 46, 64, 67–70, 159
   provision   2
   uncontrolled   67
sullage, disposal   59
superstructure   3, 160
   level of investment   64, 67
superstructures, existing, assessment of   10
surveys
   building condition   29
   building materials   29
   case studies see case studies
   co-ordination   22
   conduct of   101
   detailed   17–34, 101
   field, methods   4, 100–14, 116
   housing layout   27–28
   initial   1–13
   land   23, 76, 116, 117
   methods   100–1
   photographic   24
   scanning   100–1, 160
   short, series of   3
   site   22–23, 30
      existing development   26–27
   social   26, 27, 31, 34, 100–14
      analysis of data   34, 102–5

socio-economic see socio-economic surveys
soil   8, 24–25, 25
topographic   7

T
target population   1, 2, 17–21, 140, 160
   gender sensitivity   146, 147
   household
      attitudes
         to locality   20
         to plot characteristics   20
      characteristics   3–4, 20
      community involvement   19
      economic characteristics   3–4, 19
      housing demand   4, 21
      housing needs   3–4, 18
      identifying   3
      views of   18
technical advice   71, 76, 122
   example (Project Agency)   88–89
technical factors   82
technical notes, implementation   97
telephone service   31, 58
temperature   25
tenure see land, tenure
toilets, communal   143
topography   7, 11, 24
training, building workers   45
transportation   11, 31, 50–52
   arterial roads   50, 52, 160
   demand, modes of transport   31
   initial assessment   11
   links to adjacent road networks   11, 52
   local streets   50, 160
   new settlement projects   11, 31, 50
   options   31, 50–52
   streets
      access   50, 52, 160
      district   50, 52, 160
      hierarchy of   52
   system   11
   upgrading projects   11, 31, 50, 52
trial pits   24–25
trial-pit information   8
triangulation   134

U
upgrading, of standards   132
urban appraisal, rapid   134
urban areas
   general   159
   serviced   160
urban design, briefs   140–41
urban management   160
utilities   12, 31, 52–60, 160
   costs   28, 43, 59, 60
   detailed design   80
      drawing scales   80
      networks   59
      on-plot   80
      staged provision   41, 59
   drainage   24, 25, 59, 80
   electricity supply   31, 57–58, 59, 82
   existing, use of   31
   initial assessment   12

Index   167

installation
   and layout efficiency   124
   problems   10
networks   12, 13, 24
   costs   28, 59, 60, 80
   and street layouts   11
   new settlement projects   12, 60
objectives   52, 59
off-site   12, 22, 31
on-plot   60
   attitudes to   20
   design and costs estimates   59
on-plot sewage disposal   31
   design   38–39, 59
   economic viability   59
   and plot occupancy rate   59
   questionnaire   113–14
   selection of options   59
   social acceptability   59
   upgrading   59, 80
on-site   22
   service slab   160
options   52–60
   selection   59
phasing   41, 82
priorities   59
provision   8
   existing   12, 13, 31
   levels of   52, 59, 60
      by plot occupants   60, 80
      upgrading   60, 80
   priorities   21
reticulation   160
sanitation see sanitation
sewage/sewerage see sewage/sewerage
socio-economic survey (example)   112–14
staged provision   80
and target population   12, 59–60, 60
upgrading projects   12, 60
water supply
   basic network   12, 31
   options   52–54

V
values
   land   13, 32, 33, 37, 64
      estimating   118–19
      factors influencing market prices   118
      influences on   32
   see also costs
visits, sites   8, 10, 11

W
water
   ground   8, 24, 25
   requirements   59
   storage reservoirs   24
   surface, disposal   57
water supply
   basic network   12, 31
   options   52–54
water table   8, 24, 25
wet core   160
wind   25
World Bank   2, 67